Basic Writings on Politics and Philosophy

KARL MARX was born in 1818 to Jewish parents in the town of Treves in the Rhineland. His father, a lawyer, was Voltairean in outlook; when Karl was six years old, he had the whole family baptized as Christians. Marx studied mostly at the University of Berlin where he came especially under the influence of the left "Young Hegelians." He received his doctorate in 1841 from Jena for a dissertation on the philosophies of Democritus and Epicurus. Since his radical ideas made an academic career impossible, Marx turned to journalism, and in 1842 became the editor of the democratic newspaper *Rheinische Zeitung*. At last he was able to marry Jenny von Westphalen, a girl of a noble family, to whom he had been engaged for seven years. She bore Marx seven children, four of whom died in infancy or childhood, and was loyal to him through many years of poverty and exile. When Marx's newspaper was suppressed in 1843, he went to Paris, the center of the socialist movement, to study at first hand its theory and practice. There in 1844 he met FRIEDRICH ENGELS (1820–95), who had already arrived at a standpoint similar to Marx's. Engels, the son of a wealthy German textile manufacturer, had acquired an intimate knowledge of capitalism and the conditions of the working class while working in his father's plant at Manchester. Towards the end of 1847, in Brussels, Marx and Engels at the request of a German workers' club wrote the celebrated *Communist Manifesto*. They took part in the Revolution of 1848, during which time Marx edited the *Neue Rheinische Zeitung* in Cologne. Once more the paper was suppressed, and Marx was indicted for high treason. He was, however, acquitted; the foreman of the jury thanked him for a most instructive speech. Exile in England for many years followed. Marx avoided the emigrants' squabbles, and worked steadily at the British Museum on his writing of *Capital*, the first volume of which was published in 1867. During that time, his almost sole income was derived from articles he wrote for the then socialistic New York *Tribune*, whose European correspondent he was from 1851 to 1862. Engels, working again in the Manchester factory, faithfully contributed to Marx's support. In 1864, with the founding of the International Workingmen's Association, Marx returned to political life, and became the leading spirit of its General Council. Despite its weakness in organization, the International's impact on European history was, until its removal to New York in 1872, immense. Ailing during his last years, Marx died in 1883. Engels wrote extensively and edited his friend's manuscripts until his own death twelve years later.

Basic Writings on Politics and Philosophy

KARL MARX AND
FRIEDRICH ENGELS

Edited by Lewis S. Feuer

ANCHOR BOOKS
DOUBLEDAY & COMPANY, INC.
GARDEN CITY, NEW YORK

COVER BY SYDNEY BUTCHKES
TYPOGRAPHY BY EDWARD GOREY

The selections from *The German Ideology*, by Marx and Engels, edited by R. Pascal, published in 1939, are reprinted here by arrangement with the publisher, Lawrence and Wishart Ltd.

The selection ("Why There Is No Large Socialist Party in America") from *Letters to Americans: 1848–1895*, by Marx and Engels, translated by Leonard E. Mins, copyright 1953, is reprinted here by arrangement with International Publishers Company, Inc.

The selections from Marx's *Capital* and *Critique of Political Economy* are from translations published in the United States by Charles H. Kerr & Company.

The text of Engels' article on imperialism in Algeria, which originally appeared in the English newspaper *North Star* on January 22, 1848, is taken from *Marx-Engels Gesamtausgabe*, Erste Abteilung, Band 6, Berlin, 1932, page 387.

All other translations are from editions published by the Foreign Languages Publishing House, Moscow.

The Anchor Books edition is the first publication of *Basic Writings on Politics and Philosophy*.

Anchor Books edition: 1959
Library of Congress Catalog Card Number 59–12053

Printed in the United States of America

Contents

Introduction

LEWIS S. FEUER

A generation has gone by since Stephen Spender wrote:

> Oh young men oh young comrades
> it is too late to stay in those houses
> your fathers built where they built you to
>   build to breed
> money on money.

The revolutionary intellectual of the thirties has been replaced by the managerial intellectual of the fifties, and with this change in social temper the philosophy of Karl Marx would by many persons be consigned to the museum of their youthful indiscretions. Meanwhile, however, Marxism has become an even more endemic force in Asia and Europe than it was twenty years ago. The person who would understand the modern world must come to terms with Marx's ideas. The magnetic power of Marxism, unparalleled in the history of mankind, has drawn into its ideological orbit peoples of different continents and races, from China to Burma to Ghana, Moscow to Belgrade and Djakarta. Marxism, which declared itself the harbinger of a new international order has, in partial fulfillment of its prophecy, polarized the nations into power blocs.

Few will now deny that the communist movement, which invokes the name of Marx, has tarnished the ideal which inspired his work. But the reaction against Marxism in America has finally led to a distortion in our conception of our own past and future. Marxist ideas have had an important part in shaping our contemporary political philosophy, and we would do well not to try to banish that chapter from our consciousness. Classical American social science, in the persons of such men as Beard, Veblen, and Dewey, was not only influenced by Marx, but shared with Marx the same basic tenets. The faith of these Americans in the ordinary man, in the underlying population, was also the messianic socialist one; their faith in science as the method of liberation and their belief in the primacy of the economic factor in human history were as powerful as Marx's. Classical American social scientists were indeed historical materialists in the way they regarded their social world, and this was one reason why many of their students found an evolution towards systematic Marxism a natural development in the thirties. There has, of course, been also a powerful conservative tradition in American social science, for from its beginnings American thought has been divided into two opposed trends. If Veblen and Lester Ward were radical in their plans for reconstructing society, William G. Sumner was on hand to warn against any tampering with the existent mores. The growing radical movements, however, tended to find in Marx a fulfillment of ideas which were in large measure defined in American liberal social thought.

Marxism has often been described as a religion; it can be called the first secular world religion. Its dialectic is akin to Calvinist predestination; like other creeds, it has its sacred text, its saints, its heretics, its elect, its holy city. If Marx was its Messiah, Lenin was its St. Paul. But after all these analogies have been made, what remains to be emphasized is how different Marxism is from other religions. Unlike Christianity, for instance, its appeal has always been first to the intellectuals. Christianity was resisted by the ancient philosophers, who regarded it as an aberration of the lower classes; it spread from below upwards. Marxism, on the contrary, has been carried by the intellectuals to the proletarians and peasants. To intellectuals it has appealed as no other doctrine has because it integrated for them most fully discordant psychological motives. In Marxism we find for the first time a combination of the language of science and the language of myth—a union of mysticism and logic. Scientific criticism in the nineteenth century had deprived intellectuals of their God and left them uncertain as to the foundation of their ethics. Scientific agnosticism was an austere self-denial in a world inherently lifeless and undramatic, a world with neither purpose nor climax. Social movements had assumed the character of a superficial altruistic anodyne ungrounded in the nature of the universe. In Marxism, however, one's ideals could be taken as expressions of an underlying historical necessity in things. Here was a religion which was linked to so powerful a system of social science that endless academic books were written to confute it. Logicians in a few paragraphs could dispose of arguments for the existence of God, but dialectical materialism could challenge its critics to produce any theory which would explain anywhere near as much of social reality as it had. Here was a science which at the same time gave intellectuals a cause, a sense of mission, a conviction that their lives were worth while because history needed them. Here was a system which was both science and ethics, which called itself historical materialism and demanded idealist commitment.

No society can last long unless it provides for the motives of diverse personalities, and no philosophic system can have a universal appeal unless it incorporates the most contrary themes. A consistent philosophy can never have more than a sectarian following. Marxism as a world religion was a conjunction of incompatibles. It called upon human beings for a supreme deed of free will, that of intervening in their history with a revolutionary act and creating their own society. But it did so with a necessitarian vocabulary, so that the working class in its highest moment of freedom was fulfilling historical necessity. Freedom and determinism were joined in a dialectical unity. The language of liberty always had its determinist semantic commentary, and the mystic revolutionist became one with the scientist.

As a *secular* world religion Marxism furthermore offered its rewards on this earth. Other religions had postponed happiness as a gift in another realm, but Marxism could claim to speak for the foreseeable future. However, it also offered the pains and sorrows of asceticism. For revolutionists have always derived a satisfaction from conquering desire; they are priests of the people, and they deny themselves joys which are unshared. The revolutionist is a

Puritan, smitten with guilt if he partakes of fleshly pleasures and corrupts the purity of his consecration. And the revolutionist, uncorrupted by the social order, at war with it, can experience all the pride of his self-denial.

Marxism has had rival so-called "scientific" philosophies which have contended with it for people's allegiance: Auguste Comte in the nineteenth century, Dewey and Russell in the twentieth, have vied with Marx in every continent. But Marxism alone, in an era of crisis, could answer the psychological need for *struggle* against a personified obstacle. There were no villains in Comte's system, and he was even prepared to negotiate a fusion with the Church. Dewey summoned all men to solve their problems by intelligent discussion, while Russell affirmed that human struggles were insignificant in the cosmic order. Marxism, on the contrary, satisfied the impulses towards hatred and aggression. A religion of pure love has to make some men the bearers of evil. To do the Lord's work *against his enemies*, to fight the good fight, to "struggle," as Marx once said, is man's reality.

And finally, Marx offered the intellectuals leadership in the new world. Feudal society had been ruled by military lords, capitalist society by money-minded businessmen, but in the socialist society the intellectuals would rule in the name of the proletariat. The thinker, the planner, the teacher, the scientist, the technician, in short, the men of intellectual ability, would come into their own. The Platonic fantasy of the "philosopher king," always surviving in the intellectual's unconscious, would be finally realized in historical actuality.

What remains as the enduring contribution of Marx to philosophy and political theory? It seems fair to say, in the first place, that his case for the primacy of the economic factor in history has withstood criticism. Our social and political history does consist of responses to problems which have been generated essentially by economic disequilibria. This does not mean to say that our responses to these problems are rational in the sense of aiming at an economic optimum. Marx did tend to overlook the irrational responses which are often made. He overlooked the fact that history is as much a record of class submission as of class struggle. But he set forth an unshaken argument that the problem-generating factor in history is found in societies' economic institutions. When we add to this insight a recognition of the alternativity in human responses, we are led not to an economic determinism but to an economic indeterminism.

In this sense historical materialism remains an essential component for political understanding. We could not, for instance, explain the rise of neo-conservatism in America without bearing in mind that it came with prosperity and full employment among the intellectuals. The ugly aspects of Soviet practice, of course, repelled Americans, but evidently were not the basic cause of American political attitudes, for where economic dislocation persisted, as among Asian intellectuals, Marxist theory retained its attractive power.

Second, Marxism endures as a contribution to our political ethics. This may seem a strange thing to say, for not only does Marx ridicule ethical language as nonsense, but his Soviet adherents have used his doctrine of historical necessity to justify an era of repression and denial of human rights. Marx, as a "scientific socialist," believed he could eliminate ethics from his political philosophy and found his program solely on historical necessity. Within his system he had to suppress such questions as: "Why do I, as an individual, choose to work for the socialist world? Why do I cast my lot with the exploited workers?" And the repressed ethical question returned in the form of an answer—the happy communist culmination to the historical process. Ethics repressed returned as pseudoscience; history realized the ethical end, which the individual never could avow. All this is true, and accounts for the skewness of the Marxist vision. Nevertheless, despite his contemptuous rejection of ethical terms, Marx stands out as among the imposing ethical personalities of modern times. His action was more expressive than his word. He became the symbol of the intellectual who has not succumbed to either class or organizational pressures. He refused to be an ideologist or apologist, and he even spurned the discipline of socialist editorial boards. He was an intellectual who continued the tradition of prophetic protest. For what is a prophet? He is an intellectual who speaks with the voice of the lower classes, who articulates what they cannot say, and expresses their innermost, ofttimes crushed and unconscious, aspirations. And Marx's identification with the "masses" was as total as a person's can be; free from the ordinary kinds of self-seeking, he looms as a reproach to the acquiescent, the complacent, the place hunter, the trimmer, and the smug. Though Marx could sink to crude anti-Jewish epithets, he wore the mantle of the prophets Elijah, Amos, and Isaiah, and he foretold doom to the oppressors in the name of historical inevitability.

As a prophet using the language of social science Marx is alone among sociologists in giving meaning to the word "exploitation." This concept is not fashionable today among American social scientists; it smacks to them of the pamphleteer and soapbox orator. "Exploitation" is said to be an emotive word, scientifically meaningless. American sociologists often justify the existence of classes, and argue that they are a universal necessity on the ground that so long as jobs differ in their importance, and so long as there is a relative scarcity of talent, society will give greater rewards to those who do its more difficult tasks. There is really no exploitation, according to the "American school" (as we may call them), of the lower classes by the upper. At most, they hold, there may exist a peripheral "dysfunctionality" in the distribution of income. But to Marx "exploitation" is as characteristic of class systems as "parasitism" is of the fungi in the plant kingdom. The two ideas are equally significant as scientific terms. Just as there are organisms which live off the blood stream of others and contribute no labor of their own, there are likewise those who in the social world take something for nothing. Feudal lords, industrial captains, managerial intellectuals have all made use of their strategic position and their sheer control of force and power in society to take life's goods from the lower classes. Moreover, such exploitation can exist also among nations and races in their relations to one another; an advanced people can exploit the labor of a backward one. Forced labor, coolie labor, unfavorable terms of trade are among the devices which have been used. When Marx defined classes as involving the presence of exploitative relations, he was doing more than using words to emphasize his emotional dislikes. For the history of social institutions would be determined, in his view, precisely by the efforts of classes either to remove or impose exploitative burdens. Differences of function by social groups never create problems unless one group has the sense that it is being exploited by another. Then class struggle ensues.

Marx's vocation as the prophetic spokesman of the working class was, however, the source of his errors as well as of his insights. He could describe with unmatched eloquence the "great unfairness" which has been shown throughout history towards proletarians, serfs, slaves, and peasants. He pronounced the verdict of history's conscience—the extinction of the despoilers of the poor. But Marx also assumed that because the masses had been history's maltreated ones they were a chosen people with the highest virtues. He assumed that the proletariat would be liberal, friendly to learning, and truly the inheritors of science and art. The middle classes had produced a renaissance in thought and feeling, and Marx was confident that the working class would do likewise. The meek would inherit not only the earth, but all wisdom, knowledge, and beauty. So it was writ in history's dialectic. Marx tended to assume that suffering ennobles a class with intellectual as well as moral virtues.

The history of the masses, however, has been a history of the most consistently anti-intellectual force in society. The Bible, the book of the masses, is the supreme anti-intellectual book. It has, of course, often stirred the people with its revolutionary passages, its demand for justice, its invective against the oppressors. Cromwell's soldiers carried the book with them into battle, to give meaning to their muskets. Nevertheless, the Bible begins with curses against Adam for seeking knowledge, and it ends with populist prophets denouncing the culture of the cities. William Jennings Bryan in American history is a typical representative of the masses, with all their strengths and weaknesses, a passion for justice combined with a jealous hatred of intellectuals, the aristocrats of the mind. Plato and Aristotle exalted the sciences and pure knowledge, but though they wrote of justice they were moved by no sympathy for the slaves and downtrodden, and their writings have never been circulated as revolutionary tracts. Their "justice" rationalized the exploitative status of the upper classes. The values of free science were born in Hellenism, the values of equality and justice in Hebraism. This has been history's dualism. The lower classes could perceive truths of justice but were blind to freedom of thought. It was the American lower classes, not the upper, who gave their overwhelming support to the attacks in recent years on civil liberties. It is among the working people that one finds dominant those sects and churches most hostile to the free spirit. Cults and mysteries from antiquity to the present have been supported by the masses. And the French revolutionist who mocked at Lavoisier going to the guillotine, "The republic has no need of savants," was expressing the anti-intellectualism which has frequently prevailed among common men.

In his theory of history Marx tended to underestimate the psychological complexities of human beings which upset any simple formula of social evolution. He misunderstood the character of economic causation itself. For decisions in historical crises are determined by what we may call "psycho-economic" facts rather than by the economic data themselves. The social reality consists not only of the economic stimulus but also of the emotions, habits, attitudes, and ideas which define the character of the stimulus and select the path of response. The significant questions are: How will people look at the facts, with what emotions will they perceive and misperceive them, what inner aggressions and affections will determine their action with regard to those facts? For instance, we often read that the basic cause of the Civil War was economic —that it was a conflict between a Southern slave-owning aristocracy as against Northern capitalists and laborers. But was this conflict an irrepressible one? What stake did Northern workingmen feel themselves to have in this conflict? In New York City they rioted in 1863 against the draft laws and lynched hundreds of Negroes in the streets. The Northern merchants were linked by a multitude of business ties to the South, and resented the abolitionist agitators who endangered the Union with their moralistic fanaticism. New England, to be sure, was suffering from economic decline as its farms took second place to Western lands. In their frustration its farmers searched for different objects upon which to vent their resentment. Those who became mill hands in the burgeoning factory towns experienced all the gloom and monotony of the new industrial existence. New England became a prey to "isms," a "burnt-over" area, through which a succession of doctrines passed like successive holocausts. Temperance reform, vegetarianism, religious revivals, and the Know-Nothing movement were some of the fevers and fervors which were felt. The Know-Nothings in 1854 won not only the governorship in Massachusetts but almost the entire legislature with their program against Catholics and immigrants. A few years later all these aggressions were channeled against the South and endowed with the moral zeal of the crusade against slavery. Men who could stand no association with Negroes in their personal lives became the agents of a higher ethics in history. The twistings and turnings of the New Englanders from one cause to another have all the traits of an irrational process, and it was something of a historical contingency that the outcome was a war which freed the slaves. In Marx's philosophy all these irrationalities are obliterated and the actual outcome is given a rational interpretation as the one and only logical, historical necessity. The dialectic misreads the irrational as rational. The plight of the New Englanders, for instance, stemmed from economic causes, but the direction in which they would channel their latent aggressive energies, the way they would define their economic situation for themselves had an element of the indeterminate. This is what we mean by characterizing the causation as "psycho-economic."

Modern technology, Marx believed, is inherently "revolutionary" and intrinsically "social" in character, and consequently its whole influence would be towards making people equal as well as interdependent. The production process itself would tend to make for a co-operative society. Technological necessity had for Marx the qualities of a finally beneficent deity. In actual fact, however, modern technology has been among the principal forces working against socialism. The hierarchies of administrative control make neither for equality nor for fraternity. The new modes of technological and scientific skill which industry requires create the strategic base for new types of exploitation. The socialist ethic is something which will have to be brought to modern industry; it is not something which will arise necessarily from the machine process.

Marx's theory of classes has often been criticized as a gross simplification of social reality. In his actual historical writings Marx showed himself keenly aware of the nuances in political attitude of society's different classes and subclasses. He did tend, however, in the last analysis, to pose the basic contrast between the proletariat and the bourgeoisie. For the prophets have always been dualists, and have seen history as constituted finally by the conflict between good and evil, the children of light and the children of darkness. Nevertheless, this simple class dualism in Marx's theory is also the source of his tremendous historical insight. Different classes do not perceive the class hierarchy in the same way. The lower classes tend to look at social reality most simply; they make the fewest gradations in the social world above them, for these subtleties have no significance in their lives. Their world is made up of the well-to-do and the poor, the haves and have-nots, the exploiters and exploited. The members of the higher social strata, on the other hand, perceive a more complex social reality. They are aware of a variety of distinctions in status based on the inherited age of people's wealth, their social elegance, and moral character. This relativity of class perspectives, abundantly documented by American social scientists, leads naturally to the query: Which class perspective, if any, is more valid than the others? Marx's theory is an imaginative triumph in depicting the class structure of society as seen from the perspective of the lowest class. But can this perspective lay claim to more historical truth than others? Here Marx's answer would be clear. His bold vision does grasp more of historical reality than the more complex bourgeois schemes. For what is distinctive in the modern revolutionary era is the entry of the masses as participants in the making of history. Reality, as a stimulus to action, can be defined as how the world is perceived, and when the masses act their reality is their perspective, the world as they perceive it. The perception which guides the actions of a revolutionary working class will be precisely that described in Marx's simple portraiture. Perhaps revolutions will founder or develop in unintended ways, with new modes of class structure; Marx's theory offers little light on the stable, post-revolutionary era, when new classes differentiate themselves and the masses recede once more into the historical background. He has, however, given the phenomenology of the revolutionary consciousness, the world as it is experienced in crisis by the revolutionary workingmen. And to the extent that this class has a primary importance in historical crises, its definition of social reality will be basic, indeed, in determining the character of the efforts at social reconstruction.

A historical crisis, moreover, awakens the dormant anxieties in men. Hunger, the food anxiety, does not disturb a prosperous society, which can preoccupy itself with the activities of enjoyable living and perhaps the pursuit of competitive status. A crisis, however, restores the full significance of food and elemental security in people's lives. To hungry peoples in Asia and Africa the values of free thought, for instance, are relatively hollow and irrelevant, for their concern is primarily with the freedom to eat rather than to starve. When Marx mocked at the ethical ideas of democratic liberalism as nonsense, he was articulating the standpoint of the hungry, to whom food is the all-encompassing utility. When a large part of society begins to experience the sheer harsh threat of foodlessness, history becomes a tale told in the language of economic anxieties.

Curiously enough, although Marxism today has, in Asia, the dominant emotional attraction, its diffusion there cannot be explained within the framework of the Marxist system. The reasons for the reception of Marxism in Asia have little to do with the breakdown of the capitalist system, for in India, China, Burma, Indonesia and Viet Nam capitalism was a peripheral phenomenon. The soil for the spread of Marxism was prepared by the "good" effects of imperialism, which lowered the death rate by bringing stable government and measures of public health to Asia. Thereby it produced in Asia a tremendous pressure of population on the food resources. At the same time, the imperialist order educated a new colonial intellectual class which could not hope to find employment in the backward economies. The symbols of the Marxist philosophy became the vehicles of the resentment of Asian intellectuals. The Marxist terms were filled with a new content. The "capitalist" was identified with the Western rulers, the "proletariat" was taken as the Asian people generally, and the "class struggle" became the equivalent of racial and national liberation. The Asians were particularly receptive to Marx's apotheosis of technology in historical causation. For through building up industry they could guarantee their independence, eradicate their own inferiority feelings, and assert themselves as equal to the white men. And lastly, Marxism as a science of political leadership offered to Asian intellectuals a new ideology for their role as society's administrators.

Meanwhile American development is out of phase with the rest of the world. America, disenchanted with its own Marxist venture of the thirties, is learning the language of conservatism, and is finding itself ever more removed from the Asian and European worlds. Yet even we must re-learn the meaning of Marxism. For as freedom is reborn in Eastern Europe and Asia, it will speak in the Marxist idiom and try to disenthrall the universal humanist bearing of Marx's ideas from their Stalinist perversion. As social scientists and philosophers, furthermore, we must acknowledge that tremendous segment of reality which the Marxist philosophy has come closest to grasping.

Every period has had its own anthology of Marx and Engels. Algernon Lee thirty years ago in his Vanguard selection stressed Marx's agitational pamphlets, while Max Eastman twenty years ago gave great weight to Marx's *Capital*. We have chosen to emphasize the writings of Marx and Engels on politics and philosophy. For Marx the economist is less important today than Marx the political sociologist and philosopher of history. Marx's economic terminology has turned out to be too cumbersome for even Marxist economists to use, and his insights can be formulated more cogently and with their necessary qualifications in the language of marginal economic analysis. As a political sociologist, however, as an analyst of the class content of historical movements, Marx remains the master. Most contemporary political sociology consists of glosses to Marx. And as the bearer of a vision of man's destiny and place within the historical process Marx is pre-eminent. Among philosophers he is the supreme historical mystic by virtue of his self-identification with history. We have therefore selected for our edition material from Marx's and Engels' writings on general philosophy, ethics, religion, and mystical movements as well as from their now classical political works.

I. Manifesto of the Communist Party

KARL MARX AND FRIEDRICH ENGELS

PREFACE TO THE ENGLISH EDITION OF 1888

FRIEDRICH ENGELS

The Manifesto was published as the platform of the Communist League, a workingmen's association, first exclusively German, later on international, and, under the political conditions of the Continent before 1848, unavoidably a secret society. At a Congress of the League, held in London in November 1847, Marx and Engels were commissioned to prepare for publication a complete theoretical and practical party program. Drawn up in German, in January 1848, the manuscript was sent to the printer in London a few weeks before the French Revolution of February 24. A French translation was brought out in Paris shortly before the insurrection of June 1848. The first English translation, by Miss Helen Macfarlane, appeared in George Julian Harney's *Red Republican*, London, 1850. A Danish and a Polish edition had also been published.

The defeat of the Parisian insurrection of June 1848—the first great battle between proletariat and bourgeoisie—drove again into the background, for a time, the social and political aspirations of the European working class. Thenceforth the struggle for supremacy was again, as it had been before the revolution of February, solely between different sections of the propertied class; the working class was reduced to a fight for political elbowroom, and to the position of extreme wing of the middle-class radicals. Wherever independent proletarian movements continued to show signs of life they were ruthlessly hunted down. Thus the Prussian police hunted out the Central Board of the Communist League, then located in Cologne. The members were arrested and, after eighteen months' imprisonment, they were tried in October 1852. This celebrated "Cologne Communist trial" lasted from October 4 till November 12; seven of the prisoners were sentenced to terms of imprisonment in a fortress, varying from three to six years. Immediately after the sentence the League was formally dissolved by the remaining members. As to the Manifesto, it seemed thenceforth to be doomed to oblivion.

When the European working class had recovered sufficient strength for another attack on the ruling classes, the International Workingmen's Association sprang up. But this Association, formed with the express aim of welding into one body the whole militant proletariat of Europe and America, could not at once proclaim the principles laid down in the Manifesto. The International was bound to have a program broad enough to be acceptable to the English trade unions, to the followers of Proudhon in France, Belgium, Italy, and Spain, and to the Lassalleans[1] in Germany. Marx, who drew up this program to the satisfaction of all parties, entirely trusted to the intellectual development of the working class, which was sure to result from combined action and mutual discussion. The very events and vicissitudes of the struggle against capital, the defeats even more than the victories, could not help bringing home to men's minds the insufficiency of their various favorite nostrums and preparing the way for a more complete insight into the true conditions of working-class emancipation. And Marx was right. The International, on its breaking up in 1874, left the workers quite different men from what it had found them in 1864. Proudhonism in France, Lassalleanism in Germany were dying out, and even the conservative English trade unions, though most of them had long since severed their connection with the Inter-

[1] Lassalle personally, to us, always acknowledged himself to be a disciple of Marx and, as such, stood on the ground of the Manifesto. But in his public agitation, 1862–64, he did not go beyond demanding co-operative workshops supported by state credit.

national, were gradually advancing towards that point at which, last year at Swansea, their president could say in their name: "Continental socialism has lost its terrors for us." In fact, the principles of the Manifesto had made considerable headway among the workingmen of all countries.

The Manifesto itself thus came to the front again. The German text had been, since 1850, reprinted several times in Switzerland, England, and America. In 1872 it was translated into English in New York, where the translation was published in *Woodhull and Claflin's Weekly*. From this English version a French one was made in *Le Socialiste* of New York. Since then at least two more English translations, more or less mutilated, have been brought out in America, and one of them has been reprinted in England. The first Russian translation, made by Bakounine, was published at Herzen's *Kolokol* office in Geneva, about 1863; a second one, by the heroic Vera Zasulich, also in Geneva, 1882. A new Danish edition is to be found in *Socialdemokratisk Bibliothek*, Copenhagen, 1885; a fresh French translation in *Le Socialiste*, Paris, 1885. From this latter a Spanish version was prepared and published in Madrid, 1886. The German reprints are not to be counted; there have been twelve altogether at the least. An Armenian translation, which was to be published in Constantinople some months ago, did not see the light, I am told, because the publisher was afraid of bringing out a book with the name of Marx on it, while the translator declined to call it his own production. Of further translations into other languages I have heard, but have not seen them. Thus the history of the Manifesto reflects, to a great extent, the history of the modern working-class movement; at present it is undoubtedly the most widespread, the most international production of all socialist literature, the common platform acknowledged by millions of workingmen from Siberia to California.

Yet, when it was written, we could not have called it a *Socialist* Manifesto. By socialists, in 1847, were understood, on the one hand, the adherents of the various utopian systems: Owenites in England, Fourierists in France, both of them already reduced to the position of mere sects, and gradually dying out; on the other hand, the most multifarious social quacks, who, by all manners of tinkering, professed to redress, without any danger to capital and profit, all sorts of social grievances, in both cases men outside the working-class movement and looking rather to the "educated" classes for support. Whatever portion of the working class had become convinced of the insufficiency of mere political revolutions and had proclaimed the necessity of a total social change, that portion then called itself communist. It was a crude, rough-hewn, purely instinctive sort of communism; still, it touched the cardinal point and was powerful enough among the working class to produce the utopian communism, in France, of Cabet and, in Germany, of Weitling. Thus socialism was, in 1847, a middle-class movement, communism a working-class movement. Socialism was, on the Continent at least, "respectable"; communism was the very opposite. And as our notion, from the very beginning, was that "the emancipation of the working class must be the act of the working class itself," there could be no doubt as to which of the two names we must take. Moreover, we have, ever since, been far from repudiating it.

The Manifesto being our joint production, I consider myself bound to state that the fundamental proposition, which forms its nucleus, belongs to Marx. That proposition is that in every historical epoch the prevailing mode of economic production and exchange and the social organization necessarily following from it form the basis upon which is built up, and from which alone can be explained, the political and intellectual history of that epoch; that consequently the whole history of mankind (since the dissolution of primitive tribal society, holding land in common ownership) has been a history of class struggles, contests between exploiting and exploited, ruling and oppressed classes; that the history of these class struggles forms a series of evolutions in which, nowadays, a stage has been reached where the exploited and oppressed class—the proletariat—cannot attain its emancipation from the sway of the exploiting and ruling class—the bourgeoisie—without, at the same time, and once and for all, emancipating society at large from all exploitation, oppression, class distinctions, and class struggles.

This proposition, which, in my opinion, is destined to do

for history what Darwin's theory has done for biology, we, both of us, had been gradually approaching for some years before 1845. How far I had independently progressed towards it is best shown by my *Condition of the Working Class in England*. But when I again met Marx at Brussels, in spring 1845, he had it already worked out, and put it before me, in terms almost as clear as those in which I have stated it here.

From our joint preface to the German edition of 1872, I quote the following:

"However much the state of things may have altered during the last twenty-five years, the general principles laid down in this Manifesto are, on the whole, as correct today as ever. Here and there some detail might be improved. The practical application of the principles will depend, as the Manifesto itself states, everywhere and at all times, on the historical conditions for the time being existing, and for that reason no special stress is laid on the revolutionary measures proposed at the end of Section II. That passage would, in many respects, be very differently worded today. In view of the gigantic strides of modern industry since 1848, and of the accompanying improved and extended organization of the working class, in view of the practical experience gained, first in the February revolution, and then, still more, in the Paris Commune, where the proletariat for the first time held political power for two whole months, this program has in some details become antiquated. One thing especially was proved by the Commune, viz., that 'the working class cannot simply lay hold of the ready-made state machinery and wield it for its own purposes.' (See *The Civil War in France; Address of the General Council of the International Workingmen's Association*, London, Truelove, 1871, page 15, where this point is further developed.) Further, it is self-evident that the criticism of socialist literature is deficient in relation to the present time, because it comes down only to 1847; also, that the remarks on the relation of the communists to the various opposition parties (Section IV), although in principle still correct, yet in practice are antiquated, because the political situation has been entirely changed and the progress of history has swept from off the earth the greater portion of the political parties there enumerated.

"But then, the Manifesto has become a historical document which we have no longer any right to alter."

The present translation is by Mr. Samuel Moore, the translator of the greater portion of Marx's *Capital*. We have revised it in common, and I have added a few notes explanatory of historical allusions.

Manifesto of the Communist Party

A specter is haunting Europe—the specter of communism. All the powers of old Europe have entered into a holy alliance to exorcise this specter: Pope and Czar, Metternich and Guizot, French radicals and German police spies.

Where is the party in opposition that has not been decried as communistic by its opponents in power? Where the opposition that has not hurled back the branding reproach of communism against the more advanced opposition parties, as well as against its reactionary adversaries?

Two things result from this fact:

I. Communism is already acknowledged by all European powers to be itself a power.

II. It is high time that communists should openly, in the face of the whole world, publish their views, their aims, their tendencies, and meet this nursery tale of the specter of communism with a Manifesto of the party itself.

To this end, communists of various nationalities have assembled in London and sketched the following Manifesto, to be published in the English, French, German, Italian, Flemish, and Danish languages.

I. BOURGEOIS AND PROLETARIANS[1]

The history of all hitherto existing society[2] is the history of class struggles.

Free man and slave, patrician and plebeian, lord and serf, guild master[3] and journeyman, in a word, oppressor and oppressed, stood in constant opposition to one another, carried on an uninterrupted, now hidden, now open fight, a fight that each time ended either in a revolutionary reconstitution of society at large or in the common ruin of the contending classes.

In the earlier epochs of history we find almost everywhere a complicated arrangement of society into various orders, a manifold gradation of social rank. In ancient Rome we have patricians, knights, plebeians, slaves; in the Middle Ages, feudal lords, vassals, guild masters, journeymen, apprentices, serfs; in almost all of these classes, again, subordinate gradations.

[1] By "bourgeoisie" is meant the class of modern capitalists, owners of the means of social production and employers of wage labor. By proletariat, the class of modern wage laborers who, having no means of production of their own, are reduced to selling their labor power in order to live. [Note by Engels to the English edition of 1888.]

[2] That is, all *written* history. In 1847 the pre-history of society, the social organization existing previous to recorded history, was all but unknown. Since then Haxthausen discovered common ownership of land in Russia, Maurer proved it to be the social foundation from which all Teutonic races started in history, and by and by village communities were found to be, or to have been, the primitive form of society everywhere from India to Ireland. The inner organization of this primitive communistic society was laid bare, in its typical form, by Morgan's crowning discovery of the true nature of the *gens* and its relation to the *tribe*. With the dissolution of these primeval communities society begins to be differentiated into separate and finally antagonistic classes. I have attempted to retrace this process of dissolution in *Der Ursprung der Familie, des Privateigenthums und des Staats* [*The Origin of the Family, Private Property and the State*], second edition, Stuttgart, 1886. [Note by Engels to the English edition of 1888.]

[3] Guild master, that is, a full member of a guild, a master within, not a head of a guild. [Note by Engels to the English edition of 1888.]

The modern bourgeois society that has sprouted from the ruins of feudal society has not done away with class antagonisms. It has but established new classes, new conditions of oppression, new forms of struggle in place of the old ones.

Our epoch, the epoch of the bourgeoisie, possesses, however, this distinctive feature: it has simplified the class antagonisms. Society as a whole is more and more splitting up into two great hostile camps, into two great classes directly facing each other: bourgeoisie and proletariat.

From the serfs of the Middle Ages sprang the chartered burghers of the earliest towns. From these burgesses the first elements of the bourgeoisie were developed.

The discovery of America, the rounding of the Cape opened up fresh ground for the rising bourgeoisie. The East Indian and Chinese markets, the colonization of America, trade with the colonies, the increase in the means of exchange and in commodities generally, gave to commerce, to navigation, to industry an impulse never before known, and thereby, to the revolutionary element in the tottering feudal society, a rapid development.

The feudal system of industry, under which industrial production was monopolized by closed guilds, now no longer sufficed for the growing wants of the new markets. The manufacturing system took its place. The guild masters were pushed on one side by the manufacturing middle class; division of labor between the different corporate guilds vanished in the face of division of labor in each single workshop.

Meantime the markets kept ever growing, the demand ever rising. Even manufacture no longer sufficed. Thereupon steam and machinery revolutionized industrial production. The place of manufacture was taken by the giant, modern industry, the place of the industrial middle class by industrial millionaires, the leaders of whole industrial armies, the modern bourgeois.

Modern industry has established the world market, for which the discovery of America paved the way. This market has given an immense development to commerce, to navigation, to communication by land. This development has, in its turn, reacted on the extension of industry; and in proportion as industry, commerce, navigation, railways extended, in the same proportion the bourgeoisie developed, increased its capital, and pushed into the background every class handed down from the Middle Ages.

We see, therefore, how the modern bourgeoisie is itself the product of a long course of development, of a series of revolutions in the modes of production and of exchange.

Each step in the development of the bourgeoisie was accompanied by a corresponding political advance of that class. An oppressed class under the sway of the feudal nobility, an armed and self-governing association in the medieval commune[4]; here independent urban republic (as in Italy and Germany), there taxable "third estate" of the monarchy (as in France), afterwards, in the period of manufacture proper, serving either the semi-feudal or the absolute monarchy as a counterpoise against the nobility, and, in fact, cornerstone of the great monarchies in general, the bourgeoisie has at last, since the establishment of modern industry and of the world market, conquered for itself, in the modern representative state, exclusive political sway. The executive of the modern state is but a committee for managing the common affairs of the whole bourgeoisie.

The bourgeoisie, historically, has played a most revolutionary part.

The bourgeoisie, wherever it has got the upper hand, has put an end to all feudal, patriarchal, idyllic relations. It has pitilessly torn asunder the motley feudal ties that bound man to his "natural superiors," and has left remaining no other nexus between man and man than naked self-interest, than callous "cash payment." It has drowned the most heavenly ecstasies of religious fervor, of chivalrous enthusiasm, of Philistine sentimentalism in the icy water of egotistical calculation. It has resolved personal worth into exchange value and, in place of the numberless in-

[4] "Commune" was the name taken, in France, by the nascent towns even before they had conquered from their feudal lords and masters local self-government and political rights as the "third estate." Generally speaking, for the economic development of the bourgeoisie, England is here taken as the typical country; for its political development, France. [Note by Engels to the English edition of 1888.]

defeasible chartered freedoms, has set up that single, unconscionable freedom—free trade. In one word, for exploitation, veiled by religious and political illusions, it has substituted naked, shameless, direct, brutal exploitation.

The bourgeoisie has stripped of its halo every occupation hitherto honored and looked up to with reverent awe. It has converted the physician, the lawyer, the priest, the poet, the man of science into its paid wage laborers.

The bourgeoisie has torn away from the family its sentimental veil, and has reduced the family relation to a mere money relation.

The bourgeoisie has disclosed how it came to pass that the brutal display of vigor in the Middle Ages, which reactionists so much admire, found its fitting complement in the most slothful indolence. It has been the first to show what man's activity can bring about. It has accomplished wonders far surpassing Egyptian pyramids, Roman aqueducts, and Gothic cathedrals; it has conducted expeditions that put in the shade all former exoduses of nations and crusades.

The bourgeoisie cannot exist without constantly revolutionizing the instruments of production, and thereby the relations of production, and with them the whole relations of society. Conservation of the old modes of production in unaltered form was, on the contrary, the first condition of existence for all earlier industrial classes. Constant revolutionizing of production, uninterrupted disturbance of all social conditions, everlasting uncertainty and agitation distinguish the bourgeois epoch from all earlier ones. All fixed, fast-frozen relations, with their train of ancient and venerable prejudices and opinions, are swept away, all new-formed ones become antiquated before they can ossify. All that is solid melts into air, all that is holy is profaned, and man is at last compelled to face with sober senses his real conditions of life and his relations with his kind.

The need of a constantly expanding market for its products chases the bourgeoisie over the whole surface of the globe. It must nestle everywhere, settle everywhere, establish connections everywhere.

The bourgeoisie has through its exploitation of the world market given a cosmopolitan character to production and consumption in every country. To the great chagrin of reactionists, it has drawn from under the feet of industry the national ground on which it stood. All old-established national industries have been destroyed or are daily being destroyed. They are dislodged by new industries, whose introduction becomes a life and death question for all civilized nations, by industries that no longer work up indigenous raw material, but raw material drawn from the remotest zones; industries whose products are consumed not only at home, but in every quarter of the globe. In place of the old wants, satisfied by the productions of the country, we find new wants, requiring for their satisfaction the products of distant lands and climes. In place of the old local and national seclusion and self-sufficiency we have intercourse in every direction, universal interdependence of nations. And as in material, so also in intellectual production. The intellectual creations of individual nations become common property. National one-sidedness and narrow-mindedness become more and more impossible, and from the numerous national and local literatures there arises a world literature.

The bourgeoisie, by the rapid improvement of all instruments of production, by the immensely facilitated means of communication, draws all, even the most barbarian, nations into civilization. The cheap prices of its commodities are the heavy artillery with which it batters down all Chinese walls, with which it forces the barbarians' intensely obstinate hatred of foreigners to capitulate. It compels all nations, on pain of extinction, to adopt the bourgeois mode of production; it compels them to introduce what it calls civilization into their midst, i.e., to become bourgeois themselves. In one word, it creates a world after its own image.

The bourgeoisie has subjected the country to the rule of the towns. It has created enormous cities, has greatly increased the urban population as compared with the rural, and has thus rescued a considerable part of the population from the idiocy of rural life. Just as it has made the country dependent on the towns, so it has made barbarian and semi-barbarian countries dependent on the civilized ones, nations of peasants on nations of bourgeois, the East on the West.

The bourgeoisie keeps more and more doing away with the scattered state of the population, of the means of production, and of property. It has agglomerated population, centralized means of production, and has concentrated property in a few hands. The necessary consequence of this was political centralization. Independent, or but loosely connected provinces, with separate interests, laws, governments and systems of taxation, became lumped together into one nation, with one government, one code of laws, one national class interest, one frontier, and one customs tariff.

The bourgeoisie, during its rule of scarce one hundred years, has created more massive and more colossal productive forces than have all preceding generations together. Subjection of nature's forces to man, machinery, application of chemistry to industry and agriculture, steam navigation, railways, electric telegraphs, clearing of whole continents for cultivation, canalization of rivers, whole populations conjured out of the ground—what earlier century had even a presentiment that such productive forces slumbered in the lap of social labor?

We see then: the means of production and of exchange, on whose foundation the bourgeoisie built itself up, were generated in feudal society. At a certain stage in the development of these means of production and of exchange, the conditions under which feudal society produced and exchanged, the feudal organization of agriculture and manufacturing industry, in one word, the feudal relations of property, became no longer compatible with the already developed productive forces; they became so many fetters. They had to be burst asunder; they were burst asunder.

Into their place stepped free competition, accompanied by a social and political constitution adapted to it, and by the economic and political sway of the bourgeois class.

A similar movement is going on before our own eyes. Modern bourgeois society with its relations of production, of exchange, and of property, a society that has conjured up such gigantic means of production and of exchange, is like the sorcerer who is no longer able to control the powers of the nether world whom he has called up by his spells. For many a decade past, the history of industry and commerce is but the history of the revolt of modern productive forces against modern conditions of production, against the property relations that are the conditions for the existence of the bourgeoisie and of its rule. It is enough to mention the commercial crises that by their periodic return put on its trial, each time more threateningly, the existence of the entire bourgeois society. In these crises a great part not only of the existing products but also of the previously created productive forces are periodically destroyed. In these crises there breaks out an epidemic that in all earlier epochs would have seemed an absurdity—the epidemic of overproduction. Society suddenly finds itself put back into a state of momentary barbarism; it appears as if a famine, a universal war of devastation had cut off the supply of every means of subsistence; industry and commerce seem to be destroyed; and why? Because there is too much civilization, too much means of subsistence, too much industry, too much commerce. The productive forces at the disposal of society no longer tend to further the development of the conditions of bourgeois property; on the contrary, they have become too powerful for these conditions, by which they are fettered, and as soon as they overcome these fetters they bring disorder into the whole of bourgeois society, endanger the existence of bourgeois property. The conditions of bourgeois society are too narrow to comprise the wealth created by them. And how does the bourgeoisie get over these crises? On the one hand, by enforced destruction of a mass of productive forces; on the other, by the conquest of new markets, and by the more thorough exploitation of the old ones. That is to say, by paving the way for more extensive and more destructive crises, and by diminishing the means whereby crises are prevented.

The weapons with which the bourgeoisie felled feudalism to the ground are now turned against the bourgeoisie itself.

But not only has the bourgeoisie forged the weapons that bring death to itself; it has also called into existence the men who are to wield those weapons—the modern working class—the proletarians.

In proportion as the bourgeoisie, i.e., capital, is developed, in the same proportion is the proletariat, the modern working class, developed—a class of laborers, who live only so long as they find work, and who find work only so long as their labor increases capital. These laborers, who must sell themselves piecemeal, are a commodity, like every other article of commerce, and are consequently exposed to all the vicissitudes of competition, to all the fluctuations of the market.

Owing to the extensive use of machinery and to division of labor, the work of the proletarians has lost all individual character and, consequently, all charm for the workman. He becomes an appendage of the machine, and it is only the simplest, most monotonous, and most easily acquired knack that is required of him. Hence the cost of production of a workman is restricted, almost entirely, to the means of subsistence that he requires for his maintenance and for the propagation of his race. But the price of a commodity, and therefore also of labor, is equal to its cost of production. In proportion, therefore, as the repulsiveness of the work increases, the wage decreases. Nay, more, in proportion as the use of machinery and division of labor increases, in the same proportion the burden of toil also increases, whether by prolongation of the working hours, by increase of the work exacted in a given time, or by increased speed of the machinery, etc.

Modern industry has converted the little workshop of the patriarchal master into the great factory of the industrial capitalist. Masses of laborers, crowded into the factory, are organized like soldiers. As privates of the industrial army they are placed under the command of a perfect hierarchy of officers and sergeants. Not only are they slaves of the bourgeois class, and of the bourgeois state; they are daily and hourly enslaved by the machine, by the overlooker, and, above all, by the individual bourgeois manufacturer himself. The more openly this despotism proclaims gain to be its end and aim, the more petty, the more hateful, and the more embittering it is.

The less the skill and exertion of strength implied in manual labor, in other words, the more modern industry becomes developed, the more is the labor of men superseded by that of women. Differences of age and sex have no longer any distinctive social validity for the working class. All are instruments of labor, more or less expensive to use, according to their age and sex.

No sooner is the exploitation of the laborer by the manufacturer over, to the extent that he receives his wages in cash, than he is set upon by the other portions of the bourgeoisie, the landlord, the shopkeeper, the pawnbroker, etc.

The lower strata of the middle class—the small tradespeople, shopkeepers, and retired tradesmen generally, the handicraftsmen and peasants—all these sink gradually into the proletariat, partly because their diminutive capital does not suffice for the scale on which modern industry is carried on, and is swamped in the competition with the large capitalists, partly because their specialized skill is rendered worthless by new methods of production. Thus the proletariat is recruited from all classes of the population.

The proletariat goes through various stages of development. With its birth begins its struggle with the bourgeoisie. At first the contest is carried on by individual laborers, then by the workpeople of a factory, then by the operatives of one trade, in one locality, against the individual bourgeois who directly exploits them. They direct their attacks not against the bourgeois conditions of production, but against the instruments of production themselves; they destroy imported wares that compete with their labor, they smash to pieces machinery, they set factories ablaze, they seek to restore by force the vanished status of the workman of the Middle Ages.

At this stage the laborers still form an incoherent mass scattered over the whole country and broken up by their mutual competition. If anywhere they unite to form more compact bodies, this is not yet the consequence of their own active union, but of the union of the bourgeoisie, which class, in order to attain its own political ends, is compelled to set the whole proletariat in motion, and is moreover yet, for a time, able to do so. At this stage, therefore, the proletarians do not fight their enemies, but the enemies of their enemies, the remnants of absolute monarchy, the landowners, the non-industrial bourgeois, the petty bourgeoisie. Thus the whole historical movement is concentrated in the hands of the bourgeoisie; every victory so obtained is a victory for the bourgeoisie.

But with the development of industry the proletariat not only increases in number; it becomes concentrated in greater masses, its strength grows, and it feels that strength more. The various interests and conditions of life within the ranks of the proletariat are more and more equalized, in proportion as machinery obliterates all distinctions of labor and nearly everywhere reduces wages to the same low level. The growing competition among the bourgeois and the resulting commercial crises make the wages of the workers ever more fluctuating. The unceasing improvement of machinery, ever more rapidly developing, makes their livelihood more and more precarious; the collisions between individual workmen and individual bourgeois take more and more the character of collisions between two classes. Thereupon the workers begin to form combinations (trade unions) against the bourgeois; they club together in order to keep up the rate of wages; they found permanent associations in order to make provision beforehand for these occasional revolts. Here and there the contest breaks out into riots.

Now and then the workers are victorious, but only for a time. The real fruit of their battles lies not in the immediate result, but in the ever expanding union of the workers. This union is helped on by the improved means of communication that are created by modern industry and that place the workers of different localities in contact with one another. It was just this contact that was needed to centralize the numerous local struggles, all of the same character, into one national struggle between classes. But every class struggle is a political struggle. And that union, to attain which the burghers of the Middle Ages, with their miserable highways, required centuries, the modern proletarians, thanks to railways, achieve in a few years.

This organization of the proletarians into a class, and consequently into a political party, is continually being upset again by the competition between the workers themselves. But it ever rises up again, stronger, firmer, mightier. It compels legislative recognition of particular interests of the workers by taking advantage of the divisions among the bourgeoisie itself. Thus the ten-hour bill in England was carried.

Altogether collisions between the classes of the old society further, in many ways, the course of development of the proletariat. The bourgeoisie finds itself involved in a constant battle. At first with the aristocracy; later on, with those portions of the bourgeoisie itself whose interests have become antagonistic to the progress of industry; at all times, with the bourgeoisie of foreign countries. In all these battles it sees itself compelled to appeal to the proletariat, to ask for its help, and thus to drag it into the political arena. The bourgeoisie itself, therefore, supplies the proletariat with its own elements of political and general education: in other words, it furnishes the proletariat with weapons for fighting the bourgeoisie.

Further, as we have already seen, entire sections of the ruling classes are, by the advance of industry, precipitated into the proletariat, or are at least threatened in their conditions of existence. These also supply the proletariat with fresh elements of enlightenment and progress.

Finally, in times when the class struggle nears the decisive hour, the process of dissolution going on within the ruling class, in fact within the whole range of old society, assumes such a violent, glaring character that a small section of the ruling class cuts itself adrift and joins the revolutionary class, the class that holds the future in its hands. Just as, therefore, at an earlier period, a section of the nobility went over to the bourgeoisie, so now a portion of the bourgeoisie goes over to the proletariat, and in particular a portion of the bourgeois ideologists, who have raised themselves to the level of comprehending theoretically the historical movement as a whole.

Of all the classes that stand face to face with the bourgeoisie today, the proletariat alone is a really revolutionary class. The other classes decay and finally disappear in the face of modern industry; the proletariat is its special and essential product.

The lower-middle class, the small manufacturer, the shopkeeper, the artisan, the peasant, all these fight against the bourgeoisie, to save from extinction their existence as fractions of the middle class. They are therefore not revolutionary, but conservative. Nay, more, they are reactionary, for they try to roll back the wheel of history. If by chance they are revolutionary they are so only in view of their impending transfer into the proletariat; they thus defend not their present but their future interests, they desert their own standpoint to place themselves at that of the proletariat.

The "dangerous class," the social scum, that passively rotting mass thrown off by the lowest layers of old society, may, here and there, be swept into the movement by a proletarian revolution; its conditions of life, however, prepare it far more for the part of a bribed tool of reactionary intrigue.

In the conditions of the proletariat those of old society at large are already virtually swamped. The proletarian is without property; his relation to his wife and children has no longer anything in common with the bourgeois family relations; modern industrial labor, modern subjection to capital, the same in England as in France, in America as in Germany, has stripped him of every trace of national character. Law, morality, religion are to him so many bourgeois prejudices, behind which lurk in ambush just as many bourgeois interests.

All the preceding classes that got the upper hand sought to fortify their already acquired status by subjecting society at large to their conditions of appropriation. The proletarians cannot become masters of the productive forces of society, except by abolishing their own previous mode of appropriation, and thereby also every other previous mode of appropriation. They have nothing of their own to secure and to fortify; their mission is to destroy all previous securities for, and insurances of, individual property.

All previous historical movements were movements of minorities, or in the interest of minorities. The proletarian movement is the self-conscious, independent movement of the immense majority, in the interests of the immense majority. The proletariat, the lowest stratum of our present society, cannot stir, cannot raise itself up, without the whole superincumbent strata of official society being sprung into the air.

Though not in substance, yet in form, the struggle of the proletariat with the bourgeoisie is at first a national struggle. The proletariat of each country must, of course, first of all settle matters with its own bourgeoisie.

In depicting the most general phases of the development of the proletariat, we traced the more or less veiled civil war, raging within existing society, up to the point where that war breaks out into open revolution, and where the violent overthrow of the bourgeoisie lays the foundation for the sway of the proletariat.

Hitherto every form of society has been based, as we have already seen, on the antagonism of oppressing and oppressed classes. But in order to oppress a class certain conditions must be assured to it under which it can, at least, continue its slavish existence. The serf, in the period of serfdom, raised himself to membership in the commune, just as the petty bourgeois, under the yoke of feudal absolutism, managed to develop into a bourgeois. The modern laborer, on the contrary, instead of rising with the progress of industry, sinks deeper and deeper below the conditions of existence of his own class. He becomes a pauper, and pauperism develops more rapidly than population and wealth. And here it becomes evident that the bourgeoisie is unfit any longer to be the ruling class in society, and to impose its conditions of existence upon society as an overriding law. It is unfit to rule because it is incompetent to assure an existence to its slave within his slavery, because it cannot help letting him sink into such a state that it has to feed him instead of being fed by him. Society can no longer live under this bourgeoisie: in other words, its existence is no longer compatible with society.

The essential condition for the existence, and for the sway of the bourgeois class, is the formation and augmentation of capital; the condition for capital is wage labor. Wage labor rests exclusively on competition between the laborers. The advance of industry, whose involuntary promoter is the bourgeoisie, replaces the isolation of the laborers, due to competition, by their revolutionary combination, due to association. The development of modern industry, therefore, cuts from under its feet the very foundation on which the bourgeoisie produces and appropriates products. What the bourgeoisie, therefore, produces, above all, is its own gravediggers. Its fall and the victory of the proletariat are equally inevitable.

II. PROLETARIANS AND COMMUNISTS

In what relation do the communists stand to the proletarians as a whole?

The communists do not form a separate party opposed to other working-class parties.

They have no interests separate and apart from those of the proletariat as a whole.

They do not set up any sectarian principles of their own, by which to shape and mold the proletarian movement.

The communists are distinguished from the other working-class parties by this only: 1. In the national struggles of the proletarians of the different countries they point out and bring to the front the common interests of the entire proletariat, independent of all nationality. 2. In the various stages of development which the struggle of the working class against the bourgeoisie has to pass through, they always and everywhere represent the interests of the movement as a whole.

The communists, therefore, are on the one hand, practically, the most advanced and resolute section of the working-class parties of every country, that section which pushes forward all others; on the other hand, theoretically, they have over the great mass of the proletariat the advantage of clearly understanding the line of march, the conditions, and the ultimate general results of the proletarian movement.

The immediate aim of the communists is the same as that of all the other proletarian parties: formation of the proletariat into a class, overthrow of the bourgeois supremacy, conquest of political power by the proletariat.

The theoretical conclusions of the communists are in no way based on ideas or principles that have been invented, or discovered, by this or that would-be universal reformer.

They merely express, in general terms, actual relations springing from an existing class struggle, from a historical movement going on under our very eyes. The abolition of existing property relations is not at all a distinctive feature of communism.

All property relations in the past have continually been subject to historical change consequent upon the change in historical conditions.

The French Revolution, for example, abolished feudal property in favor of bourgeois property.

The distinguishing feature of communism is not the abolition of property generally, but the abolition of bourgeois property. But modern bourgeois private property is the final and most complete expression of the system of producing and appropriating products that is based on class antagonisms, on the exploitation of the many by the few.

In this sense the theory of the communists may be summed up in the single sentence: Abolition of private property.

We communists have been reproached with the desire of abolishing the right of personally acquiring property as the fruit of a man's own labor, which property is alleged to be the groundwork of all personal freedom, activity, and independence.

Hard-won, self-acquired, self-earned property! Do you mean the property of the petty artisan and of the small peasant, a form of property that preceded the bourgeois form? There is no need to abolish that; the development of industry has to a great extent already destroyed it, and is still destroying it daily.

Or do you mean modern bourgeois private property?

But does wage labor create any property for the laborer? Not a bit. It creates capital, i.e., that kind of property which exploits wage labor, and which cannot increase except upon condition of begetting a new supply of wage labor for fresh exploitation. Property, in its present form, is based on the antagonism of capital and wage labor. Let us examine both sides of this antagonism.

To be a capitalist is to have not only a purely personal but a social *status* in production. Capital is a collective product, and only by the united action of many members, nay, in the last resort only by the united action of all members of society, can it be set in motion.

Capital is, therefore, not a personal, it is a social power.

When, therefore, capital is converted into common property, into the property of all members of society, personal property is not thereby transformed into social property. It is only the social character of the property that is changed. It loses its class character.

Let us now take wage labor.

The average price of wage labor is the minimum wage, i.e., that quantum of the means of subsistence which is absolutely requisite to keep the laborer in bare existence as a laborer. What, therefore, the wage laborer appropriates by means of his labor merely suffices to prolong and reproduce a bare existence. We by no means intend to abolish this personal appropriation of the products of labor, an appropriation that is made for the maintenance and reproduction of human life, and that leaves no surplus wherewith to command the labor of others. All that we want to do away with is the miserable character of this appropriation, under which the laborer lives merely to increase capital, and is allowed to live only in so far as the interest of the ruling class requires it.

In bourgeois society living labor is but a means to increase accumulated labor. In communist society accumulated labor is but a means to widen, to enrich, to promote the existence of the laborer.

In bourgeois society, therefore, the past dominates the present; in communist society the present dominates the past. In bourgeois society capital is independent and has individuality, while the living person is dependent and has no individuality.

And the abolition of this state of things is called by the bourgeois abolition of individuality and freedom! And rightly so. The abolition of bourgeois individuality, bourgeois independence, and bourgeois freedom is undoubtedly aimed at.

By freedom is meant, under the present bourgeois conditions of production, free trade, free selling and buying.

But if selling and buying disappear, free selling and buying disappear also. This talk about free selling and buying, and all the other "brave words" of our bourgeoisie about freedom in general, have a meaning, if any, only in contrast with restricted selling and buying, with the fettered traders of the Middle Ages, but have no meaning when opposed to the communistic abolition of buying and selling, of the bourgeois conditions of production, and of the bourgeoisie itself.

You are horrified at our intending to do away with private property. But in your existing society private property is already done away with for nine tenths of the population; its existence for the few is solely due to its non-existence in the hands of those nine tenths. You reproach us, therefore, with intending to do away with a form of property the necessary condition for whose existence is the non-existence of any property for the immense majority of society.

In one word, you reproach us with intending to do away with your property. Precisely so; that is just what we intend.

From the moment when labor can no longer be converted into capital, money, or rent, into a social power capable of being monopolized, i.e., from the moment when individual property can no longer be transformed into bourgeois property, into capital, from that moment, you say, individuality vanishes.

You must, therefore, confess that by "individual" you mean no other person than the bourgeois, than the middle-class owner of property. This person must, indeed, be swept out of the way and made impossible.

Communism deprives no man of the power to appropriate the products of society; all that it does is to deprive him of the power to subjugate the labor of others by means of such appropriation.

It has been objected that upon the abolition of private property all work will cease and universal laziness will overtake us.

According to this, bourgeois society ought long ago have gone to the dogs through sheer idleness, for those of its members who work acquire nothing and those who acquire anything do not work. The whole of this objection is but another expression of the tautology that there can no longer be any wage labor when there is no longer any capital.

All objections urged against the communistic mode of

producing and appropriating material products have, in the same way, been urged against the communistic modes of producing and appropriating intellectual products. Just as, to the bourgeois, the disappearance of class property is the disappearance of production itself, so the disappearance of class culture is to him identical with the disappearance of all culture.

That culture, the loss of which he laments, is, for the enormous majority, a mere training to act as a machine.

But don't wrangle with us so long as you apply, to our intended abolition of bourgeois property, the standard of your bourgeois notions of freedom, culture, law, etc. Your very ideas are but the outgrowth of the conditions of your bourgeois production and bourgeois property, just as your jurisprudence is but the will of your class made into a law for all, a will whose essential character and direction are determined by the economic conditions of existence of your class.

The selfish misconception that induces you to transform into eternal laws of nature and of reason the social forms springing from your present mode of production and form of property—historical relations that rise and disappear in the progress of production—this misconception you share with every ruling class that has preceded you. What you see clearly in the case of ancient property, what you admit in the case of feudal property you are of course forbidden to admit in the case of your own bourgeois form of property.

Abolition of the family! Even the most radical flare up at this infamous proposal of the communists.

On what foundation is the present family, the bourgeois family, based? On capital, on private gain. In its completely developed form this family exists only among the bourgeoisie. But this state of things finds its complement in the practical absence of the family among the proletarians, and in public prostitution.

The bourgeois family will vanish as a matter of course when its complement vanishes, and both will vanish with the vanishing of capital.

Do you charge us with wanting to stop the exploitation

of children by their parents? To this crime we plead guilty.

But, you will say, we destroy the most hallowed of relations when we replace home education by social.

And your education! Is not that also social, and determined by the social conditions under which you educate, by the intervention, direct or indirect, of society, by means of schools, etc.? The communists have not invented the intervention of society in education; they do but seek to alter the character of that intervention, and to rescue education from the influence of the ruling class.

The bourgeois claptrap about the family and education, about the hallowed co-relation of parent and child, becomes all the more disgusting, the more, by the action of modern industry, all family ties among the proletarians are torn asunder and their children transformed into simple articles of commerce and instruments of labor.

"But you communists would introduce community of women," screams the whole bourgeoisie in chorus.

The bourgeois sees in his wife a mere instrument of production. He hears that the instruments of production are to be exploited in common and, naturally, can come to no other conclusion than that the lot of being common to all will likewise fall to the women.

He has not even a suspicion that the real point aimed at is to do away with the status of women as mere instruments of production.

For the rest, nothing is more ridiculous than the virtuous indignation of our bourgeois at the community of women which, they pretend, is to be openly and officially established by the communists. The communists have no need to introduce community of women; it has existed almost from time immemorial.

Our bourgeois, not content with having the wives and daughters of their proletarians at their disposal, not to speak of common prostitutes, take the greatest pleasure in seducing each other's wives.

Bourgeois marriage is in reality a system of wives in common and thus, at the most, what the communists might possibly be reproached with is that they desire to introduce, in substitution for a hypocritically concealed, an openly legalized community of women. For the rest, it is self-evident that the abolition of the present system of production must bring with it the abolition of the community of women springing from that system, i.e., of prostitution, both public and private.

The communists are further reproached with desiring to abolish countries and nationality.

The workingmen have no country. We cannot take from them what they have not got. Since the proletariat must first of all acquire political supremacy, must rise to be the leading class of the nation, must constitute itself *the* nation, it is, so far, itself national, though not in the bourgeois sense of the word.

National differences and antagonisms between peoples are daily more and more vanishing, owing to the development of the bourgeoisie, to freedom of commerce, to the world market, to uniformity in the mode of production and in the conditions of life corresponding thereto.

The supremacy of the proletariat will cause them to vanish still faster. United action, of the leading civilized countries at least, is one of the first conditions for the emancipation of the proletariat.

In proportion as the exploitation of one individual by another is put to an end, the exploitation of one nation by another will also be put to an end. In proportion as the antagonism between classes within the nation vanishes, the hostility of one nation to another will come to an end.

The charges against communism made from a religious, a philosophical, and, generally, from an ideological standpoint are not deserving of serious examination.

Does it require deep intuition to comprehend that man's ideas, views, and conceptions, in one word, man's consciousness, change with every change in the conditions of his material existence, in his social relations, and in his social life?

What else does the history of ideas prove than that intellectual production changes its character in proportion as material production is changed? The ruling ideas of each age have ever been the ideas of its ruling class.

When people speak of ideas that revolutionize society they do but express the fact that within the old society the elements of a new one have been created, and that the dissolution of the old ideas keeps even pace with the dissolution of the old conditions of existence.

When the ancient world was in its last throes, the ancient religions were overcome by Christianity. When Christian ideas succumbed in the eighteenth century to rationalist ideas, feudal society fought its death battle with the then revolutionary bourgeoisie. The ideas of religious liberty and freedom of conscience merely gave expression to the sway of free competition within the domain of knowledge.

"Undoubtedly," it will be said, "religious, moral, philosophical, and juridical ideas have been modified in the course of historical development. But religion, morality, philosophy, political science, and law constantly survived this change.

"There are, besides, eternal truths, such as freedom, justice, etc., that are common to all states of society. But communism abolishes eternal truths, it abolishes all religion, and all morality, instead of constituting them on a new basis; it therefore acts in contradiction to all past historical experience."

What does this accusation reduce itself to? The history of all past society has consisted in the development of class antagonisms, antagonisms that assumed different forms at different epochs.

But whatever form they may have taken, one fact is common to all past ages, viz., the exploitation of one part of society by the other. No wonder then that the social consciousness of past ages, despite all the multiplicity and variety it displays, moves within certain common forms, or general ideas, which cannot completely vanish except with the total disappearance of class antagonisms.

The communist revolution is the most radical rupture with traditional property relations; no wonder that its development involves the most radical rupture with traditional ideas.

But let us have done with the bourgeois objections to communism.

We have seen above that the first step in the revolution

by the working class is to raise the proletariat to the position of ruling class, to win the battle of democracy.

The proletariat will use its political supremacy to wrest, by degrees, all capital from the bourgeoisie, to centralize all instruments of production in the hands of the state, i.e., of the proletariat organized as the ruling class, and to increase the total of productive forces as rapidly as possible.

Of course, in the beginning this cannot be effected except by means of despotic inroads on the rights of property and on the conditions of bourgeois production; by means of measures, therefore, which appear economically insufficient and untenable, but which, in the course of the movement, outstrip themselves, necessitate further inroads upon the old social order, and are unavoidable as a means of entirely revolutionizing the mode of production.

These measures will of course be different in different countries.

Nevertheless, in the most advanced countries the following will be pretty generally applicable:

1. Abolition of property in land and application of all rents of land to public purposes.

2. A heavy progressive or graduated income tax.

3. Abolition of all right of inheritance.

4. Confiscation of the property of all emigrants and rebels.

5. Centralization of credit in the hands of the state, by means of a national bank with state capital and an exclusive monopoly.

6. Centralization of the means of communication and transport in the hands of the state.

7. Extension of factories and instruments of production owned by the state; the bringing into cultivation of wastelands, and the improvement of the soil generally in accordance with a common plan.

8. Equal liability of all to labor. Establishment of industrial armies, especially for agriculture.

9. Combination of agriculture with manufacturing industries; gradual abolition of the distinction between town and country, by a more equable distribution of the population over the country.

10. Free education for all children in public schools. Abolition of children's factory labor in its present form. Combination of education with industrial production, etc.

When, in the course of development, class distinctions have disappeared and all production has been concentrated in the hands of a vast association of the whole nation, the public power will lose its political character. Political power, properly so called, is merely the organized power of one class for oppressing another. If the proletariat during its contest with the bourgeoisie is compelled, by the force of circumstances, to organize itself as a class, if, by means of a revolution, it makes itself the ruling class and, as such, sweeps away by force the old conditions of production, then it will, along with these conditions, have swept away the conditions for the existence of class antagonisms and of classes generally, and will thereby have abolished its own supremacy as a class.

In place of the old bourgeois society, with its classes and class antagonisms, we shall have an association in which the free development of each is the condition for the free development of all.

III. SOCIALIST AND COMMUNIST LITERATURE

1. REACTIONARY SOCIALISM

a. Feudal Socialism

Owing to their historical position, it became the vocation of the aristocracies of France and England to write pamphlets against modern bourgeois society. In the French Revolution of July 1830, and in the English reform agitation, these aristocracies again succumbed to the hateful upstart. Thenceforth a serious political contest was altogether out of question. A literary battle alone remained possible. But even in the domain of literature the old cries of the Restoration period[1] had become impossible.

[1] Not the English Restoration, 1660 to 1689, but the French Restoration, 1814 to 1830. [Note by Engels to the English edition of 1888.]

In order to arouse sympathy, the aristocracy were obliged to lose sight, apparently, of their own interests, and to formulate their indictment against the bourgeoisie in the interest of the exploited working class alone. Thus the aristocracy took their revenge by singing lampoons on their new master, and whispering in his ears sinister prophecies of coming catastrophe.

In this way arose feudal socialism: half lamentation, half lampoon; half echo of the past, half menace of the future; at times, by its bitter, witty, and incisive criticism, striking the bourgeoisie to the very heart's core, but always ludicrous in its effect, through total incapacity to comprehend the march of modern history.

The aristocracy, in order to rally the people to them, waved the proletarian alms bag in front for a banner. But the people, as often as it joined them, saw on their hindquarters the old feudal coats of arms, and deserted with loud and irreverent laughter.

One section of the French Legitimists and "Young England" exhibited this spectacle.

In pointing out that their mode of exploitation was different from that of the bourgeoisie, the feudalists forget that they exploited under circumstances and conditions that were quite different and that are now antiquated. In showing that, under their rule, the modern proletariat never existed, they forget that the modern bourgeoisie is the necessary offspring of their own form of society.

For the rest, so little do they conceal the reactionary character of their criticism that their chief accusation against the bourgeoisie amounts to this, that under the bourgeois regime a class is being developed which is destined to cut up root and branch the old order of society.

What they upbraid the bourgeoisie with is not so much that it creates a proletariat as that it creates a *revolutionary* proletariat.

In political practice, therefore, they join in all coercive measures against the working class; and in ordinary life, despite their highfalutin phrases, they stoop to pick up the golden apples dropped from the tree of industry, and to barter truth, love, and honor for traffic in wool, beetroot sugar, and potato spirits.[2]

As the parson has ever gone hand in hand with the landlord, so has clerical socialism with feudal socialism.

Nothing is easier than to give Christian asceticism a socialist tinge. Has not Christianity declaimed against private property, against marriage, against the state? Has it not preached, in the place of these, charity and poverty, celibacy and mortification of the flesh, monastic life and Mother Church? Christian socialism is but the holy water with which the priest consecrates the heartburnings of the aristocrat.

b. Petty-Bourgeois Socialism

The feudal aristocracy was not the only class that was ruined by the bourgeoisie, not the only class whose conditions of existence pined and perished in the atmosphere of modern bourgeois society. The medieval burgesses and the small peasant proprietors were the precursors of the modern bourgeoisie. In those countries which are but little developed, industrially and commercially, these two classes still vegetate side by side with the rising bourgeoisie.

In countries where modern civilization has become fully developed, a new class of petty bourgeois has been formed, fluctuating between proletariat and bourgeoisie and ever renewing itself as a supplementary part of bourgeois society. The individual members of this class, however, are being constantly hurled down into the proletariat by the action of competition, and as modern industry develops they even see the moment approaching when they will completely disappear as an independent section of modern society, to be replaced, in manufactures, agriculture, and commerce, by overlookers, bailiffs, and shopmen.

[2] This applies chiefly to Germany, where the landed aristocracy and squirearchy have large portions of their estates cultivated for their own account by stewards, and are, moreover, extensive beetroot sugar manufacturers and distillers of potato spirits. The wealthier British aristocracy are, as yet, rather above that; but they, too, know how to make up for declining rents by lending their names to floaters of more or less shady joint-stock companies. [Note by Engels to the English edition of 1888.]

In countries like France, where the peasants constitute far more than half of the population, it was natural that writers who sided with the proletariat against the bourgeoisie should use, in their criticism of the bourgeois regime, the standard of the peasant and petty bourgeois, and from the standpoint of these intermediate classes should take up the cudgels for the working class. Thus arose petty-bourgeois socialism. Sismondi was the head of this school, not only in France but also in England.

This school of socialism dissected with great acuteness the contradictions in the conditions of modern production. It laid bare the hypocritical apologies of economists. It proved, incontrovertibly, the disastrous effects of machinery and division of labor, the concentration of capital and land in a few hands, overproduction and crises; it pointed out the inevitable ruin of the petty bourgeois and peasant, the misery of the proletariat, the anarchy in production, the crying inequalities in the distribution of wealth, the industrial war of extermination between nations, the dissolution of old moral bonds, of the old family relations, of the old nationalities.

In its positive aims, however, this form of socialism aspires either to restoring the old means of production and of exchange, and with them the old property relations and the old society, or to cramping the modern means of production and of exchange within the framework of the old property relations that have been, and were bound to be, exploded by those means. In either case it is both reactionary and utopian.

Its last words are: corporate guilds for manufacture; patriarchal relations in agriculture.

Ultimately, when stubborn historical facts had dispersed all intoxicating effects of self-deception, this form of socialism ended in a miserable fit of the blues.

c. German, or "True," Socialism

The socialist and communist literature of France, a literature that originated under the pressure of a bourgeoisie in power, and that was the expression of the struggle against this power, was introduced into Germany at a time when the bourgeoisie in that country had just begun its contest with feudal absolutism.

German philosophers, would-be philosophers, and *beaux esprits* eagerly seized on this literature, only forgetting that when these writings immigrated from France into Germany, French social conditions had not immigrated along with them. In contact with German social conditions, this French literature lost all its immediate practical significance, and assumed a purely literary aspect. Thus, to the German philosophers of the eighteenth century, the demands of the first French Revolution were nothing more than the demands of "practical reason" in general, and the utterance of the will of the revolutionary French bourgeoisie signified in their eyes the laws of pure will, of will as it was bound to be, of true human will generally.

The work of the German literati consisted solely in bringing the new French ideas into harmony with their ancient philosophical conscience, or rather, in annexing the French ideas without deserting their own philosophic point of view.

This annexation took place in the same way in which a foreign language is appropriated, namely, by translation.

It is well known how the monks wrote silly lives of Catholic saints *over* the manuscripts on which the classical works of ancient heathendom had been written. The German literati reversed this process with the profane French literature. They wrote their philosophical nonsense beneath the French original. For instance, beneath the French criticism of the economic functions of money they wrote *Alienation of Humanity*, and beneath the French criticism of the bourgeois state they wrote, *Dethronement of the Category of the General*, and so forth.

The introduction of these philosophical phrases at the back of the French historical criticisms they dubbed, "philosophy of action," "true socialism," "German science of socialism," "philosophical foundation of socialism," and so on.

The French socialist and communist literature was thus completely emasculated. And since it ceased in the hands of the German to express the struggle of one class with the other he felt conscious of having overcome "French one-sidedness" and of representing not true requirements, but the requirements of truth; not the interests of the proletariat, but the interests of human nature, of man in general, who belongs to no class, has no reality, who exists only in the misty realm of philosophical fantasy.

This German socialism, which took its schoolboy task so seriously and solemnly, and extolled its poor stock in trade in such mountebank fashion, meanwhile gradually lost its pedantic innocence.

The fight of the German, and especially of the Prussian, bourgeoisie against feudal aristocracy and absolute monarchy, in other words, the liberal movement, became more earnest.

By this, the long-wished-for opportunity was offered to "true" socialism of confronting the political movement with the socialist demands, of hurling the traditional anathemas against liberalism, against representative government, against bourgeois competition, bourgeois freedom of the press, bourgeois legislation, bourgeois liberty and equality, and of preaching to the masses that they had nothing to gain, and everything to lose, by this bourgeois movement. German socialism forgot, in the nick of time, that the French criticism, whose silly echo it was, presupposed the existence of modern bourgeois society, with its corresponding economic conditions of existence, and the political constitution adapted thereto, the very things whose attainment was the object of the pending struggle in Germany.

To the absolute governments, with their following of parsons, professors, country squires, and officials, it served as a welcome scarecrow against the threatening bourgeoisie.

It was a sweet finish after the bitter pills of floggings and bullets with which these same governments, just at that time, dosed the German working-class risings.

While this "true" socialism thus served the governments as a weapon for fighting the German bourgeoisie, it, at the same time, directly represented a reactionary interest, the interest of the German Philistines. In Germany the petty-bourgeois class, a relic of the sixteenth century, and since then constantly cropping up again under various forms, is the real social basis of the existing state of things.

To preserve this class is to preserve the existing state of

things in Germany. The industrial and political supremacy of the bourgeoisie threatens it with certain destruction: on the one hand, from the concentration of capital; on the other, from the rise of a revolutionary proletariat. "True" socialism appeared to kill these two birds with one stone. It spread like an epidemic.

The robe of speculative cobwebs, embroidered with flowers of rhetoric, steeped in the dew of sickly sentiment, this transcendental robe in which the German socialists wrapped their sorry "eternal truths," all skin and bone, served to wonderfully increase the sale of their goods among such a public.

And on its part, German socialism recognized more and more its own calling as the bombastic representative of the petty-bourgeois Philistine.

It proclaimed the German nation to be the model nation and the German petty Philistine to be the typical man. To every villainous meanness of this model man it gave a hidden, higher, socialistic interpretation, the exact contrary of its real character. It went to the extreme length of directly opposing the "brutally destructive" tendency of communism, and of proclaiming its supreme and impartial contempt of all class struggles. With very few exceptions, all the so-called socialist and communist publications that now (1847) circulate in Germany belong to the domain of this foul and enervating literature.

2. CONSERVATIVE, OR BOURGEOIS, SOCIALISM

A part of the bourgeoisie is desirous of redressing social grievances, in order to secure the continued existence of bourgeois society.

To this section belong economists, philanthropists, humanitarians, improvers of the condition of the working class, organizers of charity, members of societies for the prevention of cruelty to animals, temperance fanatics, hole-and-corner reformers of every imaginable kind. This form of socialism has, moreover, been worked out into complete systems.

We may cite Proudhon's *Philosophie de la Misère* [*Philosophy of Poverty*] as an example of this form.

The socialistic bourgeois want all the advantages of modern social conditions without the struggles and dangers necessarily resulting therefrom. They desire the existing state of society minus its revolutionary and disintegrating elements. They wish for a bourgeoisie without a proletariat. The bourgeoisie naturally conceives the world in which it is supreme to be the best; and bourgeois socialism develops this comfortable conception into various more or less complete systems. In requiring the proletariat to carry out such a system, and thereby to march straightway into the social New Jerusalem, it but requires in reality that the proletariat should remain within the bounds of existing society, but should cast away all its hateful ideas concerning the bourgeoisie.

A second and more practical, but less systematic, form of this socialism sought to depreciate every revolutionary movement in the eyes of the working class, by showing that no mere political reform, but only a change in the material conditions of existence, in economic relations, could be of any advantage to them. By changes in the material conditions of existence, this form of socialism, however, by no means understands abolition of the bourgeois relations of production, an abolition that can be effected only by a revolution, but administrative reforms, based on the continued existence of these relations; reforms, therefore, that in no respect affect the relations between capital and labor, but, at the best, lessen the cost and simplify the administrative work of bourgeois government.

Bourgeois socialism attains adequate expression when, and only when, it becomes a mere figure of speech.

Free trade: for the benefit of the working class. Protective duties: for the benefit of the working class. Prison reform: for the benefit of the working class. This is the last word and the only seriously meant word of bourgeois socialism.

The socialism of the bourgeoisie simply consists of the assertion that the bourgeois are bourgeois—for the benefit of the working class.

3. CRITICAL UTOPIAN SOCIALISM AND COMMUNISM

We do not here refer to that literature which, in every great modern revolution, has always given voice to the demands of the proletariat, such as the writings of Babeuf and others.

The first direct attempts of the proletariat to attain its own ends, made in times of universal excitement, when feudal society was being overthrown, these attempts necessarily failed, owing to the then undeveloped state of the proletariat, as well as to the absence of the economic conditions for its emancipation, conditions that had yet to be produced, and could be produced by the impending bourgeois epoch alone. The revolutionary literature that accompanied these first movements of the proletariat had necessarily a reactionary character. It inculcated universal asceticism and social leveling in its crudest form.

The socialist and communist systems properly so called, those of St. Simon, Fourier, Owen, and others, spring into existence in the early undeveloped period, described above, of the struggle between proletariat and bourgeoisie (see Section I, Bourgeois and Proletarians).

The founders of these systems see, indeed, the class antagonisms as well as the action of the decomposing elements in the prevailing form of society. But the proletariat, as yet in its infancy, offers to them the spectacle of a class without any historical initiative or any independent political movement.

Since the development of class antagonism keeps even pace with the development of industry, the economic situation, as they find it, does not as yet offer to them the material conditions for the emancipation of the proletariat. They therefore search after a new social science, after new social laws that are to create these conditions.

Historical action is to yield to their personal inventive action, historically created conditions of emancipation to fantastic ones, and the gradual, spontaneous class organization of the proletariat to an organization of society specially contrived by these inventors. Future history resolves itself, in their eyes, into the propaganda and the practical carrying out of their social plans.

In the formation of their plans they are conscious of caring chiefly for the interests of the working class as being the most suffering class. Only from the point of view of being the most suffering class does the proletariat exist for them.

The undeveloped state of the class struggle, as well as their own surroundings, causes socialists of this kind to consider themselves far superior to all class antagonisms. They want to improve the condition of every member of society, even that of the most favored. Hence they habitually appeal to society at large, without distinction of class; nay, by preference, to the ruling class. For how can people, when once they understand their system, fail to see in it the best possible plan of the best possible state of society?

Hence they reject all political, and especially all revolutionary, action; they wish to attain their ends by peaceful means, and endeavor, by small experiments, necessarily doomed to failure, and by the force of example, to pave the way for the new social gospel.

Such fantastic pictures of future society, painted at a time when the proletariat is still in a very undeveloped state and has but a fantastic conception of its own position, correspond with the first instinctive yearnings of that class for a general reconstruction of society.

But these socialist and communist publications contain also a critical element. They attack every principle of existing society. Hence they are full of the most valuable materials for the enlightenment of the working class. The practical measures proposed in them—such as the abolition of the distinction between town and country, of the family, of the carrying on of industries for the account of private individuals, and of the wage system, the proclamation of social harmony, the conversion of the functions of the state into a mere superintendence of production—all these proposals point solely to the disappearance of class antagonisms which were, at that time, only just cropping up, and which, in these publications, are recognized in their earliest, indistinct and undefined forms only. These proposals, therefore, are of a purely utopian character.

The significance of critical utopian socialism and communism bears an inverse relation to historical development. In proportion as the modern class struggle develops and takes definite shape, this fantastic standing apart from the contest, these fantastic attacks on it lose all practical value and all theoretical justification. Therefore, although the originators of these systems were, in many respects, revolutionary, their disciples have, in every case, formed mere reactionary sects. They hold fast by the original views of their masters, in opposition to the progressive historical development of the proletariat. They, therefore, endeavor, and that consistently, to deaden the class struggle and to reconcile the class antagonisms. They still dream of experimental realization of their social utopias, of founding isolated "*phalanstères*," of establishing "home colonies," of setting up a "Little Icaria"[3]—duodecimo editions of the New Jerusalem—and to realize all these castles in the air they are compelled to appeal to the feelings and purses of the bourgeois. By degrees they sink into the category of the reactionary conservative socialists depicted above, differing from these only by more systematic pedantry, and by their fanatical and superstitious belief in the miraculous effects of their social science.

They, therefore, violently oppose all political action on the part of the working class; such action, according to them, can only result from blind unbelief in the new gospel.

The Owenites in England and the Fourierists in France, respectively, oppose the Chartists and the Réformistes.

IV. POSITION OF THE COMMUNISTS IN RELATION TO THE VARIOUS EXISTING OPPOSITION PARTIES

Section II has made clear the relations of the communists to the existing working-class parties, such as the Chartists in England and the agrarian reformers in America.

[3] *Phalanstères* were socialist colonies on the plan of Charles Fourier; "Icaria" was the name given by Cabet to his utopia and, later on, to his American communist colony. [Note by Engels to the English edition of 1888.]

The communists fight for the attainment of the immediate aims, for the enforcement of the momentary interests of the working class, but in the movement of the present they also represent and take care of the future of that movement. In France the communists ally themselves with the social democrats,[1] against the conservative and radical bourgeoisie, reserving, however, the right to take up a critical position in regard to phrases and illusions traditionally handed down from the Great Revolution.

In Switzerland they support the radicals, without losing sight of the fact that this party consists of antagonistic elements, partly of democratic socialists, in the French sense, partly of radical bourgeois.

In Poland they support the party that insists on an agrarian revolution as the prime condition for national emancipation, that party which fomented the insurrection of Cracow in 1846.

In Germany they fight with the bourgeoisie whenever it acts in a revolutionary way, against the absolute monarchy, the feudal squirearchy, and the petty bourgeoisie.

But they never cease, for a single instant, to instill into the working class the clearest possible recognition of the hostile antagonism between bourgeoisie and proletariat, in order that the German workers may straightway use, as so many weapons against the bourgeoisie, the social and political conditions that the bourgeoisie must necessarily introduce along with its supremacy, and in order that, after the fall of the reactionary classes in Germany, the fight against the bourgeoisie itself may immediately begin.

The communists turn their attention chiefly to Germany, because that country is on the eve of a bourgeois revolution that is bound to be carried out under more advanced conditions of European civilization, and with a much more developed proletariat, than that of England was in the seventeenth and of France in the eighteenth century, and because the bourgeois revolution in Germany

[1] The party then represented in Parliament by Ledru-Rollin, in literature by Louis Blanc, in the daily press by the *Réforme*. The name of social democracy signified, with these its inventors, a section of the democratic or republican party more or less tinged with socialism. [Note by Engels to the English edition of 1888.]

will be but the prelude to an immediately following proletarian revolution.

In short, the communists everywhere support every revolutionary movement against the existing social and political order of things.

In all these movements they bring to the front, as the leading question in each, the property question, no matter what its degree of development at the time.

Finally, they labor everywhere for the union and agreement of the democratic parties of all countries.

The communists disdain to conceal their views and aims. They openly declare that their ends can be attained only by the forcible overthrow of all existing social conditions. Let the ruling classes tremble at a communistic revolution. The proletarians have nothing to lose but their chains. They have a world to win.

WORKINGMEN OF ALL COUNTRIES, UNITE!

II. *Excerpt from* A Contribution to the Critique of Political Economy

KARL MARX

In this excerpt from the Preface, Marx tells how he arrived at the materialist conception of history. Karl Marx, A *Contribution to the Critique of Political Economy*, translated from the second German edition by N. I. Stone, Chicago: Charles H. Kerr and Company, 1904, pages 10–15.—ED.

. . . some remarks as to the course of my own politico-economic studies may be in place here.

The subject of my professional studies was jurisprudence, which I pursued, however, in connection with and as secondary to the studies of philosophy and history. In 1842–43, as editor of the *Rheinische Zeitung*, I found myself embarrassed at first when I had to take part in discussions concerning so-called material interests. The proceedings of the Rhine Diet in connection with forest thefts and the extreme subdivision of landed property; the official controversy about the condition of the Mosel peasants, into which Herr von Schaper, at that time President of the Rhine Province, entered with the *Rheinische Zeitung*; finally, the debates on free trade and protection gave me the first impulse to take up the study of economic questions. At the same time a weak, quasi-philosophic echo of French socialism and communism made itself heard in the *Rheinische Zeitung* in those days when the good intentions "to go ahead" greatly outweighed knowledge of facts. I declared myself against such botching, but had to admit at once in a controversy with the *Allgemeine Augsburger Zeitung* that my previous studies did not allow me to hazard an independent judgment as to the merits of the French schools. When, therefore, the publishers of the *Rheinische Zeitung* conceived the illusion that by a less aggressive policy the paper could be saved from the death sentence pronounced upon it, I was glad to grasp that opportunity to retire to my study room from public life.

The first work undertaken for the solution of the question that troubled me was a critical revision of Hegel's *Philosophy of Law;* the Introduction to that work appeared in the *Deutsch-Französische Jahrbücher*, published in Paris in 1844. I was led by my studies to the conclusion that legal relations as well as forms of state could be neither understood by themselves nor explained by the so-called general progress of the human mind, but that they are rooted in the material conditions of life, which are summed up by Hegel after the fashion of the English and French of the eighteenth century under the name "civil society"; the anatomy of that civil society is to be sought in political economy. The study of the latter, which I had taken up in Paris, I continued at Brussels, whither I immigrated on account of an order of expulsion issued by Mr. Guizot. The general conclusion at which I arrived and which, once reached, continued to serve as the leading thread in my studies may be briefly summed up as follows: In the social production which men carry on they enter into definite relations that are indispensable and independent of their will; these relations of production correspond to a definite stage of development of their material powers of production. The sum total of these relations of production constitutes the economic structure of society—the real foundation, on which rise legal and political superstructures and to which correspond definite forms of social consciousness. The mode of production in material life determines the general character of the social, political, and spiritual processes of life. It is not the consciousness of men that determines their existence, but, on the contrary, their social existence determines their consciousness. At a certain stage of their development the material forces of production in society come into conflict with the existing relations of production, or—what is but a legal expression for the same thing—with the property relations within which they had been at work before. From forms of development of the forces of production these relations turn into their fetters. Then comes the period of social revolution. With the change of the economic foundation the entire immense superstructure is more or less rapidly transformed. In considering such transformations the distinction should always be made between the material transformation of the economic conditions of production, which can be determined with the precision of natural science, and the legal, political, religious, aesthetic, or philosophic—in short, ideological—forms in which men become conscious of this conflict and fight it out. Just as our opinion of an individual is not based on what he thinks of himself, so can we not judge such a period of transformation by its own consciousness; on the contrary, this consciousness must rather be explained from the contradictions of material life, from the existing conflict between the social forces of production and the relations of production. No social order ever disappears before all the productive forces for which there is room in it have been developed, and new, higher relations of production never appear before the material conditions of their existence have matured in the womb of the old society. Therefore mankind always takes up only such problems as it can solve, since, looking at the matter more closely, we will always find that the problem itself arises only when the material conditions necessary for its solution already exist or are at least in the process of formation. In broad outlines we can designate the Asiatic, the ancient, the feudal, and the modern bourgeois methods of production as so many epochs in the progress of the economic formation of society. The bourgeois relations of production are the last antagonistic form of the social process of production—antagonistic not in the sense of individual antagonism, but of one arising from conditions surrounding the life of individuals in society; at the same time the productive forces developing in the womb of bourgeois society create the material conditions for the solution of that antagonism. This social formation constitutes, therefore, the closing chapter of the prehistoric stage of human society.

Friedrich Engels, with whom I was continually corresponding and exchanging ideas since the appearance of his ingenious critical essay on economic categories (in the *Deutsch-Französische Jahrbücher*), came by a different road to the same conclusions as myself (see his *Condition of the Working Class in England*). When he, too, settled in Brussels in the spring of 1845, we decided to work out together the contrast between our view and the idealism of the German philosophy; in fact, to settle our accounts with our former philosophic conscience. The plan was carried out in the form of a criticism of the post-Hegelian philosophy. The manuscript in two solid octavo volumes had long reached the publisher in Westphalia when we received information that conditions had so changed as not to allow of its publication. We abandoned the manuscript to the stinging criticism of the mice the more readily since we had accomplished our main purpose—the clearing up of the question to ourselves. Of the scattered writings on various subjects in which we presented our views to the public at that time, I recall only the *Manifesto of the Communist Party*, written by Engels and myself, and the *Discourse on Free Trade*, written by myself. The leading points of our theory were first presented scientifically, though in a polemic form, in my *Misère de la Philosophie*, etc. directed against Proudhon and published in 1847. An essay on *Wage Labor*, written by me in German, and in which I put together my lectures on the subject delivered before the German Workmen's Club at Brussels, was prevented from leaving the hands of the printer by the February revolution and my expulsion from Belgium, which followed it as a consequence.

The publication of the *Neue Rheinische Zeitung* in 1848 and 1849, and the events which took place later on, interrupted my economic studies, which I could not resume before 1850 in London. The enormous material on the history of political economy which is accumulated in the British Museum; the favorable view which London offers for the observation of bourgeois society; finally, the new stage of development upon which the latter seemed to have entered with the discovery of gold in California and Australia led me to the decision to resume my studies from the very beginning and work up critically the new material. These studies partly led to what might seem side questions, over which I nevertheless had to stop for longer or shorter periods of time. Especially was the time at my disposal cut down by the imperative necessity of working for a living. My work as contributor on the leading Anglo-American newspaper, the New York *Tribune*, at which I have now been engaged for eight years, has caused very great interruption in my studies, since I engage in newspaper work proper only occasionally. Yet articles on important economic events in England and on the Continent have formed so large a part of my contributions that I have been obliged to make myself familiar with practical details which lie outside the proper sphere of political economy.

This account of the course of my studies in political economy is simply to prove that my views, whatever one may think of them, and no matter how little they agree with the interested prejudices of the ruling classes, are the result of many years of conscientious research. At the entrance to science, however, the same requirement must be put as at the entrance to hell:

Qui si convien lasciare ogni sospetto
Ogni viltà convien che qui sia morta.[1]

London, January 1859

[1] *Here must all distrust be left;*
All cowardice must here be dead.
(*The Divine Comedy of Dante Alighieri,* Canto III, translated by John Aitken Carlyle.) The words were spoken by Virgil to Dante as they entered the gate of hell.

III. On Historical Materialism

FRIEDRICH ENGELS

This essay, written in English, was the principal part of the Introduction to the English edition of *Socialism: Utopian and Scientific*, published in 1892. Marx and Engels mistakenly assign the nominalist philosophy of William of Ockham to the realist Duns Scotus.—ED.

I am perfectly aware that the contents of this work will meet with objection from a considerable portion of the British public. But if we Continentals had taken the slightest notice of the prejudices of British "respectability" we should be even worse off than we are. This book defends what we call "historical materialism," and the word "materialism" grates upon the ears of the immense majority of British readers. Agnosticism might be tolerated, but materialism is utterly inadmissible.

And yet the original home of all modern materialism, from the seventeenth century onwards, is England.

"Materialism is the natural-born son of Great Britain. Already the British schoolman, Duns Scotus, asked 'whether it was impossible for matter to think.'

"In order to effect this miracle he took refuge in God's omnipotence, i.e., he made theology preach materialism. Moreover, he was a nominalist. Nominalism, the first form of materialism, is found chiefly among the English schoolmen.

"The real progenitor of English materialism is Bacon. To him natural philosophy is the only true philosophy, and physics based upon the experience of the senses is the chief part of natural philosophy. Anaxagoras and his homoeomerae, Democritus and his atoms, he often quotes as his authorities. According to him, the senses are infallible and the source of all knowledge. All science is based on experience, and consists in subjecting the data furnished by the senses to a rational method of investigation. Induction, analysis, comparison, observation, experiment are the principal forms of such a rational method. Among the qualities inherent in matter, motion is the first and foremost, not only in the form of mechanical and mathematical motion, but chiefly in the form of an impulse, a vital spirit, a tension—or a 'qual,' to use a term of Jakob Böhme's[1]—of matter.

"In Bacon, its first creator, materialism still occludes within itself the germs of a many-sided development. On the one hand, matter, surrounded by a sensuous, poetic glamour, seems to attract man's whole entity by winning smiles. On the other, the aphoristically formulated doctrine pullulates with inconsistencies imported from theology.

"In its further evolution materialism becomes one-sided. Hobbes is the man who systematizes Baconian materialism. Knowledge based upon the senses loses its poetic blossom, it passes into the abstract experience of the mathematician; geometry is proclaimed as the queen of sciences. Materialism takes to misanthropy. If it is to overcome its opponent, misanthropic, fleshless spiritualism, and that on the latter's own ground, materialism has to chastise its own flesh and turn ascetic. Thus from a sensual it passes into an intellectual entity, but thus, too, it evolves all the consistency, regardless of consequences, characteristic of the intellect.

"Hobbes, as Bacon's continuator, argues thus: If all human knowledge is furnished by the senses, then our con-

[1] "Qual" is a philosophical play upon words. Qual literally means torture, a pain which drives to action of some kind; at the same time the mystic Böhme puts into the German word something of the meaning of the Latin *qualitas;* his "qual" was the activating principle arising from, and promoting in its turn, the spontaneous development of the thing, relation, or person subject to it, in contradistinction to a pain inflicted from without.

cepts and ideas are but the phantoms, divested of their sensual forms, of the real world. Philosophy can but give names to these phantoms. One name may be applied to more than one of them. There may even be names of names. It would imply a contradiction if, on the one hand, we maintained that all ideas had their origin in the world of sensation and, on the other, that a word was more than a word; that besides the beings known to us by our senses, beings which are one and all individuals, there existed also beings of a general, not individual, nature. An unbodily substance is the same absurdity as an unbodily body. Body, being, substance are but different terms for the same reality. *It is impossible to separate thought from matter that thinks.* This matter is the substratum of all changes going on in the world. The word 'infinite' is meaningless unless it states that our mind is capable of performing an endless process of addition. Only material things being perceptible to us, we cannot know anything about the existence of God. My own existence alone is certain. Every human passion is a mechanical movement which has a beginning and an end. The objects of impulse are what we call good. Man is subject to the same laws as nature. Power and freedom are identical.

"Hobbes had systematized Bacon without, however, furnishing a proof for Bacon's fundamental principle, the origin of all human knowledge from the world of sensation. It was Locke who, in his *Essay concerning Human Understanding,* supplied this proof.

"Hobbes had shattered the theistic prejudices of Baconian materialism; Collins, Dodwell, Coward, Hartley, Priestley similarly shattered the last theological bars that still hemmed in Locke's sensationalism. At all events, for practical materialists, deism is but an easygoing way of getting rid of religion."[2]

Thus Karl Marx wrote about the British origin of modern materialism. If Englishmen nowadays do not exactly relish the compliment he paid their ancestors, more's the pity. It is nonetheless undeniable that Bacon, Hobbes, and Locke are the fathers of that brilliant school of French

[2] Marx and Engels, *Die Heilige Familie,* Frankfurt am Main, 1845, pp. 201–4.

materialists which made the eighteenth century, in spite of all battles on land and sea won over Frenchmen by Germans and Englishmen, a pre-eminently French century, even before that crowning French Revolution, the results of which we outsiders, in England as well as in Germany, are still trying to acclimatize.

There is no denying it. About the middle of this century what struck every cultivated foreigner who set up his residence in England was what he was then bound to consider the religious bigotry and stupidity of the English respectable middle class. We, at that time, were all materialists, or at least very advanced freethinkers, and to us it appeared inconceivable that almost all educated people in England should believe in all sorts of impossible miracles, and that even geologists like Buckland and Mantell should contort the facts of their science so as not to clash too much with the myths of the Book of Genesis; while, in order to find people who dared to use their own intellectual faculties with regard to religious matters, you had to go among the uneducated, the "great unwashed," as they were then called, the working people, especially the Owenite socialists.

But England has been "civilized" since then. The exhibition of 1851 sounded the knell of English insular exclusiveness. England became gradually internationalized, in diet, in manners, in ideas; so much so that I begin to wish that some English manners and customs had made as much headway on the Continent as other Continental habits have made here. Anyhow, the introduction and spread of salad oil (before 1851 known only to the aristocracy) has been accompanied by a fatal spread of Continental skepticism in matters religious, and it has come to this, that agnosticism, though not yet considered "the thing" quite as much as the Church of England, is yet very nearly on a par, as far as respectability goes, with baptism, and decidedly ranks above the Salvation Army. And I cannot help believing that under these circumstances it will be consoling to many who sincerely regret and condemn this progress of infidelity to learn that these "newfangled notions" are not of foreign origin, are not "made in Germany," like so many other articles of daily use, but are undoubtedly Old

English, and that their British originators two hundred years ago went a good deal further than their descendants now dare to venture.

What, indeed, is agnosticism but, to use an expressive Lancashire term, "shamefaced" materialism? The agnostic's conception of nature is materialistic throughout. The entire natural world is governed by law, and absolutely excludes the intervention of action from without. "But," he adds, "we have no means either of ascertaining or of disproving the existence of some Supreme Being beyond the known universe." Now this might hold good at the time when Laplace, to Napoleon's question why in the great astronomer's *Mécanique céleste* the Creator was not even mentioned, proudly replied: *"Je n'avais pas besoin de cette hypothèse* [I had no need of this hypothesis]." But nowadays, in our evolutionary conception of the universe, there is absolutely no room for either a Creator or a Ruler, and to talk of a Supreme Being shut out from the whole existing world implies a contradiction in terms and, it seems to me, a gratuitous insult to the feelings of religious people.

Again, our agnostic admits that all our knowledge is based upon the information imparted to us by our senses. "But," he adds, "how do we know that our senses give us correct representations of the objects we perceive through them?" And he proceeds to inform us that whenever he speaks of objects or their qualities he does in reality not mean these objects and qualities, of which he cannot know anything for certain, but merely the impressions which they have produced on his senses. Now this line of reasoning seems undoubtedly hard to beat by mere argumentation. But before there was argumentation there was action. *Im Anfang war die Tat* [In the beginning was the deed]. And human action had solved the difficulty long before human ingenuity invented it. The proof of the pudding is in the eating. From the moment we turn to our own use these objects, according to the qualities we perceive in them, we put to an infallible test the correctness or otherwise of our sense perceptions. If these perceptions have been wrong, then our estimate of the use to which an object can be turned must also be wrong, and our attempt must fail. But if we succeed in accomplishing our aim, if we find that the object does agree with our idea of it, and does answer the purpose we intended it for, then that is positive proof that our perceptions of it and of its qualities, *so far*, agree with reality outside ourselves. And whenever we find ourselves face to face with a failure, then we generally are not long in making out the cause that made us fail; we find that the perception upon which we acted was either incomplete and superficial or combined with the results of other perceptions in a way not warranted by them—what we call defective reasoning. So long as we take care to train and to use our senses properly, and to keep our action within the limits prescribed by perceptions properly made and properly used, so long we shall find that the result of our action proves the conformity of our perceptions with the objective nature of the things perceived. Not in one single instance, so far, have we been led to the conclusion that our sense perceptions, scientifically controlled, induce in our minds ideas respecting the outer world that are, by their very nature, at variance with reality, or that there is an inherent incompatibility between the outer world and our sense perception of it.

But then come the Neo-Kantian agnostics and say: We may correctly perceive the qualities of a thing, but we cannot by any sensible or mental process grasp the thing-in-itself. This thing-in-itself is beyond our ken. To this Hegel, long since, has replied: If you know all the qualities of a thing, you know the thing itself; nothing remains but the fact that the said thing exists without us, and when your senses have taught you that fact you have grasped the last remnant of the thing-in-itself, Kant's celebrated, unknowable *Ding an sich*. To which it may be added that in Kant's time our knowledge of natural objects was indeed so fragmentary that he might well suspect, behind the little we knew about each of them, a mysterious thing-in-itself. But one after another these ungraspable things have been grasped, analyzed, and, what is more, *reproduced* by the giant progress of science; and what we can produce we certainly cannot consider as unknowable. To the chemistry of the first half of this century organic substances were such mysterious objects; now we learn to build them up one after another from their chemical elements without the aid of organic processes. Modern chemists declare that as soon as the chemical constitution of no matter what body is known it can be built up from its elements. We are still far from knowing the constitution of the highest organic substances, the albuminous bodies; but there is no reason why we should not, if only after centuries, arrive at the knowledge and, armed with it, produce artificial albumen. But if we arrive at that we shall at the same time have produced organic life, for life, from its lowest to its highest forms, is but the normal mode of existence of albuminous bodies.

As soon, however, as our agnostic has made these formal mental reservations he talks and acts as the rank materialist he at bottom is. He may say that, as far as *we* know, matter and motion—or, as they are now called, energy—can be neither created nor destroyed, but that we have no proof of their not having been created at some time or other. But if you try to use this admission against him in any particular case, he will quickly put you out of court. If he admits the possibility of spiritualism *in abstracto*, he will have none of it *in concreto*. As far as we know and can know, he will tell you there is no Creator and no Ruler of the universe; as far as we are concerned, matter and energy can be neither created nor annihilated; for us mind is a mode of energy, a function of the brain; all we know is that the material world is governed by immutable laws, and so forth. Thus, as far as he is a scientific man, as far as he *knows* anything, he is a materialist; outside his science, in spheres about which he knows nothing, he translates his ignorance into Greek and calls it agnosticism.

At all events, one thing seems clear: even if I was an agnostic, it is evident that I could not describe the conception of history sketched out in this little book as "historical agnosticism." Religious people would laugh at me, agnostics would indignantly ask, was I going to make fun of them? And thus I hope even British respectability will not be overshocked if I use, in English as well as in so many other languages, the term "historical materialism" to designate that view of the course of history which seeks the ultimate cause and the great moving power of all important historic events in the economic development of society, in the changes in the modes of production and exchange, in the consequent division of society into distinct classes, and in the struggles of these classes against one another.

This indulgence will perhaps be accorded to me all the sooner if I show that historical materialism may be of advantage even to British respectability. I have mentioned the fact that, about forty or fifty years ago, any cultivated foreigner settling in England was struck by what he was then bound to consider the religious bigotry and stupidity of the English respectable middle class. I am now going to prove that the respectable English middle class of that time was not quite so stupid as it looked to the intelligent foreigner. Its religious leanings can be explained.

When Europe emerged from the Middle Ages, the rising middle class of the towns constituted its revolutionary element. It had conquered a recognized position within medieval feudal organization, but this position, also, had become too narrow for its expansive power. The development of the middle class, the *bourgeoisie*, became incompatible with the maintenance of the feudal system; the feudal system, therefore, had to fall.

But the great international center of feudalism was the Roman Catholic Church. It united the whole of feudalized Western Europe, in spite of all internal wars, into one grand political system, opposed as much to the schismatic Greeks as to the Mohammedan countries. It surrounded feudal institutions with the halo of divine consecration. It had organized its own hierarchy on the feudal model and, lastly, it was itself by far the most powerful feudal lord, holding, as it did, fully one third of the soil of the Catholic world. Before profane feudalism could be successfully attacked in each country and in detail, this, its sacred central organization, had to be destroyed.

Moreover, parallel with the rise of the middle class went on the great revival of science: astronomy, mechanics, physics, anatomy, physiology were again cultivated. And the bourgeoisie, for the development of its industrial production, required a science which ascertained the physical properties of natural objects and the modes of action of the forces of nature. Now up to then science had but been the humble handmaid of the Church, had not been allowed to overstep the limits set by faith, and for that reason had been no science at all. Science rebelled against the Church; the bourgeoisie could not do without science, and, therefore, had to join in the rebellion.

The above, though touching but two of the points where the rising middle class was bound to come into collision with the established religion, will be sufficient to show, first, that the class most directly interested in the struggle against the pretensions of the Roman Church was the bourgeoisie and, second, that every struggle against feudalism, at that time, had to take on a religious disguise, had to be directed against the Church in the first instance. But if the universities and the traders of the cities started the cry, it was sure to find, and did find, a strong echo in the masses of the country people, the peasants, who everywhere had to struggle for their very existence with their feudal lords, spiritual and temporal.

The long fight of the bourgeoisie against feudalism culminated in three great, decisive battles.

The first was what is called the Protestant Reformation in Germany. The war cry raised against the Church by Luther was responded to by two insurrections of a political nature: first, that of the lower nobility under Franz von Sickingen (1523), then the great Peasants' War, 1525. Both were defeated, chiefly in consequence of the indecision of the parties most interested, the burghers of the towns—an indecision into the causes of which we cannot here enter. From that moment the struggle degenerated into a fight between the local princes and the central power, and ended by blotting out Germany, for two hundred years, from the politically active nations of Europe. The Lutheran reformation produced a new creed indeed, a religion adapted to absolute monarchy. No sooner were the peasants of northeast Germany converted to Lutheranism than they were from free men reduced to serfs.

But where Luther failed, Calvin won the day. Calvin's creed was one fit for the boldest of the bourgeoisie of his time. His predestination doctrine was the religious expression of the fact that in the commercial world of competition success or failure does not depend upon a man's activity or cleverness, but upon circumstances uncontrollable by him. It is not of him that willeth or of him that runneth, but of the mercy of unknown superior economic powers; and this was especially true at a period of economic revolution, when all old commercial routes and centers were replaced by new ones, when India and America were opened to the world, and when even the most sacred economic articles of faith—the value of gold and silver—began to totter and to break down. Calvin's church constitution was thoroughly democratic and republican, and where the kingdom of God was republicanized could the kingdoms of this world remain subject to monarchs, bishops, and lords? While German Lutheranism became a willing tool in the hands of princes, Calvinism founded a republic in Holland, and active republican parties in England and, above all, Scotland.

In Calvinism the second great bourgeois upheaval found its doctrine ready cut and dried. This upheaval took place in England. The middle class of the towns brought it on, and the yeomanry of the country districts fought it out. Curiously enough, in all the three great bourgeois risings, the peasantry furnishes the army that has to do the fighting, and the peasantry is just the class that, the victory once gained, is most surely ruined by the economic consequences of that victory. A hundred years after Cromwell the yeomanry of England had almost disappeared. Anyhow, had it not been for that yeomanry and for the plebeian element in the towns, the bourgeoisie alone would never have fought the matter out to the bitter end, and would never have brought Charles I to the scaffold. In order to secure even those conquests of the bourgeoisie that were ripe for gathering at the time, the revolution had to be carried considerably further—exactly as in 1793 in France and 1848 in Germany. This seems, in fact, to be one of the laws of evolution of bourgeois society.

Well, upon this excess of revolutionary activity there necessarily followed the inevitable reaction, which in its turn went beyond the point where it might have maintained itself. After a series of oscillations, the new center of gravity was at last attained, and became a new starting point. The grand period of English history, known to respectability under the name of "the Great Rebellion," and the struggles succeeding it, were brought to a close by the comparatively puny event entitled by Liberal historians "the Glorious Revolution."

The new starting point was a compromise between the rising middle class and the ex-feudal landowners. The latter, though called, as now, the aristocracy, had been long since on the way which led them to become what Louis Philippe in France became at a much later period, "the first bourgeois of the kingdom." Fortunately for England, the old feudal barons had killed one another during the Wars of the Roses. Their successors, though mostly scions of the old families, had been so much out of the direct line of descent that they constituted quite a new body, with habits and tendencies far more bourgeois than feudal. They fully understood the value of money, and at once began to increase their rents by turning hundreds of small farmers out and replacing them by sheep. Henry VIII, while squandering the Church lands, created fresh bourgeois landlords by wholesale; the innumerable confiscations of estates, regranted to absolute or relative upstarts, and continued during the whole of the seventeenth century, had the same result. Consequently, ever since Henry VII, the English "aristocracy," far from counteracting the development of industrial production, had, on the contrary, sought to indirectly profit thereby; and there had always been a section of the great landowners willing, from economic or political reasons, to co-operate with the leading men of the financial and industrial bourgeoisie. The compromise of 1689 was, therefore, easily accomplished. The political spoils of "pelf and place" were left to the great landowning families, provided the economic interests of the financial, manufacturing, and commercial middle class were sufficiently attended to. And these economic interests were at that time powerful enough to determine the general policy of the nation. There might be squabbles about matters of detail, but, on the whole, the aristocratic oligarchy knew too well that its own economic prosperity was irretrievably bound up with that of the industrial and commercial middle class.

From that time, the bourgeoisie was a humble but still a

recognized component of the ruling classes of England. With the rest of them it had a common interest in keeping in subjection the great working mass of the nation. The merchant or manufacturer himself stood in the position of master, or, as it was until lately called, of "natural superior" to his clerks, his workpeople, his domestic servants. His interest was to get as much and as good work out of them as he could; for this end they had to be trained to proper submission. He was himself religious; his religion had supplied the standard under which he had fought the king and the lords; he was not long in discovering the opportunities this same religion offered him for working upon the minds of his natural inferiors and making them submissive to the behests of the masters it had pleased God to place over them. In short, the English bourgeoisie now had to take a part in keeping down the "lower orders," the great producing mass of the nation, and one of the means employed for that purpose was the influence of religion.

There was another fact that contributed to strengthen the religious leanings of the bourgeoisie. That was the rise of materialism in England. This new doctrine not only shocked the pious feelings of the middle class; it announced itself as a philosophy fit only for scholars and cultivated men of the world, in contrast to religion, which was good enough for the uneducated masses, including the bourgeoisie. With Hobbes it stepped on the stage as a defender of royal prerogative and omnipotence; it called upon absolute monarchy to keep down that *puer robustus sed malitiosus* [robust but malicious boy], to wit, the people. Similarly, with the successors of Hobbes, with Bolingbroke, Shaftesbury, etc., the new deistic form of materialism remained an aristocratic, esoteric doctrine, and, therefore, hateful to the middle class both for its religious heresy and for its anti-bourgeois political connections. Accordingly, in opposition to the materialism and deism of the aristocracy, those Protestant sects which had furnished the flag and the fighting contingent against the Stuarts continued to furnish the main strength of the progressive middle class, and form even today the backbone of "the Great Liberal Party."

In the meantime materialism passed from England to

France, where it met and coalesced with another materialistic school of philosophers, a branch of Cartesianism. In France, too, it remained at first an exclusively aristocratic doctrine. But soon its revolutionary character asserted itself. The French materialists did not limit their criticism to matters of religious belief; they extended it to whatever scientific tradition or political institution they met with; and to prove the claim of their doctrine to universal application they took the shortest cut and boldly applied it to all subjects of knowledge in the giant work after which they were named—the *Encyclopédie*. Thus, in one or the other of its two forms—avowed materialism or deism—it became the creed of the whole cultured youth of France; so much so that when the Great Revolution broke out the doctrine hatched by English Royalists gave a theoretical flag to French Republicans and Terrorists, and furnished the text for the Declaration of the Rights of Man. The great French Revolution was the third uprising of the bourgeoisie, but the first that had entirely cast off the religious cloak and was fought out on undisguised political lines; it was the first, too, that was really fought out up to the destruction of one of the combatants, the aristocracy, and the complete triumph of the other, the bourgeoisie. In England the continuity of pre-revolutionary and post-revolutionary institutions, and the compromise between landlords and capitalists, found its expression in the continuity of judicial precedents and in the religious preservation of the feudal forms of the law. In France the Revolution constituted a complete breach with the traditions of the past; it cleared out the very last vestiges of feudalism, and created in the *Code Civil* a masterly adaptation of the old Roman law—that almost perfect expression of the juridical relations corresponding to the economic stage called by Marx the production of commodities—to modern capitalistic conditions; so masterly that this French revolutionary code still serves as a model for reforms of the law of property in all other countries, not excepting England. Let us, however, not forget that if English law continues to express the economic relations of capitalistic society in that barbarous feudal language which corresponds to the thing expressed, just as English spelling corresponds to English pronunciation—"*Vous écrivez Londres et vous prononcez Constantinople* [You write London and you pronounce Constantinople]," said a Frenchman—that same English law is the only one which has preserved through ages, and transmitted to America and the colonies, the best part of that old Germanic personal freedom, local self-government and independence from all interference but that of the law courts, which on the Continent has been lost during the period of absolute monarchy, and has nowhere been as yet fully recovered.

To return to our British bourgeois. The French Revolution gave him a splendid opportunity, with the help of the Continental monarchies, to destroy French maritime commerce, to annex French colonies, and to crush the last French pretensions to maritime rivalry. That was one reason why he fought it. Another was that the ways of this revolution went very much against his grain. Not only its "execrable" terrorism, but the very attempt to carry bourgeois rule to extremes. What should the British bourgeois do without his aristocracy, that taught him manners, such as they were, and invented fashions for him—that furnished officers of the army, which kept order at home, and the navy, which conquered colonial possessions and new markets abroad? There was indeed a progressive minority of the bourgeoisie, that minority whose interests were not so well attended to under the compromise; this section, composed chiefly of the less wealthy middle class, did sympathize with the Revolution, but it was powerless in Parliament.

Thus if materialism became the creed of the French Revolution, the God-fearing English bourgeois held all the faster to his religion. Had not the Reign of Terror in Paris proved what was the upshot if the religious instincts of the masses were lost? The more materialism spread from France to neighboring countries and was reinforced by similar doctrinal currents, notably by German philosophy, the more, in fact, materialism and free thought generally became on the Continent the necessary qualifications of a cultivated man, the more stubbornly the English middle class stuck to its manifold religious creeds. These creeds might differ from one another, but they were, all of them, distinctly religious, Christian creeds.

While the Revolution ensured the political triumph of the bourgeoisie in France, in England Watt, Arkwright, Cartwright, and others initiated an industrial revolution, which completely shifted the center of gravity of economic power. The wealth of the bourgeoisie increased considerably faster than that of the landed aristocracy. Within the bourgeoisie itself the financial aristocracy, the bankers, etc., were more and more pushed into the background by the manufacturers. The compromise of 1689, even after the gradual changes it had undergone in favor of the bourgeoisie, no longer corresponded to the relative position of the parties to it. The character of these parties, too, had changed; the bourgeoisie of 1830 was very different from that of the preceding century. The political power still left to the aristocracy, and used by them to resist the pretensions of the new industrial bourgeoisie, became incompatible with the new economic interests. A fresh struggle with the aristocracy was necessary; it could end only in a victory of the new economic power. First, the Reform Act was pushed through, in spite of all resistance, under the impulse of the French Revolution of 1830. It gave to the bourgeoisie a recognized and powerful place in Parliament. Then the repeal of the corn laws, which settled, once for all, the supremacy of the bourgeoisie, and especially of its most active portion, the manufacturers, over the landed aristocracy. This was the greatest victory of the bourgeoisie; it was, however, also the last it gained in its own exclusive interest. Whatever triumphs it obtained later on, it had to share with a new social power, first its ally, but soon its rival.

The industrial revolution had created a class of large manufacturing capitalists, but also a class—and a far more numerous one—of manufacturing workpeople. This class gradually increased in numbers, in proportion as the industrial revolution seized upon one branch of manufacture after another, and in the same proportion it increased in power. This power it proved as early as 1824, by forcing a reluctant Parliament to repeal the acts forbidding combinations of workmen. During the Reform agitation the workingmen constituted the Radical wing of the Reform party; the Act of 1832 having excluded them from the suffrage, they formulated their demands in the People's Charter, and constituted themselves, in opposition to the great bourgeois Anti-Corn Law party, into an independent party, the Chartists, the first workingmen's party of modern times.

Then came the Continental revolutions of February and March 1848, in which the working people played such a prominent part and, at least in Paris, put forward demands which were certainly inadmissible from the point of view of capitalist society. And then came the general reaction. First the defeat of the Chartists on April 10, 1848, then the crushing of the Paris workingmen's insurrection in June of the same year, then the disasters of 1849 in Italy, Hungary, south Germany, and at last the victory of Louis Bonaparte over Paris, December 2, 1851. For a time, at least, the bugbear of working-class pretensions was put down, but at what cost! If the British bourgeois had been convinced before of the necessity of maintaining the common people in a religious mood, how much more must he feel that necessity after all these experiences? Regardless of the sneers of his Continental compeers, he continued to spend thousands and tens of thousands, year after year, upon the evangelization of the lower orders; not content with his own native religious machinery, he appealed to Brother Jonathan, the greatest organizer in existence of religion as a trade, and imported from America revivalism, Moody and Sankey, and the like; and, finally, he accepted the dangerous aid of the Salvation Army, which revives the propaganda of early Christianity, appeals to the poor as the elect, fights capitalism in a religious way, and thus fosters an element of early Christian class antagonism, which one day may become troublesome to the well-to-do people who now find the ready money for it.

It seems a law of historical development that the bourgeoisie can in no European country get hold of political power—at least for any length of time—in the same exclusive way in which the feudal aristocracy kept hold of it during the Middle Ages. Even in France, where feudalism was completely extinguished, the bourgeoisie, as a whole, has held full possession of the government for very short periods only. During Louis Philippe's reign, 1830–48, a very small portion of the bourgeoisie ruled the kingdom; by far the larger part were excluded from the suffrage by the high qualification. Under the Second Republic, 1848–51, the whole bourgeoisie ruled, but for three years only; their incapacity brought on the Second Empire. It is only now, in the Third Republic, that the bourgeoisie as a whole have kept possession of the helm for more than twenty years, and they are already showing lively signs of decadence. A durable reign of the bourgeoisie has been possible only in countries like America, where feudalism was unknown and society at the very beginning started from a bourgeois basis. And even in France and America the successors of the bourgeoisie, the working people, are already knocking at the door.

In England the bourgeoisie never held undivided sway. Even the victory of 1832 left the landed aristocracy in almost exclusive possession of all the leading government offices. The meekness with which the wealthy middle class submitted to this remained inconceivable to me until the great Liberal manufacturer, Mr. W. A. Forster, in a public speech implored the young men of Bradford to learn French, as a means to get on in the world, and quoted from his own experience how sheepish he looked when, as a Cabinet minister, he had to move in society where French was, at least, as necessary as English! The fact was, the English middle class of that time were, as a rule, quite uneducated upstarts, and could not help leaving to the aristocracy those superior government places where other qualifications were required than mere insular narrowness and insular conceit, seasoned by business sharpness.[3] Even

[3] And even in business matters the conceit of national chauvinism is but a sorry adviser. Up to quite recently the average English manufacturer considered it derogatory for an Englishman to speak any language but his own, and felt rather proud than otherwise of the fact that "poor devils" of foreigners settled in England and took off his hands the trouble of disposing of his products abroad. He never noticed that these foreigners, mostly Germans, thus got command of a very large part of British foreign trade, imports and exports, and that the direct foreign trade of Englishmen became limited, almost entirely, to the colonies,

now the endless newspaper debates about middle-class education show that the English middle class does not yet consider itself good enough for the best education, and looks to something more modest. Thus, even after the repeal of the corn laws, it appeared a matter of course that the men who had carried the day, the Cobdens, Brights, Forsters, etc., should remain excluded from a share in the official government of the country, until twenty years afterwards a new Reform Act opened to them the door of the Cabinet. The English bourgeoisie are, up to the present day, so deeply penetrated by a sense of their social inferiority that they keep up, at their own expense and that of the nation, an ornamental caste of drones to represent the nation worthily at all state functions; and they consider themselves highly honored whenever one of themselves is found worthy of admission into this select and privileged body, manufactured, after all, by themselves.

The industrial and commercial middle class had, therefore, not yet succeeded in driving the landed aristocracy completely from political power when another competitor, the working class, appeared on the stage. The reaction after the Chartist movement and the Continental revolutions, as well as the unparalleled extension of English trade from 1848–66 (ascribed vulgarly to free trade alone, but due far more to the colossal development of railways, ocean steamers, and means of intercourse generally), had again driven the working class into the dependency of the Liberal party, of which they formed, as in pre-Chartist times, the Radical wing. Their claims to the franchise, however, gradually be-

China, the United States, and South America. Nor did he notice that these Germans traded with other Germans abroad, who gradually organized a complete network of commercial colonies all over the world. But when Germany, about forty years ago, seriously began manufacturing for export, this network served her admirably in her transformation, in so short a time, from a corn-exporting into a first-rate manufacturing country. Then, about ten years ago, the British manufacturer got frightened, and asked his ambassadors and consuls how it was that he could no longer keep his customers together. The unanimous answer was: (1) You don't learn your customer's language, but expect him to speak your own; (2) You don't even try to suit your customer's wants, habits, and tastes, but expect him to conform to your English ones.

came irresistible; while the Whig leaders of the Liberals "funked," Disraeli showed his superiority by making the Tories seize the favorable moment and introduce household suffrage in the boroughs, along with a redistribution of seats. Then followed the ballot; then in 1884 the extension of household suffrage to the counties and a fresh redistribution of seats, by which electoral districts were to some extent equalized. All these measures considerably increased the electoral power of the working class, so much so that in at least a hundred and fifty to two hundred constituencies that class now furnishes the majority of voters. But parliamentary government is a capital school for teaching respect for tradition; if the middle class look with awe and veneration upon what Lord John Manners playfully called "our old nobility," the mass of the working people then looked up with respect and deference to what used to be designated as "their betters," the middle class. Indeed, the British workman, some fifteen years ago, was the model workman, whose respectful regard for the position of his master, and whose self-restraining modesty in claiming rights for himself, consoled our German economists of the Kathedersocialist school for the incurable communistic and revolutionary tendencies of their own workingmen at home.

But the English middle class—good men of business as they are—saw farther than the German professors. They had shared their power but reluctantly with the working class. They had learned, during the Chartist years, what that *puer robustus sed malitiosus*, the people, is capable of. And since that time, they had been compelled to incorporate the better part of the People's Charter in the Statutes of the United Kingdom. Now, if ever, the people must be kept in order by moral means, and the first and foremost of all moral means of action upon the masses is and remains—religion. Hence the parsons' majorities on the school boards, hence the increasing self-taxation of the bourgeoisie for the support of all sorts of revivalism, from ritualism to the Salvation Army.

And now came the triumph of British respectability over the free thought and religious laxity of the Continental bourgeois. The workmen of France and Germany had become rebellious. They were thoroughly infected with socialism, and, for very good reasons, were not at all particular as to the legality of the means by which to secure their own ascendancy. The *puer robustus*, here, turned from day to day more *malitiosus*. Nothing remained to the French and German bourgeoisie as a last resource but to silently drop their free thought, as a youngster, when seasickness creeps upon him, quietly drops the burning cigar he brought swaggeringly on board; one by one the scoffers turned pious in outward behavior, spoke with respect of the Church, its dogmas and rites, and even conformed with the latter as far as could not be helped. French bourgeois dined *maigre* on Fridays, and German ones sat out long Protestant sermons in their pews on Sundays. They had come to grief with materialism. "*Die Religion muss dem Volk erhalten werden*"—religion must be kept alive for the people—that was the only and the last means to save society from utter ruin. Unfortunately for themselves, they did not find this out until they had done their level best to break up religion forever. And now it was the turn of the British bourgeois to sneer and to say: "Why, you fools, I could have told you that two hundred years ago!"

However, I am afraid neither the religious stolidity of the British nor the *post festum* [after the feast] conversion of the Continental bourgeois will stem the rising proletarian tide. Tradition is a great retarding force, is the *vis inertiae* of history, but, being merely passive, is sure to be broken down; and thus religion will be no lasting safeguard to capitalist society. If our juridical, philosophical, and religious ideas are the more or less remote offshoots of the economic relations prevailing in a given society, such ideas cannot, in the long run, withstand the effects of a complete change in these relations. And unless we believe in supernatural revelation, we must admit that no religious tenets will ever suffice to prop up a tottering society.

In fact, in England, too, the working people have begun to move again. They are, no doubt, shackled by traditions of various kinds. Bourgeois traditions, such as the widespread belief that there can be but two parties, Conservative and Liberal, and that the working class must work out its salvation by and through the great Liberal party. Workingmen's traditions, inherited from their first tentative efforts at independent action, such as the exclusion, from ever so many old trade unions, of all applicants who have not gone through a regular apprenticeship, which means the breeding, by every such union, of its own blacklegs. But for all that the English working class is moving, as even Professor Brentano has sorrowfully had to report to his brother Kathedersocialists. It moves, like all things in England, with a slow and measured step, with hesitation here, with more or less unfruitful, tentative attempts there; it moves now and then with an overcautious mistrust of the name of socialism, while it gradually absorbs the substance, and the movement spreads and seizes one layer of the workers after another. It has now shaken out of their torpor the unskilled laborers of the East End of London, and we all know what a splendid impulse these fresh forces have given it in return. And if the pace of the movement is not up to the impatience of some people, let them not forget that it is the working class which keeps alive the finest qualities of the English character, and that if a step in advance is once gained in England it is, as a rule, never lost afterwards. If the sons of the old Chartists, for reasons explained above, were not quite up to the mark, the grandsons bid fair to be worthy of their forefathers.

But the triumph of the European working class does not depend upon England alone. It can be secured only by the co-operation of, at least, England, France, and Germany. In both the latter countries the working-class movement is well ahead of England. In Germany it is even within measurable distance of success. The progress it has there made during the last twenty-five years is unparalleled. It advances with ever increasing velocity. If the German middle class have shown themselves lamentably deficient in political capacity, discipline, courage, energy, and perseverance, the German working class have given ample proof of all these qualities. Four hundred years ago Germany was the starting point of the first upheaval of the European middle class; as things are now, is it outside the limits of possibility that Germany will be the scene, too, of the first great victory of the European proletariat?

IV. Socialism: Utopian and Scientific

FRIEDRICH ENGELS

This booklet, composed of three chapters from Engels' book against Dühring, was first published in French in 1880. Its English translation, done by Edward Aveling, was printed in 1892.—ED.

I

Modern socialism is, in its essence, the direct product of the recognition, on the one hand, of the class antagonisms existing in the society of today between proprietors and non-proprietors, between capitalists and wage workers; on the other hand, of the anarchy existing in production. But in its theoretical form modern socialism originally appears ostensibly as a more logical extension of the principles laid down by the great French philosophers of the eighteenth century. Like every new theory, modern socialism had, at first, to connect itself with the intellectual stock in trade ready to its hand, however deeply its roots lay in material economic facts.

The great men, who in France prepared men's minds for the coming revolution, were themselves extreme revolutionists. They recognized no external authority of any kind whatever. Religion, natural science, society, political institutions—everything was subjected to the most unsparing criticism: everything must justify its existence before the judgment seat of reason or give up existence. Reason became the sole measure of everything. It was the time when, as Hegel says, the world stood upon its head[1]; first in the sense that the human head, and the principles arrived at by its thought, claimed to be the basis of all human action and association; but by and by, also, in the wider sense that the reality which was in contradiction to these principles had, in fact, to be turned upside down. Every form of society and government then existing, every old traditional notion was flung into the lumber room as irrational; the world had hitherto allowed itself to be led solely by prejudices; everything in the past deserved only pity and contempt. Now, for the first time, appeared the light of day, the kingdom of reason; henceforth superstition, injustice, privilege, oppression were to be superseded by eternal truth, eternal right, equality based on nature and the inalienable rights of man.

We know today that this kingdom of reason was nothing more than the idealized kingdom of the bourgeoisie; that this eternal right found its realization in bourgeois justice; that this equality reduced itself to bourgeois equality before the law; that bourgeois property was proclaimed as one of the essential rights of man; and that the government of reason, the *contrat social* of Rousseau, came into being, and only could come into being, as a democratic bourgeois republic. The great thinkers of the eighteenth century

[1] This is the passage on the French Revolution: "Thought, the concept of law, all at once made itself felt, and against this the old scaffolding of wrong could make no stand. In this conception of law, therefore, a constitution has now been established, and henceforth everything must be based upon this. Since the sun had been in the firmament, and the planets circled round him, the sight had never been seen of man standing upon his head—i.e., on the Idea—and building reality after this image. Anaxagoras first said that the nous, reason, rules the world; but now, for the first time, had man come to recognize that the Idea must rule the mental reality. And this was a magnificent sunrise. All thinking beings have participated in celebrating this holy day. A sublime emotion swayed men at that time, an enthusiasm of reason pervaded the world, as if now had come the reconciliation of the Divine Principle with the world." [Hegel: *Philosophy of History*, 1840, p. 535.] Is it not high time to set the anti-socialist law in action against such teachings, subversive and to the common danger, by the late Professor Hegel?

could, no more than their predecessors, go beyond the limits imposed upon them by their epoch.

But, side by side with the antagonism of the feudal nobility and the burghers, who claimed to represent all the rest of society, was the general antagonism of exploiters and exploited, of rich idlers and poor workers. It was this very circumstance that made it possible for the representatives of the bourgeoisie to put themselves forward as representing not one special class, but the whole of suffering humanity. Still further. From its origin the bourgeoisie was saddled with its antithesis: capitalists cannot exist without wage workers, and, in the same proportion as the medieval burgher of the guild developed into the modern bourgeois, the guild journeyman and the day laborer, outside the guilds, developed into the proletarian. And although, upon the whole, the bourgeoisie, in their struggle with the nobility, could claim to represent at the same time the interests of the different working classes of that period, yet in every great bourgeois movement there were independent outbursts of that class which was the forerunner, more or less developed, of the modern proletariat. For example, at the time of the German Reformation and the Peasants' War, the Anabaptists and Thomas Münzer; in the great English Revolution, the Levelers; in the great French Revolution, Babeuf.

There were theoretical enunciations corresponding with these revolutionary uprisings of a class not yet developed: in the sixteenth and seventeenth centuries, utopian pictures of ideal social conditions; in the eighteenth, actual communistic theories (Morelly and Mably). The demand for equality was no longer limited to political rights; it was extended also to the social conditions of individuals. It was not simply class privileges that were to be abolished, but class distinctions themselves. A communism, ascetic, denouncing all the pleasures of life, Spartan, was the first form of the new teaching. Then came the three great Utopians: St. Simon, to whom the middle-class movement, side by side with the proletarian, still had a certain significance; Fourier; and Owen, who in the country where capitalist production was most developed, and under the influence of the antagonisms begotten of this, worked out his proposals for the removal of class distinction systematically and in direct relation to French materialism.

One thing is common to all three. Not one of them appears as a representative of the interests of that proletariat which historical development had, in the meantime, produced. Like the French philosophers, they do not claim to emancipate a particular class to begin with, but all humanity at once. Like them, they wish to bring in the kingdom of reason and eternal justice, but this kingdom, as they see it, is as far as heaven from earth from that of the French philosophers.

For, to our three social reformers, the bourgeois world, based upon the principles of these philosophers, is quite as irrational and unjust and, therefore, finds its way to the dust hole quite as readily as feudalism and all the earlier stages of society. If pure reason and justice have not hitherto ruled the world, this has been the case only because men have not rightly understood them. What was wanted was the individual man of genius, who has now arisen and who understands the truth. That he has now arisen, that the truth has now been clearly understood, is not an inevitable event, following of necessity in the chain of historical development, but a mere happy accident. He might just as well have been born five hundred years earlier, and might then have spared humanity five hundred years of error, strife, and suffering.

We saw how the French philosophers of the eighteenth century, the forerunners of the Revolution, appealed to reason as the sole judge of all that is. A rational government, rational society were to be founded; everything that ran counter to eternal reason was to be remorselessly done away with. We saw also that this eternal reason was in reality nothing but the idealized understanding of the eighteenth-century citizen, just then evolving into the bourgeois. The French Revolution had realized this rational society and government.

But the new order of things, rational enough as compared with earlier conditions, turned out to be by no means absolutely rational. The state based upon reason completely collapsed. Rousseau's *contrat social* had found its realization in the Reign of Terror, from which the bourgeoisie, who had lost confidence in their own political capacity, had taken refuge first in the corruption of the Directorate, and, finally, under the wing of the Napoleonic despotism. The promised eternal peace was turned into an endless war of conquest. The society based upon reason had fared no better. The antagonism between rich and poor, instead of dissolving into general prosperity, had become intensified by the removal of the guild and other privileges, which had to some extent bridged it, and by the removal of the charitable institutions of the Church. The "freedom of property" from feudal fetters, now veritably accomplished, turned out to be, for the small capitalists and small proprietors, the freedom to sell their small property, crushed under the overmastering competition of the large capitalists and landlords, to these great lords, and thus, as far as the small capitalists and peasant proprietors were concerned, became "freedom *from* property." The development of industry upon a capitalistic basis made poverty and misery of the working masses conditions of existence of society. Cash payment became more and more, in Carlyle's phrase, "the sole nexus between man and man." The number of crimes increased from year to year. Formerly the feudal vices had openly stalked about in broad daylight; though not eradicated, they were now at any rate thrust into the background. In their stead the bourgeois vices, hitherto practiced in secret, began to blossom all the more luxuriantly. Trade became to a greater and greater extent cheating. The "fraternity" of the revolutionary motto was realized in the chicanery and rivalries of the battle of competition. Oppression by force was replaced by corruption; the sword, as the first social lever, by gold. The right of the first night was transferred from the feudal lords to the bourgeois manufacturers. Prostitution increased to an extent never heard of. Marriage itself remained, as before, the legally recognized form, the official cloak of prostitution, and, moreover, was supplemented by rich crops of adultery.

In a word, compared with the splendid promises of the philosophers, the social and political institutions born of the "triumph of reason" were bitterly disappointing caricatures. All that was wanting was the men to formulate this disappointment, and they came with the turn of the century. In 1802, St. Simon's Geneva letters appeared; in 1808 appeared Fourier's first work, although the groundwork of his theory dated from 1799; on January 1, 1800, Robert Owen undertook the direction of New Lanark.

At this time, however, the capitalist mode of production, and with it the antagonism between the bourgeoisie and the proletariat, was still very incompletely developed. Modern industry, which had just arisen in England, was still unknown in France. But modern industry develops, on the one hand, the conflicts which make absolutely necessary a revolution in the mode of production and the doing away with its capitalistic character—conflicts not only between the classes begotten of it, but also between the very productive forces and the forms of exchange created by it. And, on the other hand, it develops, in these very gigantic productive forces, the means of ending these conflicts. If, therefore, about the year 1800 the conflicts arising from the new social order were only just beginning to take shape, this holds still more fully as to the means of ending them. The "have-nothing" masses of Paris, during the Reign of Terror, were able for a moment to gain the mastery, and thus to lead the bourgeois revolution to victory in spite of the bourgeoisie themselves. But in doing so they only proved how impossible it was for their domination to last under the conditions then obtaining. The proletariat, which then for the first time evolved from these "have-nothing" masses as the nucleus of a new class, as yet quite incapable of independent political action, appeared as an oppressed, suffering order, to which, in its incapacity to help itself, help could, at best, be brought in from without or down from above.

This historical situation also dominated the founders of socialism. To the crude conditions of capitalistic production and the crude class conditions corresponded crude theories. The solution of the social problems, which as yet lay hidden in undeveloped economic conditions, the Utopians attempted to evolve out of the human brain. Society presented nothing but wrongs; to remove these was the task of reason. It was necessary, then, to discover a new and more perfect system of social order and to impose this upon society from without by propaganda, and, wherever it was possible, by the example of model experiments. These new social systems were foredoomed as utopian; the more completely they were worked out in detail, the more they could not avoid drifting off into pure fantasies.

These facts once established, we need not dwell a moment longer upon this side of the question, now wholly belonging to the past. We can leave it to the literary small fry to solemnly quibble over these fantasies, which today only make us smile, and to crow over the superiority of their own bald reasoning as compared with such "insanity." For ourselves, we delight in the stupendously grand thoughts and germs of thought that everywhere break out through their fantastic covering, and to which these Philistines are blind.

St. Simon was a son of the great French Revolution, at the outbreak of which he was not yet thirty. The Revolution was the victory of the third estate, i.e., of the great masses of the nation, *working* in production and in trade, over the privileged *idle* classes, the nobles and the priests. But the victory of the third estate soon revealed itself as exclusively the victory of a small part of this "estate," as the conquest of political power by the socially privileged section of it, i.e., the propertied bourgeoisie. And the bourgeoisie had certainly developed rapidly during the Revolution, partly by speculation in the lands of the nobility and of the Church, confiscated and afterwards put up for sale, and partly by frauds upon the nation by means of army contracts. It was the domination of these swindlers that, under the Directorate, brought France to the verge of ruin, and thus gave Napoleon the pretext for his *coup d'état*.

Hence to St. Simon the antagonism between the third estate and the privileged classes took the form of an antagonism between "workers" and "idlers." The idlers were not merely the old privileged classes, but also all who, without taking any part in production or distribution, lived on their incomes. And the workers were not only the wage workers, but also the manufacturers, the merchants, the bankers. That the idlers had lost the capacity for intellectual leadership and political supremacy had been proved, and was by the Revolution finally settled. That the non-possessing classes had not this capacity seemed to St. Simon proved by the experiences of the Reign of Terror. Then who was to lead and command? According to St. Simon, science and industry, both united by a new religious bond, destined to restore that unity of religious ideas which had been lost since the time of the Reformation—a necessarily mystic and rigidly hierarchic "new Christianity." But science, that was the scholars; and industry, that was, in the first place, the working bourgeois, manufacturers, merchants, bankers. These bourgeois were certainly intended by St. Simon to transform themselves into a class of public officials, of social trustees; but they were still to hold, vis-à-vis the workers, a commanding and economically privileged position. The bankers especially were to be called upon to direct the whole of social production by the regulation of credit. This conception was in exact keeping with a time in which modern industry in France and, with it, the chasm between bourgeoisie and proletariat was only just coming into existence. But what St. Simon especially lays stress upon is this: what interests him first, and above all other things, is the lot of the class that is the most numerous and the poorest (*"la classe la plus nombreuse et la plus pauvre"*).

Already in his Geneva letters St. Simon lays down the proposition that "all men ought to work." In the same work he recognizes also that the Reign of Terror was the reign of the non-possessing masses. "See," says he to them, "what happened in France at the time when your comrades held sway there; they brought about a famine." But to recognize the French Revolution as a class war, and not simply one between nobility and bourgeoisie, but between nobility, bourgeoisie, and the non-possessors, was, in the year 1802, a most pregnant discovery. In 1816 he declares that politics is the science of production, and foretells the complete absorption of politics by economics. The knowledge that economic conditions are the basis of political institutions appears here only in embryo. Yet what is here already very plainly expressed is the idea of the future conversion of political rule over men into an administration of things and a direction of processes of production—that is to say, the "abolition of the state," about which recently there has been so much noise.

St. Simon shows the same superiority over his contemporaries, when in 1814, immediately after the entry of the allies into Paris, and again in 1815, during the Hundred Days' War, he proclaims the alliance of France with England, and then of both these countries with Germany, as the only guarantee for the prosperous development and peace of Europe. To preach to the French in 1815 an alliance with the victors of Waterloo required as much courage as historical foresight.

If in St. Simon we find a comprehensive breadth of view, by virtue of which almost all the ideas of later socialists that are not strictly economic are found in him in embryo, we find in Fourier a criticism of the existing conditions of society, genuinely French and witty, but not upon that account any the less thorough. Fourier takes the bourgeoisie, their inspired prophets before the Revolution, and their interested eulogists after it at their own word. He remorselessly lays bare the material and moral misery of the bourgeois world. He confronts it with the earlier philosophers' dazzling promises of a society in which reason alone should reign, of a civilization in which happiness should be universal, of an illimitable human perfectibility, and with the rose-colored phraseology of the bourgeois ideologists of his time. He points out how everywhere the most pitiful reality corresponds with the most high-sounding phrases, and he overwhelms this hopeless fiasco of phrases with his mordant sarcasm.

Fourier is not only a critic; his imperturbably serene nature makes him a satirist, and assuredly one of the greatest satirists of all time. He depicts with equal power and charm the swindling speculations that blossomed out upon the downfall of the Revolution and the shopkeeping spirit prevalent in, and characteristic of, French commerce at that time. Still more masterly is his criticism of the bourgeois form of the relations between the sexes and the position of woman in bourgeois society. He was the first to declare that in any given society the degree of woman's emancipation is the natural measure of the general emancipation.

But Fourier is at his greatest in his conception of the

history of society. He divides its whole course, thus far, into four stages of evolution—savagery, barbarism, the patriarchate, civilization. This last is identical with the so-called civil, or bourgeois, society of today—i.e., with the social order that came in with the sixteenth century. He proves "that the civilized stage raises every vice practiced by barbarism in a simple fashion into a form of existence, complex, ambiguous, equivocal, hypocritical"—that civilization moves in "a vicious circle," in contradictions which it constantly reproduces without being able to solve them; hence it constantly arrives at the very opposite to that which it wants to attain, or pretends to want to attain, so that, e.g., "under civilization poverty is born of superabundance itself."

Fourier, as we see, uses the dialectic method in the same masterly way as his contemporary, Hegel. Using these same dialectics, he argues against the talk about illimitable human perfectibility, that every historical phase has its period of ascent and also its period of descent, and he applies this observation to the future of the whole human race. As Kant introduced into natural science the idea of the ultimate destruction of the earth, Fourier introduced into historical science that of the ultimate destruction of the human race.

While in France the hurricane of the Revolution swept over the land, in England a quieter, but not on that account less tremendous, revolution was going on. Steam and the new tool-making machinery were transforming manufacture into modern industry, and thus revolutionizing the whole foundation of bourgeois society. The sluggish march of development of the manufacturing period changed into a veritable storm-and-stress period of production. With constantly increasing swiftness the splitting up of society into large capitalists and non-possessing proletarians went on. Between these, instead of the former stable middle class, an unstable mass of artisans and small shopkeepers, the most fluctuating portion of the population, now led a precarious existence.

The new mode of production was, as yet, only at the beginning of its period of ascent; as yet it was the normal, regular method of production—the only one possible under existing conditions. Nevertheless, even then it was producing crying social abuses—the herding together of a homeless population in the worst quarters of the large towns; the loosening of all traditional moral bonds, of patriarchal subordination, of family relations; overwork, especially of women and children, to a frightful extent; complete demoralization of the working class, suddenly flung into altogether new conditions, from the country into the town, from agriculture into modern industry, from stable conditions of existence into insecure ones that changed from day to day.

At this juncture there came forward as a reformer a manufacturer twenty-nine years old—a man of almost sublime, childlike simplicity of character, and at the same time one of the few born leaders of men. Robert Owen had adopted the teaching of the materialistic philosophers: that man's character is the product, on the one hand, of heredity; on the other, of the environment of the individual during his lifetime, and especially during his period of development. In the industrial revolution most of his class saw only chaos and confusion, and the opportunity of fishing in these troubled waters and making large fortunes quickly. He saw in it the opportunity of putting into practice his favorite theory, and so of bringing order out of chaos. He had already tried it with success, as superintendent of more than five hundred men in a Manchester factory. From 1800 to 1829 he directed the great cotton mill at New Lanark, in Scotland, as managing partner, along the same lines, but with greater freedom of action and with a success that made him a European reputation. A population, originally consisting of the most diverse and, for the most part, very demoralized elements, a population that gradually grew to twenty-five hundred, he turned into a model colony, in which drunkenness, police, magistrates, lawsuits, poor laws, charity were unknown. And all this simply by placing the people in conditions worthy of human beings, and especially by carefully bringing up the rising generation. He was the founder of infant schools, and introduced them first at New Lanark. At the age of two the children came to school, where they enjoyed themselves so much that they could scarcely be got home again. While his competitors worked their people thirteen or fourteen hours a day, in New

Lanark the working day was only ten and a half hours. When a crisis in cotton stopped work for four months, his workers received their full wages all the time. And with all this the business more than doubled in value, and to the last yielded large profits to its proprietors.

In spite all this Owen was not content. The existence which he secured for his workers was, in his eyes, still far from being worthy of human beings. "The people were slaves at my mercy." The relatively favorable conditions in which he had placed them were still far from allowing a rational development of the character and of the intellect in all directions, much less of the free exercise of all their faculties. "And yet, the working part of this population of twenty-five hundred persons was daily producing as much real wealth for society as, less than half a century before, it would have required the working part of a population of six hundred thousand to create. I asked myself, what became of the difference between the wealth consumed by twenty-five hundred persons and that which would have been consumed by six hundred thousand?"[2]

The answer was clear. It had been used to pay the proprietors of the establishment 5 per cent on the capital they had laid out, in addition to over three hundred thousand pounds' clear profit. And that which held for New Lanark held to a still greater extent for all the factories in England. "If this new wealth had not been created by machinery, imperfectly as it has been applied, the wars of Europe, in opposition to Napoleon, and to support the aristocratic principles of society, could not have been maintained. And yet this new power was the creation of the working class."[3] To them, therefore, the fruits of this new power belonged. The newly created gigantic productive forces, hitherto used only to enrich individuals and to enslave the masses, offered to Owen the foundations for a reconstruction of society;

[2] From *The Revolution in Mind and Practice*, p. 21, a memorial addressed to all the "red Republicans, Communists and Socialists of Europe," and sent to the provisional government of France, 1848, and also "to Queen Victoria and her responsible advisers."

[3] *Ibid.* p. 22.

they were destined, as the common property of all, to be worked for the common good of all.

Owen's communism was based upon this purely business foundation, the outcome, so to say, of commercial calculation. Throughout it maintained this practical character. Thus in 1823 Owen proposed the relief of the distress in Ireland by communist colonies, and drew up complete estimates of costs of founding them, yearly expenditure, and probable revenue. And in his definite plan for the future the technical working out of details is managed with such practical knowledge—ground plan, front and side and bird's-eye views all included—that, the Owen method of social reform once accepted, there is from the practical point of view little to be said against the actual arrangement of details.

His advance in the direction of communism was the turning point in Owen's life. As long as he was simply a philanthropist he was rewarded with nothing but wealth, applause, honor, and glory. He was the most popular man in Europe. Not only men of his own class, but statesmen and princes listened to him approvingly. But when he came out with his communist theories, that was quite another thing. Three great obstacles seemed to him especially to block the path to social reform: private property, religion, the present form of marriage. He knew what confronted him if he attacked these—outlawry, excommunication from official society, the loss of his whole social position. But nothing of this prevented him from attacking them without fear of consequences, and what he had foreseen happened. Banished from official society, with a conspiracy of silence against him in the press, ruined by his unsuccessful communist experiments in America, in which he sacrificed all his fortune, he turned directly to the working class and continued working in their midst for thirty years. Every social movement, every real advance in England on behalf of the workers links itself to the name of Robert Owen. He forced through in 1819, after five years' fighting, the first law limiting the hours of labor of women and children in factories. He was president of the first congress at which all the trade unions of England united in a single great trade association. He introduced as transition measures to the complete communistic organization of society, on the one hand, co-operative societies for retail trade and production. These have since that time, at least, given practical proof that the merchant and the manufacturer are socially quite unnecessary. On the other hand, he introduced labor bazaars for the exchange of the products of labor through the medium of labor notes, whose unit was a single hour of work; institutions necessarily doomed to failure, but completely anticipating Proudhon's bank of exchange of a much later period, and differing entirely from this in that it did not claim to be the panacea for all social ills, but only a first step towards a much more radical revolution of society.

The Utopians' mode of thought has for a long time governed the socialist ideas of the nineteenth century, and still governs some of them. Until very recently all French and English socialists did homage to it. The earlier German communism, including that of Weitling, was of the same school. To all these socialism is the expression of absolute truth, reason, and justice, and has only to be discovered to conquer all the world by virtue of its own power. And as absolute truth is independent of time, space, and of the historical development of man, it is a mere accident when and where it is discovered. With all this, absolute truth, reason, and justice are different with the founder of each different school. And as each one's special kind of absolute truth, reason, and justice is again conditioned by his subjective understanding, his conditions of existence, the measure of his knowledge, and his intellectual training, there is no other ending possible in this conflict of absolute truths than that they shall be mutually exclusive one of the other. Hence from this nothing could come but a kind of eclectic, average socialism, which, as a matter of fact, has up to the present time dominated the minds of most of the socialist workers in France and England. Hence a mishmash allowing of the most manifold shades of opinion; a mishmash of such critical statements, economic theories, pictures of future society by the founders of different sects as excite a minimum of opposition; a mishmash which is the more easily brewed the more the definite sharp edges of the individual constituents are rubbed down in the stream of debate, like rounded pebbles in a brook.

To make a science of socialism it had first to be placed upon a real basis.

II

In the meantime, along with and after the French philosophy of the eighteenth century, had arisen the new German philosophy, culminating in Hegel. Its greatest merit was the taking up again of dialectics as the highest form of reasoning. The old Greek philosophers were all born natural dialecticians, and Aristotle, the most encyclopedic intellect of them, had already analyzed the most essential forms of dialectic thought. The newer philosophy, on the other hand, although in it, also, dialectics had brilliant exponents (e.g., Descartes and Spinoza), had, especially through English influence, become more and more rigidly fixed in the so-called metaphysical mode of reasoning, by which also the French of the eighteenth century were almost wholly dominated, at all events in their special philosophical work. Outside of philosophy in the restricted sense the French, nevertheless, produced masterpieces of dialectics. We need only call to mind Diderot's *Le Neveu de Rameau*, and Rousseau's *Discours sur l'origine et les fondements de l'inégalité parmi les hommes*. We give here, in brief, the essential character of these two modes of thought.

When we consider and reflect upon nature at large or the history of mankind or our own intellectual activity, at first we see the picture of an endless entanglement of relations and reactions, permutations and combinations, in which nothing remains what, where, and as it was, but everything moves, changes, comes into being, and passes away. We see, therefore, at first the picture as a whole, with its individual parts still more or less kept in the background; we observe the movements, transitions, connections rather than the things that move, combine, and are connected. This primitive, naïve but intrinsically correct conception of the world is that of ancient Greek philosophy, and was first clearly formulated by Heraclitus: everything is and is not, for everything is fluid, is constantly changing, constantly coming into being and passing away.

But this conception, correctly as it expresses the general character of the picture of appearances as a whole, does not suffice to explain the details of which this picture is made up, and so long as we do not understand these we have not a clear idea of the whole picture. In order to understand these details we must detach them from their natural or historical connection and examine each one separately, its nature, special causes, effects, etc. This is primarily the task of natural science and historical research: branches of science which the Greeks of classical times, on very good grounds, relegated to a subordinate position, because they had, first of all, to collect materials for these sciences to work upon. A certain amount of natural and historical material must be collected before there can be any critical analysis, comparison, and arrangement in classes, orders, and species. The foundations of the exact natural sciences were, therefore, first worked out by the Greeks of the Alexandrian period, and later on, in the Middle Ages, by the Arabs. Real natural science dates from the second half of the fifteenth century, and thence onward it had advanced with constantly increasing rapidity. The analysis of nature into its individual parts, the grouping of the different natural processes and objects in definite classes, the study of the internal anatomy of organic bodies in their manifold forms—these were the fundamental conditions of the gigantic strides in our knowledge of nature that have been made during the last four hundred years. But this method of work has also left us as legacy the habit of observing natural objects and processes in isolation, apart from their connection with the vast whole; of observing them in repose, not in motion; as constants, not as essentially variables; in their death, not in their life. And when this way of looking at things was transferred by Bacon and Locke from natural science to philosophy, it begot the narrow, metaphysical mode of thought peculiar to the last century.

To the metaphysician things and their mental reflexes, ideas, are isolated, are to be considered one after the other and apart from each other, are objects of investigation fixed, rigid, given once for all. He thinks in absolutely irreconcilable antitheses. "His communication is 'yea, yea; nay, nay'; for whatsoever is more than these cometh of evil." For him a thing either exists or does not exist; a thing cannot at the same time be itself and something else. Positive and negative absolutely exclude one another; cause and effect stand in a rigid antithesis one to the other.

At first sight this mode of thinking seems to us very luminous, because it is that of so-called sound common sense. Only sound common sense, respectable fellow that he is, in the homely realm of his own four walls, has very wonderful adventures directly he ventures out into the wide world of research. And the metaphysical mode of thought, justifiable and necessary as it is in a number of domains whose extent varies according to the nature of the particular object of investigation, sooner or later reaches a limit beyond which it becomes one-sided, restricted, abstract, lost in insoluble contradictions. In the contemplation of individual things it forgets the connection between them; in the contemplation of their existence it forgets the beginning and end of that existence; of their repose, it forgets their motion. It cannot see the wood for the trees.

For everyday purposes we know and can say, e.g., whether an animal is alive or not. But upon closer inquiry, we find that this is, in many cases, a very complex question, as the jurists know very well. They have cudgeled their brains in vain to discover a rational limit beyond which the killing of the child in its mother's womb is murder. It is just as impossible to determine absolutely the moment of death, for physiology proves that death is not an instantaneous, momentary phenomenon, but a very protracted process.

In like manner, every organic being is every moment the same and not the same; every moment it assimilates matter supplied from without and gets rid of other matter; every moment some cells of its body die and others build themselves anew; in a longer or shorter time the matter of its body is completely renewed, and is replaced by other molecules of matter, so that every organic being is always itself and yet something other than itself.

Further, we find upon closer investigation that the two poles of an antithesis, positive and negative, e.g., are as inseparable as they are opposed, and that despite all their opposition they mutually interpenetrate. And we find, in like manner, that cause and effect are conceptions which hold good only in their application to individual cases; but as soon as we consider the individual cases in their general connection with the universe as a whole they run into each other, and they become confounded when we contemplate that universal action and reaction in which causes and effects are eternally changing places, so that what is effect here and now will be cause there and then, and vice versa.

None of these processes and modes of thought enters into the framework of metaphysical reasoning. Dialectics, on the other hand, comprehends things and their representations, ideas, in their essential connection, concatenation, motion, origin, and ending. Such processes as those mentioned above are, therefore, so many corroborations of its own method of procedure.

Nature is the proof of dialectics, and it must be said for modern science that it has furnished this proof with very rich materials, increasing daily, and thus has shown that, in the last resort, nature works dialectically and not metaphysically; that she does not move in the eternal oneness of a perpetually recurring circle, but goes through a real historical evolution. In this connection Darwin must be named before all others. He dealt the metaphysical conception of nature the heaviest blow by his proof that all organic beings, plants, animals, and man himself are the products of a process of evolution going on through millions of years. But the naturalists who have learned to think dialectically are few and far between, and this conflict of the results of discovery with preconceived modes of thinking explains the endless confusion now reigning in theoretical natural science, the despair of teachers as well as learners, of authors and readers alike.

An exact representation of the universe, of its evolution, of the development of mankind, and of the reflection of this evolution in the minds of men can therefore be obtained only by the methods of dialectics, with its constant regard to the innumerable actions and reactions of life and death, of progressive or retrogressive changes. And in this spirit the new German philosophy has worked. Kant began his career by resolving the stable solar system of Newton and its eternal duration, after the famous initial impulse had once been given, into the result of a historic process, the formation of the sun and all the planets out of a rotating nebulous mass. From this he at the same time drew the conclusion that, given this origin of the solar system, its future death followed of necessity. His theory half a century later was established mathematically by Laplace, and half a century after that the spectroscope proved the existence in space of such incandescent masses of gas in various stages of condensation.

This new German philosophy culminated in the Hegelian system. In this system—and herein is its great merit—for the first time the whole world, natural, historical, intellectual, is represented as a process, i.e., as in constant motion, change, transformation, development; and the attempt is made to trace out the internal connection that makes a continuous whole of all this movement and development. From this point of view the history of mankind no longer appeared as a wild whirl of senseless deeds of violence, all equally condemnable at the judgment seat of mature philosophic reason and best forgotten as quickly as possible, but as the process of evolution of man himself. It was now the task of the intellect to follow the gradual march of this process through all its devious ways, and to trace out the inner law running through all its apparently accidental phenomena.

That the Hegelian system did not solve the problem it propounded is here immaterial. Its epoch-making merit was that it propounded the problem. This problem is one that no single individual will ever be able to solve. Although Hegel was—with St. Simon—the most encyclopedic mind of his time, yet he was limited, first, by the necessarily limited extent of his own knowledge and, second, by the limited extent and depth of the knowledge and conceptions of his age. To these limits a third must be added. Hegel was an idealist. To him the thoughts within his brain were not the more or less abstract pictures of actual things and processes, but, conversely, things and their evolution were only the realized pictures of the "Idea," existing somewhere from eternity before the world was. This way of thinking turned everything upside down, and completely reversed the actual connection of things in the world. Correctly and ingeniously as many individual groups of facts were grasped by Hegel, yet, for the reasons just given, there is much that is botched, artificial, labored—in a word, wrong—in point of detail. The Hegelian system, in itself, was a colossal miscarriage—but it was also the last of its kind. It was suffering, in fact, from an internal and incurable contradiction. Upon the one hand, its essential proposition was the conception that human history is a process of evolution, which, by its very nature, cannot find its intellectual final term in the discovery of any so-called absolute truth. But, on the other hand, it laid claim to being the very essence of this absolute truth. A system of natural and historical knowledge, embracing everything, and final for all time, is a contradiction to the fundamental law of dialectic reasoning. This law, indeed, by no means excludes, but, on the contrary, includes the idea that the systematic knowledge of the external universe can make giant strides from age to age.

The perception of the fundamental contradiction in German idealism led necessarily back to materialism, but, *nota bene*, not to the simply metaphysical, exclusively mechanical materialism of the eighteenth century. Old materialism looked upon all previous history as a crude heap of irrationality and violence; modern materialism sees in it the process of evolution of humanity, and aims at discovering the laws thereof. With the French of the eighteenth century, and even with Hegel, the conception obtained of nature as a whole, moving in narrow circles and forever immutable, with its eternal celestial bodies, as Newton, and unalterable organic species, as Linnaeus, taught. Modern materialism embraces the more recent discoveries of natural science, according to which nature also has its history in time, the celestial bodies, like the organic species that under favorable conditions people them, being born and perishing. And even if nature as a whole must still be said to move in recurrent cycles, these cycles assume infinitely larger dimensions. In both aspects modern materialism is essentially dialectic, and no longer requires the assistance of that sort of philosophy which, queenlike, pretended to rule the remaining mob of sciences. As soon as each special science is bound to make clear its position in the great totality of things and of our knowledge of things, a special science dealing with this totality is superfluous or unnecessary. That which still survives of all earlier philosophy is the science of thought and its laws—formal logic and dialectics. Everything else is subsumed in the positive science of nature and history.

While, however, the revolution in the conception of nature could be made only in proportion to the corresponding positive materials furnished by research, already much earlier certain historical facts had occurred which led to a decisive change in the conception of history. In 1831 the first working-class rising took place in Lyons; between 1838 and 1842 the first national working-class movement, that of the English Chartists, reached its height. The class struggle between proletariat and bourgeoisie came to the front in the history of the most advanced countries in Europe, in proportion to the development, upon the one hand, of modern industry; upon the other, of the newly acquired political supremacy of the bourgeoisie. Facts more and more strenuously gave the lie to the teachings of bourgeois economy as to the identity of the interests of capital and labor, as to the universal harmony and universal prosperity that would be the consequence of unbridled competition. All these things could no longer be ignored, any more than the French and English socialism, which was their theoretical, though very imperfect, expression. But the old idealist conception of history, which was not yet dislodged, knew nothing of class struggles based upon economic interests, knew nothing of economic interests; production and all economic relations appeared in it only as incidental, subordinate elements in the "history of civilization."

The new facts made imperative a new examination of all past history. Then it was seen that *all* past history, with the exception of its primitive stages, was the history of class struggles; that these warring classes of society are always the products of the modes of production and of exchange—in a word, of the *economic* conditions of their time; that the economic structure of society always furnishes the real basis, starting from which we can alone work out the ultimate explanation of the whole superstructure of juridical and political institutions as well as of the religious, philosophical, and other ideas of a given historical period. Hegel had freed history from metaphysics—he had made it dialectic; but his conception of history was essentially idealistic. But now idealism was driven from its last refuge, the philosophy of history; now a materialistic treatment of history was propounded, and a method found of explaining man's "knowing" by his "being" instead of, as heretofore, his "being" by his "knowing."

From that time forward socialism was no longer an accidental discovery of this or that ingenious brain, but the necessary outcome of the struggle between two historically developed classes—the proletariat and the bourgeoisie. Its task was no longer to manufacture a system of society as perfect as possible, but to examine the historico-economic succession of events from which these classes and their antagonism had of necessity sprung, and to discover in the economic conditions thus created the means of ending the conflict. But the socialism of earlier days was as incompatible with this materialistic conception as the conception of nature of the French materialists was with dialectics and modern natural science. The socialism of earlier days certainly criticized the existing capitalistic mode of production and its consequences. But it could not explain them, and, therefore, could not get the mastery of them. It could only simply reject them as bad. The more strongly this earlier socialism denounced the exploitation of the working class, inevitable under capitalism, the less able was it clearly to show in what this exploitation consisted and how it arose. But for this it was necessary (1) to present the capitalistic method of production in its historical connection and its inevitableness during a particular historical period, and therefore, also, to present its inevitable downfall; and (2) to lay bare its essential character, which was still a secret. This was done by the discovery of *surplus value*. It was shown that the appropriation of unpaid labor is the basis of the capitalist mode of production, and of the exploitation of the worker that occurs under it; that even if the capitalist buys the labor power of his laborer at its full value as a commodity on the market he yet extracts more value from it than he paid for, and that in the ultimate analysis this surplus value forms those sums of value from which are heaped up the constantly increasing masses of capital in the hands of the possessing classes. The genesis of capitalist production and the production of capital were both explained.

These two great discoveries, the materialistic conception of history and the revelation of the secret of capitalistic production through surplus value, we owe to Marx. With these discoveries socialism became a science. The next thing was to work out all its details and relations.

III

The materialist conception of history starts from the proposition that the production of the means to support human life—and, next to production, the exchange of things produced—is the basis of all social structure; that in every society that has appeared in history, the manner in which wealth is distributed and society divided into classes or orders is dependent upon what is produced, how it is produced, and how the products are exchanged. From this point of view the final causes of all social changes and political revolutions are to be sought not in men's brains, not in man's better insight into eternal truth and justice, but in changes in the modes of production and exchange. They are to be sought not in the *philosophy*, but in the *economics* of each particular epoch. The growing perception that existing social institutions are unreasonable and unjust, that reason has become unreason and right wrong, is only proof that in the modes of production and exchange changes have silently taken place with which the social order, adapted to earlier economic conditions, is no longer in keeping. From this it also follows that the means of getting rid of the incongruities that have been brought to light must also be present, in a more or less developed condition, within the changed modes of production themselves. These means are not to be invented by deduction from fundamental principles, but are to be discovered in the stubborn facts of the existing system of production.

What is, then, the position of modern socialism in this connection?

The present structure of society—this is now pretty generally conceded—is the creation of the ruling class of to-day, of the bourgeoisie. The mode of production peculiar to the bourgeoisie, known, since Marx, as the capitalist mode of production, was incompatible with the feudal system, with the privileges it conferred upon individuals, entire social ranks, and local corporations, as well as with the hereditary ties of subordination which constituted the framework of its social organization. The bourgeoisie broke up the feudal system and built upon its ruins the capitalist order of society, the kingdom of free competition, of personal liberty, of the equality, before the law, of all commodity owners, of all the rest of the capitalist blessings. Thenceforward the capitalist mode of production could develop in freedom. Since steam, machinery, and the making of machines by machinery transformed the older manufacture into modern industry, the productive forces evolved under the guidance of the bourgeoisie developed with a rapidity and in a degree unheard of before. But just as the older manufacture, in its time, and handicraft, becoming more developed under its influence, had come into collision with the feudal trammels of the guilds, so now modern industry, in its more complete development, comes into collision with the bounds within which the capitalistic mode of production holds it confined. The new productive forces have already outgrown the capitalistic mode of using them. And this conflict between productive forces and modes of production is not a conflict engendered in the mind of man, like that between original sin and divine justice. It exists, in fact, objectively, outside us, independently of the will and actions even of the men who have brought it on. Modern socialism is nothing but the reflex in thought of this conflict in fact; its ideal reflection in the minds, first, of the class directly suffering under it, the working class.

Now in what does this conflict consist?

Before capitalistic production, i.e., in the Middle Ages, the system of petty industry obtained generally, based upon the private property of the laborers in their means of production; in the country, the agriculture of the small peasant, free man, or serf; in the towns, the handicrafts organized in guilds. The instruments of labor—land, agricultural implements, the workshop, the tool—were the instruments of labor of single individuals, adapted for the use of one worker, and, therefore, of necessity, small, dwarfish, circumscribed. But for this very reason they belonged, as a rule, to the producer himself. To concentrate these scattered, limited means of production, to enlarge them, to turn them into the powerful levers of production of the present day—this was precisely the historic role of capitalist production and of its upholder, the bourgeoisie. In the fourth section of *Capital*, Marx has explained in detail how since the fifteenth century this has been historically worked out through the three phases of simple co-operation, manufacture, and modern industry. But the bourgeoisie, as is also shown there, could not transform these puny means of production into mighty productive forces without transforming them, at the same time, from means of production of the individual into *social* means of production workable only by a collectivity of men. The spinning wheel, the hand loom, the blacksmith's hammer were replaced by the spinning machine, the power loom, the steam hammer; the individual workshop, by the factory, implying the co-operation of hundreds and thousands of workmen. In like manner production itself changed from a series of individual into a series of social acts, and the products from individual to social products. The yarn, the cloth, the metal articles that now came out of the factory were the joint product of many workers, through whose hands they successively had to pass before they were ready. No one person could say of them: "I made that; this is *my* product."

But where, in a given society, the fundamental form of production is that spontaneous division of labor which creeps in gradually and not upon any preconceived plan, there the products take on the form of *commodities*, whose mutual exchange, buying and selling, enable the individual producers to satisfy their manifold wants. And this was the case in the Middle Ages. The peasant, e.g., sold to the artisan agricultural products and bought from him the products of handicraft. Into this society of individual producers, of commodity producers, the new mode of production thrust itself. In the midst of the old division of labor, grown up spontaneously and upon *no definite plan,* which had governed the whole of society, now arose division of labor upon a *definite plan,* as organized in the factory; side by side with *individual* production appeared *social* production. The products of both were sold in the same market, and, therefore, at prices at least approximately equal. But organization upon a definite plan was stronger than spontaneous division of labor. The factories working with the combined social forces of a collectivity of individuals produced their commodities far more cheaply than the individual small producers. Individual production succumbed in one department after another. Socialized production revolutionized all the old methods of production. But its revolutionary character was, at the same time, so little recognized that it was, on the contrary, introduced as a means of increasing and developing the production of commodities. When it arose it found ready-made, and made liberal use of, certain machinery for the production and exchange of commodities: merchants' capital, handicraft, wage labor. Socialized production thus introducing itself as a new form of the production of commodities, it was a matter of course that under it the old forms of appropriation remained in full swing and were applied to its products as well.

In the medieval stage of evolution of the production of commodities the question as to the owner of the product of labor could not arise. The individual producer, as a rule, had, from raw material belonging to himself and generally his own handiwork, produced it with his own tools, by the labor of his own hands or of his family. There was no need for him to appropriate the new product. It belonged wholly to him, as a matter of course. His property in the product was, therefore, based *upon his own labor.* Even where external help was used, this was, as a rule, of little importance, and very generally was compensated by something other than wages. The apprentices and journeymen of the guilds worked less for board and wages than for education, in order that they might become master craftsmen themselves.

Then came the concentration of the means of production and of the producers in large workshops and manufactories, their transformation into actual socialized means of production and socialized producers. But the socialized producers and means of production and their products were still treated, after this change, just as they had been before, i.e., as the means of production and the products of individuals. Hitherto the owner of the instruments of labor had himself appropriated the product because, as a rule, it was his own product and the assistance of others was the exception. Now the owner of the instruments of labor always appropriated to himself the product, although it was no longer *his* product, but exclusively the product of the *labor of others.* Thus the products now produced socially were not appropriated by those who had actually set in motion the means of production and actually produced the commodities, but by the *capitalists.* The means of production, and production itself, had become in essence socialized. But they were subjected to a form of appropriation which presupposes the private production of individuals, under which, therefore, everyone owns his own product and brings it to market. The mode of production is subjected to this form of appropriation, although it abolishes the conditions upon which the latter rests.[1]

This contradiction, which gives to the new mode of production its capitalistic character, *contains the germ of the whole of the social antagonisms of today.* The greater the mastery obtained by the new mode of production over all important fields of production and in all manufacturing countries, the more it reduced individual production to an insignificant residuum, *the more clearly was brought out*

[1] It is hardly necessary in this connection to point out that, even if the form of appropriation remains the same, the *character* of the appropriation is just as much revolutionized as production is by the changes described above. It is, of course, a very different matter whether I appropriate to myself my own product or that of another. Note in passing that wage labor, which contains the whole capitalistic mode of production in embryo, is very ancient; in a sporadic, scattered form it existed for centuries alongside of slave labor. But the embryo could duly develop into the capitalistic mode of production only when the necessary historical preconditions had been furnished.

the incompatibility of socialized production with capitalistic appropriation.

The first capitalists found, as we have said, alongside of other forms of labor, wage labor ready-made for them on the market. But it was exceptional, complementary, accessory, transitory wage labor. The agricultural laborer, though upon occasion he hired himself out by the day, had a few acres of his own land on which he could at all events live in a pinch. The guilds were so organized that the journeyman of today became the master of tomorrow. But all this changed as soon as the means of production became socialized and concentrated in the hands of capitalists. The means of production, as well as the product, of the individual producer became more and more worthless; there was nothing left for him but to turn wage worker under the capitalist. Wage labor, aforetime the exception and accessory, now became the rule and basis of all production; aforetime complementary, it now became the sole remaining function of the worker. The wage worker for a time became a wage worker for life. The number of these permanent wage workers was further enormously increased by the breaking up of the feudal system that occurred at the same time, by the disbanding of the retainers of the feudal lords, the eviction of the peasants from their homesteads, etc. The separation was made complete between the means of production, concentrated in the hands of the capitalists, on the one side, and the producers, possessing nothing but their labor power, on the other. *The contradiction between socialized production and capitalistic appropriation manifested itself as the antagonism of proletariat and bourgeoisie.*

We have seen that the capitalistic mode of production thrust its way into a society of commodity producers, of individual producers, whose social bond was the exchange of their products. But every society based upon the production of commodities has this peculiarity: that the producers have lost control over their own social interrelations. Each man produces for himself with such means of production as he may happen to have, and for such exchange as he may require to satisfy his remaining wants. No one knows how much of his particular article is coming on the market, nor how much of it will be wanted. No one knows whether his individual product will meet an actual demand, whether he will be able to make good his costs of production or even to sell his commodity at all. Anarchy reigns in socialized production.

But the production of commodities, like every other form of production, has its peculiar, inherent laws inseparable from it; and these laws work, despite anarchy, in and through anarchy. They reveal themselves in the only persistent form of social interrelations, i.e., in exchange, and here they affect the individual producers as compulsory laws of competition. They are, at first, unknown to these producers themselves, and have to be discovered by them gradually and as the result of experience. They work themselves out, therefore, independently of the producers, and in antagonism to them, as inexorable natural laws of their particular form of production. The product governs the producers.

In medieval society, especially in the earlier centuries, production was essentially directed towards satisfying the wants of the individual. It satisfied, in the main, only the wants of the producer and his family. Where relations of personal dependence existed, as in the country, it also helped to satisfy the wants of the feudal lord. In all this there was, therefore, no exchange; the products, consequently, did not assume the character of commodities. The family of the peasant produced almost everything it wanted: clothes and furniture, as well as means of subsistence. Only when it began to produce more than was sufficient to supply its own wants and the payments in kind to the feudal lord, only then did it also produce commodities. This surplus, thrown into socialized exchange and offered for sale, became commodities.

The artisans of the towns, it is true, had from the first to produce for exchange. But they, also, themselves supplied the greatest part of their own individual wants. They had gardens and plots of land. They turned their cattle out into the communal forest, which, also, yielded them timber and firing. The women spun flax, wool, and so forth. Production for the purpose of exchange, production of commodities, was only in its infancy. Hence exchange was restricted, the market narrow, the methods of production stable; there was local exclusiveness without, local unity within; the mark in the country; in the town, the guild.

But with the extension of the production of commodities, and especially with the introduction of the capitalist mode of production, the laws of commodity production, hitherto latent, came into action more openly and with greater force. The old bonds were loosened, the old exclusive limits broken through, the producers were more and more turned into independent, isolated producers of commodities. It became apparent that the production of society at large was ruled by absence of plan, by accident, by anarchy; and this anarchy grew to greater and greater height. But the chief means by aid of which the capitalist mode of production intensified this anarchy of socialized production was the exact opposite of anarchy. It was the increasing organization of production, upon a social basis, in every individual productive establishment. By this the old, peaceful, stable condition of things was ended. Wherever this organization of production was introduced into a branch of industry, it brooked no other method of production by its side. The field of labor became a battleground. The great geographical discoveries, and the colonization following upon them, multiplied markets and quickened the transformation of handicraft into manufacture. The war did not break out simply between the individual producers of particular localities. The local struggles begot in their turn national conflicts, the commercial wars of the seventeenth and the eighteenth centuries.

Finally, modern industry and the opening of the world market made the struggle universal, and at the same time gave it an unheard-of virulence. Advantages in natural or artificial conditions of production now decide the existence or non-existence of individual capitalists, as well as of whole industries and countries. He that falls is remorselessly cast aside. It is the Darwinian struggle of the individual for existence transferred from nature to society with intensified violence. The conditions of existence natural to the animal appear as the final term of human development. The contradiction between socialized production and capitalistic appropriation now presents itself as *an antagonism between the organization of production in the individual workshop and the anarchy of production in society generally.*

The capitalistic mode of production moves in these two forms of the antagonism immanent to it from its very origin. It is never able to get out of that "vicious circle" which Fourier had already discovered. What Fourier could not, indeed, see in his time is that this circle is gradually narrowing; that the movement becomes more and more a spiral, and must come to an end, like the movement of the planets, by collision with the center. It is the compelling force of anarchy in the production of society at large that more and more completely turns the great majority of men into proletarians, and it is the masses of the proletariat again who will finally put an end to anarchy in production. It is the compelling force of anarchy in social production that turns the limitless perfectibility of machinery under modern industry into a compulsory law by which every individual industrial capitalist must perfect his machinery more and more, under penalty of ruin.

But the perfecting of machinery is making human labor superfluous. If the introduction and increase of machinery means the displacement of millions of manual by a few machine workers, improvement in machinery means the displacement of more and more of the machine workers themselves. It means, in the last instance, the production of a number of available wage workers in excess of the average needs of capital, the formation of a complete industrial reserve army, as I called it in 1845,[2] available at the times when industry is working at high pressure, to be cast out upon the street when the inevitable crash comes, a constant dead weight upon the limbs of the working class in its struggle for existence with capital, a regulator for the keeping of wages down to the low level that suits the interests of capital. Thus it comes about, to quote Marx, that machinery becomes the most powerful weapon in the war of capital against the working class; that the instruments of labor constantly tear the means of subsistence out of the hands of the laborer; that the very product of the worker

[2] *The Condition of the Working Class in England.*

able to deal with political economy in a straightforward fashion, modern economic conditions did not actually exist in Germany. And as soon as these conditions did come into existence, they did so under circumstances that no longer allowed of their being really and impartially investigated within the bounds of the bourgeois horizon. In so far as political economy remains within that horizon, in so far, i.e., as the capitalist regime is looked upon as the absolutely final form of social production instead of as a passing historical phase of its evolution, political economy can remain a science only so long as the class struggle is latent or manifests itself only in isolated and sporadic phenomena.

Let us take England. Its political economy belongs to the period in which the class struggle was as yet undeveloped. Its last great representative, Ricardo, in the end, consciously makes the antagonism of class interests, of wages and profits, of profits and rent, the starting point of his investigations, naïvely taking this antagonism for a social law of nature. But by this start the science of bourgeois economy had reached the limits beyond which it could not pass. Already in the lifetime of Ricardo, and in opposition to him, it was met by criticism in the person of Sismondi.[1]

The succeeding period, from 1820 to 1830, was notable in England for scientific activity in the domain of political economy. It was the time as well of the vulgarizing and extending of Ricardo's theory, as of the contest of that theory with the old school. Splendid tournaments were held. What was done then is little known to the Continent generally, because the polemic is for the most part scattered through articles in reviews, occasional literature, and pamphlets. The unprejudiced character of this polemic—although the theory of Ricardo already serves, in exceptional cases, as a weapon of attack upon bourgeois economy—is explained by the circumstances of the time. On the one hand, modern industry itself was only just emerging from the age of childhood, as is shown by the fact that with the crisis of 1825 it for the first time opens the periodic cycle of its modern life. On the other hand, the class struggle between capital and labor is forced into the background,

[1] See my work, *Critique*, etc., p. 70.

politically by the discord between the governments and the feudal aristocracy, gathered around the Holy Alliance, on the one hand and the popular masses, led by the bourgeoisie, on the other; economically by the quarrel between industrial capital and aristocratic landed property—a quarrel that in France was concealed by the opposition between small and large landed property and that in England broke out openly after the corn laws. The literature of political economy in England at this time calls to mind the stormy forward movement in France after Dr. Quesnay's death, but only as a St. Martin's summer reminds us of spring. With the year 1830 came the decisive crisis.

In France and in England the bourgeoisie had conquered political power. Thenceforth the class struggle, practically as well as theoretically, took on more and more outspoken and threatening forms. It sounded the knell of scientific bourgeois economy. It was thenceforth no longer a question whether this theorem or that was true, but whether it was useful to capital or harmful, expedient or inexpedient, politically dangerous or not. In place of disinterested inquirers there were hired prize fighters; in place of genuine scientific research, the bad conscience and the evil intent of apologetic. Still, even the obtrusive pamphlets with which the Anti-Corn Law League, led by the manufacturers Cobden and Bright, deluged the world, have a historic interest, if no scientific one, on account of their polemic against the landed aristocracy. But since then the free trade legislation, inaugurated by Sir Robert Peel, has deprived vulgar economy of this, its last sting.

The Continental revolution of 1848–49 also had its reaction in England. Men who still claimed some scientific standing and aspired to be something more than mere sophists and sycophants of the ruling classes, tried to harmonize the political economy of capital with the claims, no longer to be ignored, of the proletariat. Hence a shallow syncretism, of which John Stuart Mill is the best representative. It is a declaration of bankruptcy by bourgeois economy, an event on which the great Russian scholar and critic, N. Tschernyschewsky, has thrown the light of a mastermind in his *Outlines of Political Economy according to Mill.*

In Germany, therefore, the capitalist mode of production came to a head after its antagonistic character had already, in France and England, shown itself in a fierce strife of classes. And meanwhile, moreover, the German proletariat had attained a much clearer class consciousness than the German bourgeoisie. Thus at the very moment when a bourgeois science of political economy seemed at last possible in Germany, it had in reality again become impossible.

Under these circumstances its professors fell into two groups. The one set, prudent, practical business folk, flocked to the banner of Bastiat, the most superficial and therefore the most adequate representative of the apologetic of vulgar economy; the other, proud of the professorial dignity of their science, followed John Stuart Mill in his attempt to reconcile irreconcilables. Just as in the classical time of bourgeois economy, so also in the time of its decline, the Germans remained mere schoolboys, imitators and followers, petty retailers and hawkers in the service of the great foreign wholesale concern.

The peculiar historic development of German society therefore forbids, in that country, all original work in bourgeois economy, but not the criticism of that economy. So far as such criticism represents a class it can represent only the class whose vocation in history is the overthrow of the capitalist mode of production and the final abolition of all classes—the proletariat.

The learned and unlearned spokesmen of the German bourgeoisie tried at first to kill *Das Kapital* by silence, as they had managed to do with my earlier writings. As soon as they found that these tactics no longer fitted in with the conditions of the time they wrote, under pretense of criticizing my book, prescriptions "for the tranquilization of the bourgeois mind." But they found in the workers' press—see, e.g., Joseph Dietzgen's articles in the *Volksstaat* —antagonists stronger than themselves, to whom (down to this very day) they owe a reply.[2]

[2] The mealymouthed babblers of German vulgar economy fell foul of the style of my book. No one can feel the literary shortcomings in *Das Kapital* more strongly than I myself. Yet I will for the benefit and the enjoyment of these gentlemen and their

An excellent Russian translation of *Das Kapital* appeared in the spring of 1872. The edition of three thousand copies is already nearly exhausted. As early as 1871, A. Sieber, professor of political economy in the University of Kiev, in his work, *David Ricardo's Theory of Value and of Capital*, referred to my theory of value, of money, and of capital as in its fundamentals a necessary sequel to the teaching of Smith and Ricardo. That which astonishes the Western European in the reading of this excellent work is the author's consistent and firm grasp of the purely theoretical position.

That the method employed in *Das Kapital* has been little understood is shown by the various conceptions, contradictory one to another, that have been formed of it.

Thus the Paris *Revue Positiviste* reproaches me in that, on the one hand, I treat economics metaphysically and, on the other hand—imagine!—confine myself to the mere critical analysis of actual facts, instead of writing recipes (Comtist ones?) for the cookshops of the future. In answer to the reproach *in re* metaphysics Professor Sieber has it: "In so far as it deals with actual theory, the method of Marx is the deductive method of the whole English school, a school whose failings and virtues are common to the best theoretic economists." M. Block—"*Les théoriciens du socialisme en Allemagne,*" *extrait du Journal des Economistes,* Juillet et Aout 1872—makes the discovery that my method is analytic and says: "*Par cet ouvrage M. Marx se classe parmi les esprits analytiques les plus éminents.* [By this work M. Marx places himself among the most eminent

---

public quote in this connection one English and one Russian notice. The *Saturday Review*, always hostile to my views, said in its notice of the first edition: "The presentation of the subject invests the driest economic questions with a certain peculiar charm." The *St. Petersburg Journal* (*Sankt-Peterburgskie Viedomosti*), in its issue of April 20, 1872, says: "The presentation of the subject, with the exception of one or two exceptionally special parts, is distinguished by its comprehensibility by the general reader, its clearness, and in spite of the scientific intricacy of the subject, by an unusual liveliness. In this respect the author in no way resembles . . . the majority of German scholars, who . . . write their books in a language so dry and obscure that the heads of ordinary mortals are cracked by it."

analytical minds.]" German reviews, of course, shriek out at "Hegelian sophistics." The *European Messenger* of St. Petersburg, in an article dealing exclusively with the method of *Das Kapital* (May number, 1872, pages 427–36), finds my method of inquiry severely realistic, but my method of presentation, unfortunately, German-dialectical. It says: "At first sight, if the judgment is based on the external form of the presentation of the subject, Marx is the most ideal of ideal philosophers, always in the German, i.e., the bad sense of the word. But in point of fact he is infinitely more realistic than all his forerunners in the work of economic criticism. He can in no sense be called an idealist." I cannot answer the writer better than by aid of a few extracts from his own criticism, which may interest some of my readers to whom the Russian original is inaccessible.

After a quotation from the preface to my *Critique of Political Economy*, Berlin, 1859, pages 11–13, where I discuss the materialistic basis of my method, the writer goes on: "The one thing which is of moment to Marx is to find the law of the phenomena with whose investigation he is concerned; and not only is that law of moment to him which governs these phenomena, in so far as they have a definite form and mutual connection within a given historical period. Of still greater moment to him is the law of their variation, of their development, i.e., of their transition from one form into another, from one series of connections into a different one. This law once discovered, he investigates in detail the effects in which it manifests itself in social life. Consequently Marx troubles himself about only one thing: to show, by rigid scientific investigation, the necessity of successive determinate orders of social conditions, and to establish, as impartially as possible, the facts that serve him for fundamental starting points. For this it is quite enough if he proves, at the same time, both the necessity of the present order of things and the necessity of another order, into which the first must inevitably pass over; and this all the same, whether men believe or do not believe it, whether they are conscious or unconscious of it. Marx treats the social movement as a process of natural history, governed by laws not only independent of human will, consciousness, and intelligence, but rather, on the contrary, determining that will, consciousness, and intelligence. . . . If in the history of civilization the conscious element plays a part so subordinate, then it is self-evident that a critical inquiry whose subject matter is civilization can, less than anything else, have for its basis any form of, or any result of, consciousness. That is to say that not the idea but the material phenomenon alone can serve as its starting point. Such an inquiry will confine itself to the confrontation and the comparison of a fact, not with ideas, but with another fact. For this inquiry the one thing of moment is that both facts be investigated as accurately as possible, and that they actually form, each with respect to the other, different momenta of an evolution; but most important of all is the rigid analysis of the series of successions, of the sequences and concatenations in which the different stages of such an evolution present themselves. But it will be said the general laws of economic life are one and the same, no matter whether they are applied to the present or the past. This Marx directly denies. According to him, such abstract laws do not exist. On the contrary, in his opinion every historical period has laws of its own. . . . As soon as society has outlived a given period of development and is passing over from one given stage to another it begins to be subject also to other laws. In a word, economic life offers us a phenomenon analogous to the history of evolution in other branches of biology. The old economists misunderstood the nature of economic laws when they likened them to the laws of physics and chemistry. A more thorough analysis of phenomena shows that social organisms differ among themselves as fundamentally as plants or animals. Nay, one and the same phenomenon falls under quite different laws in consequence of the different structure of those organisms as a whole, of the variations of their individual organs, of the different conditions in which those organs function, etc. Marx, e.g., denies that the law of population is the same at all times and in all places. He asserts, on the contrary, that every stage of development has its own law of population. . . . With the varying degree of development of productive power, social conditions and the laws governing them vary, too. While

Marx sets himself the task of following and explaining from this point of view the economic system established by the sway of capital, he is only formulating, in a strictly scientific manner, the aim that every accurate investigation into economic life must have. The scientific value of such an inquiry lies in the disclosing of the special laws that regulate the origin, existence, development, and death of a given social organism and its replacement by another and higher one. And it is this value that, in point of fact, Marx's book has."

While the writer pictures what he takes to be actually my method, in this striking and (as far as concerns my own application of it) generous way, what else is he picturing but the dialectic method?

Of course, the method of presentation must differ in form from that of inquiry. The latter has to appropriate the material in detail, to analyze its different forms of development, to trace out their inner connection. Only after this work is done can the actual movement be adequately described. If this is done successfully, if the life of the subject matter is ideally reflected as in a mirror, then it may appear as if we had before us a mere a priori construction.

My dialectic method is not only different from the Hegelian, but is its direct opposite. To Hegel the life process of the human brain, i.e., the process of thinking, which, under the name of "the Idea," he even transforms into an independent subject, is the demiurgos of the real world, and the real world is only the external, phenomenal form of "the Idea." With me, on the contrary, the ideal is nothing else than the material world reflected by the human mind and translated into forms of thought.

The mystifying side of Hegelian dialectic I criticized nearly thirty years ago, at a time when it was still the fashion. But just as I was working at the first volume of *Das Kapital*, it was the good pleasure of the peevish, arrogant, mediocre epigoni, who now talk large in cultured Germany, to treat Hegel in the same way as the brave Moses Mendelssohn in Lessing's time treated Spinoza, i.e., as a "dead dog." I therefore openly avowed myself the pupil of that mighty thinker, and even here and there, in the chapter on the theory of value, coquetted with the modes of expression peculiar to him. The mystification which dialectic suffers in Hegel's hands by no means prevents him from being the first to present its general form of working in a comprehensive and conscious manner. With him it is standing on its head. It must be turned right side up again if you would discover the rational kernel within the mystical shell.

In its mystified form dialectic became the fashion in Germany because it seemed to transfigure and to glorify the existing state of things. In its rational form it is a scandal and abomination to bourgeoisdom and its doctrinaire professors because it includes in its comprehension and affirmative recognition of the existing state of things, at the same time also, the recognition of the negation of that state, of its inevitable breaking up; because it regards every historically developed social form as in fluid movement, and therefore takes into account its transient nature not less than its momentary existence; because it lets nothing impose upon it, and is in its essence critical and revolutionary.

The contradictions inherent in the movement of capitalist society impress themselves upon the practical bourgeois most strikingly in the changes of the periodic cycle, through which modern industry runs, and whose crowning point is the universal crisis. That crisis is once again approaching, although as yet but in its preliminary stage; and by the universality of its theater and the intensity of its action it will drum dialectics even into the heads of the mushroom upstarts of the new, holy Prusso-German Empire.

Karl Marx

London, January 24, 1873

[The Exploitation of the Workers under Capitalism, and the Workers' Response]

[*Excerpts from* CHAPTER X. THE WORKING DAY]

SECTION 5. THE STRUGGLE FOR A NORMAL WORKING DAY. COMPULSORY LAWS FOR THE EXTENSION OF THE WORKING DAY FROM THE MIDDLE OF THE FOURTEENTH TO THE END OF THE SEVENTEENTH CENTURY.

What is a working day? What is the length of time during which capital may consume the labor power whose daily value it buys? How far may the working day be extended beyond the working time necessary for the reproduction of labor power itself? It has been seen that to these questions capital replies: The working day contains the full twenty-four hours, with the deduction of the few hours of repose without which labor power absolutely refuses its services again. Hence it is self-evident that the laborer is nothing else, his whole life through, than labor power, that therefore all his disposable time is by nature and law labor time, to be devoted to the self-expansion of capital. Time for education, for intellectual development, for the fulfilling of social functions and for social intercourse, for the free play of his bodily and mental activity, even the rest time of Sunday (and that in a country of Sabbatarians!)[1]

[1] In England even now occasionally in rural districts a laborer is condemned to imprisonment for desecrating the Sabbath by working in his front garden. The same laborer is punished for breach of contract if he remains away from his metal-, paper-, or glassworks on the Sunday, even if it be from a religious whim. The orthodox Parliament will hear nothing of Sabbath-breaking if it occurs in the process of expanding capital. A memorial (August 1863) in which the London day laborers in fish and poultry shops asked for the abolition of Sunday labor states that their work lasts for the first six days of the week on an average fifteen hours a day and on Sunday eight to ten hours. From this same memorial we learn also that the delicate gourmands among the aristocratic hypocrites of Exeter Hall especially encourage this "Sunday labor." These "holy ones," so zealous *in cute curanda* ["in taking care of the skin," Horace, *Epistles*, I, 2, 29], show their

—moonshine! But in its blind, unrestrainable passion, its werewolf hunger for surplus labor, capital oversteps not only the moral, but even the merely physical maximum bounds of the working day. It usurps the time for growth, development, and healthy maintenance of the body. It steals the time required for the consumption of fresh air and sunlight. It higgles over a mealtime, incorporating it where possible with the process of production itself, so that food is given to the laborer as to a mere means of production, as coal is supplied to the boiler, grease and oil to the machinery. It reduces the sound sleep needed for the restoration, reparation, refreshment of the bodily powers to just so many hours of torpor as the revival of an organism, absolutely exhausted, renders essential. It is not the normal maintenance of the labor power which is to determine the limits of the working day; it is the greatest possible daily expenditure of labor power, no matter how diseased, compulsory, and painful it may be, which is to determine the limits of the laborers' period of repose. Capital cares nothing for the length of life of labor power. All that concerns it is simply and solely the maximum of labor power that can be rendered fluent in a working day. It attains this end by shortening the extent of the laborer's life as a greedy farmer snatches increased produce from the soil by robbing it of its fertility.

The capitalistic mode of production (essentially the production of surplus value, the absorption of surplus labor) produces thus, with the extension of the working day, not only the deterioration of human labor power by robbing it of its normal moral and physical conditions of development and function. It produces also the premature exhaustion and death of this labor power itself.[2] It extends the laborer's time of production during a given period by shortening his actual lifetime.

Christianity by the humility with which they bear the overwork, the privations, and the hunger of others. *Obsequium ventris istis* (the laborers) *perniciosius est* ["For those fellows, obedience to the belly is ruinous." Horace, *Satires*, II, 7, 104].

2 "We have given in our previous reports the statements of several experienced manufacturers to the effect that overhours . . . certainly tend prematurely to exhaust the working power of the men." (*L.c.* 64, p. xiii.)

But the value of the labor power includes the value of the commodities necessary for the reproduction of the worker, or for the keeping up of the working class. If then the unnatural extension of the working day, that capital necessarily strives after in its unmeasured passion for self-expansion, shortens the length of life of the individual laborer, and therefore the duration of his labor power, the forces used up have to be replaced at a more rapid rate and the sum of the expenses for the reproduction of labor power will be greater, just as in a machine the part of its value to be reproduced every day is greater the more rapidly the machine is worn out. It would seem, therefore, that the interest of capital itself points in the direction of a normal working day.

The slaveowner buys his laborer as he buys his horse. If he loses his slave he loses capital that can be restored only by new outlay in the slave mart. But "the rice grounds of Georgia or the swamps of the Mississippi may be fatally injurious to the human constitution; but the waste of human life which the cultivation of these districts necessitates is not so great that it cannot be repaired from the teeming preserves of Virginia and Kentucky. Considerations of economy, moreover, which, under a natural system, afford some security for humane treatment by identifying the master's interest with the slave's preservation, when once trading in slaves is practiced, become reasons for racking to the uttermost the toil of the slave, for when his place can at once be supplied from foreign preserves the duration of his life becomes a matter of less moment than its productiveness while it lasts. It is accordingly a maxim of slave management, in slave-importing countries, that the most effective economy is that which takes out of the human chattel in the shortest space of time the utmost amount of exertion it is capable of putting forth. It is in tropical culture, where annual profits often equal the whole capital of plantations, that Negro life is most recklessly sacrificed. It is the agriculture of the West Indies, which has been for centuries prolific of fabulous wealth, that has engulfed millions of the African race. It is in Cuba, at this day, whose revenues are reckoned by millions, and whose planters are princes, that we see in the servile class the coarsest fare, the most exhausting and unremitting toil, and even the absolute destruction of a portion of its numbers every year."[3]

Mutato nomine de te fabula narratur ["Under a changed name, of you the tale is told." Horace, *Satires*, I, 1, 69]. For slave trade read labor market for Kentucky and Virginia, Ireland and the agricultural districts of England, Scotland, and Wales, for Africa, Germany. We heard how overwork thinned the ranks of the bakers in London. Nevertheless, the London labor market is always overstocked with German and other candidates for death in the bakeries. Pottery, as we saw, is one of the shortest-lived industries. Is there any want herefore of potters? Josiah Wedgwood, the inventor of modern pottery, himself originally a common workman, said in 1785 before the House of Commons that the whole trade employed from fifteen thousand to twenty thousand people.[4] In the year 1861 the population alone of the town centers of this industry in Great Britain numbered 101,302. "The cotton trade has existed for ninety years. . . . It has existed for three generations of the English race, and I believe I may safely say that during that period it has destroyed nine generations of factory operatives. . . ."[5]

What experience shows to the capitalist generally is a constant excess of population, i.e., an excess in relation to the momentary requirements of surplus-labor-absorbing capital, although this excess is made up of generations of human beings stunted, short-lived, swiftly replacing each other, plucked, so to say, before maturity.[6] And, indeed, experience shows to the intelligent observer with what swiftness and grip the capitalist mode of production, dating, historically speaking, only from yesterday, has seized the vital power of the people by the very root—shows how

[3] Cairnes, *The Slave Power*, pp. 110, 111.

[4] John Ward, *History of the Borough of Stoke-upon-Trent*, London, 1843, p. 42.

[5] Ferrand's speech in the House of Commons, April 27, 1863.

[6] The overworked "die off with strange rapidity; but the places of those who perish are instantly filled, and a frequent change of persons makes no alteration in the scene." (E. G. Wakefield, *England and America*, London, 1833, Vol. I, p. 55.)

the degeneration of the industrial population is only retarded by the constant absorption of primitive and physically uncorrupted elements from the country—shows how even the country laborers, in spite of fresh air and the principle of natural selection, that works so powerfully among them and permits the survival of only the strongest, are already beginning to die off.[7] Capital, that has such good reasons for denying the sufferings of the legions of workers that surround it, is in practice moved as much and as little by the sight of the coming degradation and final depopulation of the human race as by the probable fall of the earth into the sun. In every stock-jobbing swindle everyone knows that sometime or other the crash must come, but everyone hopes that it may fall on the head of his neighbor, after he himself has caught the shower of gold and placed it in safety. *Après moi le déluge!* is the watchword of every capitalist and of every capitalist nation. Hence capital is reckless of the health or length of life of the laborer, unless under compulsion from society.[8] To the outcry as to the physical and mental degradation, the pre-

[7] See: Public Health. Sixth Report of the Medical Officer of the Privy Council, 1863. Published in London, 1864. This report deals especially with the agricultural laborers. "Sutherland . . . is commonly represented as a highly improved county . . . but . . . recent inquiry has discovered that even there, in districts once famous for fine men and gallant soldiers, the inhabitants have degenerated into a meager and stunted race. In the healthiest situations, on hillsides fronting the sea, the faces of their famished children are as pale as they could be in the foul atmosphere of a London alley." (W. T. Thornton, "Overpopulation and Its Remedy." *L.c.*, pp. 74, 75.) They resemble in fact the thirty thousand "gallant Highlanders" whom Glasgow pigs together in its wynds and closes with prostitutes and thieves.

[8] "But though the health of a population is so important a fact of the national capital, we are afraid it must be said that the class of employers of labor have not been the most forward to guard and cherish this treasure. . . . The consideration of the health of the operatives was forced upon the mill owners. (*Times*, November 5, 1861.) "The men of the West Riding became the clothiers of mankind . . . the health of the workpeople was sacrificed, and the race in a few generations must have degenerated. But a reaction set in. Lord Shaftesbury's bill limited the hours of children's labor," etc. (Report of the Registrar-General, for October 1861.)

mature death, the torture of overwork, it answers: Ought these to trouble us since they increase our profits? But looking at things as a whole, all this does not, indeed, depend on the good or ill will of the individual capitalist. Free competition brings out the inherent laws of capitalist production, in the shape of external coercive laws having power over every individual capitalist.[9]

The establishment of a normal working day is the result of centuries of struggle between capitalist and laborer. The history of this struggle shows two opposed tendencies. Compare, e.g., the English factory legislation of our time with the English Labor Statutes from the fourteenth century to well into the middle of the eighteenth.[10] While the modern Factory Acts compulsorily shortened the working day, the earlier statutes tried to lengthen it by compulsion. Of course, the pretensions of capital in embryo—when, beginning to grow, it secures the right of absorbing a *quantum sufficit* of surplus labor, not merely by the force of economic relations, but by the help of the state—appear

[9] We therefore find, e.g., that in the beginning of 1863, twenty-six firms owning extensive potteries in Staffordshire, among others, Josiah Wedgwood & Sons, petition in a memorial for "some legislative enactment." Competition with other capitalists permits them no voluntary limitation of working time for children, etc. "Much as we deplore the evils before mentioned, it would not be possible to prevent them by any scheme of agreement between the manufacturers. . . . Taking all these points into consideration, we have come to the conviction that some legislative enactment is wanted." (Children's Employment Commission Report 1, 1863, p. 322.) Most recently a much more striking example offers. The rise in the price of cotton during a period of feverish activity had induced the manufacturers in Blackburn to shorten, by mutual consent, the working time in their mills during a certain fixed period. This period terminated about the end of November 1871. Meanwhile the wealthier manufacturers, who combined spinning with weaving, used the diminution of production resulting from this agreement to extend their own business and thus to make great profits at the expense of the small employers. The latter thereupon turned in their extremity to the operatives, urged them earnestly to agitate for the nine-hour system, and promised contributions in money to this end.

[10] The Labor Statutes, the like of which were enacted at the same time in France, the Netherlands, and elsewhere, were first formally repealed in England in 1813, long after the changes in methods of production had rendered them obsolete.

very modest when put face to face with the concessions that, growling and struggling, it has to make in its adult condition. It takes centuries ere the "free" laborer, thanks to the development of capitalistic production, agrees, i.e., is compelled by social conditions, to sell the whole of his active life, his very capacity for work, for the price of the necessaries of life, his birthright for a mess of pottage. Hence it is natural that the lengthening of the working day, which capital, from the middle of the fourteenth to the end of the seventeenth century, tried to impose by state measures on adult laborers, approximately coincides with the shortening of the working day, which, in the second half of the nineteenth century, has here and there been effected by the state to prevent the coining of children's blood into capital. That which today, e.g., in the State of Massachusetts, until recently the freest state of the North American republic, has been proclaimed as the statutory limit of the labor of children under twelve was in England, even in the middle of the seventeenth century, the normal working day of able-bodied artisans, robust laborers, athletic blacksmiths. . . .[11]

[11] "No child under 12 years of age shall be employed in any manufacturing establishment more than 10 hours in one day." General Statutes of Massachusetts, 63, ch. 12. (The various statutes were passed between 1836 and 1858.) "Labor performed during a period of 10 hours on any day in all cotton, woolen, silk, paper, glass, and flax factories, or in manufactories of iron and brass, shall be considered a legal day's labor. And be it enacted, that hereafter no minor engaged in any factory shall be holden or required to work more than 10 hours in any day, or 60 hours in any week; and that hereafter no minor shall be admitted as a worker under the age of 10 years in any factory within this State." State of New Jersey. An Act to limit the hours of labor, etc., 61 and 62. (Law of March 11, 1855.) "No minor who has attained the age of 12 years, and is under the age of 15 years, shall be employed in any manufacturing establishment more than 11 hours in any one day, nor before 5 o'clock in the morning, nor after 7.30 in the evening." (Revised Statutes of the State of Rhode Island, etc., ch. 39, § 23, July 1, 1857.)

SECTION 6. THE STRUGGLE FOR THE NORMAL WORKING DAY. COMPULSORY LIMITATION BY LAW OF THE WORKING TIME. THE ENGLISH FACTORY ACTS, 1833 TO 1864.

After capital had taken centuries in extending the working day to its normal maximum limit, and then beyond this to the limit of the natural day of twelve hours,[12] there followed on the birth of machinism and modern industry in the last third of the eighteenth century a violent encroachment like that of an avalanche in its intensity and extent. All bounds of morals and nature, age and sex, day and night were broken down. Even the ideas of day and night, of rustic simplicity in the old statutes, became so confused that an English judge, as late as 1860, needed a quite Talmudic sagacity to explain "judicially" what was day and what was night.[13] Capital celebrated its orgies.

As soon as the working class, stunned at first by the noise and turmoil of the new system of production, recovered, in some measure, its senses, its resistance began, and first in the native land of machinism, in England. For thirty years, however, the concessions conquered by the workpeople were purely nominal. Parliament passed five labor laws between 1802 and 1833, but was shrewd enough not to vote

[12] "It is certainly much to be regretted that any class of persons should toil twelve hours a day, which, including the time for their meals and for going to and returning from their work, amounts, in fact, to fourteen of the twenty-four hours. . . . Without entering into the question of health, no one will hesitate, I think, to admit that, *in a moral point of view*, so entire an absorption of the time of the working classes, without intermission, from the early age of thirteen, and in trades not subject to restriction much younger, must be extremely prejudicial, and is an evil greatly to be deplored. . . . For the sake, therefore, of public morals, of bringing up an orderly population, and of giving the great body of the people a reasonable enjoyment of life, it is much to be desired that in all trades some portion of every working day should be reserved for rest and leisure." (Leonard Horner in Reports of Inspector of Factories, December 1841.)

[13] See: Judgment of Mr. J. H. Otwey, Belfast. Hilary Sessions, County Antrim, 1860.

a penny for their carrying out, for the requisite officials, etc.[14]

They remained a dead letter. "The fact is, that prior to the Act of 1833 young persons and children were worked all night, all day, or both, *ad libitum.*"[15]

A normal working day for modern industry dates only from the Factory Act of 1833, which included cotton, wool, flax, and silk factories. Nothing is more characteristic of the spirit of capital than the history of the English Factory Acts from 1833 to 1864.

The Act of 1833 declares the ordinary factory working day to be from half past five in the morning to half past eight in the evening, and within these limits, a period of fifteen hours, it is lawful to employ young persons (i.e., persons between thirteen and eighteen years of age) at any time of the day, provided no one individual young person should work more than twelve hours in any one day, except in certain cases especially provided for. The sixth section of the Act provided, "That there shall be allowed in the course of every day not less than one and a half hours for meals to every such person restricted as hereinbefore provided." The employment of children under nine, with exceptions mentioned later, was forbidden; the work of children between nine and thirteen was limited to eight hours a day, night work, i.e., according to this Act, work between 8:30 P.M. and 5:30 A.M. was forbidden for all persons between 9 and 18. . . .

[14] It is very characteristic of the regime of Louis Philippe, the bourgeois king, that the one factory act passed during his reign, that of March 22, 1841, was never put in force. And this law dealt only with child labor. It fixed eight hours a day for children between eight and twelve, twelve hours for children between twelve and sixteen, etc., with many exceptions which allow night work even for children eight years old. The supervision and enforcement of this law are, in a country where every mouse is under police administration, left to the good will of the *amis du commerce*. Only since 1853, in one single department—the Département du Nord—has a paid government inspector been appointed. Not less characteristic of the development of French society generally is the fact that Louis Philippe's law stood solitary among the all-embracing mass of French laws till the Revolution of 1848.

[15] Report of Inspector of Factories, April 30, 1860, p. 50.

SECTION 7. THE STRUGGLE FOR THE NORMAL WORKING DAY. REACTION OF THE ENGLISH ACTS ON OTHER COUNTRIES.

. . . The history of the regulation of the working day in certain branches of production, and the struggle still going on in others in regard to this regulation, prove conclusively that the isolated laborer, the laborer as "free" vendor of his labor power, when capitalist production has once attained a certain stage, succumbs without any power of resistance. The creation of a normal working day is, therefore, the product of a protracted civil war, more or less dissembled, between the capitalist class and the working class. As the contest takes place in the arena of modern industry, it first breaks out in the home of that industry—England.[16] The English factory workers were the champions not only of the English, but of the modern working class generally, as their theorists were the first to throw down the gauntlet to the theory of capital.[17] Hence, the philosopher of the factory, Ure, denounces as an ineffable disgrace to the English working class that they inscribed "the slavery of the Factory Acts" on the banner which they

[16] Belgium, the paradise of Continental liberalism, shows no trace of this movement. Even in the coal and metal mines laborers of both sexes, and all ages, are consumed in perfect "freedom," at any period and through any length of time. Of every 1,000 persons employed there, 733 are men, 88 women, 135 boys, and 44 girls under sixteen; in the blast furnaces, etc., of every 1,000, 688 are men, 149 women, 98 boys, and 65 girls under sixteen. Add to this the low wages for the enormous exploitation of mature and immature labor power. The average daily pay for a man is 2s. 8d., for a woman 1s. 8d., for a boy, 1s. 2½d. As a result Belgium had in 1863, as compared with 1850, nearly doubled both the amount and the value of its exports of coal, iron, etc.

[17] Robert Owen, soon after 1810, not only maintained the necessity of a limitation of the working day in theory, but actually introduced the ten-hour day into his factory at New Lanark. This was laughed at as a communistic utopia; so were his "Combination of children's education with productive labor," and the cooperative societies of workingmen, first called into being by him. Today the first utopia is a Factory Act, the second figures as an official phrase in all Factory Acts, the third is already being used as a cloak for reactionary humbug.

bore against capital, manfully striving for "perfect freedom of labor."[18]

France limps slowly behind England. The February revolution was necessary to bring into the world the twelve-hour law,[19] which is much more deficient than its English original. For all that, the French revolutionary method has its special advantages. It once for all commands the same limit to the working day in all shops and factories without distinction, while English legislation reluctantly yields to the pressure of circumstances, now on this point, now on that, and is getting lost in a hopelessly bewildering tangle of contradictory enactments.[20] On the other hand, the French law proclaims as a principle that which in England was won only in the name of children, minors, and women, and has been only recently for the first time claimed as a general right.[21]

[18] Ure: "French translation, Philosophie des Manufactures." Paris, 1836, Vol. II, pp. 39, 40, 67, 77, etc.

[19] In the Compte Rendu of the International Statistical Congress at Paris, 1855, it is stated: "The French law, which limits the length of daily labor in factories and workshops to twelve hours, does not confine this work to definite fixed hours. For children's labor only the work time is prescribed as between 5 A.M. and 9 P.M. Therefore some of the masters use the right which this fatal silence gives them to keep their works going, without intermission, day in, day out, possibly with the exception of Sunday. For this purpose they use two different sets of workers, of whom neither is in the workshop more than twelve hours at a time, but the work of the establishment lasts day and night. The law is satisfied, but is humanity?" Besides "the destructive influence of night labor on the human organism," stress is also laid upon "the fatal influence of the association of the two sexes by night in the same badly lighted workshops."

[20] "For instance, there is within my district one occupier who, within the same curtilage, is at the same time a bleacher and dyer under the Bleaching and Dyeing Works Act, a printer under the Print Works Act, and a finisher under the Factory Act." (Report of Mr. Baker, in Reports, etc., for October 31, 1861, p. 20.) After enumerating the different provisions of these acts, and the complications arising from them, Mr. Baker says: "It will hence appear that it must be very difficult to secure the execution of these three acts of Parliament where the occupier chooses to evade the law." But what is assured to the lawyers by this is lawsuits.

[21] Thus the factory inspectors at last venture to say: "These objections [of capital to the legal limitation of the working day]

In the United States of North America every independent movement of the workers was paralyzed so long as slavery disfigured a part of the republic. Labor cannot emancipate itself in the white skin where in the black it is branded. But out of the death of slavery a new life at once arose. The first fruit of the Civil War was the eight-hour agitation, that ran with the seven-league boots of the locomotive from the Atlantic to the Pacific, from New England to California. The General Congress of Labor at Baltimore (August 16, 1866) declared: "The first and great necessity of the present, to free the labor of this country from capitalistic slavery, is the passing of a law by which eight hours shall be the normal working day in all states of the American Union. We are resolved to put forth all our strength until this glorious result is attained."[22] At the same time, the Congress of the International Workingmen's Association at Geneva, on the proposition of the London General Council, resolved that "the limitation of the working day is a preliminary condition without which all further attempts at improvement and emancipation must prove abortive . . . the Congress proposes eight hours as the legal limit of the working day."

Thus the movement of the working class on both sides of the Atlantic, which had grown instinctively out of the conditions of production themselves, endorsed the words of the English factory inspector, R. J. Saunders: "Further steps towards a reformation of society can never be carried

---

must succumb before the broad principle of the rights of labor. . . . There is a time when the master's right in his workman's labor ceases, and his time becomes his own, even if there were no exhaustion in the question." (Reports, etc., for October 31, 1862, p. 54.)

[22] "We, the workers of Dunkirk, declare that the length of time of labor required under the present system is too great, and that, far from leaving the worker time for rest and education, it plunges him into a condition of servitude but little better than slavery. That is why we decide that eight hours are enough for a working day, and ought to be legally recognized as enough; why we call to our help that powerful lever, the press . . . and why we shall consider all those that refuse us this help as enemies of the reform of labor and of the rights of the laborer." (Resolution of the Workingmen of Dunkirk, New York State, 1866.)

out with any hope of success unless the hours of labor be limited and the prescribed limit strictly enforced."[23]

It must be acknowledged that our laborer comes out of the process of production other than he entered. In the market he stood as owner of the commodity labor power face to face with other owners of commodities, dealer against dealer. The contract by which he sold to the capitalist his labor power proved, so to say, in black and white that he disposed of himself freely. The bargain concluded, it is discovered that he was no "free agent," that the time for which he is free to sell his labor power is the time for which he is forced to sell it,[24] that in fact the vampire will not loose its hold on him "so long as there is a muscle, a nerve, a drop of blood to be exploited."[25] For "protection" against "the serpent of their agonies," the laborers must put their heads together and, as a class, compel the passing of a law, an all-powerful social barrier that shall prevent the very workers from selling, by voluntary contract with capital, themselves and their families into slavery and death.[26] In place of the pompous catalogue of the "inalienable rights of man" comes the modest Magna Charta of a legally limited working day, which shall make clear "when the time which the worker sells is ended and

[23] Reports, etc., for October, 1848, p. 112.

[24] "The proceedings [the maneuvers of capital, e.g., 1848–50] have afforded, moreover, incontrovertible proof of the fallacy of the assertion so often advanced, that operatives need no protection, but may be considered as free agents in the disposal of the only property which they possess—the labor of their hands and the sweat of their brows." (Reports, etc., for April 30, 1850, p. 45.) "Free labor (if so it may be termed), even in a free country, requires the strong arm of the law to protect it." (Reports, etc., for October 31, 1864, p. 34.) "To permit, which is tantamount to compelling . . . to work fourteen hours a day with or without meals," etc. (Repts., etc., for April 30, 1863, p. 40.)

[25] Friedrich Engels, *L.c.*, p. 5.

[26] The Ten-Hour Act has, in the branches of industry that come under it, "put an end to the premature decrepitude of the former long-hour workers." (Reports, etc., for October 31, 1859, p. 47.) "Capital [in factories] can never be employed in keeping the machinery in motion beyond a limited time, without certain injury to the health and morals of the laborers employed; and they are not in a position to protect themselves." (*L.c.*, p. 8.)

when his own begins."[27] *Quantum mutatus ab illo!* [How changed from what he once was!]

CHAPTER XXVI: THE SECRET OF PRIMITIVE ACCUMULATION

We have seen how money is changed into capital, how through capital surplus value is made, and from surplus value more capital. But the accumulation of capital presupposes surplus value; surplus value presupposes capitalistic production; capitalistic production presupposes the pre-existence of considerable masses of capital and of labor power in the hands of producers of commodities. The whole movement, therefore, seems to turn in a vicious circle, out of which we can get only by supposing a primitive accumulation (previous accumulation of Adam Smith) preceding capitalistic accumulation; an accumulation not the result of the capitalist mode of production, but its starting point.

This primitive accumulation plays in political economy about the same part as original sin in theology. Adam bit the apple, and thereupon sin fell on the human race. Its origin is supposed to be explained when it is told as an anecdote of the past. In times long gone by there were two sorts of people: one, the diligent, intelligent, and, above all, frugal elite; the other, lazy rascals, spending their substance, and more, in riotous living. The legend of theological original sin tells us certainly how man came to be condemned to eat his bread in the sweat of his brow, but the history of economic original sin reveals to us that there

[27] "A still greater boon is the distinction at last made clear between the worker's own time and his master's. The worker knows now when that which he sells is ended and when his own begins; and by possessing a sure foreknowledge of this is enabled to prearrange his own minutes for his own purposes." (*L.c.*, p. 52.) "By making them masters of their own time [the Factory Acts] have given them a moral energy which is directing them to the eventual possession of political power." (*L.c.*, p. 47.) "With suppressed irony, and in very well-weighed words, the factory inspectors hint that the actual law also frees the capitalist from some of the brutality natural to a man who is a mere embodiment of capital, and that it has given him time for little 'culture.' Formerly the master had no time for anything but money; the servant had no time for anything but labor." (*L.c.*, p. 48.)

are people to whom this is by no means essential. Never mind! Thus it came to pass that the former sort accumulated wealth and the latter sort had at last nothing to sell except their own skins. And from this original sin dates the poverty of the great majority that, despite all its labor, has up to now nothing to sell but itself, and the wealth of the few that increases constantly although they have long ceased to work. Such insipid childishness is every day preached to us in the defense of property. M. Thiers, e.g., had the assurance to repeat it, with all the solemnity of a statesman, to the French people, once so *spirituel*. But as soon as the question of property crops up, it becomes a sacred duty to proclaim the intellectual food of the infant as the one thing fit for all ages and for all stages of development. In actual history it is notorious that conquest, enslavement, robbery, murder—briefly, force—play the great part. In the tender annals of political economy the idyllic reigns from time immemorial. Right and "labor" were from all time the sole means of enrichment, the present year of course always excepted. As a matter of fact, the methods of primitive accumulation are anything but idyllic.

In themselves, money and commodities are no more capital than are the means of production and of subsistence. They want transforming into capital. But this transformation itself can take place only under certain circumstances that center in this, viz., that two very different kinds of commodity possessors must come face to face and into contact: on the one hand, the owners of money, means of production, means of subsistence, who are eager to increase the sum of values they possess, by buying other people's labor power; on the other hand, free laborers, the sellers of their own labor power, and therefore the sellers of labor. Free laborers, in the double sense that neither they themselves form part and parcel of the means of production, as in the case of slaves, bondsmen, etc., nor do the means of production belong to them, as in the case of peasant proprietors; they are, therefore, free from, unencumbered by, any means of production of their own. With this polarization of the market for commodities, the fundamental conditions of capitalist production are given. The capitalist system presupposes the complete separation of the laborers from all property in the means by which they can realize their labor. As soon as capitalist production is once on its own legs it not only maintains this separation, but reproduces it on a continually extending scale. The process, therefore, that clears the way for the capitalist system can be none other than the process which takes away from the laborer the possession of his means of production: a process that transforms, on the one hand, the social means of subsistence and of production into capital; on the other, the immediate producers into wage laborers. The so-called primitive accumulation, therefore, is nothing else than the historical process of divorcing the producer from the means of production. It appears as primitive, because it forms the prehistoric stage of capital and of the mode of production corresponding with it.

The economic structure of capitalistic society has grown out of the economic structure of feudal society. The dissolution of the latter set free the elements of the former.

The immediate producer, the laborer, could dispose of his own person only after he had ceased to be attached to the soil and ceased to be the slave, serf, or bondsman of another. To become a free seller of labor power, who carries his commodity wherever he finds a market, he must further have escaped from the regime of the guilds, their rules for apprentices and journeymen, and the impediments of their labor regulations. Hence the historical movement which changes the producers into wage workers appears, on the one hand, as their emancipation from serfdom and from the fetters of the guilds, and this side alone exists for our bourgeois historians. But, on the other hand, these new freedmen became sellers of themselves only after they had been robbed of all their own means of production, and of all the guarantees of existence afforded by the old feudal arrangements. And the history of this, their expropriation, is written in the annals of mankind in letters of blood and fire.

The industrial capitalists, these new potentates, had on their part not only to displace the guild masters of handicrafts, but also the feudal lords, the possessors of the sources of wealth. In this respect their conquest of social power appears as the fruit of a victorious struggle both against feudal lordship and its revolting prerogatives and against the guilds and the fetters they laid on the free development of production and the free exploitation of man by man. The *chevaliers d'industrie*, however, only succeed in supplanting the chevaliers of the sword by making use of events of which they themselves were wholly innocent. They have risen by means as vile as those by which the Roman freedman once upon a time made himself the master of his *patronus*.

The starting point of the development that gave rise to the wage laborer as well as to the capitalist was the servitude of the laborer. The advance consisted in a change of form of this servitude, in the transformation of feudal exploitation into capitalist exploitation. To understand its march we need not go back very far. Although we come across the first beginnings of capitalist production as early as the fourteenth or fifteenth century, sporadically, in certain towns of the Mediterranean, the capitalist era dates from the sixteenth century. Wherever it appears, the abolition of serfdom has been long effected, and the highest development of the Middle Ages, the existence of sovereign towns, has been long on the wane.

In the history of primitive accumulation all revolutions are epoch-making that act as levers for the capitalist class in course of formation; but, above all, those moments when great masses of men are suddenly and forcibly torn from their means of subsistence and hurled as free and "unattached" proletarians on the labor market. The expropriation of the agricultural producer, of the peasant, from the soil is the basis of the whole process. The history of this expropriation in different countries assumes different aspects, and runs through its various phases in different orders of succession and at different periods. In England alone, which we take as our example, has it the classic form.[1]

[1] In Italy, where capitalistic production developed earliest, the dissolution of serfdom also took place earlier than elsewhere. The serf was emancipated in that country before he had acquired any prescriptive right to the soil. His emancipation at once transformed him into a free proletarian, who, moreover, found his

CHAPTER XXXII: HISTORICAL TENDENCY OF CAPITALIST ACCUMULATION

What does the primitive accumulation of capital, i.e., its historical genesis, resolve itself into? In so far as it is not immediate transformation of slaves and serfs into wage laborers, and therefore a mere change of form, it means only the expropriation of the immediate producers, i.e., the dissolution of private property based on the labor of its owner. Private property, as the antithesis to social, collective property, exists only where the means of labor and the external conditions of labor belong to private individuals. But according as these private individuals are laborers or not laborers, private property has a different character. The numberless shades that it at first sight presents correspond to the intermediate stages lying between these two extremes. The private property of the laborer in his means of production is the foundation of petty industry, whether agricultural, manufacturing, or both; petty industry, again, is an essential condition for the development of social production and of the free individuality of the laborer himself. Of course, this petty mode of production exists also under slavery, serfdom, and other states of dependence. But it flourishes, it lets loose its whole energy, it attains its adequate classical form only where the laborer is the private owner of his own means of labor set in action by himself, the peasant of the land which he cultivates, the artisan of the tool which he handles as a virtuoso. This mode of production presupposes parceling of the soil and scattering of the other means of production. As it excludes the concentration of these means of production, so also it excludes co-operation, division of labor within each separate process

---

master ready waiting for him in the towns, for the most part handed down as legacies from the Roman time. When the revolution of the world market, at about the end of the fifteenth century, annihilated northern Italy's commercial supremacy, a movement in the reverse direction set in. The laborers of the towns were driven *en masse* into the country, and gave an impulse, never before seen, to the *petite culture,* carried on in the form of gardening.

of production, the control over and the productive application of the forces of nature by society, and the free development of the social productive powers. It is compatible only with a system of production, and a society, moving within narrow and more or less primitive bounds. To perpetuate it would be, as Pecqueur rightly says, "to decree universal mediocrity." At a certain stage of development it brings forth the material agencies for its own dissolution. From that moment new forces and new passions spring up in the bosom of society, but the old social organization fetters them and keeps them down. It must be annihilated; it is annihilated. Its annihilation, the transformation of the individualized and scattered means of production into socially concentrated ones, of the pygmy property of the many into the huge property of the few, the expropriation of the great mass of the people from the soil, from the means of subsistence, and from the means of labor, this fearful and painful expropriation of the mass of the people forms the prelude to the history of capital. It comprises a series of forcible methods, of which we have passed in review only those that have been epoch-making as methods of the primitive accumulation of capital. The expropriation of the immediate producers was accomplished with merciless vandalism, and under the stimulus of passions the most infamous, the most sordid, the pettiest, the most meanly odious. Self-earned private property, which is based, so to say, on the fusing together of the isolated, independent laboring individual with the conditions of his labor, is supplanted by capitalistic private property, which rests on exploitation of the nominally free labor of others, i.e., on wage labor.[1]

As soon as this process of transformation has sufficiently decomposed the old society from top to bottom, as soon as the laborers are turned into proletarians, their means of labor into capital, as soon as the capitalist mode of pro-

[1] "*Nous sommes dans une condition tout-à-fait nouvelle de la société . . . nous tendons à séparer toute espèce de propriété d'avec toute espèce de travail.* [We are in a completely new condition of society . . . we tend to separate every kind of property from every kind of labor.]" (Sismondi, *Nouveaux Principes de l'Économie Politique,* T. II., p. 434.)

duction stands on its own feet, then the further socialization of labor and further transformation of the land and other means of production into socially exploited and, therefore, common means of production, as well as the further expropriation of private proprietors, take a new form. That which is now to be expropriated is no longer the laborer working for himself, but the capitalist exploiting many laborers. This expropriation is accomplished by the action of the immanent laws of capitalistic production itself, by the centralization of capital. One capitalist always kills many. Hand in hand with this centralization, or this expropriation of many capitalists by few, develop, on an ever extending scale, the co-operative form of the labor process, the conscious technical application of science, the methodical cultivation of the soil, the transformation of the instruments of labor into instruments of labor usable only in common, the economizing of all means of production by their use as the means of production of combined, socialized labor, the entanglement of all peoples in the net of the world market, and this, the international character of the capitalistic regime. Along with the constantly diminishing number of the magnates of capital, who usurp and monopolize all advantages of this process of transformation, grows the mass of misery, oppression, slavery, degradation, exploitation; but with this, too, grows the revolt of the working class, a class always increasing in numbers, and disciplined, united, organized by the very mechanism of the process of capitalist production itself. The monopoly of capital becomes a fetter upon the mode of production which has sprung up and flourished along with and under it. Centralization of the means of production and socialization of labor at last reach a point where they become incompatible with their capitalist integument. This integument is burst asunder. The knell of capitalist private property sounds. The expropriators are expropriated.

The capitalist mode of appropriation, the result of the capitalist mode of production, produces capitalist private property. This is the first negation of individual private property, as founded on the labor of the proprietor. But capitalist production begets, with the inexorability of a law of nature, its own negation. It is the negation of negation.

This does not re-establish private property for the producer, but gives him individual property based on the acquisitions of the capitalist era: i.e., on co-operation and the possession in common of the land and of the means of production.

The transformation of scattered private property, arising from individual labor, into capitalist private property is, naturally, a process incomparably more protracted, violent, and difficult than the transformation of capitalistic private property, already practically resting on socialized production, into socialized property. In the former case we had the expropriation of the mass of the people by a few usurpers; in the latter we have the expropriation of a few usurpers by the mass of the people.

VII. On the History of Early Christianity

FRIEDRICH ENGELS

This essay is noteworthy for Engels' explicit recognition of the religious character of the communist movement, and his endorsement of Renan's words: "If I wanted to give you an idea of the early Christian communities I would tell you to look at a local section of the International Workingmen's Association." It was first published in *Die Neue Zeit,* Volume XIII, Band 1, 1894–95, pages 4–13, 36–43.—Ed.

I

The history of early Christianity has notable points of resemblance with the modern working-class movement. Like the latter, Christianity was originally a movement of oppressed people: it first appeared as the religion of slaves and emancipated slaves, of poor people deprived of all rights, of peoples subjugated or dispersed by Rome. Both Christianity and the workers' socialism preach forthcoming salvation from bondage and misery; Christianity places this salvation in a life beyond, after death, in heaven; socialism places it in this world, in a transformation of society. Both are persecuted and baited, their adherents are despised and made the objects of exclusive laws, the former as enemies of the human race, the latter as enemies of the state, enemies of religion, the family, social order. And in spite of all persecution, nay, even spurred on by it, they forge victoriously, irresistibly ahead. Three hundred years after its appearance Christianity was the recognized state religion in the Roman world empire, and in barely sixty years socialism has won itself a position which makes its victory absolutely certain.

If, therefore, Professor Anton Menger wonders in his *Right to the Full Product of Labor* why, with the enormous concentration of landownership under the Roman emperors and the boundless sufferings of the working class of the time, which was composed almost exclusively of slaves, "socialism did not follow the overthrow of the Roman Empire in the West," it is because he cannot see that this "socialism" did in fact, as far as it was possible at the time, exist and even became dominant—in Christianity. Only this Christianity, as was bound to be the case in the historic conditions, did not want to accomplish the social transformation in this world, but beyond it, in heaven, in eternal life after death, in the impending "millennium."

The parallel between the two historic phenomena forces itself upon our attention as early as the Middle Ages, in the first risings of the oppressed peasants and particularly of the town plebeians. These risings, like all mass movements of the Middle Ages, were bound to wear the mask of religion and appeared as the restoration of early Christianity from spreading degeneration,[1] but behind the

[1] A peculiar antithesis to this was the religious risings in the Mohammedan world, particularly in Africa. Islam is a religion adapted to Orientals, especially Arabs, i.e., on one hand to townsmen engaged in trade and industry, on the other to nomadic Bedouins. Therein lies, however, the embryo of a periodically recurring collision. The townspeople grow rich, luxurious, and lax in the observation of the "law." The Bedouins, poor and hence of strict morals, contemplate with envy and covetousness these riches and pleasures. Then they unite under a prophet, a Mahdi, to chastise the apostates and restore the observation of the ritual and the true faith, and to appropriate in recompense the treasures of the renegades. In a hundred years they are naturally in the same position as the renegades were: a new purge of the faith is required, a new Mahdi arises, and the game starts again from the beginning. That is what happened from the conquest campaigns of the African Almoravids and Almohads in Spain to the last Mahdi of Khartoum, who so successfully thwarted the English. It happened in the same way or similarly with the risings in Persia and other Mohammedan countries. All these movements are clothed in religion, but they have their source in economic causes, and yet even when they are victorious they allow

religious exaltation there was every time a very tangible worldly interest. This appeared most splendidly in the organization of the Bohemian Taborites under Jan Žižka, of glorious memory, but this trait pervades the whole of the Middle Ages until it gradually fades away after the German Peasant War to revive again with the workingmen communists after 1830. The French revolutionary communists, as also in particular Weitling and his supporters, referred to early Christianity long before Renan's words: "If I wanted to give you an idea of the early Christian communities I would tell you to look at a local section of the International Workingmen's Association."

This French man of letters, who by mutilating German criticism of the Bible in a manner unprecedented even in modern journalism composed the novel on Church history *Origines du Christianisme*, did not know himself how much truth there was in the words just quoted. I should like to see the old "International" who can read, for example, the so-called Second Epistle of Paul to the Corinthians without old wounds reopening, at least in one respect. The whole epistle, from Chapter Eight onwards, echoes the eternal and oh! so well-known complaint: "*Les cotisations ne rentrent pas* [Contributions are not coming in]!" How many of the most zealous propagandists of the sixties would sympathizingly squeeze the hand of the author of that epistle, whoever he may be, and whisper: "So it was like that with you, too!" We, too—Corinthians were legion in our Association—can sing a song about contributions not coming in but tantalizing us as they floated elusively before our eyes. They were the famous "millions of the International"!

One of our best sources on the first Christians is Lucian of Samosata, the Voltaire of classic antiquity, who was equally skeptic towards every kind of religious superstition and therefore had neither pagan-religious nor political

---

the old economic conditions to persist untouched. So the old situation remains unchanged and the collision recurs periodically. In the popular risings of the Christian West, on the contrary, the religious disguise is only a flag and a mask for attacks on an economic order which is becoming antiquated. This is finally overthrown, a new one arises, and the world progresses.

grounds to treat the Christians otherwise than as some other kind of religious community. On the contrary, he mocked them all for their superstition, those who prayed to Jupiter no less than those who prayed to Christ; from his shallow, rationalistic point of view one sort of superstition was as stupid as the other. This in any case impartial witness relates among other things the life story of a certain adventurous Peregrinus, Proteus by name, from Parium in Hellespontus. When a youth, this Peregrinus made his debut in Armenia by committing fornication. He was caught in the act and lynched, according to the custom of the country. He was fortunate enough to escape, and after strangling his father in Parium he had to flee.

"And so it happened"–I quote from Schott's translation –"that he also came to hear of the astonishing learning of the Christians, with whose priests and scribes he had cultivated intercourse in Palestine. He made such progress in a short time that his teachers were like children compared with him. He became a prophet, an elder, a master of the synagogue, in a word, all in everything. He interpreted their writings and himself wrote a great number of works, so that finally people saw in him a superior being, let him lay down laws for them, and made him their overseer [bishop]. . . . On that ground [i.e., because he was a Christian] Proteus was at length arrested by the authorities and thrown into prison. . . . As he thus lay in chains, the Christians, who saw in his capture a great misfortune, made all possible attempts to free him. But they did not succeed. Then they administered to him in all possible ways with the greatest solicitude. As early as daybreak one could see aged mothers, widows, and young orphans crowding at the door of his prison; the most prominent among the Christians even bribed the warders and spent whole nights with him; they took their meals with him and read their holy books in his presence; briefly, the beloved Peregrinus" (he still went by that name) "was no less to them than a new Socrates. Envoys of Christian communities came to him even from towns in Asia Minor to lend him a helping hand, to console him, and to testify in his favor in court. It is unbelievable how quick these people are to act whenever it is a question of their community; they immediately spare neither exertion nor expense. And thus from all sides money then poured in to Peregrinus, so that his imprisonment became for him a source of great income. For the poor people persuaded themselves that they were immortal in body and in soul, and that they would live for all eternity; that was why they scorned death and many of them even voluntarily sacrificed their lives. Then their most prominent lawgiver convinced them that they would all be brothers one to another once they were converted, i.e., renounced the Greek gods, professed faith in the crucified sophist, and lived according to his prescriptions. That is why they despise all material goods without distinction and own them in common—doctrines which they have accepted in good faith, without demonstration or proof. And when a skillful impostor who knows how to make clever use of circumstances comes to them he can manage to get rich in a short time and laugh up his sleeve over these simpletons. For the rest, Peregrinus was set free by him who was then prefect of Syria."

Then, after a few more adventures:

"Our worthy set forth a second time" (from Parium) "on his peregrinations, the Christians' good disposition standing him in lieu of money for his journey: they administered to his needs everywhere, and never let him suffer want. He was fed for a time in this way. But then when he violated the laws of the Christians, too—I think he was caught eating of some forbidden food—they excommunicated him from their community."

What memories of youth come to my mind as I read this passage from Lucian! First of all, the "prophet Albrecht," who from about 1840 literally plundered the Weitling communist communities in Switzerland for several years—a tall, powerful man with a long beard, who wandered on foot through Switzerland and gathered audiences for his mysterious new gospel of world emancipation but who, after all, seems to have been a tolerably harmless hoaxer and soon died. Then his not so harmless successor, "the doctor," George Kuhlmann from Holstein, who put to profit the time when Weitling was in prison to convert the communities of French Switzerland to *his own* gospel, and for a time with such success that he even caught

August Becker, by far the cleverest but also the biggest ne'er-do-well among them. This Kuhlmann used to deliver lectures to them which were published in Geneva in 1845 under the title, *The New World, or the Kingdom of the Spirit on Earth. Proclamation.* In the introduction, written by his supporters (probably August Becker), we read:

"What was needed was a man on whose lips all our sufferings and all our longings and hopes, in a word, all that affects our time most profoundly, should find expression. . . . This man, whom our time was waiting for, has come. He is the doctor, George Kuhlmann from Holstein. He has come forward with the doctrine of the new world or the kingdom of the spirit in reality."

I hardly need to add that this doctrine of the new world is nothing more than the most vulgar sentimental nonsense, rendered in half-biblical expressions à la Lamennais and declaimed with prophet-like arrogance. But this did not prevent the good Weitlingers from carrying the swindler shoulder-high as the Asian Christians once did Peregrinus. They who were otherwise archdemocrats and extreme equalitarians, to the extent of fostering ineradicable suspicion against any schoolmaster, journalist, and any man generally who was not a manual worker as being an "erudite" who was out to exploit them, let themselves be persuaded by the melodramatically arrayed Kuhlmann that in the new world it would be the wisest of all, i.e., Kuhlmann, who would regulate the distribution of pleasures and that therefore, even then, in the old world, the disciples ought to bring pleasures by the bushel to that same wisest of all while they themselves should be content with crumbs. So Peregrinus Kuhlmann lived a splendid life of pleasure at the expense of the community—as long as it lasted. It did not last very long, of course; the growing murmurs of doubters and unbelievers and the menace of persecution by the Vaudois government put an end to the kingdom of the spirit in Lausanne—Kuhlmann disappeared.

Everybody who has known by experience the European working-class movement in its beginnings will remember dozens of similar examples. Today such extreme cases, at least in the large centers, have become impossible, but in remote districts where the movement has won new ground a small Peregrinus of this kind can still count on a temporary limited success. And just as those who have nothing to look forward to from the official world or have come to the end of their tether with it—opponents of inoculation, supporters of abstemiousness, vegetarians, anti-vivisectionists, nature healers, free-community preachers whose communities have fallen to pieces, authors of new theories on the origin of the universe, unsuccessful or unfortunate inventors, victims of real or imaginary injustice who are termed "good-for-nothing pettifoggers" by the bureaucracy, honest fools, and dishonest swindlers—all throng to the working-class parties in all countries—so it was with the first Christians. All the elements which had been set free, i.e., at a loose end, by the dissolution of the old world came one after the other into the orbit of Christianity as the only element that resisted that process of dissolution—for the very reason that it was the necessary product of that process—and that it therefore persisted and grew while the other elements were but ephemeral flies. There was no fanaticism, no foolishness, no scheming that did not flock to the young Christian communities and did not at least for a time and in isolated places find attentive ears and willing believers. And like our first communist workers' associations, the early Christians, too, took with such unprecedented gullibility to anything which suited their purpose that we are not even sure that some fragment or other of the "great number of works" that Peregrinus wrote for Christianity did not find its way into our New Testament.

II

German criticism of the Bible, so far the only scientific basis of our knowledge of the history of early Christianity, followed a double tendency.

The first tendency was that of the *Tübingen school,* in which, in the broad sense, D. F. Strauss must also be included. In critical inquiry it goes as far as a *theological* school can go. It admits that the four Gospels are not eyewitness accounts but only later adaptations of writings that have been lost; that no more than four of the Epistles attributed to the apostle Paul are authentic, etc. It strikes out of the historical narrations all miracles and contradictions, considering them as unacceptable, but from the rest it tries "to save what can be saved" and then its nature, that of a theological school, is very evident. Thus it enabled Renan, who bases himself mostly on it, to "save" still more by applying the same method and, moreover, to try to impose upon us as historically authenticated many New Testament accounts that are more than doubtful and, besides, a multitude of other legends about martyrs. In any case, all that the Tübingen school rejects as unhistorical or apocryphal can be considered as finally eliminated for science.

The other tendency has but one representative—*Bruno Bauer*. His greatest service consists not merely in having given a pitiless criticism of the Gospels and the Epistles of the apostles, but in having for the first time seriously undertaken an inquiry into not only the Jewish and Greco-Alexandrian elements but the purely Greek and Greco-Roman elements that first opened for Christianity the career of a universal religion. The legend that Christianity arose ready and complete out of Judaism and, starting from Palestine, conquered the world with its dogma already defined in the main, and its morals, has been untenable since Bruno Bauer; it can continue to vegetate only in the theological faculties and with people who wish "to keep religion alive for the people" even at the expense of science. The enormous influence which the Philonic school of Alexandria and Greco-Roman vulgar philosophy—Platonic and mainly Stoic—had on Christianity, which became the state religion under Constantine, is far from having been defined in detail, but its existence has been proved, and that is primarily the achievement of Bruno Bauer: he laid the foundation of the proof that Christianity was not imported from outside—from Judea—into the Romano-Greek world and imposed on it, but that, at least in its world-religion form, it is that world's own product. Bauer, of course, like all those who are fighting against deep-rooted prejudices, over-reached his aim in this work. In order to define through literary sources, too, Philo's and particularly Seneca's influence on emerging Christianity and to show up the authors of the New Testament formally as downright plagiarists of those philosophers he had to place the appearance of the new religion about half a century later, to reject the opposing accounts of Roman historians and take extensive liberties with historiography in general. According to him, Christianity as such appears only under the Flavians, the literature of the New Testament only under Hadrian, Antonius, and Marcus Aurelius. As a result the New Testament accounts of Jesus and his disciples are deprived for Bauer of any historical background: they are diluted in legends in which the phases of interior development and the moral struggles of the first communities are transferred to more or less fictitious persons. Not Galilee and Jerusalem, but Alexandria and Rome, according to Bauer, are the birthplaces of the new religion.

If, therefore, the Tübingen school presents to us in the remains of the New Testament stories and literature that it left untouched the extreme maximum of what science today can still accept as disputable, Bruno Bauer presents to us the maximum of what can be contested. The factual truth lies between these two limits. Whether that truth can be defined with the means at our disposal today is very doubtful. New discoveries, particularly in Rome, in the Orient, and above all in Egypt, will contribute more to this than any criticism.

But we have in the New Testament a single book the time of the writing of which can be defined within a few months, which must have been written between June 67 and January or April 68; a book, consequently, which belongs to the very beginning of the Christian era and reflects with the most naïve fidelity and in the corresponding idiomatic language the ideas of the beginning of that era. This book, therefore, in my opinion, is a far more important source from which to define what early Christianity really was than all the rest of the New Testament, which, in its present form, is of a far later date. This book is the so-called Revelation of John. And as this, apparently the most obscure book in the whole Bible, is moreover today, thanks to German criticism, the most comprehensible and the clearest, I shall give my readers an account of it.

One needs but to look into this book in order to be convinced of the state of great exaltation not only of the author but also of the "surrounding medium" in which he moved. Our Revelation is not the only one of its kind and time. From the year 164 before our era, when the first which has reached us, the so-called Book of Daniel, was written, up to about 250 of our era, the approximate date of Commodian's *Carmen*, Renan counted no fewer than fifteen extant classical Apocalypses, not counting subsequent imitations. (I quote Renan because his book is also the best known by non-specialists and the most accessible.) That was a time when even in Rome and Greece and still more in Asia Minor, Syria, and Egypt an absolutely uncritical mixture of the crassest superstitions of the most varying peoples was indiscriminately accepted and complemented by pious deception and downright charlatanism; a time in which miracles, ecstasies, visions, apparitions, divining, gold-making, cabala, and other secret magic played a primary role. It was in that atmosphere, and, moreover, among a class of people who were more inclined than any other to listen to these supernatural fantasies, that Christianity arose. For did not the Christian gnostics in Egypt during the second century of our era engage extensively in alchemy and introduce alchemistic notions into their teachings, as the Leyden papyrus documents, among others, prove? And the Chaldean and Judean *mathematici*, who, according to Tacitus, were twice expelled from Rome for magic, once under Claudius and again under Vitellius, practiced no other kind of geometry than the kind we shall find at the basis of John's Revelation.

To this we must add another thing. All the Apocalypses attribute to themselves the right to deceive their readers. Not only were they written as a rule by quite different people than their alleged authors, and mostly by people who lived much later, for example the Book of Daniel, the Book of Enoch, the Apocalypses of Ezra, Baruch, Judah, etc., and the Sibylline Books, but, as far as their main content is concerned, they prophesy only things that had already happened long before and were quite well known to the real author. Thus in the year 164, shortly before the death of Antiochus Epiphanes, the author of the Book of Daniel makes Daniel, who is supposed to have lived in the time of Nebuchadnezzar, prophesy the rise and fall of the Persian and Macedonian empires and the beginning of the Roman Empire, in order by this proof of his gift of prophecy to prepare the reader to accept the final prophecy that the people of Israel will overcome all hardships and finally be victorious. If, therefore, John's Revelation were really the work of its alleged author it would be the only exception among all apocalyptic literature.

The John who claims to be the author was, in any case, a man of great distinction among the Christians of Asia Minor. This is borne out by the tone of the message to the Seven Churches. Possibly he was the apostle John, whose historical existence, however, is not completely authenticated but is very probable. If this apostle was really the author, so much the better for our point of view. That would be the best confirmation that the Christianity of this book is real, genuine early Christianity. Let it be noted in passing that, apparently, the Revelation was not written by the same author as the Gospel or the three Epistles which are also attributed to John.

The Revelation consists of a series of visions. In the first, Christ appears in the garb of a high priest, goes in the midst of seven candlesticks representing the Seven Churches of Asia and dictates to "John" messages to the seven "angels" of those churches. Here at the very beginning we see plainly the difference between *this* Christianity and Constantine's universal religion, formulated by the Council of Nicaea. The Trinity is not only unknown, it is even impossible. Instead of the *one* Holy Ghost of later we here have the "*seven spirits of God*," construed by the rabbis from Isaiah 11:2. Christ is the son of God, the first and the last, the alpha and the omega, by no means God himself or equal to God, but, on the contrary, "the beginning of the *creation* of God," hence an emanation of God, existing from all eternity but subordinate to God, like the above-mentioned seven spirits. In Chapter 15:3 the martyrs in heaven sing "the song of Moses, the servant of God, and the song of the Lamb," glorifying God. Hence Christ here appears not only as subordinate to God but even, in a certain respect, on an equal footing with Moses. Christ is crucified in Jerusalem (11:8) but rises again (1:5, 18); he is "the Lamb" that has been sacrificed for the sins of

the world and with whose blood the faithful of all tongues and nations have been redeemed to God. Here we find the basic idea which enabled early Christianity to develop into a universal religion. All Semitic and European religions of that time shared the view that the gods offended by the actions of man could be propitiated by sacrifice; the first revolutionary basic idea (borrowed from the Philonic school) in Christianity was that by the one great voluntary sacrifice of a mediator the sins of all times and all men were atoned for once for all—in respect of the faithful. Thus the necessity of any further sacrifices was removed and with it the basis for a multitude of religious rites, but freedom from rites that made difficult or forbade intercourse with people of other confessions was the first condition of a universal religion. In spite of this the habit of sacrifice was so deeply rooted in the customs of peoples that Catholicism—which borrowed so much from paganism—found it appropriate to accommodate itself to this fact by the introduction of at least the symbolical sacrifice of the mass. On the other hand, there is no trace whatever of the dogma of original sin in our book.

But the most characteristic in these messages, as in the whole book, is that it never and nowhere occurs to the author to refer to himself and his co-believers by any other name than that of *Jews*. He reproaches the members of the sects in Smyrna and Philadelphia against whom he fulminates with the fact that they "say they are Jews, and are not, but are the synagogue of Satan"; of those in Pergamos he says they hold the doctrine of Balaam, who taught Balac to cast a stumbling block *before the children of Israel*, to eat things sacrificed unto idols, and to commit fornication. Here it is therefore not a case of conscious Christians but of people who say they are Jews. Granted, their Judaism is a new stage of development of the earlier, but for that very reason it is the only true one. Hence when the saints appeared before the throne of God, there came first 144,000 Jews, twelve thousand from each tribe, and only after them the countless masses of heathens converted to this renovated Judaism. That was how little our author was aware in the year 69 of the Christian era that he represented quite a new phase in the development of a religion which was to become one of the most revolutionary elements in the history of the human mind.

We therefore see that the Christianity of that time, which was still unaware of itself, was as different as heaven from earth from the later dogmatically fixed universal religion of the Nicene Council; one cannot be recognized in the other. Here we have neither the dogma nor the morals of later Christianity, but instead a feeling that one is struggling against the whole world and that the struggle will be a victorious one, an eagerness for the struggle and a certainty of victory which are totally lacking in Christians of today and which are to be found in our time only at the other pole of society, among the socialists.

In fact, the struggle against a world that at the beginning was superior in force, and at the same time against the innovators themselves, is common to the early Christians and the socialists. Neither of these two great movements was made by leaders or prophets—although there are prophets enough among both of them—they are mass movements. And mass movements are bound to be confused at the beginning, confused because the thinking of the masses at first moves among contradictions, lack of clarity, and lack of cohesion, and also because of the role that prophets still play in them at the beginning. This confusion is to be seen in the formation of numerous sects which fight against one another with at least the same zeal as against the common external enemy. So it was with early Christianity, so it was in the beginning of the socialist movement, no matter how much that worried the well-meaning worthies who preached unity where no unity was possible.

Was the International held together by a uniform dogma? On the contrary. There were communists of the French pre-1848 tradition, among whom again were various shades: communists of Weitling's school and others of the regenerated Communist League, Proudhonists dominating in France and Belgium, Blanquists, the German workers' party, and finally the Bakuninist anarchists, who for a while had the upper hand in Spain and Italy, to mention only the principal groups. It took a whole quarter of a century from the foundation of the International before the separation from the anarchists was final and complete everywhere and unity could be established, at least in respect of most general economic viewpoints. And that with our means of communication—railways, telegraph, giant industrial cities, the press, organized people's assemblies.

There was among the early Christians the same division into countless sects, which was the very means by which discussion and thereby later unity were achieved. We already find it in this book, which is beyond doubt the oldest Christian document, and our author fights it with the same irreconcilable ardor as the great sinful world outside. There were first of all the Nicolaitans, in Ephesus and Pergamos; those who said they were Jews but were the synagogue of Satan, in Smyrna and Philadelphia; the supporters of Balaam, who is called a false prophet, in Pergamos; those who said they were apostles and were not, in Ephesus; and finally, in Thyatira, the supporters of the false prophetess who is described as a Jezebel. We are given no more details about these sects, it being only said about the followers of Balaam and Jezebel that they ate things sacrificed to idols and committed fornication. Attempts have been made to conceive these five sects as Pauline Christians and all the messages as directed against Paul, the false apostle, the alleged Balaam and "Nicolaos." Arguments to this effect, hardly tenable, are to be found collected in Renan's *Saint Paul* (Paris, 1869, pages 303–5 and 367–70). They all tend to explain the messages by the Acts of the Apostles and the so-called Epistles of Paul, writings which, at least in their present form, are no less than sixty years younger than the Revelation, and the relevant factual data of which, therefore, are not only extremely doubtful but also totally contradictory. But the decisive thing is that it could not occur to the author to give five different names to one and the same sect and even two for Ephesus alone (false apostles and Nicolaitans) and two also for Pergamos (Balaamites and Nicolaitans), and to refer to them every time expressly as two different sects. At the same time one cannot deny the probability that there were also elements among these sects that would be termed Pauline today.

In both cases in which more details are given the accusation bears on eating meats offered to idols and on fornication, two points on which the Jews—the old ones as well as the Christian ones—were in continual dispute with converted heathens. The meat from heathen sacrifices was not only served at festal meals where refusal of the food offered would have seemed improper and could even have been dangerous, it was also sold in the public markets, where it was not always possible to ascertain whether it was pure in the eyes of the law. By fornication the Jews understood not only extranuptial sexual relations but also marriage within the degrees of relationship prohibited by the Jewish law or between a Jew and a gentile, and it is in this sense that the word is generally understood in the Acts of the Apostles 15:20 and 29. But our John has his own views on the sexual relations allowed to orthodox Jews. He says, 14:4, of the 144,000 heavenly Jews: "These are they which were not defiled with women; for they are virgins." And in fact, in our John's heaven there is not a single woman. He therefore belongs to the trend, which also often appears in other early Christian writings, that considers sexual relations generally as sinful. And when we moreover take into consideration the fact that he calls Rome the Great Whore with whom the kings of the earth have committed fornication and have become drunk with the wine of fornication and the merchants of the earth have waxed rich through the abundance of her delicacies, it becomes impossible for us to take the word in the messages in the narrow sense that theological apologists would like to attribute to it in order thus to catch at some confirmation of other passages in the New Testament. On the contrary. These passages in the messages are an obvious indication of a phenomenon common to all times of great agitation, that the traditional bonds of sexual relations, like all other fetters, are shaken off. In the first centuries of Christianity, too, there appeared often enough, side by side with asceticism which mortified the flesh, the tendency to extend Christian freedom to a more or less unrestrained intercourse between man and woman. The same thing was observed in the modern socialist movement. What unspeakable horror was felt in the then "pious nursery" of Germany at St. Simon's *réhabilitation de la chair* in the thirties, which was rendered in German as *Wiedereinsetzung des Fleisches* [reinstatement of the flesh]! And the most horrified of all were the then ruling distinguished estates (there were as yet no classes in our country), who could not live in Berlin any more than on their country estates without repeated reinstatement of their flesh! If only those good people had been able to know Fourier, who contemplated quite different pranks for the flesh! With the overcoming of utopianism, these extravagances yielded to a more rational and in reality far more radical conception, and since Germany has grown out of Heine's pious nursery and developed into the center of the socialist movement the hypocritical indignation of the distinguished pious world is laughed at.

That is all the dogmatic content of the messages. The rest consists in exhorting the faithful to be zealous in propaganda, to courageous and proud confession of their faith in face of the foe, to unrelenting struggle against the enemy both within and without—and as far as this goes, they could just as well have been written by one of the prophetically minded enthusiasts of the International.

III

The messages are but the introduction to the theme, properly so-called, of John's communication to the Seven Churches of Asia Minor and through them to the remaining reformed Judaism of the year 69, out of which Christianity later developed. And herewith we enter the innermost holy of holies of early Christianity.

What kind of people were the first Christians recruited from? Mainly from the "laboring and burdened," the members of the lowest strata of the people, as becomes a revolutionary element. And what did they consist of? In the towns of impoverished free men, all sorts of people, like the "mean whites" of the Southern slave states and the European beachcombers and adventurers in colonial and Chinese seaports, then of emancipated slaves, and, above all, actual slaves; on the large estates in Italy, Sicily, and Africa, of slaves, and in the rural districts of the provinces of small peasants who had fallen more and more into bondage through debt. There was absolutely no common road to emancipation for all these elements. For all of them paradise lay lost behind them; for the ruined free men it was the former *polis,* the town and the state at the same time, of which their forefathers had been free citizens; for the war-captive slaves, the time of freedom before their subjugation and captivity; for the small peasants, the abolished gentile social system and communal land ownership. All that had been smitten down by the leveling iron fist of conquering Rome. The largest social group that antiquity had attained was the tribe and the union of kindred tribes; among the barbarians grouping was based on alliances of families, and among the town-founding Greeks and Italians on the *polis,* which consisted of one or more kindred tribes. Philip and Alexander gave the Hellenic peninsula political unity, but that did not lead to the formation of a Greek nation. Nations became possible only through the downfall of Roman world domination. This domination had put an end once for all to the smaller unions; military might, Roman jurisdiction, and the tax-collecting machinery completely dissolved the traditional inner organization. To the loss of independence and distinctive organization was added the forcible plunder by military and civil authorities, who took the treasures of the subjugated away from them and then lent them back at usurious rates in order to extort still more out of them. The pressure of taxation and the need for money which it caused in regions dominated only or mainly by natural economy plunged the peasants into ever deeper bondage to the usurers, gave rise to great differences in fortune, making the rich richer and the poor completely destitute. Any resistance of isolated small tribes or towns to the gigantic Roman world power was hopeless. Where was the way out, salvation, for the enslaved, oppressed, and impoverished, a way out common to all these groups of people whose interests were mutually alien or even opposed? And yet it had to be found if a great revolutionary movement was to embrace them all.

This way out was found. But not in this world. In the state in which things were, it could only be a religious way out. Then a new world was disclosed. The continued life of the soul after the death of the body had gradually become a recognized article of faith throughout the Roman world. A kind of recompense or punishment of the deceased souls for their actions while on earth also received more and more general recognition. As far as recompense was concerned, admittedly the prospects were not so good: antiquity was too spontaneously materialistic not to attribute infinitely greater value to life on earth than to life in the kingdom of shadows; to live on after death was considered by the Greeks rather as a misfortune. Then came Christianity, which took recompense and punishment in the world beyond seriously and created heaven and hell, and a way out was found which would lead the laboring and burdened from this vale of woe to eternal paradise. And in fact only with the prospect of a reward in the world beyond could the Stoico-Philonic renunciation of the world and ascetics be exalted to the basic moral principle of a new universal religion which would inspire the oppressed masses with enthusiasm.

But this heavenly paradise does not open to the faithful by the mere fact of their death. We shall see that the kingdom of God, the capital of which is the New Jerusalem, can only be conquered and opened after arduous struggles with the powers of hell. But in the imagination of the early Christians these struggles were immediately ahead. John describes his book at the very beginning as the revelation of "things which must *shortly* come to pass"; and immediately afterwards, 1:3, he declares: "Blessed is he that readeth and they that hear the words of this prophecy . . . for *the time is at hand.*" To the church in Philadelphia, Christ sends the message: "Behold, I come *quickly.*" And in the last chapter the angel says he has shown John "things which must *shortly* be done," and gives him the order: "Seal not the sayings of the prophecy of this book: for the time is *at hand.*" And Christ himself says twice (22:12, 20), "I come *quickly.*" The sequel will show us how soon this coming was expected.

The visions of the Apocalypse, which the author now shows us, are copied throughout, and mostly literally, from earlier models, partly from the classical prophets of the Old Testament, particularly Ezekiel, partly from later Jewish apocalypses written after the fashion of the Book of Daniel and in particular from the Book of Enoch, which had already been written at least in part. Criticism has shown to the smallest details where our John got every picture, every menacing sign, every plague sent to unbelieving humanity, in a word, the whole of the material for his book; so that he not only shows great poverty of mind, but even himself proves that he never experienced even in imagination the alleged ecstasies and visions which he describes.

The order of these visions is briefly as follows: First, John sees God sitting on his throne, holding in his hand a book with seven seals, and before him the Lamb that has been slain and has risen from the dead (Christ) and is found worthy to open the seals of the book. The opening of the seals is followed by all sorts of miraculous menacing signs. When the fifth seal is opened, John sees under the altar of God the souls of the martyrs of Christ that were slain for the word of God and who cry with a loud voice, saying: "How long, O Lord, dost Thou not judge and avenge our blood on them that dwell on the earth?" And then white robes are given to them and they are told that they must rest for a little while yet, for more martyrs must be slain.

So here it is not yet a question of a "religion of love," of "Love your enemies, bless them that curse you," etc. Here undiluted revenge is preached, sound, honest revenge on the persecutors of the Christians. So it is in the whole of the book. The nearer the crisis comes, the heavier the plagues and punishments rain from the heavens and with all the more satisfaction John announces that the mass of humanity will not atone for their sins, that new scourges of God must lash them, that Christ must rule them with a rod of iron and tread the wine press of the fierceness and wrath of Almighty God, but that the impious still remain obdurate in their hearts. It is the natural feeling, free of all hypocrisy, that a fight is going on and that *à la guerre comme à la guerre* [in war, it's as war].

When the seventh seal is opened, there come seven angels with seven trumpets, and each time one of them sounds his trumpet new horrors occur. After the seventh blast seven more angels come onto the scene with the seven vials of the wrath of God, which they pour out upon the earth; still more plagues and punishments, mainly boring repetitions of what has already happened several times. Then comes the woman, Babylon, the Great Whore, sitting arrayed in scarlet over the waters, drunk with the blood of the saints and the martyrs of Jesus, the great City of the Seven Hills that rules over all the kings of the earth. She is sitting on a beast with seven heads and ten horns. The seven heads represent the seven hills, and also seven "kings." Of those kings "five are fallen, one is, and the other is not yet come," and after him comes again one of the first five; he was wounded to death but was healed. He will reign over the world for forty-two months, or three and a half years (half of a week of seven years), and will persecute the faithful to death and bring the rule of godlessness. But then follows the great final fight, the saints and the martyrs are avenged by the destruction of the Great Whore, Babylon, and all her followers, i.e., the main mass of mankind; the devil is cast into the bottomless pit and shut up there for a thousand years, during which Christ reigns with the martyrs risen from the dead. But after a thousand years the devil is freed again and there is another great battle of the spirits, in which he is finally defeated. Then follows the second resurrection, when the other dead also arise and appear before the throne of judgment of God (not of Christ, be it noted), and the faithful will enter a new heaven, a new earth, and a new Jerusalem for life eternal.

As this whole monument is made up of exclusively pre-Christian Jewish material it presents almost exclusively Jewish ideas. Since things started to go badly in this world for the people of Israel, from the time of the tribute to the Assyrians and Babylonians, from the destruction of the two kingdoms of Israel and Judah to the bondage under Seleucis, that is from Isaiah to Daniel, in every dark period there were prophecies of a Saviour. In Daniel, 12:1–3, there is even a prophecy about Michael, the guardian angel of the Jews, coming down on earth to save them from great trouble; many dead will come to life again, there will be a kind of last judgment, and the teachers who have taught the people justice will shine like stars for all eternity. The only Christian point is the great stress laid on the imminent reign of Christ and the glory of the faithful, particularly the martyrs who have risen from the dead.

For the interpretation of these prophecies, as far as they refer to events of that time, we are indebted to German criticism, particularly Ewald, Lücke, and Ferdinand Benary. It has been made accessible to non-theologians by Renan. We have already seen that Babylon, the Great Whore, stands for Rome, the City of the Seven Hills. We are told in Chapter 17:9–11 about the beast on which she sits that:

"The seven heads" of the beast "are seven mountains, on which the woman sitteth. And there are seven kings: five are fallen, and one is, and the other is not yet come; and when he cometh he must continue a short space. And the beast that was, and is not, even he is the eighth, and is of the seven, and goeth into perdition."

According to this, the beast is Roman world domination, represented by seven Caesars in succession, one of them having been mortally wounded and no longer reigning, but he will be healed and will return. It will be given unto him as the eighth to establish the kingdom of blasphemy and defiance of God. It will be given unto him "to make war with the saints and to overcome them. . . . And all that dwell upon the earth shall worship him, whose names are not written in the book of life of the Lamb. . . . And he causeth all, both small and great, rich and poor, free and bond, to receive a mark in their right hand, or in their foreheads: and that no man might buy or sell, save he that had the mark, or the name of the beast, or the number of his name. Here is wisdom. Let him that hath understanding count the number of the beast, for it is the number of a man; and his number is six hundred threescore and six." (13:7–18.)

We merely note that boycott is mentioned here as one of the measures to be applied against the Christians by the Roman Empire—and is therefore patently an invention of the devil—and pass on to the question who this Roman emperor is who reigned once before, was wounded to death and removed, but will return as the eighth in the series in the role of Antichrist.

Taking Augustus as the first, we have: 2. Tiberius, 3. Caligula, 4. Claudius, 5. Nero, 6. Galba. "Five are fallen, and one is." Hence Nero is already fallen and Galba is. Galba ruled from June 9, 68, to January 15, 69. But immediately after he ascended the throne, the legions of the

Rhine revolted under Vitellius, while other generals prepared military risings in other provinces. In Rome itself the praetorians rose, killed Galba, and proclaimed Otho emperor.

From this we see that our Revelation was written under Galba. Probably towards the end of his rule. Or, at the latest, during the three months (up to April 15, 69) of the rule of Otho, "the seventh." But who is the eighth, who was, and is not? That we learn from the number 666.

Among the Semites—Chaldeans and Jews—there was at the time a kind of magic based on the double meaning of letters. As about three hundred years before our era Hebrew letters were also used as symbols for numbers: a = 1, b = 2, g = 3, d = 4, etc. The cabala diviners added up the value of each letter of a name and sought from the sum to prophesy the future of the one who bore the name, e.g., by forming words or combinations of words of equal value. Secret words and the like were also expressed in this language of numbers. This art was given the Greek name *gematriah*, geometry; the Chaldeans, who pursued this as a business and were called *mathematici* by Tacitus, were later expelled from Rome under Claudius and again under Vitellius, presumably for "serious disorders."

It was by means of this mathematics that our number 666 appeared. It is a disguise for the name of one of the first five Caesars. But besides the number 666, Irenaeus, at the end of the second century, knew another reading—616, which, at all events, appeared at a time when the number puzzle was still widely known. The proof of the solution will be if it holds good for both numbers.

This solution was given by Ferdinand Benary of Berlin. The name is Nero. The number is based on נרון כסר Neron Kesar, the Hebrew spelling of the Greek Nerôn Kaisar, Emperor Nero, authenticated by means of the Talmud and Palmyrian inscriptions. This inscription was found on coins of Nero's time minted in the eastern half of the empire. And so—*n* (*nun*) = 50; *r* (*resh*) = 200; *v* (*vau*) for *o* = 6; *n* (*nun*) = 50; *k* (*kaph*) = 100; *s* (*samech*) = 60; *r* (*resh*) = 200. Total 666. If we take as a basis the Latin spelling *Nero Caesar* the second *nun* = 50 disappears and we get 666 − 50 = 616, which is Irenaeus's reading.

In fact, the whole Roman Empire suddenly broke into confusion in Galba's time. Galba himself marched on Rome at the head of the Spanish and Gallic legions to overthrow Nero, who fled and ordered an emancipated slave to kill him. But not only the praetorians in Rome plotted against Galba, the supreme commanders in the provinces did, too; new pretenders to the throne appeared everywhere and prepared to march on Rome with their legions. The empire seemed doomed to civil war, its dissolution appeared imminent. Over and above all this the rumor spread, especially in the East, that Nero had not been killed but only wounded, that he had fled to the Parthians and was about to advance with an army over the Euphrates to begin another and bloodier rule of terror. Achaia and Asia in particular were terrified by such reports. And at the very time at which the Revelation must have been written there appeared a false Nero, who settled with a fairly considerable number of supporters not far from Patmos and Asia Minor on the island of Kytnos in the Aegean Sea (now called Thermia), until he was killed while Otho still reigned. What was there to be astonished at in the fact that among the Christians, against whom Nero had begun the first great persecution, the view spread that he would return as the Antichrist and that his return and the intensified attempt at a bloody suppression of the new sect that it would involve would be the sign and prelude of the return of Christ, of the great victorious struggle against the powers of hell, of the thousand-year kingdom "shortly" to be established, the confident expectation of which inspired the martyrs to go joyfully to death?

Christian and Christian-influenced literature in the first two centuries gives sufficient indication that the secret of the number 666 was then known to many. Irenaeus no longer knew it, but, on the other hand, he and many others up to the end of the third century also knew that the returning Nero was meant by the beast of the Apocalypse. This trace is then lost, and the work which interests us is fantastically interpreted by religious-minded future-tellers; I myself as a child knew old people who, following the example of old Johann Albrecht Bengel, expected the end of the world and the last judgment in the year 1836. The prophecy was fulfilled, and to the very year. The victim of the last judgment, however, was not the sinful world, but the pious interpreters of the Revelation themselves. For in 1836, F. Benary provided the key to the number 666 and thus put a torturous end to all the prophetical calculations, that new *gematriah*.

Our John can give only a superficial description of the kingdom of heaven that is reserved for the faithful. The new Jerusalem is laid out on a fairly large scale, at least according to the conceptions of the time: it is 12,000 furlongs, or 2,227 square kilometers, so that its area is about five million square kilometers, more than half the size of the United States of America. And it is built of gold and all manner of precious stones. There God lives with his people, lightening them instead of the sun, and there shall be no more death, neither sorrow, neither shall there be any more pain. And a pure river of water of life flows through the city, and on either side of the river are trees of life, bearing twelve manner of fruits and yielding fruit every month, and the leaves of the tree "serve for the healing of the nations." (A kind of medicinal beverage, Renan thinks–*L'Antechrist*, page 542.) Here the saints shall live forever.

Such, as far as we know, was Christianity in Asia Minor, its main seat, about the year 68. No trace of any Trinity, but, on the contrary, the old one and indivisible Jehovah of later Judaism, which had exalted him from the national god of the Jews to the one and supreme God of heaven and earth, where he claims to rule over all nations, promising mercy to those who are converted and mercilessly smiting down the obdurate in accordance with the ancient *parcere subjectis ac debellare superbos*.[1] Hence this God, in person–not Christ, as in the later accounts of the Gospels and the Epistles–will judge at the last judgment. According to the Persian doctrine of emanation which was current in later Judaism, Christ the Lamb proceeds eternally from him as do also, but on a lower footing, the "seven spirits of God," who owe their existence to a misunderstanding of a poetical passage (Isaiah, 11:2). All of

[1] "Pardon the humble and make war on the proud."

them are subordinate to God, not God themselves or equal to him. The Lamb sacrifices itself to atone for the sins of the world, and for that it is considerably promoted in heaven, for its voluntary death is credited as an extraordinary feat throughout the book, not as something which proceeds necessarily from its intrinsic nature. Naturally the whole heavenly court of elders, cherubim, angels, and saints is there. In order to become a religion monotheism has ever had to make concessions to polytheism—since the time of the Zend-Avesta. With the Jews the decline to the sensuous gods of the heathens continued chronically until, after the exile, the heavenly court according to the Persian model adapted religion somewhat better to the people's fantasy, and Christianity itself, even after it had replaced the eternally self-equal immutable god of the Jews by the mysterious self-differentiating god of the Trinity, could find nothing to supplant the worship of the old gods but that of the saints; thus, according to Fallmerayer, the worship of Jupiter in Peloponnesus, Maina, and Arcadia died out only about the ninth century. (*Geschichte der Halbinsel Morea*, I, page 227.) Only the modern bourgeois period and its Protestantism did away with the saints again and at last took differentiated monotheism seriously.

In the book there is just as little mention of original sin and justification by faith. The faith of these early militant communities is quite different from that of the later victorious Church: side by side with the sacrifice of the Lamb the imminent return of Christ and the thousand-year kingdom which is shortly to dawn form its essential content, this faith survives only through active propaganda, unrelenting struggle against the internal and external enemy, the proud profession of the revolutionary standpoint before the heathen judges, and martyrdom, confident in victory.

We have seen that the author is not yet aware that he is something else than a Jew. Accordingly, there is no mention of baptism in the whole book, just as many more facts indicate that baptism was instituted in the second period of Christianity. The 144,000 believing Jews are "sealed," not baptized. It is said of the saints in heaven and the faithful upon earth that they had washed themselves of their sins and washed their robes and made them white in the blood of the Lamb; there is no mention of the water of baptism. The two prophets who precede the coming of the Antichrist in Chapter 11 do not baptize, and according to 19:10, the testimony of Jesus is not baptism but the spirit of prophecy. Baptism should naturally have been mentioned in all these cases if it had already been in vigor; we may therefore conclude with almost absolute certainty that the author did not know of it, that it first appeared when the Christians finally separated from the Jews.

Neither does our author know any more about the second sacrament, the Eucharist. If in the Lutheran text Christ promises all the Thyatirans that remain firm in the faith to come *das Abendmahl halten* with them, this creates a false impression. The Greek text has *deipnêsô*—"I shall eat supper [with him]," and the English Bible translates this correctly: "I shall *sup*" with him. There is no question here of the Eucharist even as a mere commemoration meal.

There can be no doubt that this book, with its date so originally authenticated as the year 68 or 69, is the oldest of all Christian literature. No other is written in such barbaric language, so full of Hebraisms, impossible constructions, and mistakes in grammar. Chapter 1, verse 4, for example, says literally: "Grace be unto you . . . from he that is being and that was and that is coming." Only professional theologians and other historians who have a stake in it now deny that the Gospels and the Acts of the Apostles are but later adaptations of writings which are now lost and whose feeble historical core is now unrecognizable in the maze of legend, that even the few Epistles supposed by Bruno Bauer to be "authentic" are either writings of a later date or at best adaptations of old works of unknown authors, altered by additions and insertions. It is all the more important since we are here in possession of a book whose date of writing has been determined to the nearest month, a book that displays to us Christianity in its undeveloped form. This form stands in the same relation to the fourth-century state religion, with its fully evolved dogma and mythology, as Tacitus's still unstable mythology of the Germans to the developed teaching of the gods of

Edda as influenced by Christian and antique elements. The core of the universal religion is there, but it includes, without any discrimination, the thousand possibilities of development which became realities in the countless subsequent sects. And the reason why this oldest writing of the time when Christianity was coming into being is especially valuable for us is that it shows, without any dilution, what Judaism, strongly influenced by Alexandria, contributed to Christianity. All that comes later is Western, Greco-Roman addition. It was only by the intermediary of the monotheistic Jewish religion that the cultured monotheism of later Greek vulgar philosophy could clothe itself in the religious form in which alone it could grip the masses. But once this intermediary was found it could become a universal religion only in the Greco-Roman world, and that by further development in and merging with the thought material that world had achieved.

VIII. Ludwig Feuerbach and the End of Classical German Philosophy

FRIEDRICH ENGELS

FOREWORD

In the Preface to *A Contribution to the Critique of Political Economy*, published in Berlin, 1859, Karl Marx relates how the two of us in Brussels in the year 1845 set about "to work out in common the opposition of our view" —the materialist conception of history which was elaborated mainly by Marx—"to the ideological view of German philosophy, in fact, to settle accounts with our erstwhile philosophical conscience. The resolve was carried out in the form of a criticism of post-Hegelian philosophy. The manuscript, two large octavo volumes, had long reached its place of publication in Westphalia when we received the news that altered circumstances did not allow of its being printed. We abandoned the manuscript to the gnawing criticism of the mice all the more willingly as we had achieved our main purpose—self-clarification."

Since then more than forty years have elapsed and Marx died without either of us having had an opportunity of returning to the subject. We have expressed ourselves in various places regarding our relation to Hegel, but nowhere in a comprehensive, connected account. To Feuerbach, who after all in many respects forms an intermediate link between Hegelian philosophy and our conception, we never returned.

In the meantime the Marxist world outlook has found representatives far beyond the boundaries of Germany and

Europe, and in all the literary languages of the world. On the other hand, classical German philosophy is experiencing a kind of rebirth abroad, especially in England and Scandinavia, and even in Germany itself people appear to be getting tired of the pauper's broth of eclecticism which is ladled out in the universities there under the name of philosophy.

In these circumstances a short, connected account of our relation to the Hegelian philosophy, of how we proceeded from it as well as of how we separated from it, appeared to me to be required more and more. Equally, a full acknowledgment of the influence which Feuerbach, more than any other post-Hegelian philosopher, had upon us during our period of storm and stress appeared to me to be an undischarged debt of honor. I therefore willingly seized the opportunity when the editors of the *Neue Zeit* asked me for a critical review of Starcke's book on Feuerbach. My contribution was published in that journal in the fourth and fifth numbers of 1886 and appears here in revised form as a separate publication.

Before sending these lines to press I have once again ferreted out and looked over the old manuscript of 1845–46. The section dealing with Feuerbach is not completed. The finished portion consists of an exposition of the materialist conception of history, which proves only how incomplete our knowledge of economic history still was at that time. It contains no criticism of Feuerbach's doctrine itself; for the present purpose, therefore, it was unusable. On the other hand, in an old notebook of Marx's I have found the eleven theses on Feuerbach printed here as an appendix. These are notes hurriedly scribbled down for later elaboration, absolutely not intended for publication, but invaluable as the first document in which is deposited the brilliant germ of the new world outlook.

Friedrich Engels

London, February 21, 1888

I. [THE REVOLUTION AGAINST HEGEL]

The volume[1] before us carries us back to a period which, although in time no more than a generation behind us, has become as foreign to the present generation in Germany as if it were already a hundred years old. Yet it was the period of Germany's preparation for the Revolution of 1848, and all that has happened since then in our country has been merely a continuation of 1848, merely the execution of the last will and testament of the revolution.

Just as in France in the eighteenth century, so in Germany in the nineteenth, a philosophical revolution ushered in the political collapse. But how different the two looked! The French were in open combat against all official science, against the Church and often also against the state; their writings were printed across the frontier, in Holland or England, while they themselves were often in jeopardy of imprisonment in the Bastille. On the other hand, the Germans were professors, state-appointed instructors of youth; their writings were recognized textbooks, and the terminating system of the whole development—the Hegelian system—was even raised, as it were, to the rank of a royal Prussian philosophy of state! Was it possible that a revolution could hide behind these professors, behind their obscure, pedantic phrases, their ponderous, wearisome sentences? Were not precisely those people who were then regarded as the representatives of the revolution, the liberals, the bitterest opponents of this brain-confusing philosophy? But what neither the government nor the liberals saw was seen by at least one man as early as 1833, and this man was indeed none other than Heinrich Heine.

Let us take an example. No philosophical proposition has earned more gratitude from narrow-minded governments and wrath from equally narrow-minded liberals than Hegel's famous statement: "All that is real is rational, and all that is rational is real." That was tangibly a sanctification of things that be, a philosophical benediction bestowed upon despotism, police government, Star Chamber

[1] K. N. Starcke, Ph.D., *Ludwig Feuerbach* (Stuttgart: Ferd. Enke, 1885).

proceedings, and censorship. That is how Frederick William III and his subjects understood it. But according to Hegel, certainly not everything that exists is also real without further qualification. For Hegel the attribute of reality belongs only to that which at the same time is necessary: "In the course of its development reality proves to be necessity." A particular governmental measure—Hegel himself cites the example of "a certain tax regulation"—is therefore for him by no means real without qualification. That which is necessary, however, proves itself in the last resort to be also rational; and, applied to the Prussian state of that time, the Hegelian proposition, therefore, merely means: This state is rational, corresponds to reason, in so far as it is necessary; and if it nevertheless appears to us to be evil, but still, in spite of its evil character, continues to exist, then the evil character of the government is justified and explained by the corresponding evil character of its subjects. The Prussians of that day had the government that they deserved.

Now, according to Hegel, reality is, however, in no way an attribute predicable of any given state of affairs, social or political, in all circumstances and at all times. On the contrary. The Roman Republic was real, but so was the Roman Empire, which superseded it. In 1789 the French monarchy had become so unreal, that is to say, so robbed of all necessity, so irrational, that it had to be destroyed by the Great Revolution, of which Hegel always speaks with the greatest enthusiasm. In this case, therefore, the monarchy was the unreal and the revolution the real. And so, in the course of development, all that was previously real becomes unreal, loses its necessity, its right of existence, its rationality. And in the place of moribund reality comes a new, viable reality—peacefully if the old has enough intelligence to go to its death without a struggle, forcibly if it resists this necessity. Thus the Hegelian proposition turns into its opposite through Hegelian dialectics itself: All that is real in the sphere of human history becomes irrational in the process of time, is therefore irrational by its very destination, is tainted beforehand with irrationality; and everything which is rational in the minds of men is destined to become real, however much it may contradict existing apparent reality. In accordance with all the rules of the Hegelian method of thought, the proposition of the rationality of everything which is real resolves itself into the other proposition: All that exists deserves to perish.

But precisely therein lay the true significance and the revolutionary character of the Hegelian philosophy (to which, as the close of the whole movement since Kant, we must here confine ourselves), that it once for all dealt the deathblow to the finality of all products of human thought and action. Truth, the cognition of which is the business of philosophy, was in the hands of Hegel no longer an aggregate of finished dogmatic statements, which, once discovered, had merely to be learned by heart. Truth lay now in the process of cognition itself, in the long historical development of science, which mounts from lower to ever higher levels of knowledge without ever reaching, by discovering so-called absolute truth, a point at which it can proceed no further, where it would have nothing more to do than to fold its hands and gaze with wonder at the absolute truth to which it had attained. And what holds good for the realm of philosophical knowledge holds good also for that of every other kind of knowledge, and also for practical action. Just as knowledge is unable to reach a complete conclusion in a perfect, ideal condition of humanity, so is history unable to do so; a perfect society, a perfect "state" are things which can exist only in imagination. On the contrary, all successive historical systems are only transitory stages in the endless course of development of human society from the lower to the higher. Each stage is necessary, and therefore justified for the time and conditions to which it owes its origin. But in the face of new, higher conditions, which gradually develop in its own womb, it loses its validity and justification. It must give way to a higher stage, which will also in its turn decay and perish. Just as the bourgeoisie by large-scale industry, competition, and the world market dissolves in practice all stable, time-honored institutions, so this dialectical philosophy dissolves all conceptions of final, absolute truth and of absolute states of humanity corresponding to it. For it (dialectical philosophy) nothing is final, absolute, sacred. It reveals the transitory character of everything and in everything; nothing can endure before it except the uninterrupted process of becoming and of passing away, of endless ascendancy from the lower to the higher. And dialectical philosophy itself is nothing more than the mere reflection of this process in the thinking brain. It has, of course, also a conservative side: it recognizes that definite stages of knowledge and society are justified for their time and circumstances; but only so far. The conservatism of this mode of outlook is relative; its revolutionary character is absolute—the only absolute dialectical philosophy admits.

It is not necessary, here, to go into the question of whether this mode of outlook is thoroughly in accord with the present state of natural science, which predicts a possible end even for the earth, and for its habitability a fairly certain one, which therefore recognizes that for the history of mankind, too, there is not only an ascending but also a descending branch. At any rate, we still find ourselves a considerable distance from the turning point at which the historical course of society becomes one of descent, and we cannot expect Hegelian philosophy to be concerned with a subject which natural science, in its time, had not at all placed upon the agenda as yet.

But what must, in fact, be said here is this: that in Hegel the views developed above are not so sharply delineated. They are a necessary conclusion from his method, but one which he himself never drew with such explicitness. And this, indeed, for the simple reason that he was compelled to make a system and, in accordance with traditional requirements, a system of philosophy must conclude with some sort of absolute truth. Therefore, however much Hegel, especially in his *Logic*, emphasized that this eternal truth is nothing but the logical, or the historical, process itself, he nevertheless finds himself compelled to supply this process with an end, just because he has to bring his system to a termination at some point or other. In his *Logic* he can make this end a beginning again, since here the point of conclusion, the Absolute Idea—which is absolute only in so far as he has absolutely nothing to say about it—"alienates," that is, transforms, itself into nature and comes to itself again later in the mind, that is, in thought and in history. But at the end of the whole philosophy a similar return to the beginning is possible only in one way. Namely, by conceiving of the end of history as follows: mankind arrives at the cognition of this selfsame Absolute Idea, and declares that this cognition of the Absolute Idea is reached in Hegelian philosophy. In this way, however, the whole dogmatic content of the Hegelian system is declared to be absolute truth, in contradiction to his dialectical method, which dissolves all dogmatism. Thus the revolutionary side is smothered beneath the overgrowth of the conservative side. And what applies to philosophical cognition applies also to historical practice. Mankind, which, in the person of Hegel, has reached the point of working out the Absolute Idea, must also in practice have got so far that it can carry out this Absolute Idea in reality. Hence the practical political demands of the Absolute Idea on contemporaries may not be stretched too far. And so we find at the conclusion of the *Philosophy of Right* that the Absolute Idea is to be realized in that monarchy based on social estates which Frederick William III so persistently but vainly promised to his subjects, that is, in a limited, moderate, indirect rule of the possessing classes suited to the petty-bourgeois German conditions of that time; and, moreover, the necessity of the nobility is demonstrated to us in a speculative fashion.

The inner necessities of the system are, therefore, of themselves sufficient to explain why a thoroughly revolutionary method of thinking produced an extremely tame political conclusion. As a matter of fact, the specific form of this conclusion springs from this: that Hegel was a German and, like his contemporary, Goethe, had a bit of the Philistine's queue dangling behind. Each of them was an Olympian Zeus in his own sphere, yet neither of them ever quite freed himself from German Philistinism.

But all this did not prevent the Hegelian system from covering an incomparably greater domain than any earlier system, nor from developing in this domain a wealth of thought which is astounding even today. The phenomenology of mind (which one may call a parallel of the embryology and paleontology of the mind, a development of individual consciousness through its different stages, set in the form of an abbreviated reproduction of the stages through which the consciousness of man has passed in the course of history), logic, natural philosophy, philosophy of mind, and the latter worked out in its separate, historical subdivisions: philosophy of history, of right, of religion, history of philosophy, aesthetics, etc.—in all these different historical fields Hegel labored to discover and demonstrate the pervading thread of development. And as he was not only a creative genius but also a man of encyclopedic erudition he played an epoch-making role in every sphere. It is self-evident that owing to the needs of the "system" he very often had to resort to those forced constructions about which his pygmy opponents make such a terrible fuss even today. But these constructions are only the frame and scaffolding of his work. If one does not loiter here needlessly, but presses on farther into the immense building, one finds innumerable treasures which today still possess undiminished value. With all philosophers it is precisely the "system" which is perishable; and for the simple reason that it springs from an imperishable desire of the human mind —the desire to overcome all contradictions. But if all contradictions are once for all disposed of, we shall have arrived at so-called absolute truth—world history will be at an end. And yet it has to continue, although there is nothing left for it to do—hence, a new, insoluble contradiction. As soon as we have once realized—and in the long run no one has helped us to realize it more than Hegel himself—that the task of philosophy thus stated means nothing but the task that a single philosopher should accomplish that which can be accomplished only by the entire human race in its progressive development—as soon as we realize that, there is an end to all philosophy in the hitherto accepted sense of the word. One leaves alone "absolute truth," which is unattainable along this path or by any single individual; instead one pursues attainable relative truths along the path of the positive sciences, and the summation of their results by means of dialectical thinking. At any rate, with Hegel philosophy comes to an end: on the one hand, because in his system he summed up its whole development in the most splendid fashion; and on the other hand, because, even though unconsciously, he showed us the way out of the labyrinth of systems to real positive knowledge of the world.

One can imagine what a tremendous effect this Hegelian system must have produced in the philosophy-tinged atmosphere of Germany. It was a triumphal procession which lasted for decades and which by no means came to a standstill on the death of Hegel. On the contrary, it was precisely from 1830 to 1840 that "Hegelianism" reigned most exclusively and, to a greater or lesser extent, infected even its opponents. It was precisely in this period that Hegelian views, consciously or unconsciously, most extensively penetrated the most diversified sciences and leavened even popular literature and the daily press, from which the average "educated consciousness" derives its mental pabulum. But this victory along the whole front was only the prelude to an internal struggle.

As we have seen, the doctrine of Hegel, taken as a whole, left plenty of room for giving shelter to the most diverse practical party views. And in the theoretical Germany of that time two things above all were practical: religion and politics. Whoever placed the chief emphasis on the Hegelian *system* could be fairly conservative in both spheres; whoever regarded the dialectical *method* as the main thing could belong to the most extreme opposition, both in politics and religion. Hegel himself, despite the fairly frequent outbursts of revolutionary wrath in his works, seemed on the whole to be more inclined to the conservative side. Indeed, his system had cost him much more "hard mental plugging" than his method. Towards the end of the thirties the cleavage in the school became more and more apparent. The left wing, the so-called Young Hegelians, in their fight with the pietist orthodox and the feudal reactionaries, abandoned bit by bit that philosophical-genteel reserve in regard to the burning questions of the day which up to that time had secured state toleration and even protection for their teachings. And when, in 1840, orthodox pietism and absolutist feudal reaction ascended the throne with Frederick William IV, open partisanship became unavoidable. The fight was still carried on with philosophical weapons, but no longer for abstract philosophical aims. It turned directly on the destruction of traditional religion and of the existing state. And while in the *Deutsche Jahrbücher* the practical ends were still predominantly put forward in philosophical disguise, in the *Rheinische Zeitung* of 1842 the Young Hegelian school revealed itself directly as the philosophy of the aspiring radical bourgeoisie and used the meager cloak of philosophy only to deceive the censorship.

At that time, however, politics was a very thorny field, and hence the main fight came to be directed against religion; this fight, particularly since 1840, was indirectly also political. Strauss's *Life of Jesus*, published in 1835, had provided the first impulse. The theory therein developed of the formation of the gospel myths was combated later by Bruno Bauer with proof that a whole series of evangelic stories had been fabricated by the authors themselves. The controversy between these two was carried out in the philosophical disguise of a battle between "self-consciousness" and "substance." The question whether the miracle stories of the Gospels came into being through unconscious traditional myth creation within the bosom of the community or whether they were fabricated by the evangelists themselves was magnified into the question whether, in world history, "substance" or "self-consciousness" was the decisive operative force. Finally came Stirner, the prophet of contemporary anarchism—Bakunin has taken a great deal from him—and capped the sovereign "self-consciousness" by his sovereign "ego."

We will not go further into this side of the decomposition process of the Hegelian school. More important for us is the following: the main body of the most determined Young Hegelians was, by the practical necessities of its fight against positive religion, driven back to Anglo-French materialism. This brought them into conflict with their school system. While materialism conceives nature as the sole reality, nature in the Hegelian system represents merely the "alienation" of the Absolute Idea, so to say, a degradation of the Idea. At all events, thinking and its thought product, the Idea, is here the primary, nature the derivative, which exists at all only by the condescension of the Idea. And in this contradiction they floundered as well or as ill as they could.

Then came Feuerbach's *Essence of Christianity*. With one blow it pulverized the contradiction, in that without circumlocutions it placed materialism on the throne again. Nature exists independently of all philosophy. It is the foundation upon which we human beings, ourselves products of nature, have grown up. Nothing exists outside nature and man, and the higher beings our religious fantasies have created are only the fantastic reflection of our own essence. The spell was broken, the "system" was exploded and cast aside, and the contradiction, shown to exist only in our imagination, was dissolved. One must himself have experienced the liberating effect of this book to get an idea of it. Enthusiasm was general; we all became at once Feuerbachians. How enthusiastically Marx greeted the new conception and how much—in spite of all critical reservations—he was influenced by it, one may read in *The Holy Family*.

Even the shortcomings of the book contributed to its immediate effect. Its literary, sometimes even high-flown, style secured for it a large public and was at any rate refreshing after long years of abstract and abstruse Hegelianizing. The same is true of its extravagant deification of love, which, coming after the now intolerable sovereign rule of "pure reason," had its excuse, if not justification. But what we must not forget is that it was precisely these two weaknesses of Feuerbach that "true socialism," which had been spreading like a plague in "educated" Germany since 1844, took as its starting point, putting literary phrases in the place of scientific knowledge, the liberation of mankind by means of "love" in place of the emancipation of the proletariat through the economic transformation of production—in short, losing itself in the nauseous fine writing and ecstasies of love typified by Herr Karl Grün.

Another thing we must not forget is this: the Hegelian school disintegrated, but Hegelian philosophy was not overcome through criticism; Strauss and Bauer each took one of its sides and set it polemically against the other. Feuerbach broke through the system and simply discarded it. But a philosophy is not disposed of by the mere assertion that it is false. And so powerful a work as Hegelian philosophy, which had exercised so enormous an influence on the intellectual development of the nation, could not be disposed of by simply being ignored. It had to be "sublated" in its own sense, that is, in the sense that while its form had to be annihilated through criticism, the new content which had been won through it had to be saved. How this was brought about we shall see below.

But in the meantime the Revolution of 1848 thrust the whole of philosophy aside as unceremoniously as Feuerbach had thrust aside Hegel. And in the process Feuerbach himself was also pushed into the background.

II. [IDEALISM AND MATERIALISM]

The great basic question of all philosophy, especially of more recent philosophy, is that concerning the relation of thinking and being. From the very early times when men, still completely ignorant of the structure of their own bodies, under the stimulus of dream apparitions[1] came to believe that their thinking and sensation were not activities of their bodies, but of a distinct soul which inhabits the body and leaves it at death—from this time men have been driven to reflect about the relation between this soul and the outside world. If upon death it took leave of the body and lived on, there was no occasion to invent yet another distinct death for it. Thus arose the idea of its immortality, which at that stage of development appeared not at all as a consolation, but as a fate against which it was no use fighting, and often enough, as among the Greeks, as a positive misfortune. Not religious desire for consolation, but the quandary arising from the common universal ignorance of what to do with this soul, once its existence had been accepted, after the death of the body led in a general way to the tedious notion of personal immortality. In an exactly similar manner the first gods arose through the personification of natural forces. And these gods in the further development of religions assumed more and more an extra-

[1] Among savages and lower barbarians the idea is still universal that the human forms which appear in dreams are souls which have temporarily left their bodies; the real man is, therefore, held responsible for acts committed by his dream apparition against the dreamer. Thus Imthurn found this belief current, for example, among the Indians of Guiana in 1884.

mundane form, until finally by a process of abstraction, I might almost say of distillation, occurring naturally in the course of man's intellectual development, out of the many more or less limited and mutually limiting gods there arose in the minds of men the idea of the one exclusive God of the monotheistic religions.

Thus the question of the relation of thinking to being, the relation of the spirit to nature—the paramount question of the whole of philosophy—has, no less than all religion, its roots in the narrow-minded and ignorant notions of savagery. But this question could for the first time be put forward in its whole acuteness, could achieve its full significance, only after humanity in Europe had awakened from the long hibernation of the Christian Middle Ages. The question of the position of thinking in relation to being, a question which, by the way, had played a great part also in the scholasticism of the Middle Ages, the question: Which is primary, spirit or nature?—that question, in relation to the Church, was sharpened into this: Did God create the world or has the world been in existence eternally?

The answers which the philosophers gave to this question split them into two great camps. Those who asserted the primacy of spirit to nature and, therefore, in the last instance, assumed world creation in some form or other—and among the philosophers, Hegel, for example, this creation often becomes still more intricate and impossible than in Christianity—comprised the camp of idealism. The others, who regarded nature as primary, belong to the various schools of materialism.

These two expressions, idealism and materialism, originally signify nothing else but this; and here, too, they are not used in any other sense. What confusion arises when some other meaning is put into them will be seen below.

But the question of the relation of thinking and being has yet another side: In what relation do our thoughts about the world surrounding us stand to this world itself? Is our thinking capable of the cognition of the real world? Are we able in our ideas and notions of the real world to produce a correct reflection of reality? In philosophical language this question is called the question of the identity of thinking and being, and the overwhelming majority of philosophers give an affirmative answer to this question. With Hegel, for example, its affirmation is self-evident; for what we cognize in the real world is precisely its thought content—that which makes the world a gradual realization of the Absolute Idea, which Absolute Idea has existed somewhere from eternity, independent of the world and before the world. But it is manifest without further proof that thought can know a content which is from the outset a thought content. It is equally manifest that what is to be proved here is already tacitly contained in the premises. But that in no way prevents Hegel from drawing the further conclusion from his proof of the identity of thinking and being that his philosophy, because it is correct for his thinking, is therefore the only correct one, and that the identity of thinking and being must prove its validity by mankind immediately translating his philosophy from theory into practice and transforming the whole world according to Hegelian principles. This is an illusion which he shares with well-nigh all philosophers.

In addition there is yet a set of different philosophers —those who question the possibility of any cognition, or at least of an exhaustive cognition, of the world. To them, among the more modern ones, belong Hume and Kant, and they have played a very important role in philosophical development. What is decisive in the refutation of this view has already been said by Hegel, in so far as this was possible from an idealist standpoint. The materialistic additions made by Feuerbach are more ingenious than profound. The most telling refutation of this, as of all other philosophical crotchets, is practice, namely, experiment and industry. If we are able to prove the correctness of our conception of a natural process by making it ourselves, bringing it into being out of its conditions and making it serve our own purposes into the bargain, then there is an end to the Kantian ungraspable "thing-in-itself." The chemical substances produced in the bodies of plants and animals remained just such things-in-themselves until organic chemistry began to produce them one after another, whereupon the thing-in-itself became a thing for us, as, for instance, alizarin, the coloring matter of the madder, which we no longer trouble to grow in the madder roots in the field, but produce much more cheaply and simply from coal tar. For three hundred years the Copernican solar system was a hypothesis with a hundred, a thousand, or ten thousand chances to one in its favor, but still always a hypothesis. But when Leverrier, by means of the data provided by this system, not only deduced the necessity of the existence of an unknown planet, but also calculated the position in the heavens which this planet must necessarily occupy, and when Galle really found this planet the Copernican system was proved. If, nevertheless, the Neo-Kantians are attempting to resurrect the Kantian conception in Germany and the agnostics that of Hume in England (where in fact it never became extinct), this is, in view of their theoretical and practical refutation, accomplished long ago, scientifically a regression and practically merely a shamefaced way of surreptitiously accepting materialism while denying it before the world.

But during this long period from Descartes to Hegel and from Hobbes to Feuerbach the philosophers were by no means impelled, as they thought they were, solely by the force of pure reason. On the contrary, what really pushed them forward most was the powerful and ever more rapidly onrushing progress of natural science and industry. Among the materialists this was plain on the surface, but the idealist systems also filled themselves more and more with a materialist content, and attempted pantheistically to reconcile the antithesis between mind and matter. Thus, ultimately, the Hegelian system represents merely a materialism idealistically turned upside down in method and content.

It is, therefore, comprehensible that Starcke in his characterization of Feuerbach first of all investigates the latter's position in regard to this fundamental question of the relation of thinking and being. After a short introduction, in which the views of the proceeding philosophers, particularly since Kant, are described in unnecessarily ponderous philosophical language, and in which Hegel, by an all too formalistic adherence to certain passages of his works, gets far less than his due, there follows a detailed description of the course of development of Feuerbach's "metaphysics" itself, as this course was successively reflected in those writings of this philosopher which have a bearing here. This description is industriously and lucidly elaborated; only, like the whole book, it is loaded with a ballast of philosophical phraseology by no means everywhere unavoidable, which is the more disturbing in its effect the less the author keeps to the manner of expression of one and the same school, or even of Feuerbach himself, and the more he interjects expressions of very different tendencies, especially of the tendencies now rampant and calling themselves philosophical.

The course of evolution of Feuerbach is that of a Hegelian—a never quite orthodox Hegelian, it is true—into a materialist, an evolution which at a definite stage necessitates a complete rupture with the idealist system of his predecessor. With irresistible force Feuerbach is finally driven to the realization that the Hegelian premundane existence of the Absolute Idea, the "pre-existence of the logical categories" before the world existed, is nothing more than the fantastic survival of the belief in the existence of an extramundane creator; that the material, sensuously perceptible world to which we ourselves belong is the only reality; and that our consciousness and thinking, however suprasensuous they may seem, are the product of a material, bodily organ, the brain. Matter is not a product of mind, but mind itself is merely the highest product of matter. This is, of course, pure materialism. But, having got so far, Feuerbach stops short. He cannot overcome the customary philosophical prejudice, prejudice not against the thing but against the name materialism. He says: "To me materialism is the foundation of the edifice of human essence and knowledge; but to me it is not what it is to the physiologist, to the natural scientist in the narrower sense, for example, to Moleschott, and necessarily is from their standpoint and profession, namely, the edifice itself. Backwards I fully agree with the materialists, but not forwards."

Here Feuerbach lumps together the materialism that is a general world outlook resting upon a definite conception of the relation between matter and mind and the special form in which this world outlook was expressed at a definite historical stage, namely, in the eighteenth century. More than that, he lumps it with the shallow, vulgarized form in which the materialism of the eighteenth century continues to exist today in the heads of naturalists and physicians, the form which was preached on their tours in the fifties by Büchner, Vogt, and Moleschott. But just as idealism underwent a series of stages of development, so also did materialism. With each epoch-making discovery even in the sphere of natural science it has to change its form, and after history also was subjected to materialistic treatment a new avenue of development has opened here, too.

The materialism of the last century was predominantly mechanical, because at that time, of all natural sciences, only mechanics, and indeed only the mechanics of solid bodies—celestial and terrestrial—in short, the mechanics of gravity, had come to any definite close. Chemistry at that time existed only in its infantile, phlogistic form. Biology still lay in swaddling clothes; vegetable and animal organisms had been only roughly examined, and were explained as the result of purely mechanical cause. What the animal was to Descartes, man was to the materialists of the eighteenth century—a machine. This exclusive application of the standards of mechanics to processes of a chemical and organic nature—in which processes the laws of mechanics are, indeed, also valid, but are pushed into the background by other, higher laws—constitutes the first specific but at that time inevitable limitation of classical French materialism.

The second specific limitation of this materialism lay in its inability to comprehend the universe as a process, as matter undergoing uninterrupted historical development. This was in accordance with the level of the natural science of that time, and with the metaphysical, that is, antidialectical, manner of philosophizing connected with it. Nature—so much was known—was in eternal motion. But according to the ideas of that time, this motion turned, also eternally, in a circle and therefore never moved from the spot; it produced the same results over and over again. This conception was at that time inevitable. The Kantian theory of the origin of the solar system had been put forward but recently, and was still regarded merely as a curiosity. The history of the development of the earth, geology, was still totally unknown, and the conception that the animate natural beings of today are the result of a long sequence of development from the simple to the complex could not at that time scientifically be put forward at all. The unhistorical view of nature was therefore inevitable. We have the less reason to reproach the philosophers of the eighteenth century on this account since the same thing is found in Hegel. According to him, nature, as a mere "alienation" of the Idea, is incapable of development in time—capable only of extending its manifoldness in space, so that it displays simultaneously and alongside of one another all the stages of development comprised in it, and is condemned to an eternal repetition of the same processes. This absurdity of a development in space, but outside of time—the fundamental condition of all development—Hegel imposes upon nature just at the very time when geology, embryology, the physiology of plants and animals, and organic chemistry were being built up, and when everywhere on the basis of these new sciences brilliant foreshadowings of the later theory of evolution were appearing (for instance, Goethe and Lamarck). But the system demanded it; hence the method, for the sake of the system, had to become untrue to itself.

This same unhistorical conception prevailed also in the domain of history. Here the struggle against the remnants of the Middle Ages blurred the view. The Middle Ages were regarded as a mere interruption of history by a thousand years of universal barbarism. The great progress made in the Middle Ages—the extension of the area of European culture, the viable great nations taking form there next to each other, and finally the enormous technical progress of the fourteenth and fifteenth centuries—all this was not seen. Thus a rational insight into the great historical interconnections was made impossible, and history served at best as a collection of examples and illustrations for the use of philosophers.

The vulgarizing peddlers, who in Germany in the fifties dabbled in materialism, by no means overcame this limitation of their teachers. All the advances of natural science which had been made in the meantime served them only as new proofs against the existence of a creator of the world; and, indeed, they did not in the least make it their business to develop the theory any further. Though idealism was at the end of its tether and was dealt a deathblow by the Revolution of 1848, it had the satisfaction of seeing that materialism had for the moment fallen lower still. Feuerbach was unquestionably right when he refused to take responsibility for this materialism, only he should not have confounded the doctrines of these itinerant preachers with materialism in general.

Here, however, there are two things to be pointed out. First, even during Feuerbach's lifetime natural science was still in that process of violent fermentation which only during the last fifteen years had reached a clarifying, relative conclusion. New scientific data were acquired to a hitherto unheard-of extent, but the establishing of interrelations, and thereby the bringing of order into this chaos of discoveries following closely upon each other's heels, has only quite recently become possible. It is true that Feuerbach had lived to see all three of the decisive discoveries—that of the cell, the transformation of energy, and the theory of evolution, named after Darwin. But how could the lonely philosopher, living in rural solitude, be able sufficiently to follow scientific developments in order to appreciate at their full value discoveries which natural scientists themselves at that time either still contested or did not know how to make adequate use of? The blame for this falls solely upon the wretched conditions in Germany, in consequence of which cobweb-spinning eclectic flea crackers had taken possession of the chairs of philosophy, while Feuerbach, who towered above them all, had to rusticate and grow sour in a little village. It is therefore not Feuerbach's fault that the historical conception of nature, which had now become possible and which removed all the one-sidedness of French materialism, remained inaccessible to him.

Second, Feuerbach is quite correct in asserting that exclusively natural-scientific materialism is indeed "the foundation of the edifice of human knowledge, but not the edifice itself." For we live not only in nature but also in human society, and this also no less than nature has its history of development and its science. It was therefore a question of bringing the science of society, that is, the sum total of the so-called historical and philosophical sciences, into harmony with the materialist foundation, and of reconstructing it thereupon. But it did not fall to Feuerbach's lot to do this. In spite of the "foundation" he remained here bound by the traditional idealist fetters, a fact which he recognizes in these words: "Backwards I agree with the materialists, but not forwards!" But it was Feuerbach himself who did not go "forwards" here, in the social domain, who did not get beyond his standpoint of 1840 or 1844. And this was again chiefly due to this reclusion, which compelled him, who, of all philosophers, was the most inclined to social intercourse, to produce thoughts out of his solitary head instead of in amicable and hostile encounters with other men of his caliber. Later we shall see in detail how much he remained an idealist in this sphere.

It need only be added here that Starcke looks for Feuerbach's idealism in the wrong place. "Feuerbach is an idealist; he believes in the progress of mankind." (Page 19.) "The foundation, the substructure of the whole, remains nevertheless idealism. Realism for us is nothing more than a protection against aberrations, while we follow our ideal trends. Are not compassion, love, and enthusiasm for truth and justice ideal forces?" (Page VIII.)

In the first place, idealism here means nothing but the pursuit of ideal aims. But these necessarily have to do at the most with Kantian idealism and its "categorical imperative"; however, Kant himself called his philosophy "transcendental idealism"; by no means because he dealt therein also with ethical ideals, but for quite other reasons, as Starcke will remember. The superstition that philosophical idealism is pivoted round a belief in ethical, that is, social, ideals arose outside philosophy, among the German Philistines, who learned by heart from Schiller's poems the few morsels of philosophical culture they needed. No one has criticized more severely the impotent "categorical imperative" of Kant—impotent because it demands the impossible, and therefore never attains to any reality—no one has more cruelly derided the Philistine sentimental enthusiasm for unrealizable ideals purveyed by Schiller than precisely the complete idealist Hegel. (See, for example, his *Phenomenology*.)

In the second place, we simply cannot get away from the fact that everything that sets men acting must find its way through their brains—even eating and drinking, which begin as a consequence of the sensations of hunger and thirst, transmitted through the brain, and end as a result of the sensation of satisfaction, likewise transmitted through the brain. The influences of the external world upon man express themselves in his brain, are reflected therein as feelings, thoughts, impulses, volitions—in short, as "ideal tendencies," and in this form become "ideal powers." If, then, a man is to be deemed an idealist because he follows "ideal tendencies" and admits that "ideal powers" have an influence over him, then every person who is at all normally developed is a born idealist, and how, in that case, can there still be any materialists?

In the third place, the conviction that humanity, at least at the present moment, moves on the whole in a progressive direction has absolutely nothing to do with the antagonism between materialism and idealism. The French materialists no less than the deists Voltaire and Rousseau held this conviction to an almost fanatical degree, and often enough made the greatest personal sacrifices for it. If ever anybody dedicated his whole life to the "enthusiasm for truth and justice"—using this phrase in the good sense—it was Diderot, for instance. If, therefore, Starcke declares all this to be idealism, this merely proves that the word materialism, and the whole antagonism between the two trends, has lost all meaning for him here.

The fact is that Starcke, although perhaps unconsciously, in this makes an unpardonable concession to the traditional Philistine prejudice against the word materialism resulting from its long-continued defamation by the priests. By the word materialism the Philistine understands gluttony, drunkenness, lust of the eye, lust of the flesh, arrogance, cupidity, avarice, covetousness, profit-hunting and stock-exchange swindling—in short, all the filthy vices in which he himself indulges in private. By the word idealism he understands the belief in virtue, universal philanthropy, and in a general way a "better world," of which he boasts before others but in which he himself at the utmost believes only so long as he is having the blues or is going through the bankruptcy consequent upon his customary "materialist" excesses. It is then that he sings his favorite song: What is man? Half beast, half angel.

For the rest, Starcke takes great pains to defend Feuerbach against the attacks and doctrines of the vociferous assistant professors who today go by the name of philosophers in Germany. For people who are interested in this afterbirth of classical German philosophy this is, of course, a matter of importance; for Starcke himself it may have appeared necessary. We, however, will spare the reader this.

III. [RELIGION AND ETHICS]

The real idealism of Feuerbach becomes evident as soon as we come to his philosophy of religion and ethics. He by no means wishes to abolish religion; he wants to perfect it. Philosophy itself must be absorbed in religion. "The periods of humanity are distinguished only by religious changes. A historical movement is fundamental only when it is rooted in the hearts of men. The heart is not a form of religion, so that the latter should exist *also* in the heart; the heart is the essence of religion." (Quoted by Starcke, page 168.) According to Feuerbach, religion is the relation between human beings based on the affections, the relation based on the heart, which relation until now has sought its truth in a fantastic mirror image of reality—in the mediation of one or many gods, the fantastic mirror images of human qualities—but now finds it directly and without any mediation in the love between "I" and "Thou." Thus, finally, with Feuerbach sex love becomes one of the highest forms, if not the highest form, of the practice of his new religion.

Now relations between human beings, based on affection, and especially between the two sexes, have existed as long as mankind has. Sex love in particular has undergone a development and won a place during the last eight hundred years which has made it a compulsory pivotal point of all poetry during this period. The existing positive religions have limited themselves to the bestowal of a higher consecration upon state-regulated sex love, that is, upon the marriage laws, and they could all disappear tomorrow without changing in the slightest the practice of love and friendship. Thus the Christian religion in France, as a matter of fact, so completely disappeared in the years 1793–98 that even Napoleon could not reintroduce it without opposition and difficulty; and this without any need for a substitute, in Feuerbach's sense, making itself felt in the interval.

Feuerbach's idealism consists here in this: he does not simply accept mutual relations based on reciprocal inclination between human beings, such as sex love, friendship, compassion, self-sacrifice, etc., as what they are in themselves—without associating them with any particular religion which to him, too, belongs to the past; but instead he asserts that they will attain their full value only when consecrated by the name of religion. The chief thing for him is not that these purely human relations exist, but that they shall be conceived of as the new, true religion. They are to have full value only after they have been marked with a religious stamp. Religion is derived from *religare,* and meant originally a bond. Therefore every bond between two people is a religion. Such etymological tricks are the last resort of idealist philosophy. Not what the word means according to the historical development of its actual use, but what it ought to mean according to its derivation is what counts. And so sex love and the intercourse between the sexes is apotheosized to a *religion,* merely in order that the word religion, which is so dear to idealistic memories, may not disappear from the language. The Parisian reformers of the Louis Blanc trend used to speak in precisely the same way in the forties. They likewise could conceive of a man without religion only as a monster, and used to say to us: *"Donc, l'athéisme c'est votre religion!"* [Well, then atheism is your religion!] If Feuerbach wishes to establish a true religion upon the basis of an essentially materialist conception of nature, that is the same as regarding modern chemistry as true alchemy. If religion can exist without its god, alchemy can exist without its philosopher's stone. By the way, there exists a very close connection between alchemy and religion. The philosopher's stone has many godlike properties, and the Egyptian-Greek alchemists of the first two centuries of our era had a hand in the development of Christian doctrines, as the data given by Kopp and Berthelot have proved.

Feuerbach's assertion that "the periods of humanity are distinguished only by religious changes" is decidedly false. Great historical turning points have been *accompanied* by religious changes only so far as the three world religions which have existed up to the present—Buddhism, Christianity, and Islam—are concerned. The old tribal and national religions, which arose spontaneously, did not proselytize, and lost all their power of resistance as soon as the independence of the tribe or people was lost. For the Germans it was sufficient to have simple contact with the decaying Roman world empire and with its newly adopted Christian world religion, which fitted its economic, political, and ideological conditions. Only with these world religions, arisen more or less artificially, particularly Christianity and Islam, do we find that the more general historical movements acquire a religious imprint. Even in regard to Christianity the religious stamp in revolutions of really universal significance is restricted to the first stages of the bourgeoisie's struggle for emancipation—from the thirteenth to the seventeenth century—and is to be accounted for not as Feuerbach thinks, by the hearts of men and their religious needs, but by the entire previous history of the Middle Ages, which knew no other form of ideology than precisely religion and theology. But when the bourgeoisie of the eighteenth century was strengthened enough likewise to possess an ideology of its own, suited to its own class standpoint, it made its great and conclusive revolution, the French, appealing exclusively to juristic and political ideas, and troubling itself with religion only in so far as it stood in its way. But it never occurred to it to put a new religion in place of the old. Everyone knows how Robespierre failed in his attempt.

The possibility of purely human sentiments in our intercourse with other human beings has nowadays been sufficiently curtailed by the society in which we must live, which is based upon class antagonism and class rule. We have no reason to curtail it still more by exalting these sentiments to a religion. And, similarly, the understanding of the great historical class struggles has already been sufficiently obscured by current historiography, particularly in Germany, so that there is also no need for us to make such an understanding totally impossible by transforming the history of these struggles into a mere appendix of ecclesiastical history. Already here it becomes evident how far today we have moved beyond Feuerbach. His "finest passages" in glorification of his new religion of love are totally unreadable today.

The only religion which Feuerbach examines seriously is Christianity, the world religion of the Occident, based upon monotheism. He proves that the Christian god is only a fantastic reflection, a mirror image, of man. Now this god is, however, himself the product of a tedious process of abstraction, the concentrated quintessence of the numerous earlier tribal and national gods. And man, whose image this god is, is therefore also not a real man, but likewise the quintessence of the numerous real men, man in the abstract, therefore himself again a mental image. Feuerbach, who on every page preaches sensuousness, absorption in the concrete, in actuality becomes thoroughly abstract as soon as he begins to talk of any other than mere sex relations between human beings.

Of these relations only one aspect appeals to him: morality. And here we are again struck by Feuerbach's astonishing poverty when compared with Hegel. The latter's ethics, or doctrine of moral conduct, is the philosophy of right, and embraces: (1) abstract right; (2) morality; (3) social ethics [*Sittlichkeit*], under which again are comprised: the family, civil society, and the state. Here the content is as realistic as the form is idealistic. Besides morality, the whole sphere of law, economy, politics is here included. With Feuerbach it is just the reverse. In form he is realistic, since he takes his start from man; but there is absolutely no mention of the world in which this man lives; hence this man remains always the same abstract man who occupied the field in the philosophy of religion. For this man is not born of woman; he issues, as from a chrysalis, from the god of the monotheistic religions. He therefore does not live in a real world, historically come into being and historically determined. True, he has intercourse with other men; however, each one of them is just as much an abstraction as he himself. In his philosophy of religion we still had men and women, but in his ethics even this last distinction disappears. Feuerbach, to be sure, at long intervals makes such statements as: "Man thinks differently in a palace and in a hut." "If because of hunger, of misery, you have no stuff in your body, you likewise have no stuff for morality in your head, in your mind or heart." "Politics must become our religion," etc. But Feuerbach is absolutely incapable of achieving anything with these maxims. They remain mere phrases, and even Starcke has to admit that for Feuerbach politics constituted an impassable frontier and the "science of society, sociology, was *terra incognita* to him."

He appears just as shallow, in comparison with Hegel, in his treatment of the antithesis of good and evil. "One believes one is saying something great," Hegel remarks, "if one says that 'Man is naturally good.' But one forgets that one says something far greater when one says: 'Man is naturally evil.'" With Hegel evil is the form in which the motive force of historical development presents itself. This contains the twofold meaning that, on the one hand, each new advance necessarily appears as a sacrilege against things hallowed, as a rebellion against conditions, though old and moribund, yet sanctified by custom, and that, on the other hand, it is precisely the wicked passions of man—greed and lust for power—which, since the emergence of class antagonisms, serve as levers of historical development—a fact of which the history of feudalism and of the bourgeoisie, for example, constitutes a single continual proof. But it does not occur to Feuerbach to investigate the historical role of moral evil. To him history is altogether an uncanny domain in which he feels ill at ease. Even his dictum: "Man as he sprang originally from nature was only a mere creature of nature, not a man. Man is a product of man, of culture, of history"—with him even this dictum remains absolutely sterile.

What Feuerbach has to tell us about morals can, therefore, only be extremely meager. The urge towards happiness is innate in man, and must therefore form the basis of all morality. But the urge towards happiness is subject to a double correction. First, by the natural consequences of our actions: After the debauch come the "blues," and habitual excess is followed by illness. Second, by its social consequences: If we do not respect the similar urge of other people towards happiness, they will defend themselves, and so interfere with our own urge towards happiness. Consequently, in order to satisfy our urge, we must be in a position to appreciate rightly the results of our conduct and must likewise allow others an equal right to seek happiness. Rational self-restraint with regard to ourselves, and love—again and again love!—in our intercourse with others—these are the basic laws of Feuerbach's morality; from them all others are derived. And neither the most spirited utterances of Feuerbach nor the strongest eulogies of Starcke can hide the tenuity and banality of these few propositions.

Only very exceptionally, and by no means to his and other people's profit, can an individual satisfy his urge towards happiness by preoccupation with himself. Rather, it requires preoccupation with the outside world, means to satisfy his needs, that is to say, food, an individual of the opposite sex, books, conversation, argument, activities, objects for use and working up. Feuerbach's morality either presupposes that these means and objects of satisfaction are given to every individual as a matter of course or else it offers only inapplicable good advice and is, therefore, not worth a brass farthing to people who are without these means. And Feuerbach himself states this in plain terms: "Man thinks differently in a palace and in a hut. If because of hunger, of misery, you have no stuff in your body, you likewise have no stuff for morality in your head, in your mind or heart."

Do matters fare any better in regard to the equal right of others to satisfy their urge towards happiness? Feuerbach posed this claim as absolute, as holding good for all times and circumstances. But since when has it been valid? Was there ever in antiquity between slaves and masters, or in the Middle Ages between serfs and barons, any talk about an equal right to the urge towards happiness? Was not the urge towards happiness of the oppressed class sacrificed ruthlessly and "by right of law" to that of the ruling class? Yes, that was indeed immoral; nowadays, however, equality of rights is recognized. Recognized in words ever since and inasmuch as the bourgeoisie, in its fight against feudalism and in the development of capitalist production, was compelled to abolish all privileges of estate, that is, personal privileges, and to introduce the equality of all individuals before the law, first in the sphere of private law, then gradually also in the sphere of public law. But the urge towards happiness thrives only to a trivial extent on ideal rights. To the greatest extent of all it thrives on material means, and capitalist production takes care to ensure that the great majority of those with equal rights shall get only what is essential for bare existence. Capitalist production has, therefore, little more respect, if indeed any more, for the equal right to the urge towards happiness of the majority than had slavery or serfdom. And are we better off in regard to the mental means of happiness, the educational means? Is not even "the schoolmaster of Sadowa" a mythical person?

More. According to Feuerbach's theory of morals, the stock exchange is the highest temple of moral conduct, provided only that one always speculates right. If my urge towards happiness leads me to the stock exchange, and if there I correctly gauge the consequences of my actions, so that only agreeable results and no disadvantages ensue, that is, if I always win, then I am fulfilling Feuerbach's precept. Moreover, I do not thereby interfere with the equal right of another person to pursue his happiness, for that other man went to the exchange just as voluntarily as I did and, in concluding the speculative transaction with me, he has followed his urge towards happiness as I have followed mine. If he loses his money, his action is *ipso facto* proved to have been unethical, because of his bad reckoning, and since I have given him the punishment he deserves I can even slap my chest proudly, like a modern Rhadamanthus. Love, too, rules on the stock exchange, in so far as it is not simply a sentimental figure of speech, for each finds in others the satisfaction of his own urge towards happiness, which is just what love ought to achieve and how it acts in practice. And if I gamble with correct prevision of the consequences of my operations, and therefore with success, I fulfill all the strictest injunctions of Feuerbachian morality—and become a rich man into the bargain. In other words, Feuerbach's morality is cut exactly to the pattern of modern capitalist society, little as Feuerbach himself might desire or imagine it.

But love!—yes, with Feuerbach love is everywhere and at all times the wonder-working god who should help to surmount all difficulties of practical life—and at that in a society which is split into classes with diametrically opposite interests. At this point the last relic of its revolutionary character disappears from his philosophy, leaving only the old cant: Love one another—fall into each other's arms regardless of distinctions of sex or estate—a universal orgy of reconciliation!

In short, the Feuerbachian theory of morals fares like all its predecessors. It is designed to suit all periods, all peoples, and all conditions, and precisely for that reason it is never and nowhere applicable. It remains, as regards the real world, as powerless as Kant's categorical imperative. In reality every class, even every profession, has its own morality, and even this it violates whenever it can do so with impunity. And love, which is to unite all, manifests itself in wars, altercations, lawsuits, domestic broils, divorces, and every possible exploitation of one by another.

Now how was it possible that the powerful impetus given by Feuerbach turned out to be so unfruitful for himself? For the simple reason that Feuerbach himself never contrives to escape from the realm of abstraction—for which he has a deadly hatred—into that of living reality. He clings fiercely to nature and man, but nature and man remain mere words with him. He is incapable of telling us anything definite either about real nature or real men. But from the abstract man of Feuerbach one arrives at real living men only when one considers them as participants in history. And that is what Feuerbach resisted, and therefore the year 1848, which he did not understand, meant to him merely the final break with the real world, retirement into solitude. The blame for this again falls chiefly on the conditions then obtaining in Germany, which condemned him to rot away miserably.

But the step which Feuerbach did not take had nevertheless to be taken. The cult of abstract man, which formed the kernel of Feuerbach's new religion, had to be replaced by the science of real men and of their historical development. This further development of Feuerbach's standpoint beyond Feuerbach was inaugurated by Marx in 1845 in *The Holy Family*.

IV. [NATURE AND HISTORY]

Strauss, Bauer, Stirner, Feuerbach—these were the offshoots of Hegelian philosophy, in so far as they did not abandon the field of philosophy. Strauss, after his *Life of Jesus* and *Dogmatics*, produced only literary studies in philosophy and ecclesiastical history after the fashion of Renan. Bauer achieved something only in the field of the history of the origin of Christianity, though what he did here was important. Stirner remained a curiosity, even after Bakunin blended him with Proudhon and labeled the blend "anarchism." Feuerbach alone was of significance as a philosopher. But not only did philosophy—claimed to soar above all special sciences and to be the science of sciences connecting them—remain to him an impassable barrier, an inviolable holy thing, but as a philosopher, too, he stopped halfway, was a materialist below and an idealist above. He was incapable of disposing of Hegel through criticism; he simply threw him aside as useless, while he himself, compared with the encyclopedic wealth of the Hegelian system, achieved nothing positive beyond a turgid religion of love and a meager, impotent morality.

Out of the dissolution of the Hegelian school, however, there developed still another tendency, the only one which has borne real fruit. And this tendency is essentially connected with the name of Marx.[1]

[1] Here I may be permitted to make a personal explanation. Lately repeated reference has been made to my share in this theory, and so I can hardly avoid saying a few words here to settle this point. I cannot deny that both before and during my forty-year collaboration with Marx I had a certain independent share in laying the foundations of the theory, and more particularly in its elaboration. But the greater part of its leading basic principles, especially in the realm of economics and history, and, above all, their final trenchant formulation, belong to Marx. What I contributed—at any rate, with the exception of my work in a few

The separation from Hegelian philosophy was here also the result of a return to the materialist standpoint. That means it was resolved to comprehend the real world—nature and history—just as it presents itself to everyone who approaches it free from preconceived idealist crotchets. It was decided mercilessly to sacrifice every idealist crotchet which could not be brought into harmony with the facts conceived in their own and not in a fantastic interconnection. And materialism means nothing more than this. But here the materialistic world outlook was taken really seriously for the first time, and was carried through consistently—at least in its basic features—in all domains of knowledge concerned.

Hegel was not simply put aside. On the contrary, one started out from his revolutionary side, described above, from the dialectical method. But in its Hegelian form this method was unusable. According to Hegel, dialectics is the self-development of the concept. The absolute concept does not only exist—unknown where—from eternity, it is also the actual living soul of the whole existing world. It develops into itself through all the preliminary stages which are treated at length in the *Logic* and which are all included in it. Then it "alienates" itself by changing into nature, where, without consciousness of itself, disguised as the necessity of nature, it goes through a new development, and finally comes again to self-consciousness in man. This self-consciousness then elaborates itself again in history from the crude form until finally the absolute concept again comes to itself completely in the Hegelian philosophy. According to Hegel, therefore, the dialectical development apparent in nature and history, that is, the causal interconnection of the progressive movement from the lower to the higher, which asserts itself through all zigzag movements and temporary retrogressions, is only a copy [*Abklatsch*] of the self-movement of the concept going on

---

special fields—Marx could very well have done without me. What Marx accomplished, I would not have achieved. Marx stood higher, saw further, and took a wider and quicker view than all the rest of us. Marx was a genius; we others were at best talented. Without him the theory would not be by far what it is today. It therefore rightly bears his name.

from eternity, no one knows where, but at all events independently of any thinking human brain. This ideological perversion had to be done away with. We comprehended the concepts in our heads once more materialistically—as images [*Abbilder*] of real things instead of regarding the real things as images of this or that stage of the absolute concept. Thus dialectics reduced itself to the science of the general laws of motion, both of the external world and of human thought—two sets of laws which are identical in substance, but differ in their expression in so far as the human mind can apply them consciously, while in nature, and also up to now for the most part in human history, these laws assert themselves unconsciously, in the form of external necessity, in the midst of an endless series of seeming accidents. Thereby the dialectic of concepts itself became merely the conscious reflex of the dialectical motion of the real world, and thus the dialectic of Hegel was placed upon its head; or rather, turned off its head, on which it was standing, and placed upon its feet. And this materialist dialectic, which for years has been our best working tool and our sharpest weapon, was, remarkably enough, discovered not only by us but also, independently of us and even of Hegel, by a German worker, Joseph Dietzgen.[2]

In this way, however, the revolutionary side of Hegelian philosophy was again taken up and at the same time freed from the idealist trimmings with which Hegel had prevented its consistent execution. The great basic thought that the world is not to be comprehended as a complex of ready-made *things*, but as a complex of *processes*, in which the things, apparently stable no less than their mind images in our heads, the concepts, go through an uninterrupted change of coming into being and passing away, in which, in spite of all seeming accidentality and of all temporary retrogression, a progressive development asserts itself in the end—this great fundamental thought has, especially since the time of Hegel, so thoroughly permeated ordinary consciousness that in this generality it is now scarcely

[2] See: *Das Wesen der menschlichen Kopfarbeit, dargestellt von einem Handarbeiter* [*The Nature of Human Brainwork, described by a Manual Worker*], Hamburg, Meissner.

ever contradicted. But to acknowledge this fundamental thought in words and to apply it in reality in detail to each domain of investigation are two different things. If, however, investigation always proceeds from this standpoint, the demand for final solutions and eternal truths ceases once for all; one is always conscious of the necessary limitation of all acquired knowledge, of the fact that it is conditioned by the circumstances in which it was acquired. On the other hand, one no longer permits oneself to be imposed upon by the antitheses, insuperable for the still common old metaphysics, between true and false, good and bad, identical and different, necessary and accidental. One knows that these antitheses have only a relative validity, that that which is recognized now as true has also its latent false side, which will later manifest itself, just as that which is now regarded as false has also its true side, by virtue of which it could previously have been regarded as true. One knows that what is maintained to be necessary is composed of sheer accidents and that the so-called accidental is the form behind which necessity hides itself—and so on.

The old method of investigation and thought which Hegel calls "metaphysical," which preferred to investigate *things* as given, as fixed and stable, a method the relics of which still strongly haunt people's minds, had a great deal of historical justification in its day. It was necessary first to examine things before it was possible to examine processes. One first had to know what a particular thing was before one could observe the changes it was undergoing. And such was the case with natural science. The old metaphysics, which accepted things as finished objects, arose from a natural science which investigated dead and living things as finished objects. But when this investigation had progressed so far that it became possible to take the decisive step forward of transition to the systematic investigation of the changes which these things undergo in nature itself, then the last hour of the old metaphysics struck in the realm of philosophy also. And in fact, while natural science up to the end of the last century was predominantly a *collecting* science, a science of finished things, in our century it is essentially a *systematizing* science, a science of the processes, of the origin and development of these things, and of the interconnection which binds all these natural processes into one great whole. Physiology, which investigates the processes occurring in plant and animal organisms; embryology, which deals with the development of individual organisms from germ to maturity; geology, which investigates the gradual formation of the earth's surface—all these are the offspring of our century.

But, above all, there are three great discoveries which have enabled our knowledge of the interconnection of natural processes to advance by leaps and bounds: first, the discovery of the cell as the unit from whose multiplication and differentiation the whole plant and animal body develops, so that not only is the development and growth of all higher organisms recognized to proceed according to a single general law, but also, in the capacity of the cell to change, the way is pointed out by which organisms can change their species and thus go through a more than individual development. Second, the transformation of energy, which has demonstrated to us that all the so-called forces operative in the first instance in inorganic nature—mechanical force and its complement, so-called potential energy, heat, radiation (light, or radiant heat), electricity, magnetism, and chemical energy—are different forms of manifestation of universal motion, which pass into one another in definite proportions, so that in place of a certain quantity of the one which disappears a certain quantity of another makes its appearance and thus the whole motion of nature is reduced to this incessant process of transformation from one form into another. Finally, the proof which Darwin first developed in connected form that the stock of organic products of nature environing us today, including man, is the result of a long process of evolution from a few originally unicellular germs, and that these again have arisen from protoplasm or albumen, which came into existence by chemical means.

Thanks to these three great discoveries and the other immense advances in natural science, we have now arrived at the point where we can demonstrate the interconnection between the processes in nature not only in particular spheres but also the interconnection of these particular spheres on the whole, and so can present in an approximately systematic form a comprehensive view of the interconnection in nature by means of the facts provided by empirical natural science itself. To furnish this comprehensive view was formerly the task of so-called natural philosophy. It could do this only by putting in place of the real but as yet unknown interconnections ideal, fancied ones, filling in the missing facts by figments of the mind and bridging the actual gaps merely in imagination. In the course of this procedure it conceived many brilliant ideas and foreshadowed many later discoveries, but it also produced a considerable amount of nonsense, which indeed could not have been otherwise. Today, when one needs to comprehend the results of natural scientific investigation only dialectically, that is, in the sense of their own interconnection, in order to arrive at a "system of nature" sufficient for our time—when the dialectical character of this interconnection is forcing itself against their will even into the metaphysically trained minds of the natural scientists—today natural philosophy is finally disposed of. Every attempt at resurrecting it would be not only superfluous but a *step backwards*.

But what is true of nature, which is hereby recognized also as a historical process of development, is likewise true of the history of society in all its branches and of the totality of all sciences which occupy themselves with things human (and divine). Here, too, the philosophy of history, of right, of religion, etc., has consisted in the substitution of an interconnection fabricated in the mind of the philosopher for the real interconnection to be demonstrated in the events, has consisted in the comprehension of history as a whole as well as in its separate parts as the gradual realization of ideas—and naturally always only the pet ideas of the philosopher himself. According to this, history worked unconsciously but of necessity towards a certain ideal goal set in advance—as, for example, in Hegel, towards the realization of his Absolute Idea—and the unalterable trend towards this Absolute Idea formed the inner interconnection in the events of history. A new mysterious providence—unconscious or gradually coming into consciousness—was thus put in the place of the real, still unknown interconnection. Here, therefore, just as in the realm of nature, it was necessary to do away with these fabricated, artificial interconnections by the discovery of the real ones—a task which ultimately amounts to the discovery of the general laws of motion, which assert themselves as the ruling ones in the history of human society.

In one point, however, the history of the development of society proves to be essentially different from that of nature. In nature—in so far as we ignore man's reaction upon nature—there are only blind, unconscious agencies acting upon one another, out of whose interplay the general law comes into operation. Nothing of all that happens—whether in the innumerable apparent accidents observable upon the surface or in the ultimate results which confirm the regularity inherent in these accidents happens as a consciously desired aim. In the history of society, on the contrary, the actors are all endowed with consciousness, are men acting with deliberation or passion, working towards definite goals; nothing happens without a conscious purpose, without an intended aim. But this distinction, important as it is for historical investigation, particularly of single epochs and events, cannot alter the fact that the course of history is governed by inner general laws. For here, also, on the whole, in spite of the consciously desired aims of all individuals, accident apparently reigns on the surface. That which is willed happens but rarely; in the majority of instances the numerous desired ends cross and conflict with one another, or these ends themselves are from the outset incapable of realization, or the means of attaining them are insufficient. Thus the conflicts of innumerable individual wills and individual actions in the domain of history produce a state of affairs entirely analogous to that prevailing in the realm of unconscious nature. The ends of the actions are intended, but the results which actually follow from these actions are not intended, or when they do seem to correspond to the end intended they ultimately have consequences quite other than those intended. Historical events thus appear on the whole to be likewise governed by chance. But where on the surface accident holds sway, there actually it is always governed by inner, hidden laws, and it is only a matter of discovering these laws.

Men make their own history, whatever its outcome may be, in that each person follows his own consciously desired end, and it is precisely the resultant of these many wills operating in different directions and of their manifold effects upon the outer world that constitutes history. Thus it is also a question of what the many individuals desire. The will is determined by passion or deliberation. But the levers which immediately determine passion or deliberation are of very different kinds. Partly they may be external objects, partly ideal motives, ambition, "enthusiasm for truth and justice," personal hatred, or even purely individual whims of all kinds. But, on the one hand, we have seen that the many individual wills active in history for the most part produce results quite other than those intended—often quite the opposite; that their motives, therefore, in relation to the total result are likewise of only secondary importance. On the other hand, the further question arises: What driving forces in turn stand behind these motives? What are the historical causes which transform themselves into these motives in the brains of the actors?

The old materialism never put this question to itself. Its conception of history, in so far as it has one at all, is therefore essentially pragmatic; it judges everything according to the motives of the action; it divides men who act in history into noble and ignoble, and then finds that as a rule the noble are defrauded and the ignoble are victorious. Hence it follows for the old materialism that nothing very edifying is to be got from the study of history, and for us that in the realm of history the old materialism becomes untrue to itself because it takes the ideal driving forces which operate there as ultimate causes, instead of investigating what is behind them, what are the driving forces of these driving forces. The inconsistency does not lie in the fact that *ideal* driving forces are recognized, but in the investigation not being carried further back behind these into their motive causes. On the other hand, the philosophy of history, particularly as represented by Hegel, recognizes that the ostensible and also the really operating motives of men who act in history are by no means the ultimate causes of historical events, that behind these motives are other motive powers, which have to be discovered.

But it does not seek these powers in history itself; it imports them rather from outside, from philosophical ideology into history. Hegel, for example, instead of explaining the history of ancient Greece out of its own inner interconnections, simply maintains that it is nothing more than the working out of "forms of beautiful individuality," the realization of a "work of art" as such. He says much in this connection about the old Greeks that is fine and profound, but that does not prevent us today from refusing to be put off with such an explanation, which is a mere manner of speech.

When, therefore, it is a question of investigating the driving powers which—consciously or unconsciously, and indeed very often unconsciously—lie behind the motives of men who act in history and which constitute the real ultimate driving forces of history, then it is not a question so much of the motives of single individuals, however eminent, as of those motives which set in motion great masses, whole peoples, and again whole classes of the people in each people; and this, too, not momentarily, for the transient flaring up of a straw fire which quickly dies down, but for a lasting action resulting in a great historical transformation. To ascertain the driving causes which here in the minds of acting masses and their leaders—the so-called great men—are reflected as conscious motives, clearly or unclearly, directly or in ideological, even glorified, form—that is the only path which can put us on the track of the laws holding sway both in history as a whole and at particular periods and in particular lands. Everything which sets men in motion must go through their minds, but what form it will take in the mind will depend very much upon the circumstances. The workers have by no means become reconciled to capitalist machine industry, even though they no longer simply break the machines to pieces, as they still did in 1848 on the Rhine.

But while in all earlier periods the investigation of these driving causes of history was almost impossible—on account of the complicated and concealed interconnections between them and their effects—our present period has so far simplified these interconnections that the riddle could be solved. Since the establishment of large-scale industry, that is, at least since the European peace of 1815, it has been no longer a secret to any man in England that the whole political struggle there turned on the claims to supremacy of two classes: the landed aristocracy and the bourgeoisie (middle class). In France, with the return of the Bourbons, the same fact was perceived, the historians of the Restoration period, from Thierry to Guizot, Mignet and Thiers, speak of it everywhere as the key to the understanding of all French history since the Middle Ages. And since 1830 the working class, the proletariat, has been recognized in both countries as a third competitor for power. Conditions had become so simplified that one would have had to close one's eyes deliberately not to see in the fight of these three great classes and in the conflict of their interests the driving force of modern history—at least in the two most advanced countries.

But how did these classes come into existence? If it was possible at first glance still to ascribe the origin of the great, formerly feudal landed property—at least in the first instance—to political causes, to taking possession by force, this could not be done in regard to the bourgeoisie and the proletariat. Here the origin and development of two great classes was seen to lie clearly and palpably in purely economic causes. And it was just as clear that in the struggle between landed property and the bourgeoisie, no less than in the struggle between the bourgeoisie and the proletariat, it was a question, first and foremost, of economic interests, to the furtherance of which political power was intended to serve merely as a means. Bourgeoisie and proletariat both arose in consequence of a transformation of the economic conditions, more precisely, of the mode of production. The transition, first from guild handicrafts to manufacture, and then from manufacture to large-scale industry, with steam and mechanical power, had caused the development of these two classes. At a certain stage the new productive forces set in motion by the bourgeoisie—in the first place, the division of labor and the combination of many detail laborers [*Teilarbeiter*] in one general manufactory—and the conditions and requirements of exchange developed through these productive forces became incompatible with the existing order of production handed down by history and sanctified by law, that is to say, incompatible with the privileges of the guild and the numerous other personal and local privileges (which were only so many fetters to the unprivileged estates) of the feudal order of society. The productive forces represented by the bourgeoisie rebelled against the order of production represented by the feudal landlords and the guild masters. The result is known: the feudal fetters were smashed, gradually in England, at one blow in France. In Germany the process is not yet finished. But just as, at a definite stage of its development, manufacture came into conflict with the feudal order of production, so now large-scale industry has already come into conflict with the bourgeois order of production established in its place. Tied down by this order, by the narrow limits of the capitalist mode of production, this industry produces, on the one hand, an ever increasing proletarianization of the great mass of the people and, on the other hand, an ever greater mass of unsalable products. Overproduction and mass misery, each the cause of the other—that is the absurd contradiction which is its outcome, and which of necessity calls for the liberation of the productive forces by means of a change in the mode of production.

In modern history at least it is, therefore, proved that all political struggles are class struggles and all class struggles for emancipation, despite their necessarily political form—for every class struggle is a political struggle—turn ultimately on the question of *economic* emancipation. Therefore, here at least, the state—the political order—is the subordinate, and civil society—the realm of economic relations—the decisive element. The traditional conception, to which Hegel, too, pays homage, saw in the state the determining element and in civil society the element determined by it. Appearances correspond to this. As all the driving forces of the actions of any individual person must pass through his brain and transform themselves into motives of his will in order to set him into action, so also all the needs of civil society—no matter which class happens to be the ruling one—must pass through the will of the state in order to secure general validity in the form of laws. That is the formal aspect of the matter—the one which is self-evident. The question arises, however: What is the content of this merely formal will—of the individual as well as of the state—and whence is this content derived? Why is just this willed and not something else? If we inquire into this we discover that in modern history the will of the state is, on the whole, determined by the changing needs of civil society, by the supremacy of this or that class, in the last resort by the development of the productive forces and relations of exchange.

But if even in our modern era, with its gigantic means of production and communication, the state is not an independent domain with an independent development, but one whose existence as well as development is to be explained in the last resort by the economic conditions of life of society, then this must be still truer of all earlier times, when the production of the material life of man was not yet carried on with these abundant auxiliary means, and when, therefore, the necessity of such production must have exercised a still greater mastery over men. If the state even today, in the era of big industry and of railways, is on the whole only a reflection, in concentrated form, of the economic needs of the class controlling production, then this must have been much more so in an epoch when each generation of men was forced to spend a far greater part of its aggregate lifetime in satisfying material needs, and was therefore much more dependent on them than we are today. An examination of the history of earlier periods, as soon as it is seriously undertaken from this angle, most abundantly confirms this. But, of course, this cannot be gone into here.

If the state and public law are determined by economic relations, so, too, of course is private law, which indeed in essence only sanctions the existing economic relations between individuals which are normal in the given circumstances. The form in which this happens can, however, vary considerably. It is possible, as happened in England, in harmony with the whole national development, to retain in the main the forms of the old feudal laws while giving them a bourgeois content; in fact, directly reading a bourgeois meaning into the feudal name. But, also, as happened in Western Continental Europe, Roman law, the first world law of a commodity-producing society, with its unsurpassably fine elaboration of all the essential legal relations of simple commodity owners (of buyers and sellers, debtors and creditors, contracts, obligations, etc.), can be taken as the foundation. In which case, for the benefit of a still petty-bourgeois and semi-feudal society, either it can be reduced to the level of such a society simply through judicial practice (common law) or, with the help of allegedly enlightened, moralizing jurists it can be worked into a special code of law to correspond with such a social level—a code which in these circumstances will be a bad one also from the legal standpoint (for instance, Prussian *Landrecht*). In which case, however, after a great bourgeois revolution, it is also possible for such a classic law code of bourgeois society as the French *Code Civil* to be worked out upon the basis of this same Roman Law. If, therefore, bourgeois legal rules merely express the economic life conditions of society in legal form, then they can do so well or ill, according to circumstances.

The state presents itself to us as the first ideological power over man. Society creates for itself an organ for the safeguarding of its common interests against internal and external attacks. This organ is the state power. Hardly come into being, this organ makes itself independent vis-à-vis society; and, indeed, the more so, the more it becomes the organ of a particular class, the more it directly enforces the supremacy of that class. The fight of the oppressed class against the ruling class becomes necessarily a political fight, a fight first of all against the political dominance of this class. The consciousness of the interconnection between this political struggle and its economic basis becomes dulled and can be lost altogether. While this is not wholly the case with the participants, it almost always happens with the historians. Of the ancient sources on the struggles within the Roman Republic only Appian tells us clearly and distinctly what was at issue in the last resort—namely, landed property.

But once the state has become an independent power vis-à-vis society, it produces forthwith a further ideology. It is indeed among professional politicians, theorists of public law, and jurists of private law that the connection with economic facts gets lost for fair. Since in each particular case the economic facts must assume the form of juristic motives in order to receive legal sanction; and since, in so doing, consideration of course has to be given to the whole legal system already in operation, the juristic form is, in consequence, made everything and the economic content nothing. Public law and private law are treated as independent spheres, each having its own independent historical development, each being capable of and needing a systematic presentation by the consistent elimination of all inner contradictions.

Still higher ideologies, that is, such as are still further removed from the material, economic basis, take the form of philosophy and religion. Here the interconnection between conceptions and their material conditions of existence becomes more and more complicated, more and more obscured by intermediate links. But the interconnection exists. Just as the whole Renaissance period, from the middle of the fifteenth century, was an essential product of the towns and, therefore, of the burghers, so also was the subsequently newly awakened philosophy. Its content was in essence only the philosophical expression of the thoughts corresponding to the development of the small and middle burghers into a big bourgeoisie. Among last century's Englishmen and Frenchmen, who in many cases were just as much political economists as philosophers, this is clearly evident, and we have proved it above in regard to the Hegelian school.

We will now in addition deal only briefly with religion, since the latter stands furthest away from material life and seems to be most alien to it. Religion arose in very primitive times from erroneous, primitive conceptions of men about their own nature and external nature surrounding them. Every ideology, however, once it has arisen, develops in connection with the given concept material, and develops this material further; otherwise it would not be an ideology, that is, occupation with thoughts as with independent entities, developing independently and subject only to their own laws. That the material life conditions of the persons inside whose heads this thought process goes on in the last resort determine the course of this process remains of necessity unknown to these persons, for otherwise there would be an end to all ideology. These original religious notions, therefore, which in the main are common to each group of kindred peoples, develop, after the group separates, in a manner peculiar to each people, according to the conditions of life falling to their lot. For a number of groups of peoples, and particularly for the Aryans (so-called Indo-Europeans), this process has been shown in detail by comparative mythology. The gods thus fashioned within each people were national gods, whose domain extended no farther than the national territory which they were to protect; on the other side of its boundaries other gods held undisputed sway. They could continue to exist, in imagination, only as long as the nation existed; they fell with its fall. The Roman world empire, the economic conditions of whose origin we do not need to examine here, brought about this downfall of the old nationalities. The old national gods decayed, even those of the Romans, which also were patterned to suit only the narrow confines of the city of Rome. The need to complement the world empire by means of a world religion was clearly revealed in the attempts made to provide in Rome recognition and altars for all the foreign gods to the slightest degree respectable alongside of the indigenous ones. But a new world religion is not to be made in this fashion, by imperial decree. The new world religion, Christianity, had already quietly come into being, out of a mixture of generalized Oriental, particularly Jewish, theology, and vulgarized Greek, particularly Stoic, philosophy. What it originally looked like has to be first laboriously discovered, since its official form, as it has been handed down to us, is merely that in which it became the state religion, to which purpose it was adapted by the Council of Nicaea. The fact that already after two hundred and fifty years it became the state religion suffices to show that it was the religion in correspondence with the conditions of the time. In the Middle Ages, in the same measure as feudalism developed, Christianity grew into the religious counterpart to it, with a corresponding feudal hierarchy. And when the burghers began to thrive, there developed, in opposition to feudal Catholicism, the Protestant heresy, which first appeared in southern France, among the Albigenses, at the time the cities there reached the highest point of their florescence. The Middle Ages had attached to theology all the other forms of ideology—philosophy, politics, jurisprudence—and made them subdivisions of theology. It thereby constrained every social and political movement to take on a theological form. The sentiments of the masses were fed with religion to the exclusion of all else; it was therefore necessary to put forward their own interests in a religious guise in order to produce an impetuous movement. And just as the burghers from the beginning brought into being an appendage of propertyless urban plebeians, day laborers, and servants of all kinds, belonging to no recognized social estate, precursors of the later proletariat, so likewise heresy soon became divided into a burgher-moderate heresy and a plebeian-revolutionary one, the latter an abomination to the burgher heretics themselves.

The ineradicability of the Protestant heresy corresponded to the invincibility of the rising burghers. When these burghers had become sufficiently strengthened, their struggle against the feudal nobility, which till then had been predominantly local, began to assume national dimensions. The first great action occurred in Germany—the so-called Reformation. The burghers were neither powerful enough nor sufficiently developed to be able to unite under their banner the remaining rebellious estates—the plebeians of the towns, the lower nobility, and the peasants on the land. At first the nobles were defeated; the peasants rose in a revolt which formed the peak of the whole revolutionary struggle; the cities left them in the lurch, and thus the revolution succumbed to the armies of the secular princes, who reaped the whole profit. Thenceforward Germany disappears for three centuries from the ranks of countries playing an independent active part in history. But beside the German Luther appeared the Frenchman Calvin. With true French acuity he put the bourgeois character of the Reformation in the forefront, republicanized and democratized the Church. While the Lutheran reformation in Germany degenerated and reduced the country to rack and ruin, the Calvinist reformation served as a banner for the republicans in Geneva, in Holland, and in

Scotland, freed Holland from Spain and from the German Empire, and provided the ideological costume for the second act of the bourgeois revolution, which was taking place in England. Here Calvinism justified itself as the true religious disguise of the interests of the bourgeoisie of that time, and on this account did not attain full recognition when the revolution ended in 1689 in a compromise between one part of the nobility and the bourgeoisie. The English state church was re-established; but not in its earlier form of a Catholicism which had the king for its pope, being, instead, strongly Calvinized. The old state church had celebrated the merry Catholic Sunday and had fought against the dull Calvinist one. The new, bourgeoisified church introduced the latter, which adorns England to this day.

In France the Calvinist minority was suppressed in 1685 and either Catholicized or driven out of the country. But what was the good? Already at that time the freethinker Pierre Bayle was at the height of his activity, and in 1694 Voltaire was born. The forcible measures of Louis XIV only made it easier for the French bourgeoisie to carry through its revolution in the irreligious, exclusively political form which alone was suited to a developed bourgeoisie. Instead of Protestants freethinkers took their seats in the national assemblies. Thereby Christianity entered into its final stage. It had become incapable for the future of serving any progressive class as the ideological garb of its aspirations. It became more and more the exclusive possession of the ruling classes, and these apply it as a mere means of government, to keep the lower classes within bounds. Moreover, each of the different classes uses its own appropriate religion: the landed nobility—Catholic Jesuitism or Protestant orthodoxy; the liberal and radical bourgeoisie—rationalism; and it makes little difference whether these gentlemen themselves believe in their respective religions or not.

We see, therefore: religion, once formed, always contains traditional material, just as in all ideological domains tradition forms a great conservative force. But the transformations which this material undergoes spring from class relations, that is to say, out of the economic relations of the people who execute these transformations. And here that is sufficient.

In the above it could only be a question of giving a general sketch of the Marxist conception of history, at most with a few illustrations as well. The proof must be derived from history itself, and in this regard I may be permitted to say that it has been sufficiently furnished in other writings. This conception, however, puts an end to philosophy in the realm of history, just as the dialectical conception of nature makes all natural philosophy both unnecessary and impossible. It is no longer a question anywhere of inventing interconnections from out of our brains, but of discovering them in the facts. For philosophy, which has been expelled from nature and history, there remains only the realm of pure thought, so far as it is left: the theory of the laws of the thought process itself, logic and dialectics.

With the Revolution of 1848, "educated" Germany said farewell to theory and went over to the field of practice. Small production and manufacture, based upon manual labor, were superseded by really large-scale industry. Germany again appeared on the world market. The new little German Empire abolished at least the most crying of the abuses with which this development had been obstructed by the system of petty states, the relics of feudalism, and bureaucratic management. But to the same degree that speculation abandoned the philosopher's study in order to set up its temple in the stock exchange, educated Germany lost the great aptitude for theory which had been the glory of Germany in the days of its deepest political humiliation—the aptitude for purely scientific investigation, irrespective of whether the result obtained was practically applicable or not, whether likely to offend the police authorities or not. Official German natural science, it is true, maintained its position in the front rank, particularly in the field of specialized research. But even the American journal *Science* rightly remarks that the decisive advances in the sphere of the comprehensive correlation of particular facts and their generalization into laws are now being made much more in England, instead of, as formerly, in Germany. And in the sphere of the historical sciences, philosophy included, the old fearless zeal for theory has now disappeared completely, along with classical philosophy. Inane eclecticism and an anxious concern for career and income, descending to the most vulgar job hunting, occupy its place. The official representatives of these sciences have become the undisguised ideologists of the bourgeoisie and the existing state—but at a time when both stand in open antagonism to the working class.

Only among the working class does the German aptitude for theory remain unimpaired. Here it cannot be exterminated. Here there is no concern for careers, for profit making, or for gracious patronage from above. On the contrary, the more ruthlessly and disinterestedly science proceeds, the more it finds itself in harmony with the interests and aspirations of the workers. The new tendency, which recognized that the key to the understanding of the whole history of society lies in the history of the development of labor, from the outset addressed itself by preference to the working class, and here found the response which it neither sought nor expected from officially recognized science. The German working-class movement is the inheritor of German classical philosophy.

Theses on Feuerbach

KARL MARX

I

The chief defect of all hitherto existing materialism—that of Feuerbach included—is that the thing [*Gegenstand*], reality, sensuousness, is conceived only in the form of the *object* [*Objekt*] or of *contemplation* [*Anschauung*], but not as *human sensuous activity, practice,* not subjectively. Hence it happened that the *active* side, in contradistinction to materialism, was developed by idealism—but only abstractly, since, of course, idealism does not know real, sensuous activity as such. Feuerbach wants sensuous objects really differentiated from the thought objects, but he does not conceive human activity itself as *objective* [*gegenständliche*] activity. Hence, in the *Essence of Christianity,* he regards the theoretical attitude as the only genuinely human attitude, while practice is conceived and fixed only in its dirty-judaical form of appearance. Hence he does not grasp the significance of "revolutionary," of "practical-critical," activity.

II

The question whether objective [*gegenständliche*] truth can be attributed to human thinking is not a question of theory, but is a *practical* question. In practice man must prove the truth, that is, the reality and power, the this-sidedness [*Diesseitigkeit*] of his thinking. The dispute over the reality or non-reality of thinking which is isolated from practice is a purely *scholastic* question.

III

The materialist doctrine that men are products of circumstances and upbringing, and that, therefore, changed men are products of other circumstances and changed upbringing, forgets that it is men that change circumstances, and that the educator himself needs educating. Hence this doctrine necessarily arrives at dividing society into two parts, of which one is superior to society (in Robert Owen, for example).

The coincidence of the changing of circumstances and of human activity can be conceived and rationally understood only as *revolutionizing practice.*

IV

Feuerbach starts out from the fact of religious self-alienation, the duplication of the world into a religious, imaginary world and a real one. His work consists in the dissolution of the religious world into its secular basis. He overlooks the fact that after completing this work, the chief thing still remains to be done. For the fact that the secular foundation detaches itself from itself and establishes itself in the clouds as an independent realm is really to be explained only by the self-cleavage and self-contradictoriness of this secular basis. The latter must itself, therefore, first be understood in its contradiction and then, by the removal of the contradiction, revolutionized in practice. Thus, for instance, once the earthly family is discovered to be the secret of the holy family, the former must then itself be criticized in theory and revolutionized in practice.

V

Feuerbach, not satisfied with *abstract thinking,* appeals to *sensuous contemplation,* but he does not conceive sensuousness as *practical,* human-sensuous activity.

VI

Feuerbach resolves the religious essence into the *human* essence. But the human essence is no abstraction inherent in each single individual. In its reality it is the ensemble of the social relations.

Feuerbach, who does not enter upon a criticism of this real essence, is consequently compelled:

1. To abstract from the historical process and to fix the religious sentiment [*Gemüt*] as something by itself, and to presuppose an abstract–*isolated*–human individual.

2. The human essence, therefore, can with him be comprehended only as "genus," as an internal, dumb generality which merely *naturally* unites the many individuals.

VII

Feuerbach, consequently, does not see that the "religious sentiment" is itself a *social product*, and that the abstract individual whom he analyzes belongs in reality to a particular form of society.

VIII

Social life is essentially *practical*. All mysteries which mislead theory to mysticism find their rational solution in human practice and in the comprehension of this practice.

IX

The highest point attained by *contemplative* materialism, that is, materialism which does not understand sensuousness as practical activity, is the contemplation of single individuals in "civil society."

X

The standpoint of the old materialism is "*civil*" society; the standpoint of the new is *human* society, or socialized humanity.

XI

The philosophers have only *interpreted* the world, in various ways; the point, however, is to *change* it.

IX. *Excerpts from* The German Ideology

KARL MARX AND FRIEDRICH ENGELS

The German Ideology was completed in the summer of 1846. It is a youthful work, the product of two young men in their mid-twenties, and in its exuberance still retains a Hegelian terminology, which Marx and Engels tended to discard in their later years. Historical materialism, when it was first conceived by Marx and Engels, had all the attributes of what Justice Holmes called "dramatic" thinking, with its language of "estrangement," "alienation," and "world-historical individual." Forty years later Engels wrote that the "semi-Hegelian language" he had used in the earlier period "is not only untranslatable, but has lost the greater part of its meaning even in German." (Letter to Mrs. Florence Kelley Wischnewetzky, February 25, 1886.) Marx and Engels, in their early period, held an exaggerated expectation that the division of labor would end under communism.—ED.

. . . The fact is, therefore, that definite individuals who are productively active in a definite way enter into these definite social and political relations. Empirical observation must in each separate instance bring out empirically, and without any mystification and speculation, the connection of the social and political structure with production. The social structure and the state are continually evolving out of the life process of definite individuals, but of individuals not as they may appear in their own or other people's imagination, but as they really are, i.e., as they are effective, produce materially, and are active under definite material limits, presuppositions, and conditions independent of their will.

The production of ideas, of conceptions, of consciousness is at first directly interwoven with the material activity and the material intercourse of men, the language of real life. Conceiving, thinking, the mental intercourse of men appear at this stage as the direct efflux of their material behavior. The same applies to mental production as expressed in the language of the politics, laws, morality, religion, metaphysics of a people. Men are the producers of their conceptions, ideas, etc.—real, active men, as they are conditioned by a definite development of their productive forces and of the intercourse corresponding to these, up to its furthest forms. Consciousness can never be anything else than conscious existence, and the existence of men is their actual life process. If in all ideology men and their circumstances appear upside down, as in a *camera obscura*, this phenomenon arises just as much from their historical life process as the inversion of objects on the retina does from their physical life process.

In direct contrast to German philosophy, which descends from heaven to earth, here we ascend from earth to heaven. That is to say, we do not set out from what men say, imagine, conceive, nor from men as narrated, thought of, imagined, conceived, in order to arrive at men in the flesh. We set out from real, active men, and on the basis of their real life process we demonstrate the development of the ideological reflexes and echoes of this life process. The phantoms formed in the human brain are also, necessarily, sublimates of their material life process, which is empirically verifiable and bound to material premises. Morality, religion, metaphysics, all the rest of ideology and their corresponding forms of consciousness, thus no longer retain the semblance of independence. They have no history, no development; but men, developing their material production and their material intercourse, alter, along with this, their real existence, their thinking, and the products of their thinking. Life is not determined by consciousness, but consciousness by life. In the first method of approach the starting point is consciousness taken as the living individual; in the second it is the real, living individuals themselves, as they are in actual life, and consciousness is considered solely as *their* consciousness.

This method of approach is not devoid of premises. It starts out from the real premises, and does not abandon them for a moment. Its premises are men, not in any fantastic isolation or abstract definition, but in their actual, empirically perceptible process of development under definite conditions. As soon as this active life process is described, history ceases to be a collection of dead facts, as it is with the empiricists (themselves still abstract), or an imagined activity of imagined subjects, as with the idealists.

Where speculation ends—in real life—there real, positive science begins: the representation of the practical activity, of the practical process of development of men. Empty talk about consciousness ceases, and real knowledge has to take its place. When reality is depicted, philosophy as an independent branch of activity loses its medium of existence. At best, its place can be taken only by a summing up of the most general results, abstractions which arise from the observation of the historical development of men. Viewed apart from real history, these abstractions have in themselves no value whatsoever. They can only serve to facilitate the arrangement of historical material, to indicate the sequence of its separate strata. But they by no means afford a recipe or schema, as does philosophy, for neatly trimming the epochs of history. On the contrary, our difficulties begin only when we set about the observation and the arrangement—the real depiction—of our historical material, whether of a past epoch or of the present. The removal of these difficulties is governed by premises which it is quite impossible to state here, but which only the study of the actual life process and the activity of the individuals of each epoch will make evident. We shall select here some of these abstractions, which we use to refute the ideologists, and shall illustrate them by historical examples.

(*a*) *History*

Since we are dealing with the Germans, who do not postulate anything, we must begin by stating the first premise of all human existence, and therefore of all history, the premise, namely, that men must be in a position to live in order to be able to "make history." But life involves, before everything else, eating and drinking, a habitation, clothing, and many other things. The first historical act is thus the production of the means to satisfy these needs, the production of material life itself. And indeed this is a historical act, a fundamental condition of all history, which today, as thousands of years ago, must daily and hourly be fulfilled merely in order to sustain human life. . . . The first necessity therefore in any theory of history is to observe this fundamental fact in all its significance and all its implications, and to accord it its due importance. This, as is notorious, the Germans have never done, and they have never, therefore, had an earthly basis for history and consequently never a historian. The French and the English, even if they have conceived the relation of this fact with so-called history only in an extremely one-sided fashion, particularly as long as they remained in the toils of political ideology, have nevertheless made the first attempts to give the writing of history a materialistic basis by being the first to write histories of civil society, of commerce and industry. . . .

The second fundamental point is that as soon as a need is satisfied (which implies the action of satisfying, and the acquisition of an instrument), new needs are made; and this production of new needs is the first historical act. Here we recognize immediately the spiritual ancestry of the great historical wisdom of the Germans, who, when they run out of positive material and when they can serve up neither theological nor political nor literary rubbish, do not write history at all but invent the "prehistoric era." They do not, however, enlighten us as to how we proceed from this nonsensical "prehistory" to history proper; although, on the other hand, in their historical speculation they seize upon this "prehistory" with especial eagerness because they imagine themselves safe there from interference on the part of "crude facts," and, at the same time, because there they can give full rein to their speculative impulse and set up and knock down hypotheses by the thousand.

The third circumstance which, from the very first, enters into historical development is that men, who daily remake their own life, begin to make other men, to propagate their kind: the relation between man and wife, parents and children, the *family*. The family, which to begin with is the only social relationship, becomes later, when increased needs create new social relations and the increased population new needs, a subordinate one (except in Germany) and must then be treated and analyzed according to the existing empirical data,[1] not according to "the concept of the family," as is the custom in Germany. These three aspects of social activity are not of course to be taken as three different stages, but just, as I have said, as three aspects or, to make it clear to the Germans, three "moments," which have existed simultaneously since the dawn of history and the first men, and still assert themselves in history today.

[1] The building of houses. With savages each family has of course its own cave or hut like the separate family tent of the nomads. This separate domestic economy is made only the more necessary by the further development of private property. With the agricultural peoples a communal domestic economy is just as impossible as a communal cultivation of the soil. A great advance was the building of towns. In all previous periods, however, the abolition of individual economy, which is inseparable from the abolition of private property, was impossible for the simple reason that the material conditions governing it were not present. The setting up of a communal domestic economy presupposes the development of machinery, of the use of natural forces and of many other productive forces—e.g., of water supplies, of gas lighting, steam heating, etc., the removal of the antagonism of town and country. Without these conditions a communal economy would not in itself form a new productive force; lacking any material basis and resting on a purely theoretical foundation, it would be a mere freak and would end in nothing more than a monastic economy. What was possible can be seen in the formation of towns and the erection of communal buildings for various definite purposes (prisons, barracks, etc.). That the abolition of individual economy is inseparable from the abolition of the family is self-evident.

The production of life, both of one's own in labor and of fresh life in procreation, now appears as a double relationship: on the one hand as a natural, on the other as a social relationship. By social we understand the co-operation of several individuals, no matter under what conditions, in what manner, and to what end. It follows from this that a certain mode of production or industrial stage is always combined with a certain mode of co-operation, or social stage, and this mode of co-operation is itself a "productive force." Further, that the multitude of productive forces accessible to men determines the nature of society, hence that the "history of humanity" must always be studied and treated in relation to the history of industry and exchange. But it is also clear how in Germany it is impossible to write this sort of history, because the Germans lack not only the necessary power of comprehension and the material but also the "evidence of their senses," for across the Rhine you cannot have any experience of these things since history has stopped happening. Thus it is quite obvious from the start that there exists a materialistic connection of men with one another, which is determined by their needs and their mode of production and which is as old as men themselves. This connection is ever taking on new forms and thus presents a "history" independently of the existence of any political or religious nonsense which would hold men together on its own.

Only now, after having considered four moments, four aspects of the fundamental historical relationships, do we find that man also possesses "consciousness"; but, even so, not inherent, not "pure" consciousness. From the start the "spirit" is afflicted with the curse of being "burdened" with matter, which here makes its appearance in the form of agitated layers of air, sounds—in short, of language. Language is as old as consciousness; language is practical consciousness, as it exists for other men, and for that reason is really beginning to exist for me personally as well; for language, like consciousness, arises only from the need, the necessity, of intercourse with other men. Where there exists a relationship, it exists for me: the animal has no "relations" with anything, cannot have any. For the animal, its relation to others does not exist as a relation. Consciousness is therefore from the very beginning a social product and remains so as long as men exist at all. Consciousness is at first, of course, merely consciousness concerning the immediate sensuous environment and consciousness of the limited connection with other persons and things outside the individual who is growing self-conscious. At the same time it is consciousness of nature, which first appears to men as a completely alien, all-powerful, and unassailable force, with which men's relations are purely animal and by which they are overawed like beasts; it is thus a purely animal consciousness of nature (natural religion).

We see here immediately: this natural religion or animal behavior toward nature is determined by the form of society and vice versa. Here, as everywhere, the identity of nature and man appears in such a way that the restricted relation of men to nature determines their restricted relation to one another, and their restricted relation to one another determines men's restricted relation to nature, just because nature is as yet hardly modified historically; and, on the other hand, man's consciousness of the necessity of associating with the individuals around him is the beginning of the consciousness that he is living in society at all. This beginning is as animal as social life itself at this stage. It is mere herd-consciousness, and at this point man is only distinguished from sheep by the fact that with him consciousness takes the place of instinct or that his instinct is a conscious one.

This sheeplike or tribal consciousness receives its further development and extension through increased productivity, the increase of needs, and, what is fundamental to both of these, the increase of population. With these there develops the division of labor, which was originally nothing but the division of labor in the sexual act, then that division of labor which develops spontaneously or "naturally" by virtue of natural predisposition (e.g., physical strength), needs, accidents, etc., etc. Division of labor becomes truly such only from the moment when a division of material and mental labor appears. From this moment onward consciousness *can* really flatter itself that it is something other than consciousness of existing practice, that it is *really* conceiving something without conceiving something *real*; from now on consciousness is in a position to emancipate itself from the world and to proceed to the formation of "pure" theory, theology, philosophy, ethics, etc. But even if this theory, theology, philosophy, ethics, etc., comes into contradiction with the existing relations, this can occur only as a result of the fact that existing social relations have come into contradiction with existing forces of production; this, moreover, can also occur in a particular national sphere of relations through the appearance of the contradiction, not within the national orbit, but between this national consciousness and the practice of other nations; i.e., between the national and the general consciousness of a nation.

Moreover, it is quite immaterial what consciousness starts to do on its own: out of all such muck we get only the one inference that these three moments, the forces of production, the state of society, and consciousness, can and must come into contradiction with one another, because the division of labor implies the possibility—nay, the fact—that intellectual and material activity—enjoyment and labor, production and consumption—devolve on different individuals and that the only possibility of their not coming into contradiction lies in the negation in its turn of the division of labor. It is self-evident, moreover, that "specters," "bonds," "the higher being," "concept," "scruple" are merely the idealistic, spiritual expression, the conception apparently of the isolated individual, the image of very empirical fetters and limitations, within which the mode of production of life and the form of intercourse coupled with it move.

With the division of labor, in which all these contradictions are implicit and which in its turn is based on the natural division of labor in the family and the separation of society into individual families opposed to one another, is given simultaneously the distribution, and indeed the unequal distribution (both quantitative and qualitative), of labor and its products, hence property: the nucleus, the first form, of which lies in the family, where wife and children are the slaves of the husband. This latent slavery in the family, though still very crude, is the first property, but even at this early stage it corresponds perfectly to the definition of modern economists who call it the power of disposing of the labor power of others. Division of labor and private property are, moreover, identical expressions: in the one the same thing is affirmed with reference to activity as is affirmed in the other with reference to the product of the activity.

Further, the division of labor implies the contradiction between the interest of the separate individual or the individual family and the communal interest of all individuals who have intercourse with one another. And indeed, this communal interest does not exist merely in the imagination, as "the general good," but first of all in reality, as the mutual interdependence of the individuals among whom the labor is divided. And finally, the division of labor offers us the first example of how, as long as man remains in natural society—that is, as long as a cleavage exists between the particular and the common interest—as long, therefore, as activity is not voluntarily but naturally divided, man's own deed becomes an alien power opposed to him, which enslaves him instead of being controlled by him. For as soon as labor is distributed, each man has a particular, exclusive sphere of activity which is forced upon him and from which he cannot escape. He is a hunter, a fisherman, a shepherd, or a critical critic, and must remain so if he does not want to lose his means of livelihood; while in communist society, where nobody has one exclusive sphere of activity but each can become accomplished in any branch he wishes, society regulates the general production and thus makes it possible for me to do one thing today and another tomorrow, to hunt in the morning, fish in the afternoon, rear cattle in the evening, criticize after dinner, just as I have a mind, without ever becoming hunter, fisherman, shepherd, or critic.

This crystallization of social activity, this consolidation of what we ourselves produce into an objective power above us, growing out of our control, thwarting our expectations, bringing to naught our calculations, is one of the chief factors in historical development up till now. And out of this very contradiction between the interest of the individual and that of the community the latter takes an independent form as the state, divorced from the real interests of individual and community, and at the same time as an illusory communal life, always based, however, on the real ties existing in every family and tribal conglomeration (such as flesh and blood, language, division of labor on a larger scale, and other interests) and especially, as we shall enlarge upon later, on the classes, already determined by the division of labor, which in every such mass of men separate out, and of which one dominates all the others. It follows from this that all struggles within the state, the struggle between democracy, aristocracy, and monarchy, the struggle for the franchise, etc., etc., are merely the illusory forms in which the real struggles of the different classes are fought out among one another (of this the German theoreticians have not the faintest inkling, although they have received a sufficient introduction to the subject in *The German-French Annals* and *The Holy Family*).

Further, it follows that every class which is struggling for mastery, even when its domination, as is the case with the proletariat, postulates the abolition of the old form of society in its entirety and of mastery itself, must first conquer for itself political power in order to represent its interest in turn as the general interest, a step to which in the first moment it is forced. Just because individuals seek *only* their particular interest, i.e., that not coinciding with their communal interest (for the "general good" is the illusory form of communal life), the latter will be imposed on them as an interest "alien" to them, and "independent" of them, as in its turn a particular, peculiar "general interest"; or they must meet face to face in this antagonism, as in democracy. On the other hand, too, the *practical* struggle of these particular interests, which constantly *really* run counter to the communal and illusory communal interests, makes *practical* intervention and control necessary through the illusory "general interest" in the form of the state. The social power, i.e., the multiplied productive force, which arises through the co-operation of different individuals as it is determined within the division of labor, appears to these individuals, since their co-operation is not voluntary but natural, not as their own united power, but as an alien force existing outside them, of the origin and end of which they are ignorant, which they thus cannot control, which, on the contrary, passes through a peculiar series of phases and stages independent of the will and the action of man, nay even being the prime governor of these.

This "estrangement" (to use a term which will be comprehensible to the philosophers) can, of course, be abolished given only two *practical* premises. For it to become an "intolerable" power, i.e., a power against which men make a revolution, it must necessarily have rendered the great mass of humanity "propertyless" and produced, at the same time, the contradiction of an existing world of wealth and culture, both of which conditions presuppose a great increase in productive power, a high degree of its development. And, on the other hand, this development of productive forces (which itself implies the actual empirical existence of men in their *world-historical*, instead of local, being) is absolutely necessary as a practical premise: first, for the reason that without it only *want* is made general, and with want the struggle for necessities and all the old filthy business would necessarily be reproduced; and second, because only with this universal development of productive forces is a *universal* intercourse between men established which produces in all nations simultaneously the phenomenon of the "propertyless" mass (universal competition), makes each nation dependent on the revolutions of the others, and finally has put *world-historical*, empirically universal individuals in place of local ones. Without this, (1) communism could exist only as a local event, (2) the forces of intercourse themselves could not have developed as universal, hence intolerable powers—they would have remained home-bred superstitious conditions, and (3) each extension of intercourse would abolish local communism. Empirically communism is possible only as the act of the dominant peoples "all at once," or simultaneously, which presupposes the universal development of productive forces and the world intercourse bound up with them. How otherwise could property have had a history at all, have taken on different forms, and landed property, for instance, according to the different premises given, have proceeded in France from parcellation to centralization in the hands of a few, in England from centralization in the hands of a few to parcellation, as is actually the case today? Or how does it happen that trade, which after all is nothing more than the exchange of products of various individuals and countries, rules the whole world through the relation of supply and demand—a relation which, as an English economist says, hovers over the earth like the Fate of the ancients, and with invisible hand allots fortune and misfortune to men, sets up empires and overthrows empires, causes nations to rise and to disappear—while with the abolition of the basis of private property, with the communistic regulation of production (and, implicit in this, the destruction of the alien relation between men and what they themselves produce), the power of the relation of supply and demand is dissolved into nothing, and men get exchange, production, the mode of their mutual relation, under their own control again?

Communism is for us not a stable state which is to be established, an *ideal* to which reality will have to adjust itself. We call communism the *real* movement which abolishes the present state of things. The conditions of this movement result from the premises now in existence. Besides, the world market is presupposed by the mass of propertyless workers—labor power cut off as a mass from capital or from even a limited satisfaction—and therefore no longer by the mere precariousness of labor, which, not giving an assured livelihood, is often lost through competition. The proletariat can thus exist only *world historically*, just as communism, its movement, can only have a "world-historical" existence. World-historical existence of individuals, i.e., existence of individuals which is directly linked up with world history. . . .

Our conception of history depends on our ability to expound the real process of production, starting out from the simple material production of life, and to comprehend the form of intercourse connected with this and created by this (i.e., civil society in its various stages), as the basis of all history; further, to show it in its action as state, and so, from this starting point, to explain the whole mass of different theoretical products and forms of consciousness, religion, philosophy, ethics, etc., and trace their origins and growth, by which means, of course, the whole thing can be shown in its totality (and therefore, too, the reciprocal action of these various sides on one another). It has not, like the idealistic view of history, in every period to look for a category, but remains constantly on the real ground of history; it does not explain practice from the idea, but explains the formation of ideas from material practice, and accordingly it comes to the conclusion that all forms and products of consciousness cannot be dissolved by mental criticism, by resolution into "self-consciousness" or transformation into "apparitions," "specters," "fancies," etc., but only by the practical overthrow of the actual social relations which gave rise to this idealistic humbug; that not criticism but revolution is the driving force of history, also of religion, of philosophy, and all other types of theory. It shows that history does not end by being resolved into "self-consciousness" as "spirit of the spirit," but that in it at each stage there is found a material result: a sum of productive forces, a historically created relation of individuals to nature and to one another, which is handed down to each generation from its predecessor; a mass of productive forces, different forms of capital, and conditions, which, indeed, is modified by the new generation on the one hand, but also on the other prescribes for it its conditions of life and gives it a definite development, a special character. It shows that circumstances make men just as much as men make circumstances.

This sum of productive forces, forms of capital, and social forms of intercourse, which every individual and generation finds in existence as something given, is the real basis of what the philosophers have conceived as "substance" and "essence of man," and what they have deified and attacked: a real basis which is not in the least disturbed, in its effect and influence on the development of men, by the fact that these philosophers revolt against it as "self-consciousness" and "the unique." These conditions of life, which different generations find in existence, decide also whether or not the periodically recurring revolutionary convulsion will be strong enough to overthrow the basis of all existing forms. And if these material elements of a complete revolution are not present (namely, on the one hand the existence of productive forces, on the other the formation of a revolutionary mass, which revolts not only against separate conditions of society up till then, but against the very "production of life" till then, the "total activity" on which it was based), then, as far as practical development is concerned, it is absolutely immaterial whether the "idea" of this revolution has been expressed a hundred times already, as the history of communism proves.

In the whole conception of history up to the present this real basis of history has been either totally neglected or else considered as a minor matter, quite irrelevant to the course of history. History must therefore always be written according to an extraneous standard; the real production of life seems to be beyond history, while the truly historical appears to be separated from ordinary life, something extra-superterrestrial. With this the relation of man to nature is excluded from history, and hence the antithesis of nature and history is created. The exponents of this conception of history have consequently been able to see in history only the political actions of princes and states, religious and all sorts of theoretical struggles, and in particular in each historical epoch have had to share the *illusion of that epoch*. For instance, if an epoch imagines itself to be actuated by purely "political" or "religious" motives, although "religion" and "politics" are only forms of its true motives, the historian accepts this opinion. The "idea," the "conception" of these conditioned men about their real practice is transformed into the sole determining, active force, which controls and determines their practice. When the crude form in which the division of labor appears with the Indians and Egyptians calls forth the caste system in their state and religion, the historian believes that the caste system is the power which has produced this crude social form. While the French and the English at least hold by the political illusion, which is moderately close to reality, the Germans move in the realm of the "pure spirit" and make religious illusion the driving force of history.

The Hegelian philosophy of history is the last consequence, reduced to its "finest expression," of all this German historiography, for which it is not a question of real, or even of political, interests, but of pure thoughts, which inevitably appear, even to St. Bruno, as a series of "thoughts" that devour one another and are finally swallowed up in "self-consciousness." And equally inevitably, and more logically, the course of history appears to the blessed Max Stirner, who knows not a thing about real history, as a mere tale of "knights," robbers, and ghosts, from whose visions he can, of course, save himself only by "unholiness." This conception is truly religious: it postulates religious man as the primitive man, and in its imagination puts the religious production of fancies in the place of the real production of the means of subsistence and of life itself. This whole conception of history, together with its dissolution and the scruples and qualms resulting from it, is a purely *national* affair of the Germans and has only *local* interest for the Germans, as for instance the important question treated several times of late: how really we "pass from the realm of God to the realm of man"—as if this "realm of God" had ever existed anywhere save in the imagination, and the learned gentlemen, without being aware of it, were not constantly living in the "realm of man," to which they are now seeking the way; and as if the learned pastime (for it is nothing more) of explaining the mystery of this theoretical bubble-blowing did not, on the contrary, lie in demonstrating its origin in actual earthly conditions.

Always, for these Germans, it is simply a matter of resolving the nonsense of earlier writers into some other freak, i.e., of presupposing that all this nonsense has a special meaning which can be discovered; while really it is only a question of explaining this theoretical talk from the actual existing conditions. The real, practical dissolution of these phrases, the removal of these notions from the consciousness of men, will, as we have already said, be effected by altered circumstances, not by theoretical deductions. For the mass of men, i.e., the proletariat, these theoretical notions do not exist, and hence do not require to be dissolved, and if this mass ever had any theoretical notions, e.g., religion, etc., these have now long been dissolved by circumstances. . . .

[THE METHOD OF GERMAN PHILOSOPHY]

First of all, an abstraction is made from a fact, then it is declared that the fact is based upon the abstraction. That is how to proceed if you want to appear German, profound, and speculative.

For example: Fact: The cat eats the mouse.

Reflection: Cat = nature, mouse = nature; consumption of mouse by cat = consumption of nature by nature = self-consumption of nature.

Philosophic presentation of the fact: The devouring of the mouse by the cat is based upon the self-consumption of nature.

Having thus obscured man's struggle with nature, the writer goes on to obscure man's conscious activity in relation to nature; he conceives it as the manifestation of this mere abstraction from the real conflict. . . .

X. *Excerpt from* Toward the Critique of Hegel's Philosophy of Right

KARL MARX

This essay was printed in 1844, in the *Deutsch-Französiche Jahrbücher*, of which Marx was one of the editors. Here, for the first time, Marx avowed his faith in the proletariat as the class that would dissolve the "hereto existing world" with all its forms of "self-alienation."—ED.

For Germany the *criticism of religion* is in the main complete, and criticism of religion is the premise of all criticism.

The *profane* existence of error is discredited after its *heavenly oratio pro aris et focis*[1] has been rejected. Man, who looked for a superman in the fantastic reality of heaven and found nothing there but the *reflection* of himself, will no longer be disposed to find but the *semblance* of himself, the non-human [*Unmensch*], where he seeks and must seek his true reality.

The basis of irreligious criticism is: *Man makes religion*, religion does not make man. In other words, religion is the self-consciousness and self-feeling of man, who either has not yet found himself or has already lost himself again. But *man* is no abstract being, squatting outside the world. Man is *the world of man*, the state, society. This state, this society produce religion, *a perverted world consciousness*, because they are *a perverted world*. Religion is the general theory of that world, its encyclopedic compendium, its

1 [Speech for the altars and hearths.]

logic in a popular form, its spiritualistic *point d'honneur*, its enthusiasm, its moral sanction, its solemn completion, its universal ground for consolation and justification. It is *the fantastic realization* of the human essence because the *human essence* has no true reality. The struggle against religion is therefore mediately the fight against *the other world*, of which religion is the spiritual *aroma*.

Religious distress is at the same time the *expression* of real distress and the *protest* against real distress. Religion is the sigh of the oppressed creature, the heart of a heartless world, just as it is the spirit of an unspiritual situation. It is the *opium* of the people.

The abolition of religion as the *illusory* happiness of the people is required for their *real* happiness. The demand to give up the illusions about its condition is the *demand to give up a condition which needs illusions*. The criticism of religion is therefore *in embryo the criticism of the vale of woe*, the *halo* of which is religion.

Criticism has plucked the imaginary flowers from the chain not so that man will wear the chain without any fantasy or consolation, but so that he will shake off the chain and cull the living flower. The criticism of religion disillusions man, to make him think and act and shape his reality like a man who has been disillusioned and has come to reason, so that he will revolve round himself and therefore round his true sun. Religion is only the illusory sun, which revolves round man as long as he does not revolve round himself.

The task of history, therefore, once the *world beyond the truth* has disappeared, is to establish the *truth of this world*. The immediate *task of philosophy*, which is at the service of history, once the *saintly form* of human self-alienation has been unmasked, is to unmask self-alienation in its *unholy forms*. Thus the criticism of heaven turns into the criticism of the earth, the *criticism of religion* into the *criticism of right*, and the *criticism of theology* into the *criticism of politics*. . . .

But no particular class in Germany has the consistency, the penetration, the courage, or the ruthlessness that could mark it out as the negative representative of society. No more has any estate the breadth of soul that identifies itself, even for a moment, with the soul of the nation, the geniality that inspires material might to political violence, or that revolutionary daring which flings at the adversary the defiant words: *I am nothing, but I must be everything.* The main stem of German morals and honesty, of the classes as well as of individuals, is rather that *modest egoism* which asserts its limitedness and allows it to be asserted against itself. The relation of the various sections of German society is therefore not dramatic but epic. Each of them begins to be aware of itself and begins to camp beside the others with all its particular claims not as soon as it is oppressed, but as soon as the circumstances of the time relations, without the section's own participation, create a social substratum on which it can in turn exert pressure. Even the *moral self-feeling of the German middle class* rests only on the consciousness that it is the common representative of the Philistine mediocrity of all the other classes. It is therefore not only the German kings who accede to the throne malapropos, it is every section of civil society which goes through a defeat before it celebrates victory and develops its own limitations before it overcomes the limitations facing it, asserts its narrow-hearted essence before it has been able to assert its magnanimous essence; thus the very opportunity of a great role has passed away before it is at hand, and every class, once it begins the struggle against the class opposed to it, is involved in the struggle against the class below it. Hence the higher nobility is struggling against the monarchy, the bureaucrat against the nobility, and the bourgeois against them all, while the proletariat is already beginning to find itself struggling against the bourgeoisie. The middle class hardly dares to grasp the thought of emancipation from its own standpoint when the development of the social conditions and the progress of political theory already declare that standpoint antiquated, or at least problematic. . . .

Where, then, is the *positive* possibility of a German emancipation?

Answer: In the formation of a class with *radical chains,* a class of civil society which is not a class of civil society, an estate which is the dissolution of all estates, a sphere which has a universal character by its universal suffering and claims no *particular right* because no *particular wrong* but *wrong generally* is perpetrated against it; which can invoke no *historical* but only its *human* title, which does not stand in any one-sided opposition to the consequences but in all-round opposition to the presuppositions of the German political system; a sphere, finally, which cannot emancipate itself without emancipating itself from all other spheres of society, and thereby emancipating all other spheres of society, which, in a word, is the *complete loss* of man, and hence can win itself only through the *complete re-winning of man.* This dissolution of society as a particular estate is the *proletariat.*

The proletariat is beginning to appear in Germany as a result of the rising *industrial* movement. For it is not the *naturally arising* poor but the *artificially impoverished,* not the human masses mechanically oppressed by the gravity of society but the masses resulting from the *drastic dissolution* of society, mainly of the middle estate, that form the proletariat, although, as is easily understood, the naturally arising poor and the Christian Germanic serfs gradually join its ranks.

By heralding the *dissolution of the hereto existing world order* the proletariat merely proclaims the *secret of its own existence,* for it is the *actual* dissolution of that world order. By demanding the *negation of private property* the proletariat merely raises to the rank of a *principle of society* what society has raised to the rank of *its* principle, what is already incorporated in *it* as the negative result of society without its own participation. The proletarian then finds himself possessing the same right in regard to the world which is coming into being as the *German king* in regard to the world which has come into being when he calls the people *his* people as he calls the horse *his* horse. By declaring the people his private property the king merely proclaims that the private owner is king.

As philosophy finds its *material* weapon in the proletariat, so the proletariat finds its *spiritual* weapon in philosophy. And once the lightning of thought has squarely struck this ingenuous soil of the people, the emancipation of the *Germans* into *men* will be accomplished.

Let us sum up the result:

The only *practically* possible liberation of Germany is liberation from the standpoint of *the* theory which proclaims man to be the highest essence of man. In Germany emancipation from the *Middle Ages* is possible only as emancipation from the *partial* victories over the Middle Ages as well. In Germany *no* kind of bondage can be shattered without *every* kind of bondage being shattered. The *fundamental* Germany cannot revolutionize without revolutionizing *from the foundation. The emancipation of the German* is *the emancipation of man.* The *head* of this emancipation is *philosophy,* its *heart* is the *proletariat.* Philosophy cannot be made a reality without the abolition of the proletariat, the proletariat cannot be abolished without philosophy being made a reality.

When all inner requisites are fulfilled, the *day of German resurrection* will be proclaimed by the *crowing of the Gallic cock.*

XI. *Excerpt from* The Communism of the Paper *Rheinischer Beobachter*

KARL MARX

This article, which contains Marx's attack on "the social principles of Christianity," was published in the *Deutsche-Brüsseler-Zeitung,* No. 73, September 12, 1847.—Ed.

. . . Besides income tax, the consistorial councilor has another means of introducing communism as he conceives it:

"What is the alpha and omega of Christian faith? The dogma of original sin and the redemption. And therein lies the link of solidarity between men at its highest potential; one for all and all for one."

Happy people! The *cardinal question* is solved forever. Under the double wings of the Prussian eagle and the Holy Ghost the proletariat will find two inexhaustible sources of life: first, the surplus of income tax over and above the ordinary and extraordinary needs of the state, a surplus which is equal to nought; second, the revenues from the heavenly domains of original sin and the redemption, which are also equal to nought. These two noughts provide a splendid ground for one third of the nation, who have no ground for their subsistence, and a wonderful support for another third, which is on the decline. In any case, the imaginary surpluses, original sin and the redemption, will appease the hunger of the people in quite a different way than the long speeches of the liberal deputies!

Further we read:

"In the Our Father we say: 'lead us not into temptation.' And we must practice towards our neighbor what we ask for ourselves. But our social conditions tempt man, and excessive need incites to crime."

And we, the honorable bureaucrats, judges, and consistorial councilors of the Prussian state, take this into consideration by having people racked on the wheel, beheaded, imprisoned, and flogged, and thereby "lead" the proletarians "into temptation" to have us later similarly racked on the wheel, beheaded, imprisoned, and flogged. And that will not fail to happen.

"Such conditions," the consistorial councilor declares, "a Christian state *cannot* tolerate; it must find a remedy for them."

Yes, with absurd prattle on society's duties of solidarity, with imaginary surpluses and unprovided bills drawn on God the Father, Son and Co.

"We can also be spared the already boring talk about communism," our observant consistorial councilor asserts. "If only those whose calling it is to develop the social principles of Christianity do so, the communists will soon be put to silence."

The social principles of Christianity have now had eighteen hundred years to develop, and need no further development by Prussian consistorial councilors.

The social principles of Christianity justified the slavery of antiquity, glorified the serfdom of the Middle Ages, and equally know, when necessary, how to defend the oppression of the proletariat, although they make a pitiful face over it.

The social principles of Christianity preach the necessity of a ruling and an oppressed class, and all they have for the latter is the pious wish the former will be charitable.

The social principles of Christianity transfer the consistorial councilors' adjustment of all infamies to heaven, and thus justify the further existence of those infamies on earth.

The social principles of Christianity declare all vile acts of the oppressors against the oppressed to be either the just punishment of original sin and other sins or trials that the Lord in his infinite wisdom imposes on those redeemed.

The social principles of Christianity preach cowardice,

self-contempt, abasement, submission, humility, in a word all the qualities of the *canaille;* and the proletariat, not wishing to be treated as *canaille,* needs its courage, its self-esteem, its pride, and its sense of independence more than its bread.

The social principles of Christianity are cringing, but the proletariat is revolutionary.

So much for the social principles of Christianity.

To continue:

"We acknowledged social reform as the noblest calling of the monarchy."

Did we? There has been no question of that so far. But grant it. And in what does the social reform of the monarchy consist? In putting into force an income tax purloined from the organs of liberalism and supposed to provide a surplus that the Finance Minister knows nothing about; in the fiasco of the *Landrentenbanken,* in the Prussian East Railway, and in the first place in the profit of an enormous capital of original sin and redemption!

"The interest of the monarchy itself advises that." How low monarchy must have sunk!

"That is demanded by the need of society"—which at present requires protective barriers far more than dogmas.

"That is recommended by the Gospel." It is recommended by everything in general, except the frightfully desolate state of the Prussian treasury, that abyss which will have irretrievably swallowed up the fifteen Russian millions within three years. The Gospel, by the way, recommends much, including castration as the beginning of social reform for itself (Matthew 25). . . .

XII. *Excerpts from* Herr Eugen Dühring's Revolution in Science

FRIEDRICH ENGELS

During the years 1877 and 1878, Engels wrote a series of polemical articles against a professor at the University of Berlin, Eugen Dühring. Though marred by their polemical cast, they provided the most complete exposition of the philosophy of Marx and Engels, and were subsequently published as a book. Engels read the whole manuscript to Marx, who approved of it as a statement of their common views. The following excerpts are an example of the method of historical materialism applied to moral ideas. Engels tries to define freedom of the will in a way that will make it compatible with historical necessity. The translation is by Emile Burns.—ED.

From CHAPTER IX: MORALITY AND LAW: ETERNAL TRUTHS

The conceptions of good and bad have varied so much from nation to nation and from age to age that they have often been in direct contradiction to each other. But all the same, someone may object, good is not bad and bad is not good; if good is confused with bad, there is an end to all morality and everyone can do and leave undone whatever he cares. . . . If it were such an easy business, there certainly would be no dispute at all over good and bad; everyone would know what was good and what was bad. But how do things stand today? What morality is preached to us today? There is first Christian feudal morality, inherited from past centuries of faith; and this again has two main subdivisions, Catholic and Protestant moralities, each of which in turn has no lack of further subdivisions, from the Jesuit Catholic and orthodox Protestant to loose "advanced" moralities. Alongside of these we find the modern bourgeois morality, and with it, too, the proletarian morality of the future, so that in the most advanced European countries alone the past, present, and future provide three great groups of moral theories which are in force simultaneously and alongside of each other. Which is then the true one? Not one of them, in the sense of having absolute validity, but certainly that morality which contains the maximum of durable elements is the one which, in the present, represents the overthrow of the present, represents the future—that is, the proletarian.

But when we see that the three classes of modern society, the feudal aristocracy, the bourgeoisie, and the proletariat, have their special morality, we can only draw the one conclusion, that men, consciously or unconsciously, derive their moral ideas in the last resort from the practical relations on which their class position is based—from the economic relations in which they carry on production and exchange.

But nevertheless there is much that is common to the three moral theories mentioned above. Is this not at least a portion of a morality which is externally fixed? These moral theories represent three different stages of the same historical development, and have therefore a common historical background, and for that reason alone they necessarily have much in common. Even more. In similar or approximately similar stages of economic development moral theories must of necessity be more or less in agreement. From the moment when private property in movable objects developed, in all societies in which this private property existed there must be this moral law in common: Thou shalt not steal. Does this law thereby become an eternal moral law? By no means. In a society in which the motive for stealing has been done away with, in which therefore at the very most only lunatics would ever steal, how the teacher of morals would be laughed at who tried solemnly to proclaim the eternal truth: Thou shalt not steal!

We therefore reject every attempt to impose on us any moral dogma whatsoever as an eternal, ultimate, and forever immutable moral law on the pretext that the moral world, too, has its permanent principles which transcend history and the differences between nations. We maintain, on the contrary, that all former moral theories are the product, in the last analysis, of the economic stage which society reached at that particular epoch. And as society has hitherto moved in class antagonisms, morality has always been a class morality; either it has justified the domination and the interests of the ruling class or, as soon as the oppressed class has become powerful enough, it has represented the revolt against this domination and the future interests of the oppressed. That in this process there has, on the whole, been progress in morality, as in all other branches of human knowledge, cannot be doubted. But we have not yet passed beyond class morality. A really human morality, which transcends class antagonisms and their legacies in thought, becomes possible only at a stage of society which has not only overcome class contradictions but has even forgotten them in practical life. And now it is possible to appreciate the presumption shown by Herr Dühring in advancing his claim, from the midst of the old class society and on the eve of a social revolution, to impose on the future classless society an eternal morality which is independent of time and changes in reality. Even assuming—what we do not know up to now—that he understands the structure of the society of the future at least in its main outlines.

Finally, one more revelation which is "absolutely original" but for that reason no less "going to the roots of things." With regard to the origin of evil, we have "the fact that the *type of the cat*, with the guile associated with it, is found in animal form, and the similar fact that a similar type of character is found also in human beings. . . . There is therefore nothing mysterious about evil, unless someone wants to scent out something mysterious in the existence of a cat, or of any animal of prey." Evil is—the cat. The devil therefore has no horns or cloven hoof, but claws and green eyes. And Goethe committed an unpardonable error in presenting Mephistopheles as a black dog instead of the said cat. Evil is the cat! That is morality, not only for all worlds, but also—for cats!

From CHAPTER X: MORALITY AND LAW: EQUALITY

. . . The idea of equality . . . thanks to Rousseau, played a theoretical and, during and since the Great Revolution, a practical political role, and even today still plays an important agitational role in the socialist movement of almost every country. The establishment of its scientific content will also determine its value for proletarian agitation.

The idea that all men, as men, have something in common, and that they are therefore equal so far as these common characteristics go, is of course primeval. But the modern demand for equality is something entirely different from that; this consists rather in deducing from those common characteristics of humanity, from that equality of men as men, a claim to equal political or social status for all human beings, or at least for all citizens of a state or all members of a society. Before the original conception of relative equality could lead to the conclusion that men should have equal rights in the state and in society, before this conclusion could appear to be something even natural and self-evident, however, thousands of years had to pass and did pass. In the oldest natural communities equality of rights existed at most for members of the community; women, slaves, and strangers were excluded from this equality as a matter of course. Among the Greeks and Romans the inequalities of men were of greater importance than any form of equality. It would necessarily have seemed idiotic to the ancients that Greeks and barbarians, free men and slaves, citizens and dependents, Roman citizens and Roman subjects (to use a comprehensive term) should have a claim to equal political status. Under the Roman Empire all these distinctions gradually disappeared, except the distinction between free men and slaves, and there arose, for the free men at least, that equality as between private individuals on the basis of which Roman law developed—the completest elaboration of law based on private property which we know. But so long as the distinction between free men and slaves existed, there could be no talk of drawing legal conclusions from the fact of general equality *as men*; and we saw this again, quite recently, in the slave-owning states of the North American Union.

Christianity knew only *one* point in which all men were equal: that all were equally born in original sin—which corresponded perfectly with its character as the religion of the slaves and the oppressed. Apart from this it recognized, at most, the equality of the elect, which, however, was stressed only at the very beginning. The traces of common ownership which are also found in the early stages of the new religion can be ascribed to the solidarity of a proscribed sect rather than to really equalitarian ideas. Within a very short time the establishment of the distinction between priests and laymen put an end even to this tendency to Christian equality. The overrunning of Western Europe by the Germans abolished for centuries all ideas of equality, through the gradual building up of such a complicated social and political hierarchy as had never before existed. But at the same time the invasion drew Western and Central Europe into the course of historical development, created for the first time a compact cultural area, and within this area also for the first time a system of predominantly national states exerting mutual influence on each other and mutually holding each other in check. Thereby it prepared the ground on which alone the question of the equal status of men, of the rights of man, could at a later period be raised.

The feudal Middle Ages also developed in its womb the class which was destined in the future course of its evolution to be the standard-bearer of the modern demand for equality: the bourgeoisie. Itself in its origin one of the "estates" of the feudal order, the bourgeoisie developed the predominantly handicraft industry and the exchange of products within feudal society to a relatively high level when at the end of the fifteenth century the great maritime discoveries opened to it a new and more far-reaching career. Trade beyond the confines of Europe, which had previously been carried on only between Italy and the Levant, was now extended to America and India, and soon surpassed in importance both the mutual exchange between the various European countries and the internal trade within each separate country. American gold and silver flooded Europe and forced its way like a disintegrating element into every fissure, hole, and pore of feudal society. Handicraft industry could no longer satisfy the rising demand; in the leading industries of the most advanced countries it was replaced by manufacture.

But this mighty revolution in the economic conditions of society was not followed by any immediate corresponding change in its political structure. The state order remained feudal, while society became more and more bourgeois. Trade on a large scale, that is to say, international, and, even more, world trade, requires free owners of commodities who are unrestricted in their movements and have equal rights as traders to exchange their commodities on the basis of laws that are equal for them all, at least in each separate place. The transition from handicraft to manufacture presupposes the existence of a number of free workers—free on the one hand from the fetters of the guild and on the other from the means whereby they could themselves utilize their labor power—workers who could contract with their employers for the hire of their labor power and, as parties to the contract, have rights equal with his. And finally the equality and equal status of all human labor, because and in so far as it is *human* labor, found its unconscious but clearest expression in the law of value of modern bourgeois economy, according to which the value of a commodity is measured by the socially necessary labor embodied in it.[1] But where economic relations required freedom and equality of rights, the political system opposed them at every step with guild restrictions and special privileges. Local privileges, differential duties, exceptional laws of all kinds in trade affected not only foreigners or people living in the colonies, but often enough also whole categories of the nationals of each country; the privileges of the guilds everywhere and ever anew formed barriers to the path of development of manufacture. Nowhere was the

[1] This tracing of the origin of the modern ideas of equality to the economic conditions of bourgeois society was first developed by Marx in *Capital*. [Note by F. Engels.]

path open and the chances equal for all the bourgeois competitors—and yet this was the first and ever more pressing need.

The demand for liberation from feudal fetters, and the establishment of equality of rights by the abolition of feudal inequalities, was bound soon to assume wider dimensions from the moment when the economic advance of society first placed it on the order of the day. If it was raised in the interests of industry and trade, it was also necessary to demand the same equality of rights for the great mass of the peasantry, who, in every degree of bondage from total serfdom upwards, were compelled to give the greater part of their labor time to their feudal lord without payment and in addition to pay innumerable other dues to him and to the state. On the other hand, it was impossible to avoid the demand for the abolition also of feudal privileges, the freedom from taxation of the nobility, the political privileges of the various feudal estates. And as people were no longer living in a world empire such as the Roman Empire had been, but in a system of independent states dealing with each other on an equal footing and at approximately the same stage of bourgeois development, it was a matter of course that the demand for equality should assume a general character reaching out beyond the individual state, that freedom and equality should be proclaimed as *human rights*. And it is significant of the specifically bourgeois character of these human rights that the American Constitution, the first to recognize the rights of man, in the same breath confirmed the slavery of the colored races then existing in America: class privileges were prescribed, race privileges sanctioned.

As is well known, however, from the moment when, like a butterfly from the chrysalis, the bourgeoisie arose out of the burghers of the feudal period, when this "estate" of the Middle Ages developed into a class of modern society, it was always and inevitably accompanied by its shadow, the proletariat. And in the same way the bourgeois demand for equality was accompanied by the proletarian demand for equality. From the moment when the bourgeois demand for the abolition of class privileges was put forward, alongside of it appeared the proletarian demand for the abolition of the *classes themselves*—at first in religious form, basing itself on primitive Christianity, and later drawing support from the bourgeois equalitarian theories themselves. The proletarians took the bourgeoisie at their word: equality must not be merely apparent, must not apply merely to the sphere of the state, but must also be real, must be extended to the social and economic spheres. And especially since the French bourgeoisie, from the Great Revolution on, brought bourgeois equality to the forefront, the French proletariat answered blow for blow with the demand for social and economic equality, and equality became the battle cry, particularly of the French proletariat.

The demand for equality in the mouth of the proletariat has therefore a double meaning. It is either—as was the case at the very start, for example in the Peasants' War—the spontaneous reaction against the crying social inequalities, against the contrast of rich and poor, the feudal lords and their serfs, surfeit and starvation; as such, it is the simple expression of the revolutionary instinct, and finds its justification in that, and indeed only in that. Or, on the other hand, the proletarian demand for equality has arisen as the reaction against the bourgeois demand for equality, drawing more or less correct and more far-reaching demands from this bourgeois demand, and serving as an agitational means in order to rouse the workers against the capitalists on the basis of the capitalists' own assertions; and in this case it stands and falls with bourgeois equality itself. In both cases the real content of the proletarian demand for equality is the demand for the *abolition of classes*. Any demand for equality which goes beyond that, of necessity passes into absurdity. . . .

The idea of equality, therefore, both in its bourgeois and in its proletarian form, is itself a historical product, the creation of which required definite historical conditions, which in turn themselves presuppose a long previous historical development. It is therefore anything but an eternal truth. And if today it is taken for granted by the general public—in one sense or another—if, as Marx says, it "already possesses the fixity of a popular prejudice," this is not the consequence of its axiomatic truth, but the result of the general diffusion and the continued appropriateness of the ideas of the eighteenth century. . . .

From CHAPTER XI: MORALITY AND LAW: FREEDOM AND NECESSITY

. . . It is difficult to deal with morality and law without coming up against the question of so-called free will, of human responsibility, and the relation between freedom and necessity. And the philosophy of reality also has not only one but even two solutions of this problem.

"All false theories of freedom must be replaced by what we know from experience is the nature of the relation between rational judgment on the one hand and instinctive impulse on the other, a relation which, so to speak, unites them into a single mean force. The fundamental facts of this form of dynamics must be drawn from observation and, for the calculation in advance of events which have not yet occurred, must also be estimated *as closely as possible,* in general both as to their nature and magnitude. In this way the vain delusions of inner freedom, which have been a source of worry and anxiety for thousands of years, are not only cleared away forever, but are also replaced by something positive, which can be made use of for the practical regulation of life." On this basis freedom consists in rational judgment pulling a man to the right while irrational impulses pull him to the left, and in this parallelogram of forces the actual movement follows the direction of the diagonal. Freedom is therefore the mean between judgment and impulse, reason and unreason, and its degree in each individual case can be determined on the basis of experience by a "personal equation," to use an astronomical expression. But a few pages later on we find: "We base moral responsibility on freedom, which, however, in our view means nothing more than susceptibility to conscious motives in accordance with our natural and acquired intelligence. All such motives operate with the inevitable force of natural law, notwithstanding our awareness of the possible contradiction in the actions; but it is precisely on this inevitable compulsion that we rely when we bring in the moral lever."

This second definition of freedom, which quite unceremoniously gives a knockout blow to the other, is again nothing but an extremely superficial rendering of the Hegelian conception of the matter. Hegel was the first to state correctly the relation between freedom and necessity. To him freedom is the appreciation of necessity. "Necessity is *blind* only *in so far as it is not understood.*" Freedom does not consist in the dream of independence of natural laws, but in the knowledge of these laws, and in the possibility this gives of systematically making them work towards definite ends. This holds good in relation both to the laws of external nature and to those which govern the bodily and mental life of men themselves—two classes of laws which we can separate from each other at most only in thought, but not in reality. Freedom of the will therefore means nothing but the capacity to make decisions with real knowledge of the subject. Therefore the *freer* a man's judgment is in relation to a definite question, with so much the greater *necessity* is the content of this judgment determined; while the uncertainty, founded on ignorance, which seems to make an arbitrary choice among many different and conflicting possible decisions, shows by this precisely that it is not free, that is is controlled by the very object it should itself control. Freedom therefore consists in the control over ourselves and over external nature which is founded on knowledge of natural necessity; it is therefore necessarily a product of historical development. The first men who separated themselves from the animal kingdom were in all essentials as unfree as the animals themselves, but each step forward in civilization was a step towards freedom. On the threshold of human history stands the discovery that mechanical motion can be transformed into heat: the production of fire by friction; at the close of the development so far gone through stands the discovery that heat can be transformed into mechanical motion: the steam engine. And, in spite of the gigantic and liberating revolution in the social world which the steam engine is carrying through—and which is not yet half completed—it is beyond question that the generation of fire by friction was of even greater effectiveness for the liberation of mankind. For the generation of fire by friction gave man for the first time control over one of the forces of nature, and thereby separated him forever from the animal kingdom. The steam engine will never bring about such a mighty leap forward in human development, however important it may seem in our eyes as representing all those immense productive forces dependent on it—forces which alone make possible a state of society in which there are no longer class distinctions or anxiety over the means of subsistence for the individual, and in which for the first time there can be talk of real human freedom and of an existence in harmony with the established laws of nature. But how young the whole of human history still is, and how ridiculous it would be to attempt to ascribe any absolute validity to our present views, is evident from the simple fact that all past history can be characterized as the history of the epoch from the practical discovery of the transformation of mechanical motion into heat up to that of the transformation of heat into mechanical motion.

XIII. *Excerpts from* The Class Struggles in France, 1848 to 1850

KARL MARX

[These articles were published by Marx in a monthly magazine *Neue Rheinische Zeitung, Politisch-ökonomische Revue* which he and Engels tried to establish in 1850.]

I

THE DEFEAT OF JUNE 1848

With the exception of only a few chapters, every more important part of the annals of the revolution from 1848 to 1849 carries the heading: *Defeat of the Revolution!*

What succumbed in these defeats was not the revolution. It was the pre-revolutionary traditional appendages, results of social relationships which had not yet come to the point of sharp class antagonisms—persons, illusions, conceptions, projects from which the revolutionary party before the February revolution was not free, from which it could be freed not by the *victory of February*, but only by a series of *defeats.*

In a word, the revolution made progress, forged ahead, not by its immediate tragicomic achievements, but, on the contrary, by the creation of a powerful, united counter-revolution, by the creation of an opponent in combat with whom, only, the party of revolt ripened into a really revolutionary party.

To prove this is the task of the following pages.

After the July revolution [of 1830], when the liberal banker Laffitte led his godfather, the Duke of Orleans, in triumph to the Hôtel de Ville, he let fall the words: "*From now on the bankers will rule.*" Laffitte had betrayed the secret of the revolution.

It was not the French bourgeoisie that ruled under Louis Philippe, but *one section* of it: bankers, stock-exchange kings, railway kings, owners of coal and iron mines and forests, a part of the landed proprietors that rallied round them—the so-called *finance aristocracy*. It sat on the throne, it dictated laws in the Chambers, it distributed public offices, from cabinet portfolios to tobacco bureau posts.

The *industrial bourgeoisie*, properly so called, formed part of the official opposition, i.e., it was represented only as a minority in the Chambers. Its opposition was expressed all the more resolutely, the more unalloyed the autocracy of the finance aristocracy became, and the more it itself imagined that its domination over the working class was ensured after the mutinies of 1832, 1834, and 1839, which had been drowned in blood. *Grandin*, Rouen manufacturer and the most fanatical instrument of bourgeois reaction in the Constituent as well as in the Legislative National Assembly, was the most violent opponent of Guizot in the Chamber of Deputies. *Léon Faucher*, later known for his impotent efforts to climb into prominence as the Guizot of the French counterrevolution, in the last days of Louis Philippe waged a war of the pen for industry against speculation and its trainbearer, the government. *Bastiat* agitated in the name of Bordeaux and the whole of wine-producing France against the ruling system.

The *petty bourgeoisie* of all gradations, and the *peasantry* also, were completely excluded from political power. Finally, in the official opposition or entirely outside the *pays légal*, there were the *ideological* representatives and spokesmen of the above classes, their savants, lawyers, doctors, etc.—in a word, their so-called *men of talent*.

Owing to its financial straits, the July monarchy was dependent from the beginning on the big bourgeoisie, and its dependence on the big bourgeoisie was the inexhaustible source of increasing financial straits. It was impossible to subordinate the administration of the state to the interests of national production without balancing the budget, without establishing a balance between state expenditures and revenues. And how was this balance to be established without limiting state extravagance, i.e., without encroaching on interests which were so many props of the ruling system, and without redistributing taxes, i.e., without shifting a considerable share of the burden of taxation onto the shoulders of the big bourgeoisie itself?

Moreover, the faction of the bourgeoisie that ruled and legislated through the Chambers had a *direct interest in the indebtedness of the state*. The *state deficit* was really the main object of its speculation and the chief source of its enrichment. At the end of each year, a new deficit. After expiry of four of five years, a new loan. And every new loan offered new opportunities to the finance aristocracy for defrauding the state, which was kept artificially on the verge of bankruptcy—it had to negotiate with the bankers under the most unfavorable conditions. Each new loan gave a further opportunity, that of plundering the public, which invested its capital in state bonds by means of stock-exchange manipulations, into the secrets of which the government and the majority in the Chambers were initiated. In general, the fluctuations in state credits and the possession of state secrets gave the bankers and their associates in the Chambers and on the throne the possibility of evoking sudden, extraordinary fluctuations in the quotations of state bonds, the result of which was always bound to be the ruin of a mass of smaller capitalists and the fabulously rapid enrichment of the big gamblers. As the state deficit was in the direct interest of the ruling section of the bourgeoisie, it is clear why the *extraordinary* state expenditure in the last years of Louis Philippe's reign was far more than double the extraordinary state expenditure under Napoleon, indeed reached a yearly sum of nearly four hundred million francs, whereas the whole average annual export of France seldom attained a volume amounting to seven hundred and fifty million francs. The enormous sums which, in this way, flowed through the hands of the state facilitated, moreover, swindling contracts for deliveries, bribery, defalcations, and all kinds of roguery. The defrauding of the state, practiced wholesale in connection with loans, was repeated retail in public works. What occurred in the relations between Chamber and government became multiplied in the relations between individual departments and individual *entrepreneurs*.

The ruling class exploited the *building of railways* in the same way as it exploited state expenditures in general and state loans. The Chambers piled the main burdens on the state, and secured the golden fruits to the speculating finance aristocracy. One recalls the scandals in the Chamber of Deputies, when by chance it leaked out that all the members of the majority, including a number of ministers, had been interested as shareholders in the very railway constructions which as legislators they caused to be carried out afterwards at the cost of the state.

On the other hand, the smallest financial reform was wrecked due to the influence of the bankers. For example, the *postal reform*. Rothschild protested. Was it permissible for the state to curtail sources of revenue out of which interest was to be paid on its ever increasing debt?

The July monarchy was nothing other than a joint-stock company for the exploitation of France's national wealth, the dividends on which were divided among ministers, Chambers, two hundred and forty thousand voters and their adherents. Louis Philippe was the director of this company—Robert Macaire on the throne. Trade, industry, agriculture, shipping, the interests of the industrial bourgeoisie, were bound to be continually endangered and prejudiced under this system. *Gouvernement à bon marché*, cheap government, was what it had inscribed in the July days on its banner.

Since the finance aristocracy made the laws, was at the head of the administration of the state, had command of all the organized public authorities, dominated public opinion through the actual state of affairs and through the press, the same prostitution, the same shameless cheating, the same mania to get rich were repeated in every sphere, from the court to the Café Borgne—to get rich not by production, but by pocketing the already available wealth of others. Clashing every moment with the bourgeois laws themselves, an unbridled assertion of unhealthy and dissolute appetites manifested itself, particularly at the top of bourgeois society—lusts wherein wealth derived from gambling naturally seeks its satisfaction, where pleasure becomes debauched, where money, filth, and blood commingle. The finance aristocracy, in its mode of acquisition as well as in its pleasures, is nothing but the *resurrection of the* lumpenproletariat *transported to the heights of bourgeois society.*

And the non-ruling factions of the French bourgeoisie cried: "Corruption!" The people cried: "*À bas les grands voleurs! à bas les assassins!*" [Down with the big thieves, down with the assassins!] when in 1847, on the most prominent stages of bourgeois society, the same scenes were publicly enacted as regularly led the *lumpenproletariat* to brothels, to workhouses and lunatic asylums, to the bar of justice, to the dungeon and to the scaffold. The industrial bourgeoisie saw its interests endangered, the petty bourgeoisie was filled with moral indignation, the imagination of the people was offended, Paris was flooded with pamphlets—"*La Dynastie Rothschild,*" "*Les Juifs rois de l'époque,*" ["The Rothschild dynasty," "The Jewish kings of the epoch"] etc.—in which the rule of the finance aristocracy was denounced and stigmatized with greater or less wit.

Rien pour la gloire! [Glory brings no profit!] *La paix partout et toujours!* [Peace everywhere and always!] "War depresses the quotations of the 3 and 4 per cents!" the France of the Bourse jobbers had inscribed on her banner. Her foreign policy was therefore lost in a series of mortifications to French national sentiment, which reacted all the more vigorously when the rape of Poland was brought to its conclusion with the incorporation of Cracow by Austria, and when Guizot came out actively on the side of the Holy Alliance in the Swiss separatist war. The victory of the Swiss liberals in this mimic war raised the self-respect of the bourgeois opposition in France; the bloody uprising of the people in Palermo worked like an electric shock on the paralyzed masses of the people, and awoke their great revolutionary memories and passions.[1]

The eruption of the general discontent was finally accelerated and the mood for revolt ripened by *two economic world events.*

The *potato blight* and the *crop failures* of 1845 and 1846 increased the general ferment among the people. The dearth of 1847 called forth bloody conflicts in France as well as on the rest of the Continent. As against the shameless orgies of the finance aristocracy, the struggle of the people for the prime necessities of life! At Buzançais hunger rioters executed; in Paris oversatiated swindlers snatched from the courts by the royal family!

The second great economic event which hastened the outbreak of the revolution was a *general commercial and industrial crisis* in England. Already heralded in the autumn of 1845 by the wholesale reverses of the speculators in railway shares, staved off during 1846 by a number of incidents such as the impending abolition of the corn duties, the crisis finally burst in the autumn of 1847 with the bankruptcy of the London wholesale grocers, on the heels of which followed the insolvencies of the land banks and the closing of the factories in the English industrial districts. The aftereffect of this crisis on the Continent had not yet spent itself when the February revolution broke out.

The devastation of trade and industry caused by the economic epidemic made the autocracy of the finance aristocracy still more unbearable. Throughout the whole of France the bourgeois opposition *agitated at banquets* for an *electoral reform* which should win for it the majority in the Chambers and overthrow the Ministry of the Bourse. In Paris the industrial crisis had, moreover, the particular result of throwing a number of manufacturers and big traders, who under the existing circumstances could no

[1] Annexation of Cracow by Austria, in agreement with Russia and Prussia, on November 11, 1846. Swiss separatist war [*Sonderbundskrieg*], November 4 to 28, 1847. Rising in Palermo, January 12, 1848; at the end of January, nine days' bombardment of the town by the Neapolitans. [Note by F. Engels to the edition of 1895.]

longer do any business in the foreign market, onto the home market. They set up large establishments, the competition of which ruined the small grocers and shopkeepers *en masse*. Hence the innumerable bankruptcies among this section of the Paris bourgeoisie, and hence their revolutionary action in February. It is well known how Guizot and the Chambers answered the reform proposals with an unambiguous challenge, how Louis Philippe too late resolved on a ministry led by Barrot, how things went as far as hand-to-hand fighting between the people and the army, how the army was disarmed by the passive conduct of the National Guard, how the July monarchy had to give way to a provisional government.

The provisional government which emerged from the February barricades necessarily mirrored in its composition the different parties which shared in the victory. It could not be anything but a *compromise between the different classes* which together had overturned the July throne, but whose interests were mutually antagonistic. The *great majority* of its members consisted of representatives of the bourgeoisie. The republican petty bourgeoisie was represented by Ledru-Rollin and Flocon, the republican bourgeoisie by the people from the *National*, the dynastic opposition by Cremieux, Dupont de l'Eure, etc. The working class had only two representatives, Louis Blanc and Albert. Finally, Lamartine in the provisional government; this was actually no real interest, no definite class; this was the February revolution itself, the common uprising with its illusions, its poetry, its visionary content, and its phrases. For the rest, the spokesman of the February revolution, by his position and his views, belonged to the *bourgeoisie*.

If Paris, as a result of political centralization, rules France, the workers, in moments of revolutionary earthquakes, rule Paris. The first act in the life of the provisional government was an attempt to escape from this overpowering influence by an appeal from intoxicated Paris to sober France. Lamartine disputed the right of the barricade fighters to proclaim a republic on the ground that only the majority of Frenchmen had that right; they must await their votes, the Parisian proletariat must not besmirch its victory by a usurpation. The bourgeoisie allows the proletariat only one usurpation—that of fighting.

Up to noon of February 25 the republic had not yet been proclaimed; on the other hand, all the ministries had already been divided among the bourgeois elements of the provisional government and among the generals, bankers, and lawyers of the *National*. But the workers were determined this time not to put up with any bamboozlement like that of July 1830. They were ready to take up the fight anew, and to get a republic by force of arms. With this message, *Raspail* betook himself to the Hôtel de Ville. In the name of the Parisian proletariat he *commanded* the provisional government to proclaim a republic; if this order of the people was not fulfilled within two hours, he would return at the head of two hundred thousand men. The bodies of the fallen were scarcely cold, the barricades were not yet cleared away, the workers not yet disarmed, and the only force which could be opposed to them was the National Guard. Under these circumstances the doubts born of considerations of state policy and the juristic scruples of conscience entertained by the provisional government suddenly vanished. The time limit of two hours had not yet expired when all the walls of Paris were resplendent with the gigantesque historical words:

République française! Liberté, Egalité, Fraternité!

Even the memory of the limited aims and motives which drove the bourgeoisie into the February revolution was extinguished by the proclamation of the republic on the basis of universal suffrage. Instead of only a few sections of the bourgeoisie all classes of French society were suddenly hurled into the orbit of political power, forced to leave the boxes, the stalls, and the gallery and to act in person upon the revolutionary stage! With the constitutional monarchy also vanished the semblance of a state power independently confronting bourgeois society as well as the whole series of subordinate struggles which this semblance of power called forth!

By dictating the republic to the provisional government, and through the provisional government to the whole of France, the proletariat stepped into the foreground forthwith as an independent party, but at the same time challenged the whole of bourgeois France to enter the lists against it. What it won was the terrain for the fight for its revolutionary emancipation, but by no means this emancipation itself.

The first thing that the February republic had to do was rather to *complete the rule of the bourgeoisie* by allowing, besides the finance aristocracy, *all the propertied classes* to enter the orbit of political power. The majority of the great landowners, the Legitimists, were emancipated from the political nullity to which they had been condemned by the July monarchy. Not for nothing had the *Gazette de France* agitated in common with the opposition papers; not for nothing had Larochejaquelin taken the side of the revolution in the session of the Chamber of Deputies on February 24. The nominal proprietors, who form the great majority of the French people, the *peasants,* were put by universal suffrage in the position of arbiters of the fate of France. The February republic finally brought the rule of the bourgeoisie clearly into view, since it struck off the crown behind which capital kept itself concealed.

Just as the workers in the July days had fought for and won the *bourgeois monarchy,* so in the February days they fought for and won the *bourgeois republic.* Just as the July monarchy had to proclaim itself a *monarchy surrounded by republican institutions,* so the February republic was forced to proclaim itself a *republic surrounded by social institutions.* The Paris proletariat *compelled* this concession, too.

Marche, a worker, dictated the decree by which the newly formed provisional government pledged itself to guarantee the workers a livelihood by means of work, to provide work for all citizens, etc. And when, a few days later, it forgot its promises and seemed to have lost sight of the proletariat, a mass of twenty thousand workers marched on the Hôtel de Ville with the cry: "*We want the organization of work! We want our own Ministry of Labor!*" Reluctantly, and after long debate, the provisional government nominated a permanent special commission charged with *finding* means of improving the lot of the working classes! This commission consisted of delegates from the corporations of Paris artisans, and was presided over by Louis Blanc and Albert. The Luxembourg Palace was assigned to it as its meeting place. In this way the representatives of the working class were exiled from the seat of the provisional government, the bourgeois section of which retained the real state power and the reins of administration exclusively in its hands; and *side by side* with the Ministries of Finance, Trade, and Public Works, *side by side* with the Bank and the Bourse, there arose a *socialist synagogue* whose high priests, Louis Blanc and Albert, had the task of discovering the promised land, of preaching the new gospel, and of providing work for the Paris proletariat. Unlike any profane state power, they had no budget, no executive authority at their disposal. They were supposed to use their heads to break the pillars of bourgeois society. While at the Palais de Luxembourg they sought the philosopher's stone, in the Hôtel de Ville they minted the current coinage.

And yet the claims of the Paris proletariat, so far as they went beyond the bourgeois republic, could win no other existence than the nebulous one of the Luxembourg Commission.

In common with the bourgeoisie the workers had made the February revolution, and *alongside* the bourgeoisie they sought to put through their interests, just as they had installed a worker in the provisional government itself alongside the bourgeois majority. *Organization of work!* But the existing, the bourgeois organization of work is wage labor. Without it there is no capital, no bourgeoisie, no bourgeois society. *Their own Ministry of Labor!* But the Ministries of Finance, of Trade, of Public Works—are not these the *bourgeois* Ministries of Labor? And *alongside* these a *proletarian* Ministry of Labor had to be a ministry of impotence, a ministry of pious wishes, a Luxembourg Commission. Just as the workers thought they would be able to emancipate themselves side by side with the bourgeoisie, so they thought they would be able to consummate a proletarian revolution within the national walls of France, side by side with the remaining bourgeois nations. But French production relations are conditioned by the foreign trade of France, by her position on the world market and the laws thereof; how was France to break them without a European revolutionary war, which would strike back at the despot of the world market, England?

As soon as it has risen up, a class in which the revolutionary interests of society are concentrated finds the content and the material for its revolutionary activity directly in its own situation: foes to be laid low, measures dictated by the needs of the struggle to be taken; the consequences of its own deeds drive it on. It makes no theoretical inquiries into its own task. The French working class had not attained this level; it was still incapable of accomplishing its own revolution.

The development of the industrial proletariat is, in general, conditioned by the development of the industrial bourgeoisie. Only under its rule does the proletariat gain that extensive national existence which can raise its revolution to a national one and does it itself create the modern means of production, which become just so many means of its revolutionary emancipation. Only its rule tears up the material roots of feudal society and levels the ground on which alone a proletarian revolution is possible. In France industry is more developed and the bourgeoisie more revolutionary than elsewhere on the Continent. But was not the February revolution leveled directly against the finance aristocracy? This fact proved that the industrial bourgeoisie did not rule France. The industrial bourgeoisie can rule only where modern industry shapes all property relations to suit itself, and industry can win this power only when it has conquered the world market, for national bounds are not wide enough for its development. But French industry, to a great extent, maintains its command even of the national market only through a more or less modified system of prohibitive duties. While, therefore, the French proletariat, at the moment of a revolution, possesses in Paris actual power and influence which spur it on to a drive beyond its means, in the rest of France it is crowded into separate, scattered industrial centers, being almost lost in the superior numbers of peasants and petty bourgeois. The struggle against capital in its developed, modern form, in its culminating phase, the struggle of the industrial wage workers against the industrial bourgeois, is in France a partial phenomenon, which after the February days could so much the less supply the national content of the revolution, since the struggle against capital's secondary modes of exploitation, that of the peasants against the usury in mortgages or of the petty bourgeois against the wholesale dealer, banker, and manufacturer, in a word, against bankruptcy, was still hidden in the general uprising against the finance aristocracy. Nothing is more understandable, then, than that the Paris proletariat sought to put through its own interests *side by side* with those of the bourgeoisie instead of enforcing them as the revolutionary interests of society itself, and that it let the *red* flag be lowered to the *tricolor*. The French workers could not take a step forward, could not touch a hair of the bourgeois order, until the course of the revolution had aroused the mass of the nation, peasants and petty bourgeois, standing between the proletariat and the bourgeoisie, against this order, against the rule of capital, and had forced it to attach itself to the proletariat as its protagonist. The workers could buy this victory only through the tremendous defeat of June.

The Luxembourg Commission, this creation of the Paris workers, must be given the credit for having disclosed from a Europe-wide tribune the secret of the revolution of the nineteenth century: the *emancipation of the proletariat*. The *Moniteur* turned red with rage when it had to propagate officially the "wild ravings" which up to that time lay buried in the apocryphal writings of the socialists and reached the ear of the bourgeoisie only from time to time as remote, half-terrifying, half-ludicrous legends. Europe awoke astonished from its bourgeois doze. Therefore, in the minds of the proletarians, who confused the finance aristocracy with the bourgeoisie in general; in the imagination of the good old republicans, who denied the very existence of classes or, at most, admitted them as a result of the constitutional monarchy; in the hypocritical phrases of the sections of the bourgeoisie which up to now had been excluded from power, the *rule of the bourgeoisie* was abolished with the introduction of the republic. At that time all the royalists were transformed into republicans and all the millionaires of Paris into workers. The phrase which corresponded to this imagined abolition of class relations was *fraternité*, universal fraternization and brotherhood. This pleasant abstraction from class antagonisms, this sentimental reconciliation of contradictory class interests, this fancied elevation above the class struggle, this *fraternité*, was the real catchword of the February revolution. The classes were divided by a mere *misunderstanding*, and Lamartine baptized the provisional government on February 24 "un gouvernement qui suspende *ce malentendu terrible qui existe entre les différentes classes* [a government that removes *this terrible misunderstanding which exists between the different classes*]." The Paris proletariat reveled in this magnanimous intoxication of fraternity.

The provisional government, on its part, once it was compelled to proclaim the republic, did everything to make it acceptable to the bourgeoisie and to the provinces. The bloody terror of the first French Republic was disavowed by the abolition of the death penalty for political offenses; the press was opened to all opinions; the army, the courts, the administration remained with a few exceptions in the hands of their old dignitaries; none of the July monarchy's great offenders was brought to book. The bourgeois republicans of the *National* amused themselves by exchanging monarchist names and costumes for old republican ones. To them the republic was only a new ball dress for the old bourgeois society. The young republic sought its chief merit not in frightening, but rather in constantly taking fright itself, and in winning existence and disarming resistance by the soft compliance and non-resistance of its existence. At home to the privileged classes, abroad to the despotic powers, it was loudly announced that the republic was of a peaceful nature. Live and let live was its professed motto. In addition thereto, shortly after the February revolution, the Germans, Poles, Austrians, Hungarians, and Italians revolted, each people in accordance with its immediate situation. Russia and England—the latter itself agitated, the former cowed—were not prepared. The republic, therefore, had no *national* enemy to face. Consequently there were no great foreign complications which could fire the energies, hasten the revolutionary process, drive the provisional government forward or throw it overboard. The Paris proletariat, which looked upon the republic as its own creation, naturally acclaimed each act of the provisional government which facilitated the lodgment of the latter in bourgeois society. It willingly allowed itself to be employed on police service by Caussidière in order to protect property in Paris, just as it allowed Louis Blanc to arbitrate wage disputes between workers and masters. It made it a *point d'honneur* to preserve the bourgeois honor of the republic unblemished in the eyes of Europe.

The republic encountered no resistance either abroad or at home. This disarmed it. Its task was no longer the revolutionary transformation of the world, but consisted only in adapting itself to the relations of bourgeois society. Concerning the fanaticism with which the provisional government undertook this task, there is no more eloquent testimony than its *financial measures.*

Public credit and *private credit* were naturally shattered. *Public credit* rests on confidence that the state will allow itself to be exploited by the wolves of finance. But the old state had vanished and the revolution was directed above all against the finance aristocracy. The vibrations of the last European commercial crisis had not yet ceased. Bankruptcy still followed bankruptcy.

Private credit was therefore paralyzed, circulation restricted, production at a standstill before the February revolution broke out. The revolutionary crisis increased the commercial crisis. And if private credit rests on confidence that bourgeois production in the entire scope of its relations, that the bourgeois order, will not be touched, will remain inviolate, what effect must a revolution have had which questioned the basis of bourgeois production and the economic slavery of the proletariat, which set up against the Bourse the sphinx of the Luxembourg? The uprising of the proletariat is the abolition of bourgeois credit, for it is the abolition of bourgeois production and its order. Public credit and private credit are the economic thermometer by which the intensity of a revolution can be measured. *The more they fall, the more the fervor and generative force of the revolution rise.*

The provisional government wanted to strip the republic of its anti-bourgeois appearance. And so it had, above all, to try to peg the *exchange value* of this new form of state, its *quotation* on the Bourse. With the republic currently quoted on the Bourse, private credit necessarily rose again.

In order to allay the very *suspicion* that it would not or could not honor the obligations assumed by the monarchy, in order to build up confidence in bourgeois morality and the republic's capacity to pay, the provisional government took refuge in a boast as undignified as it was childish. *In advance* of the legal date of payment it paid out the interest on the 5 per cent, 4½ per cent, and 4 per cent bonds to the state creditors. The bourgeois aplomb, the self-assurance of the capitalists, suddenly awoke when they saw the anxious haste with which it was sought to buy their confidence.

The financial embarrassment of the provisional government was naturally not lessened by a theatrical stroke which robbed it of its stock of ready cash. The financial pinch could no longer be concealed, and *petty bourgeois, domestic servants, and workers* had to pay for the pleasant surprise which had been prepared for the state creditors.

It was announced that no more money could be drawn on *savings-bank books* for an amount of over one hundred francs. The sums deposited in the savings banks were confiscated and by decree transformed into unredeemable state debt. This embittered the already hard pressed *petty bourgeois* against the republic. Since he received state debt certificates in place of his savings-bank books, he was forced to go to the Bourse in order to sell them and thus deliver himself directly into the hands of the Bourse jobbers, against whom he had made the February revolution.

The finance aristocracy, which ruled under the July monarchy, had its high church in the *Bank*. Just as the Bourse governs state credit, the Bank governs *commercial credit*.

Directly threatened not only in its rule but in its very existence by the February revolution, the Bank tried from the outset to discredit the republic by making the lack of credit general. It suddenly stopped the credits of the bankers, the manufacturers, and the merchants. As it did not immediately call forth a counterrevolution, this maneuver necessarily reacted on the Bank itself. The capitalists drew out the money which they had deposited in the vaults of the Bank. The possessors of bank notes rushed the pay office in order to exchange them for gold and silver.

The provisional government could have forced the Bank into *bankruptcy* without forcible interference, in a legal manner; it would only have had to remain passive and leave the Bank to its fate. The *bankruptcy of the Bank* would have been the deluge which in a trice would have swept from French soil the finance aristocracy, the most powerful and dangerous enemy of the republic, the golden pedestal of the July monarchy. And once the Bank was bankrupt, the bourgeoisie itself would have had to regard it as a last desperate attempt at rescue if the government had formed a national bank and subjected national credit to the control of the nation.

The provisional government, on the contrary, fixed a *compulsory quotation* for the notes of the Bank. It did more. It transformed all provincial banks into branches of the Banque de France and allowed it to cast its net over the whole of France. Later it pledged the *state forests* to the Bank as a guarantee for a loan that it contracted from it. In this way the February revolution directly strengthened and enlarged the bankocracy which it should have overthrown.

Meanwhile the provisional government was writhing under the incubus of a growing deficit. In vain it begged for patriotic sacrifices. Only the workers threw it their alms. Recourse had to be had to a heroic measure, to the imposition of a *new tax*. But who was to be taxed? The Bourse wolves, the bank kings, the state creditors, the *rentiers,* the manufacturers? That was not the way to ingratiate the republic with the bourgeoisie. That would have meant, on the one hand, to endanger state credit and commercial credit while, on the other, attempts were made to purchase them with such great sacrifices and humiliations. But someone had to fork out the cash. Who was sacrificed to bourgeois credit? *Jacques le bonhomme,* the *peasant.*

The provisional government imposed an additional tax of forty-five centimes in the franc on the four direct taxes. The government press cajoled the Paris proletariat into believing that this tax would fall chiefly on the big landed proprietors, on the possessors of the milliard granted by the Restoration. But in truth it hit the *peasant class* above all, i.e., the large majority of the French people. *They had to pay the costs of the February revolution;* in them the counterrevolution gained its main material. The forty-five-centime tax was a question of life and death for the French peasant; he made it a life-and-death question for the republic. From that moment *the republic* meant to the French peasant the *forty-five-centime tax,* and he saw in the Paris proletariat the spendthrift who did himself well at his expense.

Whereas the Revolution of 1789 began by shaking the feudal burdens off the peasants, the Revolution of 1848 announced itself to the rural population by the imposition of a new tax, in order not to endanger capital and to keep its state machine going.

There was only one means by which the provisional government could set aside all these inconveniences and jerk the state out of its old rut—a *declaration of state bankruptcy.* Everyone recalls how Ledru-Rollin in the National Assembly subsequently recited the virtuous indignation with which he repudiated this presumptuous proposal of the Bourse Jew Fould, now French Finance Minister. Fould had handed him the apple from the tree of knowledge.

By honoring the bills drawn on the state by the old bourgeois society the provisional government succumbed to the latter. It had become the hard-pressed debtor of bourgeois society instead of confronting it as the pressing creditor that had to collect the revolutionary debts of many years. It had to consolidate the shaky bourgeois relationships in order to fulfill obligations which are only to be fulfilled within these relationships. Credit became a condition of life for it, and the concessions to the proletariat, the promises made to it, became so many *fetters* which *had* to be struck off. The emancipation of the workers—even as a *phrase*—became an unbearable danger to the new republic, for it was a standing protest against the restoration of credit, which rests on undisturbed and untroubled recognition of the existing economic class relations. Therefore it was necessary *to have done with the workers.*

The February revolution had cast the army out of Paris. The National Guard, i.e., the bourgeoisie in its different gradations, constituted the sole power. Alone, however, it did not feel itself a match for the proletariat. Moreover, it was forced gradually and piecemeal to open its ranks and admit armed proletarians, albeit after the most tenacious resistance and after setting up a hundred different obstacles. There consequently remained but one way out: *to play off one part of the proletariat against the other.*

For this purpose the provisional government formed twenty-four battalions of *Mobile Guards*, each a thousand strong, composed of young men from fifteen to twenty years. They belonged for the most part to the *lumpenproletariat*, which in all big towns forms a mass sharply differentiated from the industrial proletariat, a recruiting ground for thieves and criminals of all kinds, living on the crumbs of society, people without a definite trade, vagabonds, *gens sans aveu et sans feu* [people without tie or home], varying according to the degree of civilization of the nation to which they belong, but never renouncing their *lazzaroni* [dregs] character; at the youthful age at which the provisional government recruited them, thoroughly malleable, as capable of the most heroic deeds and the most exalted sacrifices as of the basest banditry and the foulest corruption. The provisional government paid them one franc fifty centimes a day, i.e., it bought them. It gave them their own uniform, i.e., it made them outwardly distinct from the blouse-wearing workers. In part it had assigned them officers from the standing army as leaders; in part they themselves elected young sons of the bourgeoisie whose rodomontades about death for the fatherland and devotion to the republic captivated them.

And so the Paris proletariat was confronted with an army, drawn from its own midst, of twenty-four thousand young, strong, foolhardy men. It gave cheers for the Mobile Guard on its marches through Paris. It acknowledged it to be its foremost fighters on the barricades. It regarded it as the *proletarian* guard, in contradistinction to the bourgeois National Guard. Its error was pardonable.

Besides the Mobile Guard, the government decided to rally round itself an army of industrial workers. A hundred thousand workers, thrown on the streets by the crisis and the revolution, were enrolled by the Minister Marie in so-called national workshops. Under this grandiose name was hidden nothing but the employment of the workers on tedious, monotonous, unproductive *earthworks* at a wage of twenty-three sous. *English workhouses in the open*—that is what these national workshops were. The provisional government believed that it had formed, in them, *a second proletarian army against the workers themselves.* But the bourgeoisie was mistaken in the national workshops, just as the workers were mistaken in the Mobile Guard. It had created an *army for mutiny.*

But one purpose was achieved.

Ateliers nationaux—that was the name of the people's workshops, which Louis Blanc preached in the Luxembourg Palace. Marie's *ateliers,* devised in direct *antagonism* to the Luxembourg, offered occasion, thanks to the common name, for a plot of errors worthy of the Spanish comedy of servants. The provisional government itself surreptitiously spread the report that these national workshops were the discovery of Louis Blanc, and this seemed the more plausible because Louis Blanc, the prophet of the national workshops, was a member of the provisional government. And in the half-naïve, half-intentional confusion of the Paris bourgeoisie, in the artificially molded opinion of France and of Europe, these workhouses were the first realization of socialism, which was put into the pillory with them.

In their appellation, though not in their content, the *national workshops* were the embodied protest of the proletariat against bourgeois industry, bourgeois credit, and the bourgeois republic. The whole hate of the bourgeoisie was therefore turned upon them. It had found in them the point against which it could direct the attack, as soon as it was strong enough to break openly with the February illusions. All the discontent, all the ill-humor of the *petty bourgeois,* too, was directed against these national workshops, the common target. With real fury they reckoned up the sums that the proletarian loafers swallowed up, while their own situation was becoming daily more unbearable. "A state pension for sham labor, so that's socialism!" they grumbled to themselves. They sought the reason for their misery in the national workshops, the declamations of the Luxembourg, the street demonstrations of the Paris workers. And no one was more fanatic about the alleged machinations of the communists than the petty bourgeoisie, who hovered hopelessly on the brink of bankruptcy.

Thus in the approaching melee between bourgeoisie and proletariat all the advantages, all the decisive posts, all the middle sections of society were in the hands of the bourgeoisie at the same time that the waves of the February revolution rose high over the whole Continent and each new post brought a new bulletin of revolution, now from Italy, now from Germany, now from the remotest parts of Southeastern Europe, and maintained the general ecstasy of the people, giving it constant testimony of a victory that it had already forfeited.

March 17 and *April 16* were the first skirmishes in the big class struggle which the bourgeois republic hid under its wings.

March 17 revealed the ambiguous situation of the proletariat, which permitted of no decisive act. Its demonstration originally pursued the purpose of pushing the provisional government back onto the path of revolution, of effecting the exclusion of its bourgeois members, according to circumstances, and of compelling the postponement of the election days for the National Assembly and the National Guard. But on March 16 the bourgeoisie represented in the National Guard staged a hostile demonstration against the provisional government. With the cry: "*À bas Ledru-Rollin!*" it surged to the Hôtel de Ville. And the people were forced, on March 17, to shout: "Long live Ledru-Rollin! Long live the provisional government!" They were forced to take sides *against* the bourgeoisie in support of the bourgeois republic, which seemed to them to be in danger. They strengthened the provisional government instead of subordinating it to themselves. March 17 went off in a melodramatic scene, and whereas the Paris proletariat on this day once more displayed its giant body the bourgeoisie, both inside and outside the provisional government, was all the more determined to smash it.

April 16 was a *misunderstanding* engineered by the provisional government in alliance with the bourgeoisie. The workers had gathered in great numbers in the Field of Mars and in the Hippodrome, preparatory to making their selections for the general staff of the National Guard. Suddenly throughout Paris, from one end to the other, a rumor spread as quickly as lightning, to the effect that the workers had met armed in the Field of Mars, under the leadership of Louis Blanc, Blanqui, Cabet, and Raspail, in order to march thence on the Hôtel de Ville, overthrow the provisional government, and proclaim a communist government. The general alarm is sounded—Ledru-Rollin, Marrast, and Lamartine later contended for the honor of having initiated this—and in an hour a hundred thousand men are under arms; the Hôtel de Ville is occupied at all points by the National Guard; the cry: "Down with the communists! Down with Louis Blanc, with Blanqui, with Raspail, with Cabet!" thunders throughout Paris. Innumerable deputations pay homage to the provisional government, all ready to save the fatherland and society. When the workers finally appear before the Hôtel de Ville, in order to hand over to the provisional government a patriotic collection which they have made in the Field of Mars, they learn to their amazement that bourgeois Paris has defeated their shadow in a very carefully calculated sham battle. The terrible attempt of April 16 furnished the excuse *for recalling the army to Paris*—the real purpose of the clumsily staged comedy—and for the reactionary federalist demonstrations in the provinces.

On May 4 the *National Assembly*, the result of the *direct general elections*, convened. Universal suffrage did not possess the magic power which republicans of the old school had ascribed to it. They saw in the whole of France, at least in the majority of Frenchmen, *citoyens* with the same interests, the same understanding, etc. This was their *cult of the people*. Instead of their *imaginary* people the elections brought the *real* people to the light of day, i.e., representatives of the different classes into which it falls. We have seen why peasants and petty bourgeois had to vote under the leadership of a bourgeoisie spoiling for a fight and of big landowners frantic for restoration. But if universal suffrage was not the miracle-working magic wand for which the republican worthies had taken it, it possessed the incomparably higher merit of unchaining the class struggle, of letting the various middle sections of bourgeois society rapidly get over their illusions and disappointments, of tossing all the sections of the exploiting class at one throw to the apex of the state, and thus tearing from them their treacherous mask, whereas the monarchy with its property qualifications let only certain sections of the bourgeoisie compromise themselves, allowing the others to lie hidden behind the scenes and surrounding them with the halo of a common opposition.

In the Constituent National Assembly, which met on May 4, the *bourgeois republicans*, the republicans of the *National*, had the upper hand. Even Legitimists and Orleanists at first dared to show themselves only under the mask of bourgeois republicanism. The fight against the proletariat could be undertaken only in the name of the republic.

The republic dates from May 4, not from February 25, i.e., the republic recognized by the French people; it is not the republic which the Paris proletariat thrust upon the provisional government, not the republic with social institutions, not the vision which hovered before the fighters on the barricades. The republic proclaimed by the National Assembly, the sole legitimate republic, is a republic which is no revolutionary weapon against the bourgeois order, but rather its political reconstitution, the political reconsolidation of bourgeois society, in a word, *a bourgeois republic*. This contention resounded from the tribune of the National Assembly, and in the entire republican and antirepublican bourgeois press it found its echo.

And we have seen how the February republic in reality was not and could not be other than a *bourgeois* republic; how the provisional government, nevertheless, was forced by the immediate pressure of the proletariat to announce it as a *republic with social institutions*; how the Paris proletariat was still incapable of going beyond the bourgeois republic otherwise than in its *fancy*, in *imagination*; how everywhere it acted in its service when it really came to action; how the promises made to it became an unbearable danger for the new republic; how the whole life process of the provisional government was comprised in a continuous fight against the demands of the proletariat.

In the National Assembly all France sat in judgment upon the Paris proletariat. The Assembly broke immediately with the social illusions of the February revolution; it roundly proclaimed the *bourgeois republic*, nothing but the bourgeois republic. It at once excluded the representatives of the proletariat, Louis Blanc and Albert, from the Executive Commission appointed by it; it threw out the proposal of a special Labor Ministry, and received with wild applause the statement of the Minister Trélat: "The question now is merely one of *bringing labor back to its old conditions*."

But all this was not enough. The February republic was won by the workers with the passive support of the bourgeoisie. The proletarians rightly regarded themselves as the victors of February, and they made the arrogant claims of victors. They had to be vanquished in the streets, they had to be shown that they were worsted as soon as they did not fight *with* the bourgeoisie, but *against* the bourgeoisie. Just as the February republic, with its socialist concessions, required a battle of the proletariat, united with the bourgeoisie, against monarchy, so a second battle was necessary in order to sever the republic from the socialist concessions, in order to officially work out the *bourgeois republic* as dominant. Arms in hand, the bourgeoisie had to refute the demands of the proletariat. And the real birthplace of the bourgeois republic is not the *February victory*; it is the *June defeat*.

The proletariat hastened the decision when, on the fifteenth of May, it pushed its way into the National Assembly, sought in vain to recapture its revolutionary influence, and only delivered its energetic leaders to the jailers of the bourgeoisie. "*Il faut en finir* [This situation must end]!" With this cry the National Assembly gave vent to its determination to force the proletariat into a decisive struggle. The Executive Commission issued a series of provocative decrees, such as that prohibiting congregations of people, etc. The workers were directly provoked, insulted, and derided from the tribune of the Constituent National Assembly. But the real point of the attack was, as we have seen, the national workshops. The Constituent Assembly imperiously pointed these out to the Executive Commission, which only waited to hear its own plan proclaimed the command of the National Assembly.

The Executive Commission began by making admission to the national workshops more difficult, by turning the day wage into a piece wage, by banishing workers not born in Paris to Sologne, ostensibly for the construction of earthworks. These earthworks were only a rhetorical formula with which to gloss over their exile, as the workers, returning disillusioned, announced to their comrades. Finally, on June 21, a decree appeared in the *Moniteur* which ordered the forcible expulsion of all unmarried workers from the national workshops, or their enrollment in the army.

The workers were left no choice; they had to starve or start to fight. They answered on June 22 with the tremendous insurrection in which the first great battle was fought between the two classes that split modern society. It was a fight for the preservation or annihilation of the *bourgeois* order. The veil that shrouded the republic was torn asunder.

It is well known how the workers, with unexampled bravery and ingenuity, without leaders, without a common plan, without means, and, for the most part, lacking weapons, held in check for five days the army, the Mobile Guard, the Paris National Guard, and the National Guard that streamed in from the provinces. It is well known how the bourgeoisie compensated itself for the mortal anguish it suffered by unheard-of brutality, massacring over three thousand prisoners.

The official representatives of French democracy were steeped in republican ideology to such an extent that it was only some weeks later that they began to have an inkling of the significance of the June fight. They were stupefied by the gunpowder smoke in which their fantastic republic had dissolved.

The immediate impression which the news of the June defeat made on us, the reader will allow us to describe in the words of the *Neue Rheinische Zeitung*:

> The last official remnant of the February revolution,

the Executive Commission, has melted away, like an apparition, before the seriousness of events. The fireworks of Lamartine have turned into the war rockets of Cavaignac. *Fraternité*, the fraternity of antagonistic classes, of which one exploits the other, this *fraternité*, proclaimed in February, written in capital letters on the brow of Paris, on every prison, on every barracks—its true, unadulterated, its prosaic expression is *civil war*, civil war in its most frightful form, the war of labor and capital. This fraternity flamed in front of all the windows of Paris on the evening of June 25, when the Paris of the bourgeoisie was illuminated, while the Paris of the proletariat burned, bled, moaned. Fraternity endured just as long as the interests of the bourgeoisie were in fraternity with the interests of the proletariat. Pedants of the old revolutionary traditions of 1793; socialist doctrinaires who begged at the doors of the bourgeoisie on behalf of the people and were allowed to preach long sermons and to compromise themselves as long as the proletarian lion had to be lulled to sleep; republicans who demanded the old bourgeois order in its entirety, with the exception of the crowned head; adherents of the dynasty among the opposition upon whom accident foisted the overthrow of the dynasty instead of a change of ministers; Legitimists who did not want to cast aside the livery but to change its cut—these were the allies with whom the people made its February.

The February revolution was the *beautiful* revolution, the revolution of universal sympathy, because the antagonisms which had flared up in it against the monarchy slumbered peacefully side by side, still *undeveloped*, because the social struggle which formed its background had won only an airy existence, an existence of phrases, of words. The *June revolution* is the *ugly* revolution, the repulsive revolution, because deeds have taken the place of phrases, because the republic uncovered the head of the monster itself by striking off the crown that shielded and concealed it.

"*Order!*" was the battle cry of Guizot. "*Order!*" cried Sebastiani, the follower of Guizot, when Warsaw became Russian. "*Order!*" shouted Cavaignac, the brutal echo of the French National Assembly and of the republican bourgeoisie. "*Order!*" thundered his grapeshot as it ripped up the body of the proletariat. None of the numerous revolutions of the French bourgeoisie since 1789 was an attack on *order*, for they allowed the rule of the class, they allowed the slavery of the workers, they allowed the *bourgeois* order to endure, no matter how often the political form of this rule and of this slavery changed. June has violated this order. Woe to June! (*N. Rh.* Z., June 29, 1848.)

"Woe to June!" re-echoes Europe.

The Paris proletariat was *forced* into the June insurrection by the bourgeoisie. In this lay its doom. Its immediate, avowed needs did not drive it to engage in a fight for the forcible overthrow of the bourgeoisie, nor was it equal to this task. The *Moniteur* had to inform it officially that the time was past when the republic saw any occasion to bow and scrape to its illusions, and only its defeat convinced it of the truth that the slightest improvement in its position remains a *utopia within* the bourgeois republic, a utopia that becomes a crime as soon as it wants to realize it. In place of its demands, exuberant in form, but petty and even bourgeois still in content, the concession of which it wanted to wring from the February republic, there appeared the bold slogan of revolutionary struggle: *Overthrow of the bourgeoisie! Dictatorship of the working class!*

By making its burial place the birthplace of the *bourgeois republic* the proletariat compelled the latter to come out forthwith in its pure form as the state whose admitted object it is to perpetuate the rule of capital, the slavery of labor. Having constantly before its eyes the scarred, irreconcilable, invincible enemy—invincible because his existence is the condition of the bourgeoisie's own life—bourgeois rule, freed from all fetters, was bound to turn immediately into *bourgeois terrorism*. With the proletariat removed for the time being from the stage and bourgeois dictatorship recognized officially, the middle sections of bourgeois society, the petty bourgeoisie and the peasant class, had to adhere more and more closely to the proletariat as their position became more unbearable and their antagonism to the bourgeoisie more acute. Just as earlier they had to find the cause of their misery in its upsurge, so now in its defeat.

The June insurrection raised the self-assurance of the bourgeoisie all over the Continent, and caused it to league itself openly with the feudal monarchy against the people; but who was the first victim of this alliance? The Continental bourgeoisie itself. The June defeat prevented it from consolidating its rule, and from bringing the people, half satisfied and half out of humor, to a standstill at the lowest stage of the bourgeois revolution.

Finally, the defeat of June divulged to the despotic powers of Europe the secret that France must under all conditions maintain peace abroad in order to be able to wage civil war at home. Thus the peoples who had begun the fight for their national independence were abandoned to the superior power of Russia, Austria, and Prussia, but, at the same time, the fate of these national revolutions was subordinated to the fate of the proletarian revolution, and they were robbed of their apparent independence, their independence of the great social revolution. The Hungarian shall not be free, nor the Pole, nor the Italian, as long as the worker remains a slave!

Finally, with the victories of the Holy Alliance, Europe has taken on a form that makes every fresh proletarian upheaval in France directly coincide with a *world war*. The new French revolution is forced to leave its national soil forthwith and *conquer the European terrain*, on which alone the social revolution of the nineteenth century can be accomplished.

Thus only the June defeat has created all the conditions under which France can seize the *initiative* of the European revolution. Only after baptism in the blood of the *June insurgents* did the tricolor become the flag of the European revolution—the *red flag*.

And we exclaim: "*The revolution is dead! Long live the revolution!*"

London, January 1850

II

JUNE 13, 1849

February 25, 1848, had granted the *republic* to France, June 25 thrust the *revolution* upon her. And revolution, after June, meant *overthrow of bourgeois society*, whereas before February it had meant *overthrow of the form of government*.

The June fight had been led by the *republican* faction of the bourgeoisie; with victory, political power inevitably fell to its share. The state of siege laid Paris, gagged, unresisting, at its feet, and in the provinces there was a moral state of siege, the threatening, brutal arrogance of the victorious bourgeoisie and the unleashed property fanaticism of the peasants. No danger, therefore, from *below!*

The crash of the revolutionary force of the workers was simultaneously a crash of the political influence of the *democratic republicans*, i.e., of the republicans in the sense of the *petty bourgeoisie*, who were represented in the Executive Commission by Ledru-Rollin, in the Constituent National Assembly by the party of the Mountain, and in the press by the *Réforme*. Together with the bourgeois republicans they had conspired on April 16 against the proletariat, together with them they had warred against it in the June days. Thus they themselves blasted the background against which their party stood out as a power, for the petty bourgeoisie can preserve a revolutionary attitude to the bourgeoisie only as long as the proletariat stands behind it. They were dismissed. The sham alliance concluded with them reluctantly and with mental reservations during the epoch of the provisional government and the Executive Commission was openly broken by the bourgeois republicans. Spurned and repulsed as allies, they sank down to subordinate henchmen of the tricolormen, from whom they could not wring any concessions, but whose domination they had to support whenever it, and with it the republic, seemed to be put in jeopardy by the anti-republican bourgeois factions. Lastly, these factions, the Orleanists and the Legitimists, were from the very beginning in a minority in the Constituent National Assembly. Before the June days they dared to react only under the mask of bourgeois republicanism; the June victory allowed for a moment the whole of bourgeois France to greet its deliverer in Cavaignac, and when, shortly after the June days, the anti-republicans reconstituted themselves as an independent party, the military dictatorship and the state of siege in Paris permitted it to put out its antennae only very timidly and cautiously.

Since 1830 the *bourgeois republican* faction, with its writers, its speakers, its men of talent and ambition, its deputies, generals, bankers, and lawyers, had grouped itself round a Parisian journal, the *National.* In the provinces this journal had its branch newspapers. The coterie of the *National* was the *dynasty of the tricolor republic.* It immediately took possession of all state dignities, of the ministries, the prefecture of police, the post office directorship, the positions of prefect, the higher army officers' posts now become vacant. At the head of the executive power stood its general, *Cavaignac;* its editor-in-chief, Marrast, became permanent president of the Constituent National Assembly. As master of ceremonies he at the same time did the honors, in his salons, of the respectable republic.

Even revolutionary French writers, awed, as it were, by the republican tradition, have strengthened the mistaken belief that the royalists dominated the Constituent National Assembly. On the contrary, after the June days the Constituent Assembly remained the *exclusive representative of bourgeois republicanism,* and it emphasized this aspect all the more resolutely, the more the influence of the tricolor republicans collapsed outside the Assembly. If the question was one of maintaining the *form* of the bourgeois republic, then the Assembly had the votes of the democratic republicans at its disposal; if one of maintaining the *content,* then even its mode of speech no longer separated it from the royalist bourgeois factions. For it is the interests of the bourgeoisie, the material conditions of its class rule and class exploitation that form the content of the bourgeois republic.

Therefore it was not royalism but bourgeois republicanism that was realized in the life and work of this Constituent Assembly, which in the end did not die, and was not killed, but simply decayed.

For the entire duration of its rule, as long as it gave its performance of state on the proscenium, an unbroken sacrificial feast was being staged in the background—the continual sentencing by courts-martial of the imprisoned June insurgents or their deportation without trial. The Constituent Assembly had the tact to admit that in the June insurgents it was not judging criminals but wiping out enemies.

The first act of the Constituent National Assembly was the setting up of a *commission of inquiry* into the events of June and of May 15, and into the part played by the socialist and democratic party leaders during these days. The inquiry was directly aimed at Louis Blanc, Ledru-Rollin, and Caussidière. The bourgeois republicans burned with impatience to rid themselves of these rivals. They could have entrusted the venting of their spleen to no more suitable subject than M. Odilon Barrot, the former chief of the dynastic opposition, the incarnation of liberalism, the *nullité grave*, the profoundly shallow person who not only had a dynasty to revenge, but even had to settle accounts with the revolutionaries for thwarting his premiership. A sure guarantee of his relentlessness. This Barrot was therefore appointed chairman of the commission of inquiry, and he constructed a complete legal process against the February revolution, which may be summarized thus: March 17, *demonstration*; April 16, *conspiracy*; May 15, *attempt*; June 23, *civil war!* Why did he not stretch his erudite criminologist's researches as far back as February 24? The *Journal des Débats* answered: February 24—that is the *foundation of Rome*. The origin of states gets lost in a myth, in which one may believe, but which one may not discuss. Louis Blanc and Caussidière were handed over to the courts. The National Assembly completed the work of purging itself which it had begun on May 15.

The plan formed by the provisional government, and again taken up by Goudchaux, of taxing capital—in the form of a mortgage tax—was rejected by the Constituent Assembly; the law that limited the working day to ten hours was repealed; imprisonment for debt was once more introduced; the large section of the French population that can neither read nor write was excluded from jury service. Why not from the franchise also? Journals again had to deposit caution money; the right of association was restricted.

But in their haste to give back to the old bourgeois relationships their old guarantees, and to wipe out every trace left behind by the waves of the revolution, the bourgeois republicans encountered a resistance which threatened them with unexpected danger.

No one had fought more fanatically in the June days for the salvation of property and the restoration of credit than the Parisian petty bourgeois—keepers of cafés and restaurants, *marchands de vins*, small traders, shopkeepers, handicraftsmen, etc. The shopkeeper had pulled himself together and marched against the barricades in order to restore the traffic which leads from the streets into the shop. But behind the barricade stood the customers and the debtors; before it, the creditors of the shop. And when the barricades were thrown down and the workers were crushed and the shopkeepers, drunk with victory, rushed back to their shops, they found the entrance barred by a savior of property, an official agent of credit, who presented them with threatening letters: Overdue promissory note! Overdue house rent! Overdue bond! Overwhelmed shop! Overwhelmed shopkeeper!

Salvation of property! But the house in which they lived was not their property; the shop which they kept was not their property; the commodities in which they dealt were not their property. Neither their business nor the plate from which they ate, nor the bed on which they slept, belonged to them any longer. It was precisely from them that *this property had to be saved*—for the house owner who let the house, for the banker who discounted the promissory note, for the capitalist who made the advances in cash, for the manufacturer who entrusted the sale of his commodities to these retailers, for the wholesale dealer who had credited the raw materials to these handicraftsmen. *Restoration of credit!* But credit, having regained strength, proved itself a vigorous and jealous god, for it turned the debtor who could not pay out of his four walls, together with wife and child, surrendered his sham property to capital, and threw the man himself into the debtors' prison, which had once more reared its head threateningly over the corpses of the June insurgents.

The petty bourgeois saw with horror that by striking down the workers they had delivered themselves unresisting into the hands of their creditors. Their bankruptcy, which since February had been dragging on in chronic fashion and had been apparently ignored, was openly declared after June. . . .

For a moment the army and the peasant class had believed that, simultaneously with the military dictatorship, war abroad and *gloire* had been placed on the order of the day in France. But Cavaignac was not the dictatorship of the saber over bourgeois society; he was the dictatorship of the bourgeoisie through the saber. And of the soldier they now required only the gendarme. Under the stern features of antique-republican resignation Cavaignac concealed humdrum submission to the humiliating conditions of his bourgeois office. "*L'argent n'a pas de maître* [Money has no master]!" He, as well as the Constituent Assembly in general, idealized this old election cry of the *tiers état* [Third Estate] by translating it into political speech: "The bourgeoisie has no king; the true form of its rule is the republic."

And the "great organic work" of the Constituent National Assembly consisted in working out this *form*, in producing a republican *constitution*. The re-christening of the Christian calendar as a republican one, of the saintly Bartholomew as the saintly Robespierre, made no more change in the wind and weather than this constitution made or was intended to make in bourgeois society. . . .

The first draft of the constitution, made before the June days, still contained the *droit au travail*, the right to work, the first clumsy formula wherein the revolutionary aspirations of the proletariat are summarized. It was transformed into the *droit à l'assistance*, the right to public relief; and what modern state does not feed its paupers in some form or other? The right to work is, in the bourgeois sense, an absurdity, a miserable, pious wish. But behind the right to work stands the power over capital; behind the power over capital the appropriation of the means of production, their subjection to the associated working class, and, therefore, the abolition of wage labor as well as of capital and of their mutual relations. Behind the *right to work* stood the June insurrection. The Constituent Assembly, which in fact put the revolutionary proletariat *hors la loi*, outside the law, had, on principle, to throw the *proletariat's* formula out of the constitution, the law of laws, had to pronounce its anathema upon the right to work. But it did not stop there. As Plato banned the poets from his republic, so it banished forever from its republic—the *progressive tax*. And the progressive tax is not only a bourgeois measure, which can be carried out within the existing relations of production to a greater or lesser degree; it was the only means of binding the middle strata of bourgeois society to the "*respectable*" republic, of reducing the state debt, of holding the anti-republican majority of the bourgeoisie in check. . . .

The most comprehensive contradiction of this constitution, however, consists in the following: The classes whose social slavery the constitution is to perpetuate, proletariat, peasantry, petty bourgeoisie, it puts in possession of political power through universal suffrage. And from the class whose old social power it sanctions, the bourgeoisie, it withdraws the political guarantees of this power. It forces the political rule of the bourgeoisie into democratic conditions, which at every moment help the hostile classes to victory and jeopardize the very foundations of bourgeois society. From the former classes it demands that they should not go forward from political to social emancipation; from the others that they should not go back from social to political restoration.

These contradictions perturbed the bourgeois republicans but little. To the extent that they ceased to be *indispensable*—and they were indispensable only as the protagonists of the old society against the revolutionary proletariat—they fell, a few weeks after their victory, from the position of a *party* to that of a *coterie*. And they treated the constitution as a big *intrigue*. What was to be constituted in it was, above all, the rule of the coterie. . . .

December 10, 1848, was the day of the *peasant insurrection*. Only from this day does the February of the

French peasants date. The symbol that expressed their entry into the revolutionary movement, clumsily cunning, knavishly naïve, doltishly sublime, a calculated superstition, a pathetic burlesque, a cleverly stupid anachronism, a world-historic piece of buffoonery, and an undecipherable hieroglyphic for the understanding of the civilized—this symbol bore the unmistakable features of the class that represents barbarism within civilization. The republic had announced itself to this class with the *tax collector*; it announced itself to the republic with the *emperor*. Napoleon was the only man who had exhaustively represented the interests and the imagination of the peasant class, newly created in 1789. By writing his name on the front page of the republic it declared war abroad and the enforcing of its class interests at home. Napoleon was to the peasants not a person but a program. With banners, with beat of drums and blare of trumpets, they marched to the polling booths, shouting: "*Plus d'impôts, à bas les riches, à bas la république, vive l'empereur* [No more taxes, down with the rich, down with the republic, long live the emperor]!" Behind the emperor was hidden the peasant war. The republic that they voted down was the *republic of the rich*.

December 10 was the *coup d'état* of the peasants, which overthrew the existing government. And from that day on, when they had taken a government from France and given one to her, their eyes were fixed steadily on Paris. For a moment active heroes of the revolutionary drama, they could no longer be forced back into the passive and spineless role of the chorus.

The other classes helped to complete the election victory of the peasants. To the *proletariat* the election of Napoleon meant the deposition of Cavaignac, the overthrow of the Constituent Assembly, the dismissal of bourgeois republicanism, the rescission of the June victory. To the *petty bourgeoisie* Napoleon meant the rule of the debtors over the creditors. For the majority of the *big bourgeoisie* the election of Napoleon meant an open breach with the faction of which it had had to make use, for a moment, against the revolution, but which became intolerable to it as soon as this faction sought to consolidate the position of the moment into a constitutional position. Napoleon in place of Cavaignac meant to the majority the monarchy in place of the republic, the beginning of the royalist restoration, a shy hint at Orleans, the lily hidden beneath the violet. Lastly, the *army* voted for Napoleon against the Mobile Guard, against the peace idyl, for war.

Thus it happened, as the *Neue Rheinische Zeitung* stated, that the most simple-minded man in France acquired the most multifarious significance. Just because he was nothing he could signify everything save himself. . . .

III

CONSEQUENCES OF JUNE 13, 1849

Little by little we have seen peasants, petty bourgeois, the middle classes in general, stepping alongside the proletariat, driven into open antagonism to the official republic and treated by it as antagonists. *Revolt against bourgeois dictatorship, need of a change in society, adherence to democratic-republican institutions as organs of their movement, grouping round the proletariat as the decisive revolutionary power*—these are the common characteristics of the *so-called party of social democracy, the party of the red republic*. This *party of anarchy*, as its opponents christened it, is no less a coalition of different interests than the *party of order*. From the smallest reform of the old social disorder to the overthrow of the old social order, from bourgeois liberalism to revolutionary terrorism—as far apart as this lie the extremes that form the starting point and the finishing point of the party of anarchy. . . .

So swiftly had the march of the revolution ripened conditions, that the friends of reform of all shades, the most moderate claims of the middle classes, were compelled to group themselves round the banner of the most extreme party of revolution, round the *red flag*.

Yet, manifold as the *socialism* of the different large sections of the party of anarchy was, according to the economic conditions and the total revolutionary requirements of their class or fraction of a class arising out of these, in one point it is in harmony: in proclaiming itself as *the means of emancipating the proletariat* and the emancipation of the latter as its *object*. Deliberate deception on the part of some; self-deception on the part of the others, who give out the world transformed according to their own needs as the best world for all, as the realization of all revolutionary claims, and the abolition of all revolutionary collisions.

Behind the *general* socialist phrases of the "*party of anarchy*," which sound rather alike, there is concealed the socialism of the *National*, of the *Presse* and the *Siècle*, which more or less consistently wants to overthrow the rule of the finance aristocracy and to free industry and trade from their hitherto existing fetters. This is the socialism of industry, of trade, and of agriculture, whose bosses in the party of order deny these interests, in so far as they no longer coincide with their private monopolies. Socialism proper, *petty-bourgeois socialism*, socialism *par excellence*, is distinct from this *bourgeois socialism*, to which, as to every variety of socialism, a section of the workers and petty bourgeois naturally rallies. Capital hounds this class chiefly as its *creditor*, so it demands *credit institutions*; capital crushes it by *competition*, so it demands *associations* supported by the state; capital overwhelms it by *concentration*, so it demands *progressive taxes*, limitations on inheritance, taking over of large construction projects by the state, and other measures that *forcibly stem the growth of capital*. Since it dreams of the peaceful achievement of its socialism—allowing, perhaps, for a second February revolution, lasting a brief day or so—the coming historical process naturally appears to it as an *application of systems*, which the thinkers of society, whether in companies or as individual inventors, devise or have devised. Thus they become the eclectics or adepts of the existing socialist *systems*, of *doctrinaire socialism*, which was the theoretical expression of the proletariat only as long as it had not yet developed further, into a free historical movement of its own.

While this *utopia, doctrinaire socialism*, which subordinates the total movement to one of its moments, which puts in place of common, social production the brainwork of individual pedants and, above all, in fantasy does away with the revolutionary struggle of the classes and its requirements by small conjurer's tricks or great sentimentality; while this doctrinaire socialism, which at bottom only idealizes present society, takes a picture of it without shadows and wants to achieve its ideal athwart the realities of society; while the proletariat surrenders this socialism to the petty bourgeoisie; while the struggle of the different socialist leaders among themselves sets forth each of the so-called systems as a pretentious adherence to one of the transit points of the social revolution as against another—the *proletariat* rallies more and more round *revolutionary socialism*, round *communism*, for which the bourgeoisie has itself invented the name of *Blanqui*. This socialism is the *declaration of the permanence of the revolution*, the *class dictatorship* of the proletariat as the necessary transit point to the *abolition of class differences generally*, to the abolition of all the production relations on which they rest, to the abolition of all the social relations that correspond to these production relations, to the revolutionizing of all the ideas that result from these social relations. . . .

XIV. *Excerpts from* The Eighteenth Brumaire of Louis Bonaparte

KARL MARX

AUTHOR'S PREFACE TO THE SECOND EDITION

My friend *Joseph Weydemeyer*,[1] whose death was so untimely, intended to publish a political weekly in New York starting from January 1, 1852. He invited me to provide this weekly with a history of the *coup d'état*. Down to the middle of February, I accordingly wrote him weekly articles under the title, *The Eighteenth Brumaire of Louis Bonaparte*. Meanwhile Weydemeyer's original plan had fallen through. Instead in the spring of 1852 he began to publish a monthly, *Die Revolution*, the first number of which consists of my *Eighteenth Brumaire*. A few hundred copies of this found their way into Germany at that time, without, however, getting into the actual book trade. A German publisher of extremely radical pretensions to whom I offered the sale of my book was most virtuously horrified at a "presumption" so "contrary to the times."

From the above facts it will be seen that the present work took shape under the immediate pressure of events and its historical material does not extend beyond the month of February (1852). Its re-publication now is due in part to the demand of the book trade, in part to the urgent requests of my friends in Germany.

Of the writings dealing with the same subject approximately *at the same time* as mine, only two deserve notice:

[1] Military commandant of the St. Louis district during the American Civil War. [Note by Marx.]

Victor Hugo's *Napoleon the Little* and Proudhon's *Coup d'État*.

Victor Hugo confines himself to bitter and witty invective against the responsible publisher of the *coup d'état*. The event itself appears in his work like a bolt from the blue. He sees in it only the violent act of a single individual. He does not notice that he makes this individual great instead of little by ascribing to him a personal power of initiative such as would be without parallel in world history. Proudhon, for his part, seeks to represent the *coup d'état* as the result of an antecedent historical development. Unnoticeably, however, his historical construction of the *coup d'état* becomes a historical *apologia* for its hero. Thus he falls into the error of our so-called *objective* historians. I, on the contrary, demonstrate how the *class struggle* in France created circumstances and relationships that made it possible for a grotesque mediocrity to play a hero's part.

A revision of the present work would have robbed it of its peculiar coloring. Accordingly, I have confined myself to mere correction of printer's errors and to striking out allusions now no longer intelligible.

The concluding words of my work: "But when the imperial mantle finally falls on the shoulders of Louis Bonaparte, the bronze statue of Napoleon will crash from the top of the Vendôme Column," have already been fulfilled.

Colonel Charras opened the attack on the Napoleon cult in his work on the campaign of 1815. Subsequently, and particularly in the last few years, French literature made an end of the Napoleon legend with the weapons of historical research, of criticism, of satire, and of wit. Outside France this violent breach with the traditional popular belief, this tremendous mental revolution, has been little noticed and still less understood.

Lastly, I hope that my work will contribute towards eliminating the school-taught phrase now current, particularly in Germany, of so-called *Caesarism*. In this superficial historical analogy the main point is forgotten, namely, that in ancient Rome the class struggle took place only within a privileged minority, between the free rich and the free poor, while the great productive mass of the population, the slaves, formed the purely passive pedestal for these combatants. People forget *Sismondi's* significant saying: The Roman proletariat lived at the expense of society, while modern society lives at the expense of the proletariat. With so complete a difference between the material, economic conditions of the ancient and the modern class struggles, the political figures produced by them can likewise have no more in common with one another than the Archbishop of Canterbury has with the high priest Samuel.

Karl Marx

London, June 23, 1869

THE EIGHTEENTH BRUMAIRE OF LOUIS BONAPARTE

Hegel remarks somewhere that all facts and personages of great importance in world history occur, as it were, twice. He forgot to add: the first time as tragedy, the second as farce. Caussidière for Danton, Louis Blanc for Robespierre, the *Montagne* of 1848 to 1851 for the *Montagne* of 1793 to 1795, the nephew for the uncle. And the same caricature occurs in the circumstances attending the second edition of the eighteenth Brumaire!

Men make their own history, but they do not make it just as they please; they do not make it under circumstances chosen by themselves, but under circumstances directly encountered, given, and transmitted from the past. The tradition of all the dead generations weighs like a nightmare on the brain of the living. And just when they seem engaged in revolutionizing themselves and things, in creating something that has never yet existed, precisely in such periods of revolutionary crisis they anxiously conjure up the spirits of the past to their service and borrow from them names, battle cries, and costumes in order to present the new scene of world history in this time-honored disguise and this borrowed language. Thus Luther donned the mask of the apostle Paul, the Revolution of 1789 to 1814 draped itself alternately as the Roman Republic and the Roman Empire, and the Revolution of 1848 knew nothing better to do than to parody, now 1789, now the revolutionary tradition of 1793 to 1795. In like manner a beginner who has learned a new language always translates it back into his mother tongue, but he has assimilated the spirit of the new language and can freely express himself in it only when he finds his way in it without recalling the old and forgets his native tongue in the use of the new.

Consideration of this conjuring up of the dead of world history reveals at once a salient difference. Camille Desmoulins, Danton, Robespierre, St. Just, Napoleon, the heroes as well as the parties and the masses of the old French Revolution performed the task of their time in Roman costume and with Roman phrases, the task of unchaining and setting up modern *bourgeois* society. The first ones knocked the feudal basis to pieces and mowed off the feudal heads which had grown on it. The other created inside France the conditions under which alone free competition could be developed, parceled landed property exploited, and the unchained industrial productive power of the nation employed; and beyond the French borders he everywhere swept the feudal institutions away, so far as was necessary to furnish bourgeois society in France with a suitable up-to-date environment on the European continent. The new social formation once established, the antediluvian colossi disappeared and with them resurrected Romanity—the Brutuses, Gracchi, Publicolas, the tribunes, the senators, and Caesar himself. Bourgeois society in its sober reality had begotten its true interpreters and mouthpieces in the Says, Cousins, Royer-Collards, Benjamin Constants, and Guizots; its real military leaders sat behind the office desks, and the hogsheaded Louis XVIII was its political chief. Wholly absorbed in the production of wealth and in peaceful competitive struggle, it no longer comprehended that ghosts from the days of Rome had watched over its cradle. But unheroic as bourgeois society is, it nevertheless took heroism, sacrifice, terror, civil war, and battles of peoples to bring it into being. And in the classically austere traditions of the Roman Republic its gladiators found the ideals and the art forms, the self-deceptions that they needed in order to conceal from themselves the bourgeois limitations of the content of their struggles and to keep their enthusiasm on the high plane of the great historical tragedy. Similarly, at another stage of development, a century earlier, Cromwell and the English people had borrowed speech, passions, and illusions from the Old Testament for their bourgeois revolution. When the real aim had been achieved, when the bourgeois transformation of English society had been accomplished, Locke supplanted Habakkuk.

Thus the awakening of the dead in those revolutions served the purpose of glorifying the new struggles, not of parodying the old; of magnifying the given task in imagination, not of fleeing from its solution in reality; of finding once more the spirit of revolution, not of making its ghost walk about again.

From 1848 to 1851 only the ghost of the old revolution walked about, from Marrast, the *républicain en gants jaunes*, who disguised himself as the old Bailly, down to the adventurer, who hides his commonplace repulsive features under the iron death mask of Napoleon. An entire people, which had imagined that by means of a revolution it had imparted to itself an accelerated power of motion, suddenly finds itself set back into a defunct epoch and, in order that no doubt as to the relapse may be possible, the old dates arise again, the old chronology, the old names, the old edicts, which had long become a subject of antiquarian erudition, and the old minions of the law, who had seemed long decayed. The nation feels like that mad Englishman in Bedlam who fancies that he lives in the times of the ancient Pharaohs and daily bemoans the hard labor that he must perform in the Ethiopian mines as a gold digger, immured in this subterranean prison, a dimly burning lamp fastened to his head, the overseer of the slaves behind him with a long whip, and at the exits a confused welter of barbarian mercenaries, who understand neither the forced laborers in the mines nor one another, since they speak no common language. "And all this is expected of me," sighs the mad Englishman, "of me, a freeborn Briton, in order to make gold for the old Pharaohs." "In order to pay the debts of the Bonaparte family," sighs the French nation. The Englishman, so long as he was in his right mind, could not get rid of the fixed idea of making gold. The French, so long as they were engaged in revolution, could not get rid of the memory of Napoleon, as the election of December 10 proved. They hankered to return from the perils of revolution to the fleshpots of Egypt, and December 2, 1851, was the answer. They have not only a caricature of the old Napoleon, they have the old Napoleon himself, caricatured as he must appear in the middle of the nineteenth century.

The social revolution of the nineteenth century cannot draw its poetry from the past, but only from the future. It cannot begin with itself before it has stripped off all superstition in regard to the past. Earlier revolutions required recollections of past world history in order to drug themselves concerning their own content. In order to arrive at its own content the revolution of the nineteenth century must let the dead bury their dead. There the phrase went beyond the content; here the content goes beyond the phrase.

The February revolution was a surprise attack, a *taking* of the old society *unawares,* and the people proclaimed this unexpected *stroke* as a deed of world importance, ushering in a new epoch. On December 2 the February revolution is conjured away by a cardsharper's trick, and what seems overthrown is no longer the monarchy but the liberal concessions that were wrung from it by centuries of struggle. Instead of *society* having conquered a new content for itself, it seems that the *state* only returned to its oldest form, to the shamelessly simple domination of the saber and the cowl. This is the answer to the *coup de main* of February 1848, given by the *coup de tête* of December 1851. Easy come, easy go. Meanwhile the interval of time has not passed by unused. During the years 1848 to 1851 French society has made up, and that by an abbreviated because revolutionary method, for the studies and experiences which, in a regular, so to speak, textbook course of development would have had to precede the February revolution, if it was to be more than a ruffling of the surface. Society now seems to have fallen back behind its point of departure; it has in truth first to create for itself the revolutionary point of departure, the situation, the relations, the conditions under which alone modern revolution becomes serious.

Bourgeois revolutions, like those of the eighteenth century, storm swiftly from success to success; their dramatic effects outdo each other; men and things seem set in sparkling brilliants; ecstasy is the everyday spirit; but they are short-lived; soon they have attained their zenith, and a long crapulent depression lays hold of society before it learns soberly to assimilate the results of its storm-and-stress period. On the other hand, proletarian revolutions, like those of the nineteenth century, criticize themselves constantly, interrupt themselves continually in their own course, come back to the apparently accomplished in order to begin it afresh, deride with unmerciful thoroughness the inadequacies, weaknesses, and paltrinesses of their first attempts, seem to throw down their adversary only in order that he may draw new strength from the earth and rise again, more gigantic, before them, recoil ever and anon from the indefinite prodigiousness of their own aims, until a situation has been created which makes all turning back impossible, and the conditions themselves cry out:

Hic Rhodus, hic salta![1]
Here is the rose, here dance!

For the rest, every fairly competent observer, even if he had not followed the course of French developments step by step, must have had a presentiment that an unheard-of fiasco was in store for the revolution. It was enough to hear the self-complacent howl of victory with which Messieurs the democrats congratulated each other on the expected gracious consequences of the second Sunday in May 1852. In their minds the second Sunday in May 1852 had become a fixed idea, a dogma, like the day on which Christ should reappear and the millennium begin, in the minds of the Chiliasts. As ever, weakness had taken refuge in a belief in miracles, fancied the enemy overcome when he was only conjured away in imagination, and it lost all understanding of the present in a passive glorification of the future that was in store for it and of the deeds it had *in petto* but which it merely did not want to carry out as yet. Those heroes who seek to disprove their demonstrated incapacity

[1] "Here is Rhodes, jump here!" from the Latin version of a fable by Aesop.

by mutually offering each other their sympathy and getting together in a crowd had tied up their bundles, collected their laurel wreaths in advance, and were just then engaged in discounting on the exchange market the republics *in partibus* for which they had already providently organized the government personnel with all the calm of their unassuming disposition. December 2 struck them like a thunderbolt from a clear sky, and the peoples that in periods of pusillanimous depression gladly let their inward apprehension be drowned out by the loudest bawlers will perchance have convinced themselves that the times are past when the cackle of geese could save the Capitol.

The Constitution, the National Assembly, the dynastic parties, the blue and the red republicans, the heroes of Africa, the thunder from the platform, the sheet lightning of the daily press, the entire literature, the political names and the intellectual reputations, the civil law and the penal code, the *liberté, égalité, fraternité* and the second Sunday in May 1852—all has vanished like a phantasmagoria before the spell of a man whom even his enemies do not make out to be a magician. Universal suffrage seems to have survived only for a moment, in order that with its own hand it may make its last will and testament before the eyes of all the world and declare in the name of the people itself: All that exists deserves to perish.

It is not enough to say, as the French do, that their nation was taken unawares. A nation and a woman are not forgiven the unguarded hour in which the first adventurer that came along could violate them. The riddle is not solved by such turns of speech, but merely formulated differently. It remains to be explained how a nation of thirty-six million can be surprised and delivered unresisting into captivity by three swindlers.

Let us recapitulate in general outline the phases that the French revolution went through from February 24, 1848, to December 1851.

Three main periods are unmistakable: *the February period;* May 4, 1848, to May 28, 1849: *the period of the constitution of the republic,* or *of the Constituent National Assembly;* May 28, 1849, to December 2, 1851: *the period of the constitutional republic* or *of the Legislative National Assembly.*

The *first period,* from February 24, or the overthrow of Louis Philippe, to May 4, 1848, the meeting of the Constituent Assembly, the *February period* proper, may be described as the *prologue* to the revolution. Its character was officially expressed in the fact that the government improvised by it itself declared that it was *provisional* and, like the government, everything that was mooted, attempted, or enunciated during this period proclaimed itself to be only *provisional.* Nothing and nobody ventured to lay claim to the right of existence and of real action. All the elements that had prepared or determined the revolution, the dynastic opposition, the republican bourgeoisie, the democratic-republican petty bourgeoisie, and the social-democratic workers, provisionally found their place in the February *government.*

It could not be otherwise. The February days originally intended an electoral reform by which the circle of the politically privileged among the possessing class itself was to be widened and the exclusive domination of the aristocracy of finance overthrown. When it came to the actual conflict, however, when the people mounted the barricades, the National Guard maintained a passive attitude, the army offered no serious resistance, and the monarchy ran away, the republic appeared to be a matter of course. Every party construed it in its own way. Having secured it arms in hand, the proletariat impressed its stamp upon it and proclaimed it to be a *social republic.* There was thus indicated the general content of the modern revolution, a content which was in most singular contradiction to everything that, with the material available, with the degree of education attained by the masses, under the given circumstances and relations, could be immediately realized in practice. On the other hand, the claims of all the remaining elements that had collaborated in the February revolution were recognized by the lion's share that they obtained in the government. In no period do we, therefore, find a more confused mixture of high-flown phrases and actual uncertainty and clumsiness, of more enthusiastic striving for innovation and more deeply rooted domination of the old routine, of more apparent harmony of the whole of society and more profound estrangement of its elements. While the Paris proletariat still reveled in the vision of the wide prospects that had opened before it and indulged in seriously meant discussions on social problems, the old powers of society grouped themselves, assembled, reflected, and found unexpected support in the mass of the nation, the peasants and petty bourgeois, who all at once stormed onto the political stage, after the barriers of the July monarchy had fallen.

The *second period*, from May 4, 1848, to the end of May 1849, is the period of the *constitution*, the *foundation, of the bourgeois republic*. Directly after the February days not only had the dynastic opposition been surprised by the republicans and the republicans by the socialists, but all France by Paris. The National Assembly, which met on May 4, 1848, had emerged from the national elections and represented the nation. It was a living protest against the pretensions of the February days, and was to reduce the results of the revolution to the bourgeois scale. In vain the Paris proletariat, which immediately grasped the character of this National Assembly, attempted on May 15, a few days after it met, forcibly to negate its existence, to dissolve it, to disintegrate again into its constituent parts the organic form in which the proletariat was threatened by the reacting spirit of the nation. As is known, May 15 had no other result save that of removing Blanqui and his comrades, that is, the real leaders of the proletarian party, from the public stage for the entire duration of the cycle we are considering.

The *bourgeois monarchy* of Louis Philippe can be followed only by a *bourgeois republic*, that is to say, whereas a limited section of the bourgeoisie ruled in the name of the king, the whole of the bourgeoisie will now rule on behalf of the people. The demands of the Paris proletariat are utopian nonsense, to which an end must be put. To this declaration of the Constituent National Assembly the Paris proletariat replied with the *June insurrection*, the most colossal event in the history of European civil wars. The bourgeois republic triumphed. On its side stood the aristocracy of finance, the industrial bourgeoisie, the middle class, the petty bourgeois, the army, the *lumpenproletariat* organized as the Mobile Guard, the intellectual lights, the clergy, and the rural population. On the side of the Paris proletariat stood none but itself. More than three thousand insurgents were butchered after the victory, and fifteen thousand were transported without trial. With this defeat the proletariat passes into the *background* of the revolutionary stage. It attempts to press forward again on every occasion, as soon as the movement appears to make a fresh start, but with ever decreased expenditure of strength and always slighter results. As soon as one of the social strata situated above it gets into revolutionary ferment, the proletariat enters into an alliance with it and so shares all the defeats that the different parties suffer, one after another. But these subsequent blows become the weaker, the greater the surface of society over which they are distributed. The more important leaders of the proletariat in the Assembly and in the press successively fall victims to the courts, and ever more equivocal figures come to head it. In part it throws itself into *doctrinaire experiments, exchange banks, and workers' associations, hence into a movement in which it renounces the revolutionizing of the old world by means of the latter's own great, combined resources and seeks, rather, to achieve its salvation behind society's back, in private fashion, within its limited conditions of existence, and hence necessarily suffers shipwreck.* It seems to be unable either to rediscover revolutionary greatness in itself or to win new energy from the connections newly entered into, until *all classes* with which it contended in June themselves lie prostrate beside it. But at least it succumbs with the honors of the great, world-historic struggle; not only France, but all Europe trembles at the June earthquake, while the ensuing defeats of the upper classes are so cheaply bought that they require barefaced exaggeration by the victorious party to be able to pass for events at all, and become the more ignominious the further the defeated party is removed from the proletarian party.

The defeat of the June insurgents, to be sure, had now prepared, had leveled the ground on which the bourgeois republic could be founded and built up, but it had shown at the same time that in Europe the questions at issue are other than that of "republic or monarchy." It had revealed that here *bourgeois republic* signifies the unlimited despotism of one class over other classes. It had proved that in countries with an old civilization, with a developed formation of classes, with modern conditions of production, and with an intellectual consciousness in which all traditional ideas have been dissolved by the work of centuries *the republic* signifies *in general only the political form of the revolution of bourgeois society* and not its *conservative form of life*, as, for example, in the United States of North America, where, though classes already exist they have not yet become fixed, but continually change and interchange their elements in constant flux, where the modern means of production, instead of coinciding with a stagnant surplus population, rather compensate for the relative deficiency of heads and hands, and where, finally, the feverish, youthful movement of material production, which has to make a new world its own, has left neither time nor opportunity for abolishing the old spirit world.

During the June days all classes and parties had united in the *party of order* against the proletarian class as the *party of anarchy*, of socialism, of communism. They had "saved" society from "*the enemies of society*." They had given out the watchwords of the old society, "*property, family, religion, order*," to their army as passwords, and had proclaimed to the counterrevolutionary crusaders: "In this sign thou shalt conquer!" From that moment, as soon as one of the numerous parties which had gathered under this sign against the June insurgents has sought to hold the revolutionary battlefield in its own class interest, it has gone down before the cry: "Property, family, religion, order." Society is saved just as often as the circle of its rulers contracts, as a more exclusive interest is maintained against a wider one. Every demand of the simplest bourgeois financial reform, of the most ordinary liberalism, of the most formal republicanism, of the most shallow democracy is simultaneously castigated as an "attempt on society" and stigmatized as "socialism." And, finally, the high priests of "the religion of order" themselves are driven with kicks from their Pythian tripods, hauled out of their beds in the darkness of night, put in prison vans, thrown into dungeons, or sent into exile; their temple is razed to the ground, their mouths are sealed, their pens broken, their law torn to pieces in the name of religion, of property, of the family, of order. Bourgeois fanatics for order are shot down on their balconies by mobs of drunken soldiers, their domestic sanctuaries profaned, their houses bombarded for amusement—in the name of property, of the family, of religion, and of order. Finally, the scum of bourgeois society forms the *holy phalanx of order* and the hero Crapulinski installs himself in the Tuileries as the "*savior of society.*"

Only in the course of development, however, could the consequences of the change of ministers come to light. To begin with, Bonaparte had taken a step forward only to be driven backward all the more conspicuously. His brusque message was followed by the most servile declaration of allegiance to the National Assembly. As often as the ministers dared to make a diffident attempt to introduce his personal fads as legislative proposals, they themselves seemed to carry out, against their will only and compelled by their position, comical commissions of whose fruitlessness they were persuaded in advance. As often as Bonaparte blurted out his intentions behind the ministers' backs and played with his "*idées napoléoniennes,*" his own ministers disavowed him from the tribune of the National Assembly. His usurpatory longings seemed to make themselves heard only in order that the malicious laughter of his opponents might not be muted. He behaved like an unrecognized genius, whom all the world takes for a simpleton. Never did he enjoy the contempt of all classes in fuller measure than during this period. Never did the bourgeoisie rule more absolutely, never did it display more ostentatiously the insignia of domination.

I have not here to write the history of its legislative activity, which is summarized during this period in two laws: in the law re-establishing the *wine tax*, and the *education law* abolishing unbelief. If wine drinking was made harder for the French, they were presented all the more plentifully with the water of true life. If in the law on the wine tax the bourgeoisie declared the old, hateful French tax system to be inviolable, it sought through the education law to ensure among the masses the old state of mind that put up with the tax system. One is astonished to see the Orleanists, the liberal bourgeois, these old apostles of Voltaireanism and eclectic philosophy, entrust to their hereditary enemies, the Jesuits, the superintendence of the French mind. However, in regard to the pretenders to the throne, Orleanists and Legitimists could part company; they understood that to secure their united rule necessitated the uniting of the means of repression of two epochs, that the means of subjugation of the July monarchy had to be supplemented and strengthened by the means of subjugation of the Restoration.

The peasants, disappointed in all their hopes, crushed more than ever by the low level of grain prices on the one hand and by the growing burden of taxes and mortgage debts on the other, began to bestir themselves in the Departments. They were answered by a drive against the schoolmasters, who were made subject to the clergy, by a drive against the *maires*, who were made subject to the prefects, and by a system of espionage, to which all were made subject. In Paris and the large towns reaction itself has the physiognomy of its epoch and challenges more than it strikes down. In the countryside it becomes dull, coarse, petty, tiresome, and vexatious, in a word, the *gendarme*. One comprehends how three years of the regime of the *gendarme*, consecrated by the regime of the priest, were bound to demoralize immature masses.

Whatever amount of passion and declamation might be employed by the party of order against the minority from the tribune of the National Assembly, its speech remained as monosyllabic as that of the Christians, whose words were to be: Yea, yea; nay, nay! As monosyllabic on the platform as in the press. Flat as a riddle whose answer is known in advance. Whether it was a question of the right of petition or the tax on wine, freedom of the press or free trade, the clubs or the municipal charter, protection of personal liberty or regulation of the state budget, the watchword constantly recurs, the theme remains always the same, the verdict is ever ready and invariably reads: "*Socialism!*"

Even bourgeois liberalism is declared *socialistic*, bourgeois enlightenment socialistic, bourgeois financial reform socialistic. It was socialistic to build a railway where a canal already existed, and it was socialistic to defend oneself with a cane when one was attacked with a rapier.

This was not merely a figure of speech, fashion, or party tactics. The bourgeoisie had a true insight into the fact that all the weapons which it had forged against feudalism turned their points against itself, that all the means of education which it had produced rebelled against its own civilization, that all the gods which it had created had fallen away from it. It understood that all the so-called bourgeois liberties and organs of progress attacked and menaced its *class rule* at its social foundation and its political summit simultaneously, and had therefore become "*socialistic.*" In this menace and this attack it rightly discerned the secret of socialism, whose import and tendency it judges more correctly than so-called socialism knows how to judge itself; the latter can, accordingly, not comprehend why the bourgeoisie callously hardens its heart against it, whether it sentimentally bewails the sufferings of mankind or in Christian spirit prophesies the millennium and universal brotherly love, or in humanistic style twaddles about mind, education, and freedom, or in doctrinaire fashion excogitates a system for the conciliation and welfare of all classes. What the bourgeoisie did not grasp, however, was the logical conclusion that its *own parliamentary regime*, that its *political rule* in general, was now also bound to meet with the general verdict of condemnation as being *socialistic*. As long as the rule of the bourgeois class had not been organized completely, as long as it had not acquired its pure political expression, the antagonism of the other classes, likewise, could not appear in its pure form, and where it did appear could not take the dangerous turn that transforms every struggle against the state power into a struggle against capital. If in every stirring of life in society it saw "tranquillity" imperiled, how could it want to maintain at the head of society a *regime of unrest*, its own regime, the *parliamentary regime*, this regime that, according to the expression of one of its spokesmen, lives in struggle and by struggle? The parliamentary regime lives by discussion; how shall it forbid discussion? Every interest, every social institution is here transformed into general ideas, debated as ideas; how shall any interest, any institution sustain itself above thought and impose itself as an article of faith? The struggle of the orators on the platform evokes the struggle of the scribblers of the press; the debating club in Parliament is necessarily supplemented by debating clubs in the salons and the pothouses; the representatives, who constantly appeal to public opinion, give public opinion the right to speak its real mind in petitions. The parliamentary regime leaves everything to the decision of majorities; how shall the great majorities outside Parliament not want to decide? When you play the fiddle at the top of the state, what else is to be expected but that those down below dance?

Thus, by now stigmatizing as *"socialistic"* what it had previously extolled as *"liberal,"* the bourgeoisie confesses that its own interests dictate that it should be delivered from the danger of its *own rule;* that in order to restore tranquillity in the country its bourgeois Parliament must, first of all, be given its quietus; that in order to preserve its social power intact its political power must be broken; that the individual bourgeois can continue to exploit the other classes and to enjoy undisturbed property, family, religion, and order only on condition that his class be condemned along with the other classes to like political nullity; that in order to save its purse it must forfeit the crown, and the sword that is to safeguard it must at the same time be hung over its own head as a sword of Damocles.

On the threshold of the February revolution the *social republic* appeared as a phrase, as a prophecy. In the June days of 1848 it was drowned in the blood of the *Paris proletariat,* but it haunts the subsequent acts of the drama like a ghost. The *democratic republic* announces its arrival. On June 13, 1849, it is dissipated together with its *petty bourgeois,* who have taken to their heels, but in its flight it blows its own trumpet with redoubled boastfulness. The *parliamentary republic,* together with the bourgeoisie, takes possession of the entire stage; it enjoys its existence to the full, but December 2, 1851, buries it to the accompaniment of the anguished cry of the royalists in coalition: "Long live the republic!"

The French bourgeoisie balked at the domination of the working proletariat; it has brought the *lumpenproletariat* to domination, with the chief of the Society of December 10 at the head. The bourgeoisie kept France in breathless fear of the future terrors of red anarchy; Bonaparte discounted this future for it when, on December 4, he had the eminent bourgeois of the Boulevard Montmartre and the Boulevard des Italiens shot down at their windows by the liquor-inspired army of order. It apotheosized the sword; the sword rules it. It destroyed the revolutionary press; its own press has been destroyed. It placed popular meetings under police supervision; its salons are under the supervision of the police. It disbanded the democratic National Guards; its own National Guard is disbanded. It imposed a state of siege; a state of siege is imposed upon it. It supplanted the juries by military commissions; its juries are supplanted by military commissions. It subjected public education to the sway of the priests; the priests subject it to their own education. It transported people without trial; it is being transported without trial. It repressed every stirring in society by means of the state power; every stirring in its society is suppressed by means of the state power. Out of enthusiasm for its purse it rebelled against its own politicians and men of letters; its politicians and men of letters are swept aside, but its purse is being plundered now that its mouth has been gagged and its pen broken. The bourgeoisie never wearied of crying out to the revolution what St. Arsenius cried out to the Christians: "*Fuge, tace, quiesce* [Flee, be silent, keep still]!" Bonaparte cries to the bourgeoisie: "*Fuge, tace, quiesce* [Flee, be silent, keep still]!"

The French bourgeoisie had long ago found the solution to Napoleon's dilemma: "*Dans cinquante ans l'Europe sera républicaine ou cosaque* [In fifty years Europe will be either republican or Cossack]." It had found the solution to it in the "*république cosaque.*" No Circe, by means of black magic, has distorted that work of art, the bourgeois republic, into a monstrous shape. That republic has lost nothing but the semblance of respectability. Present-day France was contained in a finished state within the parliamentary republic. It required only a bayonet thrust for the bubble to burst and the monster to spring forth before our eyes.

Why did the Paris proletariat not rise in revolt after December 2?

The overthrow of the bourgeoisie had as yet been only decreed; the decree had not been carried out. Any serious insurrection of the proletariat would at once have put fresh life into the bourgeoisie, would have reconciled it with the army and ensured a second June defeat for the workers.

On December 4 the proletariat was incited by bourgeois and *épicier* to fight. On the evening of that day several legions of the National Guard promised to appear, armed and uniformed, on the scene of battle. For the bourgeois and the *épicier* had got wind of the fact that in one of his decrees of December 2, Bonaparte abolished the secret ballot and enjoined them to record their "yes" or "no" in the official registers after their names. The resistance of December 4 intimidated Bonaparte. During the night he caused placards to be posted on all the street corners of Paris, announcing the restoration of the secret ballot. The bourgeois and the *épicier* believed that they had gained their end. Those who failed to appear next morning were the bourgeois and the *épicier*.

By a *coup de main* during the night of December 1 to 2, Bonaparte had robbed the Paris proletariat of its leaders, the barricade commanders. An army without officers, averse to fighting under the banner of the *Montagnards* because of the memories of June 1848 and 1849 and May 1850, it left to its vanguard, the secret societies, the task of saving the insurrectionary honor of Paris, which the bourgeoisie had so unresistingly surrendered to the soldiery that, later on, Bonaparte could sneeringly give as his motive for disarming the National Guard—his fear that its arms would be turned against it itself by the anarchists!

"C'est le triomphe complet et définitif du socialisme [This is the complete and definitive triumph of socialism]!" Thus Guizot characterized December 2. But if the overthrow of the parliamentary republic contains within itself the germ of the triumph of the proletarian revolution, its immediate and palpable result was *the victory of Bona-*

parte over Parliament, of the executive power over the legislative power, of force without phrases over the force of phrases. In Parliament the nation made its general will the law, that is, it made the law of the ruling class its general will. Before the executive power it renounces all will of its own and submits to the superior command of an alien will, to authority. The executive power, in contrast to the legislative power, expresses the heteronomy of a nation, in contrast to its autonomy. France, therefore, seems to have escaped the despotism of a class only to fall back beneath the despotism of an individual, and, what is more, beneath the authority of an individual without authority. The struggle seems to be settled in such a way that all classes, equally impotent and equally mute, fall on their knees before the rifle butt.

But the revolution is thoroughgoing. It is still journeying through purgatory. It does its work methodically. By December 2, 1851, it had completed one half of its preparatory work; it is now completing the other half. First it perfected the parliamentary power, in order to be able to overthrow it. Now that it has attained this it perfects the *executive power*, reduces it to its purest expression, isolates it, sets it up against itself as the sole target, in order to concentrate all its forces of destruction against it. And when it has done this second half of its preliminary work, Europe will leap from its seat and exultantly exclaim: "Well grubbed, old mole!"

This executive power, with its enormous bureaucratic and military organization, with its ingenious state machinery, embracing wide strata, with a host of officials numbering a half million, besides an army of another half million, this appalling parasitic body, which enmeshes the body of French society like a net and chokes all its pores, sprang up in the days of the absolute monarchy, with the decay of the feudal system, which it helped to hasten. The seignorial privileges of the landowners and towns became transformed into so many attributes of the state power, the feudal dignitaries into paid officials and the motley pattern of conflicting medieval plenary powers into the regulated plan of a state authority whose work is divided and centralized as in a factory. The first French Revolution, with its task of breaking all separate local, territorial, urban, and provincial powers in order to create the civil unity of the nation, was bound to develop what the absolute monarchy had begun, centralization, but at the same time the extent, the attributes, and the agents of governmental power. Napoleon perfected this state machinery. The Legitimist monarchy and the July monarchy added nothing but a greater division of labor, growing in the same measure as the division of labor within bourgeois society created new groups of interests, and, therefore, new material for state administration. Every *common* interest was straightway severed from society, counterpoised to it as a higher, *general* interest, snatched from the activity of society's members themselves, and made an object of government activity, from a bridge, a schoolhouse, and the communal property of a village community to the railways, the national wealth, and the national university of France. Finally, in its struggle against the revolution, the parliamentary republic found itself compelled to strengthen, along with the repressive measures, the resources and centralization of governmental power. All revolutions perfected this machine instead of smashing it. The parties that contended in turn for domination regarded the possession of this huge state edifice as the principal spoils of the victor.

But under the absolute monarchy, during the first revolution, under Napoleon bureaucracy was only the means of preparing the class rule of the bourgeoisie. Under the Restoration, under Louis Philippe, under the parliamentary republic it was the instrument of the ruling class, however much it strove for power of its own.

Only under the second Bonaparte does the state seem to have made itself completely independent. As against civil society, the state machine has consolidated its position so thoroughly that the chief of the Society of December 10 suffices for its head, an adventurer blown in from abroad, raised on the shield by a drunken soldiery, which he has bought with liquor and sausages, and which he must continually ply with sausage anew. Hence the downcast despair, the feeling of most dreadful humiliation and degradation that oppresses the breast of France and makes her catch her breath. She feels dishonored.

And yet the state power is not suspended in mid-air. Bonaparte represents a class, and the most numerous class of French society at that, the *small-holding* [*Parzellen*] *peasants*.

Just as the Bourbons were the dynasty of big landed property and just as the Orleans' were the dynasty of money, so the Bonapartes are the dynasty of the peasants, that is, the mass of the French people. Not the Bonaparte who submitted to the bourgeois parliament, but the Bonaparte who dispersed the bourgeois parliament is the chosen of the peasantry. For three years the towns had succeeded in falsifying the meaning of the election of December 10 and in cheating the peasants out of the restoration of the empire. The election of December 10, 1848, has been consummated only by the *coup d'état* of December 2, 1851.

The small-holding peasants form a vast mass, the members of which live in similar conditions but without entering into manifold relations with one another. Their mode of production isolates them from one another instead of bringing them into mutual intercourse. The isolation is increased by France's bad means of communication and by the poverty of the peasants. Their field of production, the small holding, admits of no division of labor in its cultivation, no application of science, and, therefore, no diversity of development, no variety of talent, no wealth of social relationships. Each individual peasant family is almost self-sufficient; it itself directly produces the major part of its consumption, and thus acquires its means of life more through exchange with nature than in intercourse with society. A small holding, a peasant and his family; alongside them another small holding, another peasant and another family. A few score of these make up a village, and a few score of villages make up a Department. In this way the great mass of the French nation is formed by simple addition of homologous magnitudes, much as potatoes in a sack form a sack of potatoes. In so far as millions of families live under economic conditions of existence that separate their mode of life, their interests, and their culture from those of the other classes and put them in hostile opposition to the latter, they form a class. In so far as there is merely a local interconnection among these small-holding peasants and the identity of their interests begets no community, no national bond, and no political organization among them, they do not form a class. They are consequently incapable of enforcing their class interest in their own name, whether through a parliament or through a convention. They cannot represent themselves, they must be represented. Their representative must at the same time appear as their master, as an authority over them, as an unlimited government power that protects them against the other classes and sends them rain and sunshine from above. The political influence of the small-holding peasants, therefore, finds its final expression in the executive power subordinating society to itself.

Historical tradition gave rise to the belief of the French peasants in the miracle that a man named Napoleon would bring all the glory back to them. And an individual turns up who gives himself out as the man because he bears the name of Napoleon, in consequence of the Code Napoléon, which lays down that *la recherche de la paternité est interdite*. [Research into paternity is forbidden.] After a vagabondage of twenty years and after a series of grotesque adventures the legend finds fulfillment and the man becomes Emperor of the French. The fixed idea of the nephew was realized because it coincided with the fixed idea of the most numerous class of the French people.

But, it may be objected, what about the peasant risings in half of France, the raids on the peasants by the army, the mass incarceration and transportation of peasants?

Since Louis XIV, France has experienced no similar persecution of the peasants "on account of demagogic practices."

But let there be no misunderstanding. The Bonaparte dynasty represents not the revolutionary, but the conservative peasant; not the peasant that strikes out beyond the condition of his social existence, the small holding, but rather the peasant who wants to consolidate this holding, not the country folk who, linked up with the towns, want to overthrow the old order through their own energies, but on the contrary, those who, in stupefied seclusion within this old order, want to see themselves and their small holdings saved and favored by the ghost of the empire. It represents not the enlightenment, but the superstition of the peasant; not his judgment, but his prejudice; not his future, but his past; not his modern Cevennes, but his modern Vendée.

The three-year rigorous rule of the parliamentary republic had freed a part of the French peasants from the Napoleonic illusion and had revolutionized them, even if only superficially; but the bourgeoisie violently repressed them as often as they set themselves in motion. Under the parliamentary republic the modern and the traditional consciousness of the French peasant contended for mastery. This progress took the form of an incessant struggle between the schoolmasters and the priests. The bourgeoisie struck down the schoolmasters. For the first time the peasants made efforts to behave independently in the face of the activity of the government. This was shown in the continual conflict between the *maires* and the prefects. The bourgeoisie deposed the *maires*. Finally, during the period of the parliamentary republic, the peasants of different localities rose against their own offspring, the army. The bourgeoisie punished them with states of siege and punitive expeditions. And this same bourgeoisie now cries out about the stupidity of the masses, the vile multitude, that has betrayed it to Bonaparte. It has itself forcibly strengthened the empire sentiments [*Imperialismus*] of the peasant class, it conserved the conditions that form the birthplace of this peasant religion. The bourgeoisie, to be sure, is bound to fear the stupidity of the masses as long as they remain conservative and the insight of the masses as soon as they become revolutionary.

In the risings after the *coup d'état* a part of the French peasants protested, arms in hand, against their own vote of December 10, 1848. The school they had gone through since 1848 had sharpened their wits. But they had made themselves over to the underworld of history; history held them to their word, and the majority was still so prejudiced that in precisely the reddest Departments the peasant population voted openly for Bonaparte. In its view, the National Assembly had hindered his progress. He had now merely broken the fetters that the towns had imposed on the will of the countryside. In some parts the peasants even entertained the grotesque notion of a convention side by side with Napoleon.

After the first revolution had transformed the peasants from semi-villeins into freeholders, Napoleon confirmed and regulated the conditions on which they could exploit undisturbed the soil of France which had only just fallen to their lot and slake their youthful passion for property. But what is now causing the ruin of the French peasant is his small holding itself, the division of the land, the form of property which Napoleon consolidated in France. It is precisely the material conditions which made the feudal peasant a small-holding peasant and Napoleon an emperor. Two generations have sufficed to produce the inevitable result: progressive deterioration of agriculture, progressive indebtedness of the agriculturist. The "Napoleonic" form of property, which at the beginning of the nineteenth century was the condition for the liberation and enrichment of the French country folk, has developed in the course of this century into the law of their enslavement and pauperization. And precisely this law is the first of the "*idées napoléoniennes*" which the second Bonaparte has to uphold. If he still shares with the peasants the illusion that the cause of their ruin is to be sought not in this small-holding property itself but outside it, in the influence of secondary circumstances, his experiments will burst like soap bubbles when they come in contact with the relations of production.

The economic development of small-holding property has radically changed the relation of the peasants to the other classes of society. Under Napoleon the fragmentation of the land in the countryside supplemented free competition and the beginning of big industry in the towns. The peasant class was the ubiquitous protest against the landed aristocracy, which had just been overthrown. The roots that small-holding property struck in French soil deprived feudalism of all nutriment. Its landmarks formed the natural fortifications of the bourgeoisie against any surprise attack on the part of its old overlords. But in the course of the nineteenth century the feudal lords were replaced by urban usurers; the feudal obligation that went with the land was replaced by the mortgage; aristocratic landed property was replaced by bourgeois capital. The small holding of the peasant is now only the pretext that allows the capitalist to draw profits, interest, and rent from the soil, while leaving it to the tiller of the soil himself to see how he can extract his wages. The mortgage debt burdening the soil of France imposes on the French peasantry payment of an amount of interest equal to the annual interest on the entire British national debt. Small-holding property, in this enslavement by capital to which its development inevitably pushes forward, has transformed the mass of the French nation into troglodytes. Sixteen million peasants (including women and children) dwell in hovels, a large number of which have but one opening, others only two, and the most favored only three. And windows are to a house what the five senses are to the head. The bourgeois order, which at the beginning of the century set the state to stand guard over the newly arisen small holding and manured it with laurels, has become a vampire that sucks out its blood and brains and throws them into the alchemistic cauldron of capital. The Code Napoléon is now nothing but a *codex* of distraints, forced sales, and compulsory auctions. To the four million (including children, etc.) officially recognized paupers, vagabonds, criminals, and prostitutes in France must be added five million who hover on the margin of existence and either have their haunts in the countryside itself or, with their rags and their children, continually desert the countryside for the towns and the towns for the countryside. The interests of the peasants, therefore, are no longer, as under Napoleon, in accord with, but in opposition to the interests of the bourgeoisie, to capital. Hence the peasants find their natural ally and leader in the *urban proletariat*, whose task is the overthrow of the bourgeois order. But *strong and unlimited government*—and this is the second "*idée napoléonienne*" which the second Napoleon has to carry out—is called upon to defend this "material" order by force. This "*ordre matériel*" also serves as the catchword in all of Bonaparte's proclamations against the rebellious peasants.

Besides the mortgage which capital imposes on it, the small holding is burdened by *taxes*. Taxes are the source of life for the bureaucracy, the army, the priests, and the court, in short, for the whole apparatus of the executive power. Strong government and heavy taxes are identical. By its very nature small-holding property forms a suitable basis for an all-powerful and innumerable bureaucracy. It creates a uniform level of relationships and persons over the whole surface of the land. Hence it also permits of uniform action from a supreme center on all points of this uniform mass. It annihilates the aristocratic intermediate grades between the mass of the people and the state power. On all sides, therefore, it calls forth the direct interference of this state power and the interposition of its immediate organs. Finally, it produces an unemployed surplus population for which there is no place either on the land or in the towns, and which accordingly reaches out for state offices as a sort of respectable alms and provokes the creation of state posts. By the new markets which he opened at the point of the bayonet, by the plundering of the Continent, Napoleon repaid the compulsory taxes with interest. These taxes were a spur to the industry of the peasant, whereas now they rob his industry of its last resources and complete his inability to resist pauperism. And an enormous bureaucracy, well gallooned and well fed, is the "*idée napoléonienne*" which is most congenial of all to the second Bonaparte. How could it be otherwise, seeing that alongside the actual classes of society he is forced to create an artificial caste, for which the maintenance of his regime becomes a bread-and-butter question? Accordingly, one of his first financial operations was the raising of officials' salaries to their old level and the creation of new sinecures.

Another "*idée napoléonienne*" is the domination of the *priests* as an instrument of government. But while in its accord with society, in its dependence on natural forces and its submission to the authority which protected it from above the small holding that had newly come into being was naturally religious, the small holding that is ruined by debts, at odds with society and authority, and driven beyond its own limitations naturally becomes irreligious. Heaven was quite a pleasing accession to the narrow strip of land just won, more particularly as it makes the weather; it becomes an insult as soon as it is thrust forward as substitute for the small holding. The priest then appears as only the anointed bloodhound of the earthly police—another "*idée napoléonienne.*" On the next occasion, the expedition against Rome will take place in France itself, but in a sense opposite to that of M. de Montalembert.

Lastly, the culminating point of the "*idées napoléoniennes*" is the preponderance of the *army*. The army was the *point d'honneur* of the small-holding peasants; it was they themselves transformed into heroes, defending their new possessions against the outer world, glorifying their recently won nationhood, plundering and revolutionizing the world. The uniform was their own state dress; war was their poetry; the small holding, extended and rounded off in imagination, was their fatherland, and patriotism the ideal form of the sense of property. But the enemies against whom the French peasant has now to defend his property are not the Cossacks; they are the *huissiers* and the tax collectors. The small holding lies no longer in the so-called fatherland, but in the register of mortgages. The army itself is no longer the flower of the peasant youth; it is the swamp flower of the peasant *lumpenproletariat*. It consists in large measure of *remplaçants*, of substitutes, just as the second Bonaparte is himself only a *remplaçant*, the substitute for Napoleon. It now performs its deeds of valor by hounding the peasants in masses like chamois, by doing *gendarme* duty, and if the internal contradictions of his system chase the chief of the Society of December 10 over the French border, his army, after some acts of brigandage, will reap not laurels, but thrashings.

One sees *all* "idées napoléoniennes" *are ideas of the undeveloped small holding in the freshness of its youth*; for the small holding that has outlived its day, they are an absurdity. They are only the hallucinations of its death struggle, words that are transformed into phrases, spirits transformed into ghosts. But the parody of the empire [*das Imperialismus*] was necessary to free the mass of the French nation from the weight of tradition and to work out in pure form the opposition between the state power and society. With the progressive undermining of small-holding property, the state structure erected upon it collapses. The centralization of the state that modern society requires arises only on the ruins of the military bureaucratic government machinery which was forged in opposition to feudalism.

The condition of the French peasants provides us with the answer to the riddle of the *general elections of December 20 and 21*, which bore the second Bonaparte up Mount Sinai not to receive laws, but to give them.

Manifestly the bourgeoisie had now no choice but to elect Bonaparte. When the puritans at the Council of Constance complained of the dissolute lives of the popes and wailed about the necessity of moral reform, Cardinal Pierre d'Ailly thundered at them: "Only the devil in person can still save the Catholic Church, and you ask for angels." In like manner, after the *coup d'état*, the French bourgeoisie cried: "Only the chief of the Society of December 10 can still save bourgeois society! Only theft can still save property; only perjury, religion; bastardy, the family; disorder, order!"

As the executive authority which has made itself an independent power, Bonaparte feels it to be his mission to safeguard "bourgeois order." But the strength of this bourgeois order lies in the middle class. He looks on himself, therefore, as the representative of the middle class, and issues decrees in this sense. Nevertheless, he is somebody solely due to the fact that he has broken the political power of this middle class and daily breaks it anew. Consequently he looks on himself as the adversary of the political and literary power of the middle class. But by protecting its material power he generates its political power anew. The cause must accordingly be kept alive, but the effect, where it manifests itself, must be done away with. But this cannot pass off without slight confusions of cause and effect, since in their interaction both lose their distinguishing features. New decrees that obliterate the border line. As against the bourgeoisie, Bonaparte looks on himself, at the same time, as the representative of the peasants and of the people in general, who wants to make the lower classes of the people happy within the frame of bourgeois society. New decrees that cheat the "true socialists" of their statecraft in advance. But, above all, Bonaparte looks on himself as the chief of the Society of December 10, as the representative of the *lumpenproletariat*, to which he himself, his *entourage*, his government, and his army belong, and whose prime consideration is to benefit itself and draw California lottery prizes from the state treasury. And he vindicates his position as chief of the Society of December 10 with decrees, without decrees, and despite decrees.

This contradictory task of the man explains the contradictions of his government, the confused groping about which seeks now to win, now to humiliate first one class and then another and arrays all of them uniformly against him, whose practical uncertainty forms a highly comical contrast to the imperious, categorical style of the government decrees, a style which is faithfully copied from the uncle.

Industry and trade, hence the business affairs of the middle class, are to prosper in hothouse fashion under the strong government. The grant of innumerable railway concessions. But the Bonapartist *lumpenproletariat* is to enrich itself. The initiated play *tripotage* on the Bourse with the railway concessions. But no capital is forthcoming for the railways. Obligation of the Bank to make advances on railway shares. But, at the same time, the Bank is to be exploited for personal ends and therefore must be cajoled. Release of the Bank from the obligation to publish its report weekly. Leonine agreement of the Bank with the government. The people are to be given employment. Initiation of public works. But the public works increase the obligations of the people in respect of taxes. Hence reduction of the taxes by an onslaught on the *rentiers*, by conversion of the 5 per cent bonds to 4½ per cents. But, once more, the middle class must receive a *douceur*. Therefore doubling of the wine tax for the people, who buy it *en détail*, and halving of the wine tax for the middle class, who drink it *en gros*. Dissolution of the actual workers' associations, but promises of miracles of association in the future. The peasants are to be helped. Mortgage banks that expedite their getting into debt and accelerate the concentration of property. But these banks are to be used to make money out of the confiscated estates of the house of Orleans. No capitalist wants to agree to this condition, which is not in the decree, and the mortgage bank remains a mere decree, etc.

Bonaparte would like to appear as the patriarchal benefactor of all classes. But he cannot give to one class without taking from another. Just as at the time of the Fronde it was said of the Duke of Guise that he was the most *obligeant* man in France because he had turned all his estates into his partisans' obligations to him, so Bonaparte would fain be the most *obligeant* man in France and turn all the property, all the labor of France into a personal obligation to himself. He would like to steal the whole of France in order to be able to make a present of her to France or, rather, in order to be able to buy France anew with French money, for as the chief of the Society of December 10 he must needs buy what ought to belong to him. And all the state institutions, the Senate, the Council of State, the legislative body, the Legion of Honor, the soldiers' medals, the washhouses, the public works, the railways, the *état major* of the National Guard to the exclusion of privates, and the confiscated estates of the house of Orleans—all become parts of the institution of purchase. Every place in the army and in the government machine becomes a means of purchase. But the most important feature of this process, whereby France is taken in order to give to her, is the percentages that find their way into the pockets of the head and the members of the Society of December 10 during the turnover. The witticism with which Countess L., the mistress of M. de Morny, characterized the confiscation of the Orleans' estates: "*C'est le premier vol*[2] *de l'aigle,*" is applicable to every flight of this *eagle*, which is more like a *raven*. He himself and his adherents call out to one another daily like that Italian Carthusian admonishing the miser who, with boastful display, counted up the goods on which he could yet live for years to come: "*Tu fai conto sopra i beni, bisogna prima far il conto sopra gli anni* [Thou countest thy goods, thou shouldst first count thy years]." Lest they make a mistake in the years, they count the minutes. A bunch of blokes push their way forward to the court, into the ministries, to the head of the administration and the army, a crowd of the best of whom it must be said that no one knows whence

[2] *Vol* means flight and theft. [Note by Marx.]

he comes, a noisy, disreputable, rapacious bohème that crawls into gallooned coats with the same grotesque dignity as the high dignitaries of Soulouque. One can visualize clearly this upper stratum of the Society of December 10 if one reflects that *Véron-Crevel*[3] is its preacher of morals and *Granier de Cassagnac* its thinker. When Guizot, at the time of his ministry, utilized this Granier on a hole-and-corner newspaper against the dynastic opposition, he used to boast of him with the quip: "*C'est le roi des drôles* [He is the king of buffoons]." One would do wrong to recall the regency or Louis XV in connection with Louis Bonaparte's court and clique. For "often already, France has experienced a government of mistresses, but never before a government of *hommes entretenus* [kept men]."

Driven by the contradictory demands of his situation and being at the same time, like a conjurer, under the necessity of keeping the public gaze fixed on himself, as Napoleon's substitute, by springing constant surprises, that is to say, under the necessity of executing a *coup d'état en miniature* every day, Bonaparte throws the entire bourgeois economy into confusion, violates everything that seemed inviolable to the Revolution of 1848, makes some tolerant of revolution, others desirous of revolution, and produces actual anarchy in the name of order, while at the same time stripping its halo from the entire state machine, profanes it and makes it at once loathsome and ridiculous. The cult of the Holy Tunic of Treves he duplicates at Paris in the cult of the Napoleonic imperial mantle. But when the imperial mantle finally falls on the shoulders of Louis Bonaparte, the bronze statue of Napoleon will crash from the top of the Vendôme Column.

[3] In his work, *Cousine Bette*, Balzac delineates the thoroughly dissolute Parisian Philistine in Crevel, a character which he draws after the model of Dr. Véron, the proprietor of the *Constitutionnel.* [Note by Marx.]

XV. *Excerpts from* The Civil War in France

KARL MARX

INTRODUCTION BY FRIEDRICH ENGELS

I did not anticipate that I would be asked to prepare a new edition of the address of the General Council of the International on *The Civil War in France*, and to write an introduction to it. Therefore I can only touch briefly here on the most important points.

I am prefacing the longer work mentioned above by the two shorter addresses of the General Council on the Franco-Prussian War. In the first place, because the second of these, which itself cannot be fully understood in full without the first, is referred to in *The Civil War*. But also because these two addresses, likewise drafted by Marx, are, no less than *The Civil War*, outstanding examples of the author's remarkable gift, first proved in *The Eighteenth Brumaire of Louis Bonaparte*, for grasping clearly the character, the import, and the necessary consequences of great historical events, at a time when these events are still in progress before our eyes or have only just taken place. And, finally, because today we in Germany are still having to endure the consequences which Marx predicted would follow from these events.

Has that which was declared in the first address not come to pass: that if Germany's defensive war against Louis Bonaparte degenerated into a war of conquest against the French people all the misfortunes which befell Germany after the so-called wars of liberation would revive again with renewed intensity? Have we not had a further twenty years of Bismarck's rule, the exceptional law and socialist-baiting taking the place of the prosecutions of demagogues, with the same arbitrary action of the police and with literally the same staggering interpretations of the law?

And has not the prediction been proved to the letter, that the annexation of Alsace-Lorraine would "force France into the arms of Russia," and that after this annexation Germany must either become the avowed servant of Russia or must, after some short respite, arm for a new war, and, moreover, "a race war against the combined Slavonic and Roman races"? Has not the annexation of the French provinces driven France into the arms of Russia? Has not Bismarck for fully twenty years vainly wooed the favor of the czar, wooed it with services even lowlier than those which little Prussia, before it became the "first power in Europe," was wont to lay at Holy Russia's feet? And is there not every day still hanging over our heads the Damocles sword of war, on the first day of which all the chartered covenants of princes will be scattered like chaff, a war of which nothing is certain but the absolute uncertainty of its outcome, a race war which will subject the whole of Europe to devastation by fifteen or twenty million armed men, and which is not raging already only because even the strongest of the great military states shrinks before the absolute incalculability of its final result?

All the more is it our duty to make again accessible to the German workers these brilliant proofs, now half forgotten, of the farsightedness of international working-class policy in 1870.

What is true of these two addresses is also true of *The Civil War in France.* On May 28 the last fighters of the Commune succumbed to superior forces on the slopes of Belleville; and only two days later, on May 30, Marx read to the General Council the work in which the historical significance of the Paris Commune is delineated in short, powerful strokes, but with such trenchancy and, above all, such truth as have never again been attained in all the mass of literature on this subject.

Thanks to the economic and political development of France since 1789, Paris has been placed for the last fifty years in such a position that no revolution could break out there without assuming a proletarian character, that is to say, without the proletariat, which had bought victory with its blood, advancing its own demands after victory. These demands were more or less unclear and even confused, corresponding to the state of development reached by the workers of Paris at the particular period, but in the last resort they all amounted to the abolition of the class antagonism between capitalists and workers. It is true that no one knew how this was to be brought about. But the demand itself, however indefinitely it still was couched, contained a threat to the existing order of society; the workers who put it forward were still armed; therefore the disarming of the workers was the first commandment for the bourgeois, who were at the helm of the state. Hence, after every revolution won by the workers, a new struggle, ending with the defeat of the workers.

This happened for the first time in 1848. The liberal bourgeois of the parliamentary opposition held banquets for securing a reform of the franchise, which was to ensure supremacy for their party. Forced more and more, in their struggle with the government, to appeal to the people, they gradually had to yield precedence to the radical and republican strata of the bourgeoisie and petty bourgeoisie. But behind these stood the revolutionary workers, and since 1830 these had acquired far more political independence than the bourgeois, and even the republicans, suspected. At the moment of the crisis between the government and the opposition the workers began street fighting; Louis Philippe vanished, and with him the franchise reform; and in its place arose the republic, and indeed one which the victorious workers themselves designated as a "social" republic. No one, however, was clear as to what this social republic was to imply; not even the workers themselves. But they now had arms and were a power in the state. Therefore, as soon as the bourgeois republicans in control felt something like firm ground under their feet, their first aim was to disarm the workers. This took place by driving them into the insurrection of June 1848 by direct breach of faith, by open defiance and the attempt to banish the unemployed to a distant province. The government had taken care to have an overwhelming superiority of force.

After five days' heroic struggle the workers were defeated. And then followed a blood bath among the defenseless prisoners, the like of which has not been seen since the days of the civil wars which ushered in the downfall of the Roman Republic. It was the first time that the bourgeoisie showed to what insane cruelties of revenge it will be goaded the moment the proletariat dares to take its stand against the bourgeoisie as a separate class, with its own interests and demands. And yet 1848 was only child's play compared with the frenzy of the bourgeoisie in 1871.

Punishment followed hard at heel. If the proletariat was not yet able to rule France, the bourgeoisie could no longer do so. At least not at that period, when the greater part of it was still monarchically inclined, and it was divided into three dynastic parties and a fourth, republican party. Its internal dissensions allowed the adventurer Louis Bonaparte to take possession of all the commanding points—army, police, administrative machinery—and, on December 2, 1851, to explode the last stronghold of the bourgeoisie, the National Assembly. The Second Empire began—the exploitation of France by a gang of political and financial adventurers, but at the same time also an industrial development such as had never been possible under the narrow-minded and timorous system of Louis Philippe, with the exclusive domination of only a small section of the big bourgeoisie. Louis Bonaparte took the political power from the capitalists under the pretext of protecting them, the bourgeois, from the workers, and on the other hand the workers from them; but in return his rule encouraged speculation and industrial activity—in a word, the upsurgence and enrichment of the whole bourgeoisie to an extent hitherto unknown. To an even greater extent, it is true, corruption and mass thievery developed, clustering around the imperial court and drawing their heavy percentages from this enrichment.

But the Second Empire was the appeal to French chauvinism, was the demand for the restoration of the frontiers of the First Empire, which had been lost in 1814, or at least those of the First Republic. A French empire within the frontiers of the old monarchy and, in fact, within the even more amputated frontiers of 1815—such a thing was impossible for any length of time. Hence the necessity for occasional wars and extensions of frontiers. But no extension of frontiers was so dazzling to the imagination of the French chauvinists as the extension to the German left bank of the Rhine. One square mile on the Rhine was more to them than ten in the Alps, or anywhere else. Given the Second Empire, the demand for the restoration of the left bank of the Rhine, either all at once or piecemeal, was merely a question of time. The time came with the Austro-Prussian war of 1866; cheated of the anticipated "territorial compensation" by Bismarck and by his own overcunning, hesitant policy, there was now nothing left for Napoleon but war, which broke out in 1870 and drove him first to Sedan, and thence to Wilhelmshöhe.

The necessary consequence was the Paris revolution of September 4, 1870. The empire collapsed like a house of cards, and the republic was again proclaimed. But the enemy was standing at the gates; the armies of the empire were either hopelessly encircled at Metz or held captive in Germany. In this emergency the people allowed the Paris deputies to the former legislative body to constitute themselves into a "government of national defense." This was the more readily conceded, since, for the purposes of defense, all Parisians capable of bearing arms had enrolled in the National Guard and were armed, so that now the workers constituted a great majority. But very soon the antagonism between the almost completely bourgeois government and the armed proletariat broke into open conflict. On October 31 workers' battalions stormed the town hall and captured part of the membership of the government. Treachery, the government's direct breach of its undertakings, and the intervention of some petty-bourgeois battalions set them free again, and in order not to occasion the outbreak of civil war inside a city besieged by a foreign military power the former government was left in office.

At last, on January 28, 1871, starved Paris capitulated. But with honors unprecedented in the history of war. The forts were surrendered, the city wall stripped of guns, the weapons of the regiments of the line and of the Mobile Guard were handed over, and they themselves considered prisoners of war. But the National Guard kept its weapons and guns, and only entered into an armistice with the victors. And these did not dare enter Paris in triumph. They dared only to occupy a tiny corner of Paris, which, into the bargain, consisted partly of public parks, and even this they occupied for only a few days! And during this time they, who had maintained their encirclement of Paris for 131 days, were themselves encircled by the armed workers of Paris, who kept a sharp watch that no "Prussian" should overstep the narrow bounds of the corner ceded to the foreign conqueror. Such was the respect which the Paris workers inspired in the army before which all the armies of the empire had laid down their arms; and the Prussian *Junkers*, who had come to take revenge at the home of the revolution, were compelled to stand by respectfully and salute precisely this armed revolution!

During the war the Paris workers had confined themselves to demanding the vigorous prosecution of the fight. But now, when peace had come after the capitulation of Paris, now Thiers, the new supreme head of the government, was compelled to realize that the rule of the propertied classes—big landowners and capitalists—was in constant danger so long as the workers of Paris had arms in their hands. His first action was an attempt to disarm them. On March 18 he sent troops of the line with orders to rob the National Guard of the artillery belonging to it, which had been constructed during the siege of Paris and had been paid for by public subscription. The attempt failed; Paris mobilized as one man for resistance, and war between Paris and the French Government sitting at Versailles was declared. On March 26 the Paris Commune was elected and on March 28 it was proclaimed. The Central Committee of the National Guard, which up to then had carried on the government, handed in its resignation to the Commune after it had first decreed the abolition of the scandalous Paris "morality police." On March 30 the Commune abolished conscription and the standing army, and declared the sole armed force to be the National Guard, in which all citizens capable of bearing arms were to be enrolled. It remitted all payments of rent for dwelling houses from October 1870 until April, the amounts already paid to be booked as future rent payments, and stopped all sales of articles pledged in the municipal loan office. On the same day the foreigners elected to the Commune were confirmed in office, because "the flag of the Commune is the flag of the World Republic." On April 1 it was decided that the highest salary to be received by any employee of the Commune, and therefore also by its members themselves, was not to exceed six thousand francs (forty-eight hundred marks). On the following day the Commune decreed the separation of the church from the state, and the abolition of all state payments for religious purposes as well as the transformation of all church property into national property, as a result of which, on April 8, the exclusion from the schools of all religious symbols, pictures, dogmas, prayers—in a word, "of all that belongs to the sphere of the individual's conscience"—was ordered and gradually put into effect. On the fifth, in reply to the shooting, day after day, of captured Commune fighters by the Versailles troops, a decree was issued for the imprisonment of hostages, but it was never carried into execution. On the sixth the guillotine was brought out by the 137th Battalion of the National Guard and publicly burned, amid great popular rejoicing. On the twelfth the Commune decided that the victory column on the Place Vendôme, which had been cast from captured guns by Napoleon after the war of 1809, should be demolished as a symbol of chauvinism and incitement to national hatred. This was carried out on May 16. On April 16 it ordered a statistical tabulation of factories which had been closed down by the manufacturers, and the working out of plans for the operation of these factories by the workers formerly employed in them, who were to be organized in co-operative societies, and also plans for the organization of these co-operatives into one great union. On the twentieth it abolished night work for bakers, and also the employment offices, which since the Second Empire had been run as a monopoly by creatures appointed by the police—labor exploiters of the first rank; these offices were transferred to the mayoralties of the twenty *arrondissements* of Paris. On April 30 it ordered the closing of the pawnshops, on the ground that they were a private exploitation of the workers, and were in contradiction with the right of the workers to their instruments of labor and to credit. On May 5 it ordered the razing of the Chapel of Atonement, which had been built in expiation of the execution of Louis XVI.

Thus from March 18 onwards the class character of the Paris movement, which had previously been pushed into the background by the fight against the foreign invaders, emerged sharply and clearly. As almost only workers, or recognized representatives of the workers, sat in the Commune, its decisions bore a decidedly proletarian character. Either these decisions decreed reforms which the republican bourgeoisie had failed to pass solely out of cowardice, but which provided a necessary basis for the free activity of the working class–such as the realization of the principle that, *in relation to the state*, religion is a purely private matter–or the Commune promulgated decrees which were in the direct interest of the working class and in part cut deeply into the old order of society. In a beleaguered city, however, it was possible to make at most a start in the realization of all this. And from the beginning of May onwards all their energies were taken up by the fight against the armies assembled by the Versailles government in ever growing numbers.

On April 7 the Versailles troops had captured the Seine crossing at Neuilly, on the western front of Paris; on the other hand, in an attack on the southern front on the eleventh they were repulsed with heavy losses by General Eudes. Paris was continually bombarded, and, moreover, by the very people who had stigmatized as a sacrilege the bombardment of the same city by the Prussians. These same people now begged the Prussian Government for the hasty return of the French soldiers taken prisoner at Sedan and Metz, in order that they might recapture Paris for them. From the beginning of May the gradual arrival of these troops gave the Versailles forces a decided superiority. This already became evident when, on April 23, Thiers broke off the negotiations for the exchange, proposed by the Commune, of the Archbishop of Paris and a whole number of other priests held as hostages in Paris, for only one man, Blanqui, who had twice been elected to the Commune but was a prisoner in Clairvaux. And even more from the changed language of Thiers; previously procrastinating and equivocal, he now suddenly became insolent, threatening, brutal. The Versailles forces took the redoubt of Moulin Saquet on the southern front, on May 3; on the ninth, Fort Issy, which had been completely reduced to ruins by gunfire; on the fourteenth, Fort Vanves. On the western front they advanced gradually, capturing the numerous villages and buildings which extended up to the city wall, until they reached the main defenses; on the twenty-first, thanks to treachery and the carelessness of the National Guards stationed there, they succeeded in forcing their way into the city. The Prussians, who held the northern and eastern forts, allowed the Versailles troops to advance across the land north of the city, which was forbidden ground to them under the armistice, and thus to march forward, attacking on a wide front, which the Parisians naturally thought covered by the armistice, and therefore held only weakly. As a result of this only a weak resistance was put up in the western half of Paris, in the luxury city proper; it grew stronger and more tenacious the nearer the incoming troops approached the eastern half, the working-class city proper. It was only after eight days' fighting that the last defenders of the Commune succumbed on the heights of Belleville and Menilmontant; and then the massacre of defenseless men, women, and children, which had been raging all through the week on an increasing scale, reached its zenith. The breechloaders could no longer kill fast enough; the vanquished were shot down in hundreds by *mitrailleuse* fire. The "Wall of the Federals" at the Père Lachaise cemetery, where the final mass murder was consummated, is still standing today, a mute but eloquent testimony to the frenzy of which the ruling class is capable as soon as the working class dares to stand up for its rights. Then, when the slaughter of them all proved to be impossible, came the mass arrests, the shooting of victims arbitrarily selected from the prisoners' ranks, and the removal of the rest to great camps, where they awaited trial by court-martial. The Prussian troops surrounding the northeastern half of Paris had orders not to allow any fugitives to pass, but the officers often shut their eyes when the soldiers paid more obedience to the dictates of humanity than to those of the Supreme Command; particular honor is due to the Saxon army corps, which behaved very humanely and let through many who were obviously fighters for the Commune.

If today, after twenty years, we look back at the activity and historical significance of the Paris Commune of 1871, we shall find it necessary to make a few additions to the account given in *The Civil War in France*.

The members of the Commune were divided into a majority, the Blanquists, who had also been predominant in the Central Committee of the National Guard, and a minority, members of the International Workingmen's Association, chiefly consisting of adherents of the Proudhon school of socialism. The great majority of the Blanquists were at that time socialists only by revolutionary, proletarian instinct; only a few had attained greater clarity on principles, through Vaillant, who was familiar with German scientific socialism. It is therefore comprehensible that in the economic sphere much was left undone which, according to our view today, the Commune ought to have done. The hardest thing to understand is certainly the holy awe with which they remained standing respectfully outside the gates of the Bank of France. This was also a serious political mistake. The Bank in the hands of the Commune—this would have been worth more than ten thousand hostages. It would have meant the pressure of the whole of the French bourgeoisie on the Versailles government in favor of peace with the Commune. But what is still more wonderful is the correctness of much that nevertheless was done by the Commune, composed as it was of Blanquists and Proudhonists. Naturally the Proudhonists were chiefly responsible for the economic decrees of the Commune, both for their praiseworthy and their unpraiseworthy aspects; as the Blanquists were for its political commissions and omissions. And in both cases the irony of history willed—as is usual when doctrinaires come to the helm—that both did the opposite of what the doctrines of their school prescribed.

Proudhon, the socialist of the small peasant and master craftsman, regarded association with positive hatred. He said of it that there was more bad than good in it; that it was by nature sterile, even harmful, because it was a fetter on the freedom of the worker; that it was a pure dogma, unproductive and burdensome, in conflict as much with the freedom of the worker as with economy of labor; that its disadvantages multiplied more swiftly than its advantages; that, compared with it, competition, division of labor, and private property gave economic strength. Only in the exceptional cases—as Proudhon called them—of large-scale industry and large establishments, such as railways, was the association of workers in place. (See *General Idea of the Revolution*, third sketch.)

By 1871 large-scale industry had already so much ceased to be an exceptional case even in Paris, the center of artistic handicrafts, that by far the most important decree of the Commune instituted an organization of large-scale industry and even of manufacture which was not only to be based on the association of the workers in each factory, but also to combine all these associations in one great union; in short, an organization which, as Marx quite rightly says in *The Civil War*, must necessarily have led in the end to communism, that is to say, the direct opposite of the Proudhon doctrine. And, therefore, the Commune was the grave of the Proudhon school of socialism. Today this school has vanished from French working-class circles; here, among the possibilists no less than among the "Marxists," Marx's theory now rules unchallenged. Only among the "radical" bourgeoisie are there still Proudhonists.

The Blanquists fared no better. Brought up in the school of conspiracy, and held together by the strict discipline which went with it, they started out from the viewpoint that a relatively small number of resolute, well-organized men would be able, at a given favorable moment, not only to seize the helm of state, but also, by a display of great, ruthless energy, to maintain power until they succeeded in sweeping the mass of the people into the revolution and ranging them round the small band of leaders. This involved, above all, the strictest, dictatorial centralization of all power in the hands of the new revolutionary government. And what did the Commune, with its majority of these same Blanquists, actually do? In all its proclamations to the French in the provinces it appealed to them to form a free federation of all French communes with Paris, a national organization which for the first time was really to be created by the nation itself. It was precisely the oppressing power of the former centralized government, army, political police, bureaucracy, which Napoleon had created in 1798 and which since then had been taken over by every new government as a welcome instrument and used against its opponents—it was precisely this power which was to fall everywhere, just as it had already fallen in Paris.

From the very outset the Commune was compelled to recognize that the working class, once come to power, could not go on managing with the old state machine; that in order not to lose again its only just conquered supremacy this working class must, on the one hand, do away with all the old repressive machinery previously used against it itself and, on the other, safeguard itself against its own deputies and officials, by declaring them all, without exception, subject to recall at any moment. What had been the characteristic attribute of the former state? Society had created its own organs to look after its common interests, originally through simple division of labor. But these organs, at whose head was the state power, had in the course of time, in pursuance of their own special interests, transformed themselves from the servants of society into the masters of society. This can be seen, for example, not only in the hereditary monarchy, but equally so in the democratic republic. Nowhere do "politicians" form a more separate and powerful section of the nation than precisely in North America. There each of the two major parties which alternately succeed each other in power is itself in turn controlled by people who make a business of politics, who speculate on seats in the legislative assemblies of the Union as well as of the separate states, or who make a living by carrying on agitation for their party and on its victory are rewarded with positions. It is well known how the Americans have been trying for thirty years to shake off this yoke, which has become intolerable, and how in spite of it all they continue to sink ever deeper in this swamp of corruption. It is precisely in America that we see best how there takes place this process of the state power making itself independent in relation to society, whose mere instrument it was originally intended to be. Here there exists no dynasty, no nobility, no standing army, beyond the few men keeping watch on the Indians, no bureaucracy with permanent posts or the right to pensions. And nevertheless we find here two great gangs of political speculators, who alternately take possession of the state power and exploit it by the most corrupt means and for the most corrupt ends—and the nation is powerless against these two great cartels of politicians, who are ostensibly its servants, but in reality dominate and plunder it.

Against this transformation of the state and the organs of the state from servants of society into masters of society —an inevitable transformation in all previous states—the Commune made use of two infallible means. In the first place, it filled all posts—administrative, judicial, and educational—by election on the basis of universal suffrage of all concerned, subject to the right of recall at any time by the same electors. And, in the second place, all officials, high or low, were paid only the wages received by other workers. The highest salary paid by the Commune to anyone was six thousand francs. In this way an effective barrier to place hunting and careerism was set up, even apart from the binding mandates to delegates to representative bodies which were added besides.

This shattering [*Sprengung*] of the former state power and its replacement by a new and truly democratic one is described in detail in the third section of *The Civil War*. But it was necessary to dwell briefly here once more on some of its features, because in Germany particularly the superstitious belief in the state has been carried over from philosophy into the general consciousness of the bourgeoisie and even of many workers. According to the philosophical conception, the state is the "realization of the Idea," or the kingdom of God on earth; translated into philosophical terms, the sphere in which eternal truth and justice are or should be realized. And from this follows a superstitious reverence for the state and everything connected with it, which takes root the more readily since people are accustomed from childhood to imagine that the affairs and interests common to the whole of society could not be looked after otherwise than as they have been looked after in the past, that is, through the state and its lucratively positioned officials. And people think they have taken quite an extraordinarily bold step forward when they have rid themselves of belief in hereditary monarchy and swear by the democratic republic. In reality, however, the state is nothing but a machine for the oppression of one class by another, and indeed in the democratic republic no less than in the monarchy; and at best an evil inherited by the proletariat after its victorious struggle for class supremacy, whose worst sides the victorious proletariat, just like the Commune, cannot avoid having to lop off at once as much as possible until such time as a generation reared in new, free social conditions is able to throw the entire lumber of the state on the scrap heap.

Of late the social-democratic Philistine has once more been filled with wholesome terror at the words: dictatorship of the proletariat. Well and good, gentlemen; do you want to know what this dictatorship looks like? Look at the Paris Commune. That was the dictatorship of the proletariat.

F. Engels

London, on the twentieth anniversary
of the Paris Commune, March 18, 1891

III

On the dawn of the eighteenth of March, Paris arose to the thunderburst of "*Vive la Commune!*" What is the Commune, that sphinx so tantalizing to the bourgeois mind?

"The proletarians of Paris," said the Central Committee in its manifesto of the eighteenth of March, "amidst the failures and treasons of the ruling classes, have understood that the hour has struck for them to save the situation by taking into their own hands the direction of public affairs. . . . They have understood that it is their imperious duty and their absolute right to render themselves masters of their own destinies, by seizing upon the government power." But the working class cannot simply lay hold of the ready-made state machinery and wield it for its own purposes.

The centralized state power, with its ubiquitous organs of standing army, police, bureaucracy, clergy, and judicature—organs wrought after the plan of a systematic and hierarchic division of labor—originates from the days of absolute monarchy, serving nascent middle-class society as a mighty weapon in its struggles against feudalism. Still, its development remained clogged by all manner of medieval rubbish, seignorial rights, local privileges, municipal and guild monopolies and provincial constitutions. The gigantic broom of the French Revolution of the eighteenth century swept away all these relics of bygone times, thus clearing simultaneously the social soil of its last hindrances to the superstructure of the modern state edifice raised under the First Empire, itself the offspring of the coalition wars of old semi-feudal Europe against modern France. During the subsequent regimes the government, placed under parliamentary control—that is, under the direct control of the propertied classes—became not only a hotbed of huge national debts and crushing taxes; with its irresistible allurements of place, pelf, and patronage, it not only became the bone of contention between the rival factions and adventurers of the ruling classes, but its political character changed simultaneously with the economic changes of society. At the same pace at which the progress of modern industry developed, widened, intensified the class antagonism between capital and labor, the state power assumed more and more the character of the national power of capital over labor, of a public force organized for social enslavement, of an engine of class despotism. After every revolution marking a progressive phase in the class struggle the purely repressive character of the state power stands out in bolder and bolder relief. The Revolution of 1830, resulting in the transfer of government from the landlords to the capitalists, transferred it from the more remote to the more direct antagonists of the workingmen. The bourgeois republicans, who, in the name of the revolution of February, took the state power, used it for the June massacres, in order to convince the working class that "social" republic meant the republic ensuring their social subjection, and in order to convince the royalist bulk of the bourgeois and landlord class that they might safely leave the cares and emoluments of government to the bourgeois "republicans." However, after their one heroic exploit of June, the bourgeois republicans had, from the front, to fall back to the rear of the "party of order"–a combination formed by all the rival fractions and factions of the appropriating class in their now openly declared antagonism to the producing classes. The proper form of their joint-stock government was the *parliamentary republic*, with Louis Bonaparte for its president. Theirs was a regime of avowed class terrorism and deliberate insult toward the "vile multitude." If the parliamentary republic, as M. Thiers said, "divided them [the different fractions of the ruling class] least," it opened an abyss between that class and the whole body of society outside their spare ranks. The restraints by which their own divisions had, under former regimes, still checked the state power were removed by their union, and in view of the threatening upheaval of the proletariat, they now used that state power mercilessly and ostentatiously as the national war engine of capital against labor. In their uninterrupted crusade against the producing masses they were, however, bound not only to invest the executive with continually increased powers of repression, but at the same time to divest their own parliamentary stronghold–the National Assembly–one by one, of all its own means of defense against the executive. The executive, in the person of Louis Bonaparte, turned them out. The natural offspring of the "party of order" republic was the Second Empire.

The empire, with the *coup d'état* for its certificate of birth, universal suffrage for its sanction, and the sword for its scepter, professed to rest upon the peasantry, the large mass of producers not directly involved in the struggle of capital and labor. It professed to save the working class by breaking down Parliamentarism and, with it, the undisguised subservience of government to the propertied classes. It professed to save the propertied classes by upholding their economic supremacy over the working class; and, finally, it professed to unite all classes by reviving for all the chimera of national glory. In reality it was the only form of government possible at a time when the bourgeoisie had already lost, and the working class had not yet acquired, the faculty of ruling the nation. It was acclaimed throughout the world as the savior of society. Under its sway bourgeois society, freed from political cares, attained a development unexpected even by itself. Its industry and commerce expanded to colossal dimensions, financial swindling celebrated cosmopolitan orgies, the misery of the masses was set off by a shameless display of gorgeous, meretricious, and debased luxury. The state power, apparently soaring high above society, was at the same time itself the greatest scandal of that society and the very hotbed of all its corruptions. Its own rottenness and the rottenness of the society it had saved were laid bare by the bayonet of Prussia, herself eagerly bent upon transferring the supreme seat of that regime from Paris to Berlin. Imperialism is, at the same time, the most prostitute and the ultimate form of the state power which nascent middle-class society had commenced to elaborate as a means of its own emancipation from feudalism and which full-grown bourgeois society had finally transformed into a means for the enslavement of labor by capital.

The direct antithesis to the empire was the Commune. The cry of "social republic," with which the revolution of February was ushered in by the Paris proletariat, did but express a vague aspiration after a republic that was not only to supersede the monarchical form of class rule, but class rule itself. The Commune was the positive form of that republic.

Paris, the central seat of the old government power and, at the same time, the social stronghold of the French working class, had risen in arms against the attempt of Thiers and the rurals to restore and perpetuate that old government power bequeathed to them by the empire. Paris could resist only because, in consequence of the siege, it had got rid of the army and replaced it by a National Guard, the bulk of which consisted of workingmen. This fact was now to be transformed into an institution. The first decree of the Commune, therefore, was the suppression of the standing army and the substitution for it of the armed people.

The Commune was formed of the municipal councilors,

chosen by universal suffrage in the various wards of the town, responsible and revocable at short terms. The majority of its members were naturally workingmen, or acknowledged representatives of the working class. The Commune was to be a working, not a parliamentary, body, executive and legislative at the same time. Instead of continuing to be the agent of the central government the police was at once stripped of its political attributes and turned into the responsible and at all times revocable agent of the Commune. So were the officials of all other branches of the Administration. From the members of the Commune downwards the public service had to be done at *workmen's wages*. The vested interests and the representation allowances of the high dignitaries of state disappeared along with the high dignitaries themselves. Public functions ceased to be the private property of the tools of the central government. Not only municipal administration, but the whole initiative hitherto exercised by the state was put into the hands of the Commune.

Having once got rid of the standing army and the police, the physical force elements of the old government, the Commune was anxious to break the spiritual force of repression, the "parson power," by the disestablishment and disendowment of all churches as proprietary bodies. The priests were sent back to the recesses of private life, there to feed upon the alms of the faithful in imitation of their predecessors, the Apostles. The whole of the educational institutions were opened to the people gratuitously, and at the same time cleared of all interference of church and state. Thus not only was education made accessible to all, but science itself freed from the fetters which class prejudice and governmental force had imposed upon it.

The judicial functionaries were to be divested of that sham independence which had but served to mask their abject subservience to all succeeding governments to which, in turn, they had taken, and broken, the oaths of allegiance. Like the rest of public servants, magistrates and judges were to be elective, responsible, and revocable.

The Paris Commune was, of course, to serve as a model to all the great industrial centers of France. The communal regime once established in Paris and the secondary centers, the old centralized government would in the provinces, too, have to give way to the self-government of the producers. In a rough sketch of national organization which the Commune had no time to develop, it states clearly that the commune was to be the political form of even the smallest country hamlet, and that in the rural districts the standing army was to be replaced by a national militia, with an extremely short term of service. The rural communes of every district were to administer their common affairs by an assembly of delegates in the central town, and these district assemblies were again to send deputies to the national delegation in Paris, each delegate to be at any time revocable and bound by the *mandat impératif* [formal instructions] of his constituents. The few but important functions which still would remain for a central government were not to be suppressed, as has been intentionally misstated, but were to be discharged by communal, and therefore strictly responsible, agents. The unity of the nation was not to be broken, but, on the contrary, to be organized by the communal constitution, and to become a reality by the destruction of the state power which claimed to be the embodiment of that unity independent of, and superior to, the nation itself, from which it was but a parasitic excrescence. While the merely repressive organs of the old government power were to be amputated, its legitimate functions were to be wrested from an authority usurping pre-eminence over society itself and restored to the responsible agents of society. Instead of deciding once in three or six years which member of the ruling class was to misrepresent the people in Parliament, universal suffrage was to serve the people, constituted in communes, as individual suffrage serves every other employer in the search for the workmen and managers for his business. And it is well known that companies, like individuals, in matters of real business generally know how to put the right man in the right place, and if they for once make a mistake to redress it promptly. On the other hand, nothing could be more foreign to the spirit of the Commune than to supersede universal suffrage by hierarchic investiture.

It is generally the fate of completely new historical creations to be mistaken for the counterpart of older and even defunct forms of social life, to which they may bear a certain likeness. Thus, this new Commune, which breaks the modern state power, has been mistaken for a reproduction of the medieval communes, which first preceded, and afterwards became the substratum of, that very state power. The communal constitution has been mistaken for an attempt to break up into a federation of small states, as dreamed of by Montesquieu and the Girondins, that unity of great nations which, if originally brought about by political force, has now become a powerful coefficient of social production. The antagonism of the Commune against the state power has been mistaken for an exaggerated form of the ancient struggle against overcentralization. Peculiar historical circumstances may have prevented the classical development, as in France, of the bourgeois form of government, and may have allowed, as in England, the completion of the great central state organs by corrupt vestries, jobbing councilors, and ferocious poor-law guardians in the towns, and virtually hereditary magistrates in the counties. The communal constitution would have restored to the social body all the forces hitherto absorbed by the state parasite feeding upon, and clogging the free movement of, society. By this one act it would have initiated the regeneration of France. The provincial French middle class saw in the Commune an attempt to restore the sway their order had held over the country under Louis Philippe, and which, under Louis Napoleon, was supplanted by the pretended rule of the country over the towns. In reality the communal constitution brought the rural producers under the intellectual lead of the central towns of their districts, and these secured to them, in the workingmen, the natural trustees of their interests. The very existence of the Commune involved, as a matter of course, local municipal liberty, but no longer as a check upon the now superseded state power. It could only enter into the head of a Bismarck, who, when not engaged in his intrigues of blood and iron, always likes to resume his old trade, so befitting his mental caliber, of contributor to *Kladderadatsch* (the Berlin *Punch*); it could only enter into such a head to ascribe to the Paris Commune aspirations after that caricature of the old French municipal organization of 1791 the Prussian municipal constitution which degrades the town governments to mere secondary wheels in the police machinery of the Prussian state. The Commune made that catchword of bourgeois revolutions, "cheap government," a reality by destroying the two greatest sources of expenditure—the standing army and state functionarism. Its very existence presupposed the non-existence of monarchy, which, in Europe at least, is the normal encumbrance and indispensable cloak of class rule. It supplied the republic with the basis of really democratic institutions. But neither cheap government nor the "true republic" was its ultimate aim; they were its mere concomitants.

The multiplicity of interpretations to which the Commune has been subjected and the multiplicity of interests which have construed it in their favor show that it was a thoroughly expansive political form, while all previous forms of government had been emphatically repressive. Its true secret was this. It was essentially a working-class government, the product of the struggle of the producing against the appropriating class, the political form at last discovered under which to work out the economic emancipation of labor.

Except on this last condition, the communal constitution would have been an impossibility and a delusion. The political rule of the producer cannot coexist with the perpetuation of his social slavery. The Commune was therefore to serve as a lever for uprooting the economic foundations upon which rests the existence of classes, and therefore of class rule. With labor emancipated, every man becomes a workingman and productive labor ceases to be a class attribute.

It is a strange fact. In spite of all the tall talk and all the immense literature, for the last sixty years, about emancipation of labor, no sooner do the workingmen anywhere take the subject into their own hands with a will than uprises at once all the apologetic phraseology of the mouthpieces of present society with its two poles of capital and wage slavery (the landlord now is but the sleeping partner of the capitalist), as if capitalist society was still in its purest state of virgin innocence, with its antagonisms still undeveloped, with its delusions still unexploded, with its prostitute realities not yet laid bare. The Commune, they exclaim, intends to abolish property, the basis of all civilization! Yes, gentlemen, the Commune intended to abolish that class property which makes the labor of the many the wealth of the few. It aimed at the expropriation of the expropriators. It wanted to make individual property a truth by transforming the means of production, land and capital, now chiefly the means of enslaving and exploiting labor, into mere instruments of free and associated labor. But this is communism, "impossible" communism! Why, those members of the ruling classes who are intelligent enough to perceive the impossibility of continuing the present system—and they are many—have become the obtrusive and fullmouthed apostles of co-operative production. If co-operative production is not to remain a sham and a snare; if it is to supersede the capitalist system; if united co-operative societies are to regulate national production upon a common plan, thus taking it under their own control and putting an end to the constant anarchy and periodical convulsions which are the fatality of capitalist production, what else, gentlemen, would it be but communism, "possible" communism?

The working class did not expect miracles from the Commune. They have no ready-made utopias to introduce *par décret du peuple* [by decree of the people]. They know that in order to work out their own emancipation, and along with it that higher form to which present society is irresistibly tending by its own economic agencies, they will have to pass through long struggles, through a series of historic processes, transforming circumstances and men. They have no ideals to realize but to set free the elements of the new society with which old collapsing bourgeois society itself is pregnant. In the full consciousness of their historic mission, and with the heroic resolve to act up to it, the working class can afford to smile at the coarse invective of the gentlemen's gentlemen with the pen and inkhorn, and at the didactic patronage of well-wishing bourgeois doctrinaires, pouring forth their ignorant platitudes and sectarian crotchets in the oracular tone of scientific infallibility.

When the Paris Commune took the management of the revolution in its own hands; when plain workingmen for the first time dared to infringe upon the government privilege of their "natural superiors," and under circumstances of unexampled difficulty performed their work modestly, conscientiously, and efficiently—performed it at salaries the highest of which barely amounted to one fifth of what, according to high scientific authority [Professor Huxley], is the minimum required for a secretary to a certain metropolitan school board—the old world writhed in convulsions of rage at the sight of the red flag, the symbol of the republic of labor, floating over the Hôtel de Ville.

And yet this was the first revolution in which the working class was openly acknowledged as the only class capable of social initiative, even by the great bulk of the Paris middle class—shopkeepers, tradesmen, merchants—the wealthy capitalists alone excepted. The Commune had saved them by a sagacious settlement of that ever recurring cause of dispute among the middle classes themselves—the debtor and creditor accounts. The same portion of the middle class, after they had assisted in putting down the workingmen's insurrection of June 1848, had been at once unceremoniously sacrificed to their creditors by the then Constituent Assembly. But this was not their only motive for now rallying round the working class. They felt that there was but one alternative—the Commune, or the empire—under whatever name it might reappear. The empire had ruined them economically by the havoc it made of public wealth, by the wholesale financial swindling it fostered, by the props it lent to the artificially accelerated centralization of capital, and the concomitant expropriation of their own ranks. It had suppressed them politically, it had shocked them morally by its orgies, it had insulted their Voltaireanism by handing over the education of their children to the *frères Ignorantins*, it had revolted their national feeling as Frenchmen by precipitating them headlong into a war which left only one equivalent for the ruins it made—the disappearance of the empire. In fact, after the exodus from Paris of the high Bonapartist and capitalist *bohème* the true middle-class party of order came out in the shape of the "union républicaine," enrolling themselves under the colors of the Commune and defending it against the willful misconstruction of Thiers. Whether the gratitude of this great body of the middle class will stand the present severe trial, time must show.

The Commune was perfectly right in telling the peasants that "its victory was their only hope." Of all the lies hatched at Versailles and re-echoed by the glorious European penny-a-liner, one of the most tremendous was that the rurals represented the French peasantry. Think only of the love of the French peasant for the men to whom, after 1815, he had to pay the milliard of indemnity. In the eyes of the French peasant the very existence of a great landed proprietor is in itself an encroachment on his conquests of 1789. The bourgeois, in 1848, had burdened his plot of land with the additional tax of forty-five cents in the franc, but then he did so in the name of the revolution, while now he fomented a civil war against the revolution, to shift onto the peasant's shoulders the chief load of the five billions of indemnity to be paid to the Prussian. The Commune, on the other hand, in one of its first proclamations, declared that the true originators of the war would be made to pay its cost. The Commune would have delivered the peasant of the blood tax—would have given him a cheap government—transformed his present bloodsuckers, the notary, advocate, executor, and other judicial vampires, into salaried communal agents, elected by, and responsible to, himself. It would have freed him of the tyranny of the *garde champêtre*, the gendarme, and the prefect; would have put enlightenment by the schoolmaster in the place of stultification by the priest. And the French peasant is, above all, a man of reckoning. He would find it extremely reasonable that the pay of the priest, instead of being extorted by the taxgatherer, should depend only upon the spontaneous action of the parishioners' religious instincts. Such were the great immediate boons which the rule of the Commune—and that rule alone—held out to the French peasantry. It is, therefore, quite superfluous here to expatiate upon the more complicated but vital problems which the Commune alone was able, and at the same time compelled, to solve in favor of the peasant, viz., the hypothecary debt, lying like an incubus upon his parcel of soil, the *prolétariat foncier* (the rural proletariat), daily growing upon it, and his expropriation from it enforced, at a more and more rapid rate, by the very development of modern agriculture and the competition of capitalist farming.

The French peasant had elected Louis Bonaparte president of the republic; but the party of order created the empire. What the French peasant really wants he commenced to show in 1849 and 1850, by opposing his *maire* to the government's prefect, his schoolmaster to the government's priest, and himself to the government's gendarme. All the laws made by the party of order in January and February 1850 were avowed measures of repression against the peasant. The peasant was a Bonapartist, because the Great Revolution, with all its benefits to him, was, in his eyes, personified in Napoleon. This delusion, rapidly breaking down under the Second Empire (and in its very nature hostile to the rurals), this prejudice of the past, how could it have withstood the appeal of the Commune to the living interests and urgent wants of the peasantry?

The rurals—this was, in fact, their chief apprehension—knew that three months' free communication of communal Paris with the provinces would bring about a general rising of the peasants, and hence their anxiety to establish a police blockade around Paris, so as to stop the spread of the rinderpest.

If the Commune was thus the true representative of all the healthy elements of French society, and therefore the truly national government, it was, at the same time, as a workingmen's government, as the bold champion of the emancipation of labor, emphatically international. Within sight of the Prussian Army, that had annexed to Germany two French provinces, the Commune annexed to France the working people all over the world.

The Second Empire had been the jubilee of cosmopolitan blacklegism, the rakes of all countries rushing in at its call for a share in its orgies and in the plunder of the French people. Even at this moment the right hand of Thiers is Ganesco, the foul Wallachian, and his left hand is Markovsky, the Russian spy. The Commune admitted all foreigners to the honor of dying for an immortal cause. Between the foreign war lost by their treason and the civil war fomented by their conspiracy with the foreign invader, the bourgeoisie had found the time to display their patriotism by organizing police hunts upon the Germans in France. The Commune made a German workingman its Minister of Labor. Thiers, the bourgeoisie, the Second Empire, had continually deluded Poland by loud professions of sympathy, while in reality betraying her to, and doing the dirty work of, Russia. The Commune honored the heroic sons of Poland by placing them at the head of the defenders of Paris. And, to broadly mark the new era of history it was conscious of initiating, under the eyes of the conquering Prussians on the one side and of the Bonapartist army, led by Bonapartist generals, on the other, the Commune pulled down that colossal symbol of martial glory, the Vendôme Column.

The great social measure of the Commune was its own working existence. Its special measures could but betoken the tendency of a government of the people by the people. Such were the abolition of the night work of journeymen bakers; the prohibition, under penalty, of the employers' practice to reduce wages by levying upon their workpeople fines under manifold pretexts—a process in which the employer combines in his own person the parts of legislator, judge, and executor, and filches the money to boot. Another measure of this class was the surrender, to associations of workmen, under reserve of compensation, of all closed workshops and factories, no matter whether the respective capitalists had absconded or preferred to strike work.

The financial measures of the Commune, remarkable for their sagacity and moderation, could be only such as were compatible with the state of a besieged town. Considering the colossal robberies committed upon the city of Paris by the great financial companies and contractors, under the protection of Haussmann, the Commune would have had an incomparably better title to confiscate their property than Louis Napoleon had against the Orleans family. The Hohenzollern and the English oligarchs, who both have derived a good deal of their estates from church plunder, were, of course, greatly shocked at the Commune clearing but eight thousand francs out of secularization.

While the Versailles government, as soon as it had recovered some spirit and strength, used the most violent means against the Commune; while it put down the free expression of opinion all over France, even to the forbidding of meetings of delegates from the large towns; while it subjected Versailles and the rest of France to an espionage far surpassing that of the Second Empire; while it burned by its gendarme inquisitors all papers printed at Paris, and sifted all correspondence from and to Paris; while in the National Assembly the most timid attempts to put in a word for Paris were howled down in a manner unknown even to the *Chambre introuvable* of 1816; with the savage warfare of Versailles outside, and its attempts at corruption and conspiracy inside Paris, would the Commune not have shamefully betrayed its trust by affecting to keep up all the decencies and appearances of liberalism, as in a time of profound peace? Had the government of the Commune been akin to that of M. Thiers, there would have been no more occasion to suppress party of order papers at Paris than there was to suppress communal papers at Versailles.

It was irritating indeed to the rurals that at the very same time they declared the return to the church to be the only means of salvation for France, the infidel Commune unearthed the peculiar mysteries of the Picpus nunnery, and of the Church of St. Laurent. It was a satire upon M. Thiers that, while he showered grand crosses upon the Bonapartist generals in acknowledgment of their mastery in losing battles, signing capitulations, and turning cigarettes at Wilhelmshöhe, the Commune dismissed and arrested its generals whenever they were suspected of neglecting their duties. The expulsion from and arrest by the Commune of one of its members who had slipped in under a false name and had undergone at Lyons six days' imprisonment for simple bankruptcy, was it not a deliberate insult hurled at the forger, Jules Favre, then still the Foreign Minister of France, still selling France to Bismarck, and still dictating his orders to that paragon Government of Belgium? But indeed the Commune did not pretend to infallibility, the invariable attribute of all governments of the old stamp. It published its doings and sayings, it initiated the public into all its shortcomings.

In every revolution there intrude, at the side of its true agents, men of a different stamp; some of them survivors of and devotees to past revolutions, without insight into the present movement, but preserving popular influence by their known honesty and courage, or by the sheer force of tradition; others mere bawlers, who, by dint of repeating year after year the same set of stereotyped declamations against the government of the day, have sneaked into the reputation of revolutionists of the first water. After the eighteenth of March some such men did also turn up, and in some cases contrived to play pre-eminent parts. As far as their power went, they hampered the real action of the working class, exactly as men of that sort have hampered the full development of every previous revolution. They are an unavoidable evil; with time they are shaken off, but time was not allowed to the Commune.

Wonderful, indeed, was the change the Commune had wrought in Paris! No longer any trace of the meretricious Paris of the Second Empire. No longer was Paris the rendezvous of British landlords, Irish absentees, American ex-slaveholders and shoddy men, Russian ex-serf owners, and Wallachian boyars. No more corpses at the morgue, no nocturnal burglaries, scarcely any robberies; in fact, for the first time since the days of February 1848, the streets of Paris were safe, and that without any police of any kind. "We," said a member of the Commune, "hear no longer of assassination, theft, and personal assault; it seems, indeed, as if the police had dragged along with it to Versailles all its conservative friends." The *cocottes* had refound the scent of their protectors—the absconding men of family, religion, and, above all, of property. In their stead the real women of Paris showed again at the surface—heroic, noble, and devoted, like the women of antiquity. Working, thinking, fighting, bleeding Paris—almost forgetful, in its incubation of a new society, of the cannibals at its gates—radiant in the enthusiasm of its historic initiative!

Opposed to this new world at Paris behold the old world at Versailles—that assembly of the ghouls of all defunct regimes, Legitimists and Orleanists, eager to feed upon the carcass of the nation—with a tail of antediluvian republicans, sanctioning, by their presence in the Assembly, the slaveholders' rebellion, relying for the maintenance of their parliamentary republic upon the vanity of the senile mountebank at its head, and caricaturing 1789 by holding their ghastly meetings in the Jeu de Paume. There it was, this Assembly, the representative of everything dead in France, propped up to the semblance of life by nothing but the swords of the generals of Louis Bonaparte. Paris all truth, Versailles all lie; and that lie vented through the mouth of Thiers.

Thiers tells a deputation of the mayors of the Seine-et-Oise: "You may rely upon my word, which I have *never* broken!" He tells the Assembly itself that it was "the most freely elected and most liberal Assembly France ever possessed"; he tells his motley soldiery that it was "the admiration of the world, and the finest army France ever possessed"; he tells the provinces that the bombardment of Paris by him was a myth: "If some cannon shots have been fired, it is not the deed of the army of Versailles, but of some insurgents trying to make believe that they are fighting, while they dare not show their faces." He again tells the provinces that "the artillery of Versailles does not bombard Paris, but only cannonades it." He tells the Archbishop of Paris that the pretended executions and reprisals (!) attributed to the Versailles troops were all moonshine. He tells Paris that he was only anxious "to free it from the hideous tyrants who oppress it," and that, in fact, the Paris of the Commune was "but a handful of criminals."

The Paris of M. Thiers was not the real Paris of the "vile multitude," but a phantom Paris, the Paris of the *francs-fileurs* [absconders], the Paris of the boulevards, male and female—the rich, the capitalist, the gilded, the idle Paris, now thronging with its lackeys, its blacklegs, its literary *bohème*, and its *cocottes* at Versailles, St. Denis, Rueil, and St. Germain; considering the civil war but an agreeable diversion, eying the battle going on through telescopes, counting the rounds of cannon, and swearing by their own honor and that of their prostitutes that the performance was far better got up than it used to be at the

Porte St. Martin. The men who fell were really dead, the cries of the wounded were cries in good earnest, and, besides, the whole thing was so intensely historical.

This is the Paris of M. Thiers, as the emigration of Coblenz was the France of M. de Calonne.

IV

The first attempt of the slaveholders' conspiracy to put down Paris by getting the Prussians to occupy it was frustrated by Bismarck's refusal. The second attempt, that of the eighteenth of March, ended in the rout of the army and the flight to Versailles of the government, which ordered the whole administration to break up and follow in its track. By the semblance of peace negotiations with Paris, Thiers found the time to prepare for war against it. But where to find an army? The remnants of the line regiments were weak in number and unsafe in character. His urgent appeal to the provinces to succor Versailles, by their National Guards and volunteers, met with a flat refusal. Brittany alone furnished a handful of Chouans fighting under a white flag, every one of them wearing on his breast the heart of Jesus in white cloth and shouting "*Vive le roi* [Long live the king]!" Thiers was, therefore, compelled to collect, in hot haste, a motley crew, composed of sailors, marines, pontifical Zouaves, Valentin's gendarmes, and Pietri's *sergents-de-ville* and *mouchards*. This army, however, would have been ridiculously ineffective without the installments of imperialist war prisoners, which Bismarck granted in numbers just sufficient to keep the civil war going and the Versailles government in abject dependence on Prussia. During the war itself the Versailles police had to look after the Versailles army, while the gendarmes had to drag it on by exposing themselves at all posts of danger. The forts which fell were not taken, but bought. The heroism of the Federals convinced Thiers that the resistance of Paris was not to be broken by his own strategic genius and the bayonets at his disposal.

Meanwhile his relations with the provinces became more and more difficult. Not one single address of approval came in to gladden Thiers and his rurals. Quite the contrary.

Deputations and addresses demanding, in a tone anything but respectful, conciliation with Paris on the basis of the unequivocal recognition of the republic, the acknowledgment of the communal liberties, and the dissolution of the National Assembly, whose mandate was extinct, poured in from all sides, and in such numbers that Dufaure, Thiers' Minister of Justice, in his circular of April 23 to the public prosecutors, commanded them to treat "the cry of conciliation" as a crime! In regard, however, of the hopeless prospect held out by his campaign, Thiers resolved to shift his tactics by ordering, all over the country, municipal elections to take place on the thirtieth of April, on the basis of the new municipal law dictated by himself to the National Assembly. What with the intrigues of his prefects, what with police intimidation, he felt quite sanguine of imparting, by the verdict of the provinces, to the National Assembly that moral power it had never possessed, and of getting at last from the provinces the physical force required for the conquest of Paris.

His bandit warfare against Paris, exalted in his own bulletins, and the attempts of his ministers at the establishment, throughout France, of a reign of terror, Thiers was from the beginning anxious to accompany with a little by-play of conciliation, which had to serve more than one purpose. It was to dupe the provinces, to inveigle the middle-class element in Paris, and, above all, to afford the professed republicans in the National Assembly the opportunity of hiding their treason against Paris behind their faith in Thiers. On the twenty-first of March, when still without an army, he had declared to the Assembly: "Come what may, I will not send an army to Paris." On the twenty-seventh of March he rose again. "I have found the republic an accomplished fact, and I am firmly resolved to maintain it." In reality he put down the revolution at Lyons and Marseilles in the name of the republic, while the roars of his rurals drowned the very mention of its name at Versailles. After this exploit he toned down the "accomplished fact" into a hypothetical fact. The Orleans princes, whom he had cautiously warned off Bordeaux, were now, in flagrant breach of the law, permitted to intrigue at Dreux. The concessions held out by Thiers in his interminable interviews with the delegates from Paris and the provinces, although constantly varied in tone and color, according to time and circumstances, did in fact never come to more than the prospective restriction of revenge to the "handful of criminals implicated in the murder of Lecomte and Clément Thomas," on the well-understood premise that Paris and France were unreservedly to accept M. Thiers himself as the best of possible republics, as he, in 1830, had done with Louis Philippe. Even these concessions he not only took care to render doubtful by the official comments put upon them in the Assembly through his ministers. He had his Dufaure to act. Dufaure, this old Orleanist lawyer, had always been the justiciar of the state of siege, as now in 1871, under Thiers, so in 1839 under Louis Philippe, and in 1849 under Louis Bonaparte's presidency. While out of office he made a fortune by pleading for the Paris capitalists, and made political capital by pleading against the laws he himself had originated. He now hurried through the National Assembly not only a set of repressive laws, which were, after the fall of Paris, to extirpate the last remnants of republican liberty in France; he foreshadowed the fate of Paris by abridging the, for him, too slow procedure of court-martial, and by a newfangled, Draconic code of deportation. The Revolution of 1848, abolishing the penalty of death for political crimes, has replaced it by deportation. Louis Bonaparte did not dare, at least not in theory, to re-establish the regime of the guillotine. The rural Assembly, not yet bold enough even to hint that the Parisians were not rebels, but assassins, therefore had to confine its prospective vengeance against Paris to Dufaure's new code of deportation. Under all these circumstances Thiers himself could not have gone on with his comedy of conciliation, had it not, as he intended it to do, drawn forth shrieks of rage from the rurals, whose ruminating mind did understand neither the play nor its necessities of hypocrisy, tergiversation, and procrastination.

In sight of the impending municipal elections of the thirtieth of April, Thiers enacted one of his great conciliation scenes on the twenty-seventh of April. Amidst a flood of sentimental rhetoric he exclaimed from the tribune of the Assembly: "There exists no conspiracy against the republic but that of Paris, which compels us to shed French blood. I repeat it again and again. Let those impious arms fall from the hands which hold them, and chastisement will be arrested at once by an act of peace excluding only the small number of criminals." To the violent interruption of the rurals he replied: "Gentlemen, tell me, I implore you, am I wrong? Do you really regret that I could have stated the truth that the criminals are only a handful? Is it not fortunate in the midst of our misfortunes that those who have been capable of shedding the blood of Clément Thomas and General Lecomte are but rare exceptions?"

France, however, turned a deaf ear to what Thiers flattered himself to be a parliamentary siren's song. Out of seven hundred thousand municipal councilors returned by the thirty-five thousand communes still left to France, the united Legitimists, Orleanists, and Bonapartists did not carry eight thousand. The supplementary elections which followed were still more decidedly hostile. Thus, instead of getting from the provinces the badly needed physical force, the National Assembly lost even its last claim to moral force, that of being the expression of the universal suffrage of the country. To complete the discomfiture, the newly chosen municipal councils of all the cities of France openly threatened the usurping Assembly at Versailles with a counter Assembly at Bordeaux.

Then the long-expected moment of decisive action at last came for Bismarck. He peremptorily summoned Thiers to send to Frankfort plenipotentiaries for the definitive settlement of peace. In humble obedience to the call of his master Thiers hastened to dispatch his trusty Jules Favre, backed by Pouyer-Quertier. Pouyer-Quertier, an "eminent" Rouen cotton spinner, a fervent and even servile partisan of the Second Empire, had never found any fault with it save its commercial treaty with England, prejudicial to his own shop interest. Hardly installed at Bordeaux as Thiers' Minister of Finance, he denounced that "unholy" treaty, hinted at its near abrogation, and even had the effrontery to try, although in vain (having counted without Bismarck), the immediate enforcement of the old protective duties against Alsace, where, he said, no previous international treaties stood in the way. This man, who considered counterrevolution as a means to put down wages at Rouen, and the surrender of French provinces as a means to bring up the price of his wares in France, was he not *the one* predestined to be picked out by Thiers as the helpmate of Jules Favre in his last and crowning treason?

On the arrival at Frankfort of this exquisite pair of plenipotentiaries bully Bismarck at once met them with the imperious alternative: Either the restoration of the empire or the unconditional acceptance of his own peace terms! These terms included a shortening of the intervals in which the war indemnity was to be paid and the continued occupation of the Paris forts by Prussian troops until Bismarck should feel satisfied with the state of things in France, Prussia thus being recognized as the supreme arbiter in internal French politics! In return for this he offered to let loose, for the extermination of Paris, the captive Bonapartist army, and to lend them the direct assistance of Emperor William's troops. He pledged his good faith by making payment of the first installment of the indemnity dependent on the "pacification" of Paris. Such a bait was, of course, eagerly swallowed by Thiers and his plenipotentiaries. They signed the treaty of peace on the tenth of May, and had it endorsed by the Versailles Assembly on the eighteenth.

In the interval between the conclusion of peace and the arrival of the Bonapartist prisoners Thiers felt the more bound to resume his comedy of conciliation, as his republican tools stood in sore need of a pretext for blinking their eyes at the preparations for the carnage of Paris. As late as the eighth of May he replied to a deputation of middle-class conciliators: "Whenever the insurgents will make up their minds for capitulation, the gates of Paris will be flung wide open during a week for all except the murderers of Generals Clément Thomas and Lecomte."

A few days afterwards, when violently interpellated on these promises by the rurals, he refused to enter into any explanations; not, however, without giving them this significant hint: "I tell you there are impatient men among you, men who are in too great a hurry. They must have another eight days; at the end of these eight days there will be no more danger, and the task will be proportionate to their courage and to their capacities." As soon as MacMahon was able to assure him that he could shortly enter Paris, Thiers declared to the Assembly that he would "enter Paris with the *laws* in [his] hands, and demand a full expiation from the wretches who had sacrificed the lives of soldiers and destroyed public monuments." As the moment of decision drew near, he said—to the Assembly: "I shall be pitiless!"—to Paris that it was doomed, and to his Bonapartist banditti that they had state license to wreak vengeance upon Paris to their hearts' content. At last, when treachery had opened the gates of Paris to General Douai, on the twenty-first of May, Thiers, on the twenty-second, revealed to the rurals the "goal" of his conciliation comedy, which they had so obstinately persisted in not understanding. "I told you a few days ago that we were approaching *our goal;* today I come to tell you *the goal* is reached. The victory of order, justice, and civilization is at last won!"

So it was. The civilization and justice of bourgeois order comes out in its lurid light whenever the slaves and drudges of that order rise against their masters. Then this civilization and justice stand forth as undisguised savagery and lawless revenge. Each new crisis in the class struggle between the appropriator and the producer brings out this fact more glaringly. Even the atrocities of the bourgeois in June 1848 vanish before the ineffable infamy of 1871. The self-sacrificing heroism with which the population of Paris—men, women, and children—fought for eight days after the entrance of the Versaillese as much reflects the grandeur of their cause as the infernal deeds of the soldiery reflect the innate spirit of that civilization of which they are the mercenary vindicators. A glorious civilization, indeed, the great problem of which is how to get rid of the heaps of corpses it made after the battle was over!

To find a parallel for the conduct of Thiers and his bloodhounds we must go back to the times of Sulla and the two Triumvirates of Rome. The same wholesale slaughter in cold blood; the same disregard, in massacre, of age and sex; the same system of torturing prisoners; the same proscriptions, but this time of a whole class; the same savage hunt after concealed leaders, lest one might escape; the same denunciations of political and private enemies; the same indifference to the butchery of entire strangers to the feud. There is but this difference, that the Romans had no *mitrailleuses* for the dispatch, in the lump, of the proscribed, and that they had not "the law in their hands," nor on their lips the cry of "civilization."

And after those horrors look upon the other, still more hideous, face of that bourgeois civilization as described by its own press!

"With stray shots," writes the Paris correspondent of a London Tory paper, "still ringing in the distance, and untended wounded wretches dying amidst the tombstones of Père la Chaise—with six thousand terror-stricken insurgents wandering in an agony of despair in the labyrinth of the catacombs and wretches hurried through the streets to be shot down in scores by the *mitrailleuse*—it is revolting to see the cafés filled with the votaries of absinthe, billiards, and dominoes; female profligacy perambulating the boulevards, and the sound of revelry disturbing the night from the *cabinets particuliers* of fashionable restaurants."

M. Edouard Hervé writes in the *Journal de Paris*, a Versaillist journal suppressed by the Commune: "The way in which the population of Paris [!] manifested its satisfaction yesterday was rather more than frivolous, and we fear it will grow worse as time progresses. Paris has now a fete day appearance, which is sadly out of place; and, unless we are to be called the *Parisiens de la décadence*, this sort of thing must come to an end." And then he quotes the passage from Tacitus: " 'Yet, on the morrow of that horrible struggle, even before it was completely over, Rome—degraded and corrupt—began once more to wallow in the voluptuous slough which was destroying its body and polluting its soul—*alibi proelia et vulnera; alibi balnea popinaeque* [here fights and wounds, there baths and restaurants].' " M. Hervé only forgets to say that the "population of Paris" he speaks of is but the population of the Paris of M. Thiers—the *francs-fileurs* returning in throngs from Versailles, St. Denis, Rueil, and St. Germain—*the* Paris of the "Decline."

In all its bloody triumphs over the self-sacrificing champions of a new and better society, that nefarious civilization, based upon the enslavement of labor, drowns the moans of its victims in a hue and cry of calumny, reverberated by a world-wide echo. The serene workingmen's Paris of the Commune is suddenly changed into a pandemonium by the bloodhounds of "order." And what does this tremendous change prove to the bourgeois mind of all countries? Why, that the Commune has conspired against civilization! The Paris people die enthusiastically for the Commune in numbers unequaled in any battle known to history. What does that prove? Why, that the Commune was not the people's own government but the usurpation of a handful of criminals! The women of Paris joyfully give up their lives at the barricades and on the place of execution. What does this prove? Why, that the demon of the Commune has changed them into Megaeras and Hecates! The moderation of the Commune during two months of undisputed sway is equaled only by the heroism of its defense. What does that prove? Why, that for months the Commune carefully hid, under a mask of moderation and humanity, the bloodthirstiness of its fiendish instincts, to be let loose in the hour of its agony!

The workingmen's Paris, in the act of its heroic self-holocaust, involved in its flames buildings and monuments. While tearing to pieces the living body of the proletariat its rulers must no longer expect to return triumphantly into the intact architecture of their abodes. The government of Versailles cries: "Incendiarism!" and whispers this cue to all its agents, down to the remotest hamlet, to hunt up its enemies everywhere as suspect of professional incendiarism. The bourgeoisie of the whole world, which looks complacently upon the wholesale massacre after the battle, is convulsed by horror at the desecration of brick and mortar!

When governments give state licenses to their navies to "kill, *burn*, and destroy," is that a license for incendiarism? When the British troops wantonly set fire to the Capitol at Washington and to the summer palace of the Chinese emperor, was that incendiarism? When the Prussians, not for military reasons, but out of the mere spite of revenge, burned down, with the help of petroleum, towns like Châteaudun and innumerable villages, was that incendiarism? When Thiers, during six weeks, bombarded Paris, under the pretext that he wanted to set fire to those houses only in which there were people, was that incendiarism? In war fire is an arm as legitimate as any. Buildings held by the enemy are shelled to set them on fire. If their defenders have to retire they themselves light the flames to prevent the attack from making use of the buildings. To be burned down has always been the inevitable fate of all buildings situated in the front of battle of all the regular armies of the world. But in the war of the enslaved against their enslavers, the only justifiable war in history, this is by no means to hold good! The Commune used fire strictly as a means of defense. They used it to stop up to the Versailles troops those long, straight avenues which Haussmann had expressly opened to artillery fire; they used it to cover their retreat, in the same way as the Versaillese, in their advance, used their shells, which destroyed at least as many buildings as the fire of the Commune. It is a matter of dispute, even now, which buildings were set fire to by the defense and which by the attack. And the defense resorted to fire only then, when the Versaillese troops had already commenced their wholesale murdering of prisoners. Besides, the Commune had, long before, given full public notice that if driven to extremities they would bury themselves under the ruins of Paris and make Paris a second Moscow, as the government of defense, but only as a cloak for its treason, had promised to do. For this purpose Trochu had found them the petroleum. The Commune knew that its opponents cared nothing for the lives of the Paris people, but cared much for their own Paris buildings. And Thiers, on the other hand, had given them notice that he would be implacable in his vengeance. No sooner had he got his army ready on one side and the Prussians shutting up the trap on the other than he proclaimed: "I shall be pitiless! The expiation will be complete, and justice will be stern!" If the acts of the Paris workingmen were vandalism, it was the vandalism of defense in despair, not the vandalism of triumph, like that which the Christians perpetrated upon the really priceless art treasures of heathen antiquity; and even that vandalism has been justified by the historian as an unavoidable and comparatively trifling concomitant to the titanic struggle between a new society arising and an old one breaking down. It was still less the vandalism of Haussmann, razing historic Paris to make place for the Paris of the sight-seer!

But the execution by the Commune of the sixty-four hostages, with the Archbishop of Paris at their head! The bourgeoisie and its army in June 1848 re-established a custom which had long disappeared from the practice of war—the shooting of their defenseless prisoners. This brutal custom has since been more or less strictly adhered to by the suppressors of all popular commotions in Europe and India, thus proving that it constitutes a real "progress of civilization!" On the other hand, the Prussians, in France, had re-established the practice of taking hostages—innocent men, who, with their lives, were to answer to them for the acts of others. When Thiers, as we have seen, from the very beginning of the conflict, enforced the humane practice of shooting down the communal prisoners, the Commune, to protect their lives, was obliged to resort to the Prussian practice of securing hostages. The lives of the hostages had been forfeited over and over again by the continued shooting of prisoners on the part of the Versaillese. How could they be spared any longer after the carnage with which MacMahon's praetorians celebrated their entrance into Paris? Was even the last check upon the unscrupulous ferocity of bourgeois governments—the taking of hostages—to be made a mere sham of? The real murderer of Archbishop Darboy is Thiers. The Commune again and again had offered to exchange the archbishop, and ever so many priests in the bargain, against the single Blanqui, then in the hands of Thiers. Thiers obstinately refused. He knew that with Blanqui he would give to the Commune a head, while the archbishop would serve his purpose best in the shape of a corpse. Thiers acted upon the precedent of Cavaignac. How, in June 1848, did not Cavaignac and his men of order raise shouts of horror by stigmatizing the insurgents as the assassins of Archbishop Affre! They knew perfectly well that the archbishop had been shot by the soldiers of order. M. Jacquemet, the archbishop's vicar-general, present on the spot, had immediately afterwards handed them his evidence to that effect.

All this chorus of calumny, which the party of order never fail, in their orgies of blood, to raise against their victims, only proves that the bourgeois of our days considers himself the legitimate successor to the baron of old, who thought every weapon in his own hand fair against the plebeian, while in the hands of the plebeian a weapon of any kind constituted in itself a crime.

The conspiracy of the ruling class to break down the revolution by a civil war carried on under the patronage of the foreign invader—a conspiracy which we have traced from the very fourth of September down to the entrance of MacMahon's praetorians through the gate of St. Cloud—culminated in the carnage of Paris. Bismarck gloats over the ruins of Paris, in which he saw perhaps the first installment of that general destruction of great cities he had prayed for when still a simple rural in the Prussian *Chambre introuvable* of 1849. He gloats over the cadavers of the Paris proletariat. For him this is not only the extermination of revolution, but the extinction of France, now decapitated in reality, and by the French Government itself. With the shallowness characteristic of all successful statesmen he sees but the surface of this tremendous historic event. Whenever before has history exhibited the spectacle of a conqueror crowning his victory by turning into not only the gendarme, but the hired bravo of the conquered government? There existed no war between Prussia and the Commune of Paris. On the contrary, the Commune had accepted the peace preliminaries and Prussia had announced her neutrality. Prussia was, therefore, no belligerent. She acted the part of a bravo, a cowardly bravo, because incurring no danger; a hired bravo, because stipulating beforehand the payment of her blood money of five hundred millions on the fall of Paris. And thus, at last, came out the true character of the war, ordained by Providence as a chastisement of godless and debauched France by pious and moral Germany! And this unparalleled breach of the law of nations, even as understood by the old-world lawyers, instead of arousing the "civilized" governments of Europe to declare the felonious Prussian Government the mere tool of the St. Petersburg Cabinet, an outlaw among nations, only incites them to consider whether the few victims who escape the double cordon around Paris are not to be given up to the hangman at Versailles!

That after the most tremendous war of modern times the conquering and the conquered hosts should fraternize for the common massacre of the proletariat—this unparalleled event does indicate, not, as Bismarck thinks, the final repression of a new society upheaving, but the crumbling into dust of bourgeois society. The highest heroic effort of which old society is still capable is national war, and this is now proved to be a mere governmental humbug, intended to defer the struggle of classes, and to be thrown aside as soon as that class struggle bursts out into civil war. Class rule is no longer able to disguise itself in a national uniform; the national governments are *one* as against the proletariat!

After Whitsunday 1871 there can be neither peace nor truce possible between the workingmen of France and the appropriators of their product. The iron hand of a mercenary soldiery may keep for a time both classes tied down in common oppression. But the battle must break out again and again in ever growing dimensions, and there can be no doubt as to who will be the victor in the end—the appropriating few, or the immense working majority. And the French working class is only the advanced guard of the modern proletariat.

While the European governments thus testify, before Paris, to the international character of class rule, they cry down the International Workingmen's Association—the international counterorganization of labor against the cosmopolitan conspiracy of capital—as the fountainhead of all these disasters. Thiers denounced it as the despot of labor, pretending to be its liberator. Picard ordered that all communications between the French Internationals and those abroad should be cut off; Count Jaubert, Thiers' mummified accomplice of 1835, declares it the great problem of all civilized governments to weed it out. The rurals roar against it, and the whole European press joins the chorus. An honorable French writer, completely foreign to our Association, speaks as follows: "The members of the Central Committee of the National Guard, as well as the greater part of the members of the Commune, are the most active, intelligent, and energetic minds of the International Workingmen's Association . . . men who are thoroughly honest, sincere, intelligent, devoted, pure, and fanatical in the *good* sense of the word." The police-tinged bourgeois mind naturally imagines to itself the International Workingmen's Association as acting in the manner of a secret conspiracy, its central body ordering, from time to time, explosions in different countries. Our Association is, in fact, nothing but the international bond between the most advanced workingmen in the various countries of the civilized world. Wherever, in whatever shape, and under whatever conditions the class struggle obtains any consistency, it is but natural that members of our Association should stand in the foreground. The soil out of which it grows is modern society itself. It cannot be stamped out by any amount of carnage. To stamp it out the governments would have to stamp out the despotism of capital over labor—the condition of their own parasitical existence.

Workingmen's Paris, with its Commune, will be forever celebrated as the glorious harbinger of a new society. Its martyrs are enshrined in the great heart of the working class. Its exterminators history has already nailed to that eternal pillory from which all the prayers of their priests will not avail to redeem them.

London, May 30, 1871

[AN AFTERTHOUGHT ON THE PARIS COMMUNE]

MARX TO F. DOMELA-NIEUWENHUIS

London, February 22, 1881

. . . One thing you can at any rate be sure of: a socialist government does not come into power in a country unless conditions are so developed that it can immediately take the necessary measures for intimidating the mass of the bourgeoisie sufficiently to gain time—the first *desideratum*—for permanent action.

Perhaps you will refer me to the Paris Commune; but apart from the fact that this was merely the rising of a city under exceptional conditions, the majority of the Commune was in no wise socialist, nor could it be. With a modicum of common sense, however, it could have reached a compromise with Versailles useful to the whole mass of the people—the only thing that could be reached at the time. The appropriation of the Bank of France alone would have been enough to put an end with terror to the vaunt of the Versailles people, etc. . . .

XVI. *Excerpt from* The Origin of the Family, Private Property and the State

FRIEDRICH ENGELS

The first edition of this book was published in 1884. It is largely an exposition of the researches of the American anthropologist, Lewis H. Morgan, in the light of the materialist conception of history.—Ed.

As the state arose from the need to hold class antagonisms in check, but as it arose, at the same time, in the midst of the conflict of these classes, it is, as a rule, the state of the most powerful, economically dominant class, which, through the medium of the state, becomes also the politically dominant class, and thus acquires new means of holding down and exploiting the oppressed class. Thus the state of antiquity was above all the state of the slaveowners for the purpose of holding down the slaves, as the feudal state was the organ of the nobility for holding down the peasant serfs and bondsmen, and the modern representative state is an instrument of exploitation of wage labor by capital. By way of exception, however, periods occur in which the warring classes balance each other so nearly that the state power, as ostensible mediator, acquires, for the moment, a certain degree of independence of both. Such was the absolute monarchy of the seventeenth and eighteenth centuries, which held the balance between the nobility and the class of burghers; such was the Bonapartism of the first, and still more of the second French empire, which played off the proletariat against the bourgeoisie and the bourgeoisie against the proletariat. The latest performance of this kind, in which ruler and ruled appear equally ridiculous, is the new German Empire of the Bismarck nation: here capitalists and workers are balanced against each other and equally cheated for the benefit of the impoverished Prussian cabbage *Junkers*.

In most of the historical states the rights of citizens are, besides, apportioned according to their wealth, thus directly expressing the fact that the state is an organization of the possessing class for its protection against the non-possessing class. It was so already in the Athenian and Roman classification according to property. It was so in the medieval feudal state, in which the alignment of political power was in conformity with the amount of land owned. It is seen in the electoral qualifications of the modern representative states. Yet this political recognition of property distinctions is by no means essential. On the contrary, it marks a low stage of state development. The highest form of the state, the democratic republic, which under our modern conditions of society is more and more becoming an inevitable necessity, and is the form of state in which alone the last decisive struggle between proletariat and bourgeoisie can be fought out—the democratic republic officially knows nothing any more of property distinctions. In it wealth exercises its power indirectly, but all the more surely. On the one hand, in the form of the direct corruption of officials, of which America provides the classical example; on the other hand, in the form of an alliance between government and stock exchange, which becomes the easier to achieve the more the public debt increases and the more joint-stock companies concentrate in their hands not only transport but also production itself, using the stock exchange as their center. The latest French republic, as well as the United States, is a striking example of this; and good old Switzerland has contributed its share in this field. But that a democratic republic is not essential for this fraternal alliance between government and stock exchange is proved by England and also by the new German Empire, where one cannot tell who was elevated more by universal suffrage, Bismarck or Bleichröder. And lastly, the possessing class rules directly through the medium of universal suffrage. As long as the oppressed class, in our case therefore the proletariat, is not yet ripe to emancipate itself, it will in its majority regard the existing order of society as the only one possible and, politically, will form the tail of the capitalist class, its extreme left wing. To the extent, however, that this class matures for its self-emancipation, it constitutes itself as its own party and elects its own representatives, and not those of the capitalists. Thus universal suffrage is the gauge of the maturity of the working class. It cannot and never will be anything more in the present-day state, but that is sufficient. On the day the thermometer of universal suffrage registers boiling point among the workers, both they and the capitalists will know what to do.

The state, then, has not existed from all eternity. There have been societies that did without it, that had no conception of the state and state power. At a certain stage of economic development, which was necessarily bound up with the cleavage of society into classes, the state became a necessity, owing to this cleavage. We are now rapidly approaching a stage in the development of production at which the existence of these classes not only will have ceased to be a necessity, but will become a positive hindrance to production. They will fall as inevitably as they arose at an earlier stage. Along with them the state will inevitably fall. The society that will organize production on the basis of a free and equal association of the producers will put the whole machinery of state where it will then belong: into the museum of antiquities, by the side of the spinning wheel and the bronze ax.

XVII. Letters on Historical Materialism

FRIEDRICH ENGELS

These letters were written by Engels during the last years of his life, in reply to correspondents who raised questions concerning the meaning of historical materialism. Engels acknowledged that he and Marx had overemphasized the role of the economic factor in history. Nevertheless, he still held that the mode of production was the ultimate determining element in history, and he tried to clarify the meaning of this assertion. His analysis of "ideology" as characterized by a "false consciousness" was pathfinding. Engels rebuked those "Marxist" scholars who try to make of historical materialism a dogmatic substitute for the study of the facts.—ED.

ENGELS TO CONRAD SCHMIDT

London, August 5, 1890

. . . I saw a review of Paul Barth's book[1] by that bird of ill omen, Moritz Wirth, in the Vienna *Deutsche Worte*, and *this* criticism left on my mind an unfavorable impression of the book itself, as well. I will have a look at it, but I must say that if "little Moritz" is right when he quotes Barth as stating that the sole example of the dependence of philosophy, etc., on the material conditions of existence which he can find in all Marx's works is that Descartes declares animals to be machines, then I am sorry for the

[1] Paul Barth, *The Philosophy of History of Hegel and the Hegelians up to Marx and Hartmann.*

man who can write such a thing. And if this man has not yet discovered that while the material mode of existence is the *primum agens* this does not preclude the ideological spheres from reacting upon it in their turn, though with a secondary effect, he cannot possibly have understood the subject he is writing about. However, as I have said, all this is secondhand and little Moritz is a dangerous friend. The materialist conception of history has a lot of them nowadays, to whom it serves as an excuse for *not* studying history. Just as Marx used to say, commenting on the French "Marxists" of the late seventies: "All I know is that I am not a Marxist."

There has also been a discussion in the *Volkstribüne* about the distribution of products in future society, whether this will take place according to the amount of work done or otherwise. The question has been approached very "materialistically" in opposition to certain idealistic phraseology about justice. But strangely enough, it has not struck anyone that, after all, the method of distribution essentially depends on *how much* there is to distribute, and that this must surely change with the progress of production and social organization, so that the method of distribution may also change. But to everyone who took part in the discussion, "socialist society" appeared not as something undergoing continuous change and progress, but as a stable affair fixed once for all, which must, therefore, have a method of distribution fixed once for all. All one can reasonably do, however, is (1) try and discover the method of distribution to be used *at the beginning* and (2) try and find the *general tendency* of the further development. But about this I do not find a single word in the whole debate.

In general, the word "materialistic" serves many of the younger writers in Germany as a mere phrase with which anything and everything is labeled without further study, that is, they stick on this label and then consider the question disposed of. But our conception of history is above all a guide to study, not a lever for construction after the manner of the Hegelian. All history must be studied afresh, the conditions of existence of the different formations of society must be examined individually before the attempt is made to deduce from them the political, civil-law, aesthetic, philosophic, religious, etc., views corresponding to them. Up to now but little has been done here because only a few people have got down to it seriously. In this field we can utilize heaps of help—it is immensely big—and anyone who will work seriously can achieve much and distinguish himself. But instead of this too many of the younger Germans simply make use of the phrase "historical materialism" (and *everything* can be turned into a phrase) only in order to get their own relatively scanty historical knowledge—for economic history is still in its swaddling clothes! —constructed into a neat system as quickly as possible, and they then deem themselves something very tremendous. And after that a Barth can come along and attack the thing itself, which in his circle has indeed been degraded to a mere phrase.

However, all this will right itself. We are strong enough in Germany now to stand a lot. One of the greatest services which the anti-socialist law did us was to free us from the obtrusiveness of the German intellectual who had got tinged with socialism. We are now strong enough to digest the German intellectual, too, who is giving himself great airs again. You, who have really done something, must have noticed yourself how few of the young literary men who fasten themselves onto the party give themselves the trouble to study economics, the history of economics, the history of trade, of industry, of agriculture, of the formations of society. How many know anything of Maurer except his name! The self-sufficiency of the journalist must serve for everything here, and the result looks like it. It often seems as if these gentlemen think anything is good enough for the workers. If these gentlemen only knew that Marx thought his best things were still not good enough for the workers, how he regarded it as a crime to offer the workers anything but the very best! . . .

ENGELS TO JOSEPH BLOCH

London, September 21–22, 1890

. . . According to the materialist conception of history, the *ultimately* determining element in history is the production and reproduction of real life. More than this neither Marx nor I has ever asserted. Hence if somebody twists this into saying that the economic element is the *only* determining one he transforms that proposition into a meaningless, abstract, senseless phrase. The economic situation is the basis, but the various elements of the superstructure—political forms of the class struggle and its results, to wit: constitutions established by the victorious class after a successful battle, etc., juridical forms, and even the reflexes of all these actual struggles in the brains of the participants, political, juristic, philosophical theories, religious views, and their further development into systems of dogmas—also exercise their influence upon the course of the historical struggles and in many cases preponderate in determining their *form*. There is an interaction of all these elements in which, amidst all the endless host of accidents (that is, of things and events whose inner interconnection is so remote or so impossible of proof that we can regard it as non-existent, as negligible), the economic movement finally asserts itself as necessary. Otherwise the application of the theory to any period of history would be easier than the solution of a simple equation of the first degree.

We make our history ourselves, but, in the first place, under very definite assumptions and conditions. Among these the economic ones are ultimately decisive. But the political ones, etc., and indeed even the traditions which haunt human minds also play a part, although not the decisive one. The Prussian state also arose and developed from historical, ultimately economic, causes. But it could scarcely be maintained without pedantry that among the many small states of north Germany, Brandenburg was specifically determined by economic necessity to become the great power embodying the economic, linguistic, and, after the Reformation, also the religious difference between North and South, and not by other elements as well (above all, by its entanglement with Poland, owing to the possession of Prussia, and hence with international political relations—which were indeed also decisive in the formation of the Austrian dynastic power). Without making oneself ridiculous it would be a difficult thing to explain in terms of economics the existence of every small state in Germany, past and present, or the origin of the High German consonant permutations, which widened the geographic partition wall formed by the mountains from the Sudetic range to the Taunus to form a regular fissure across all Germany.

In the second place, however, history is made in such a way that the final result always arises from conflicts between many individual wills, of which each in turn has been made what it is by a host of particular conditions of life. Thus there are innumerable intersecting forces, an infinite series of parallelograms of forces which give rise to one resultant—the historical event. This may again itself be viewed as the product of a power which works as a whole *unconsciously* and without volition. For what each individual wills is obstructed by everyone else, and what emerges is something that no one willed. Thus history has proceeded hitherto in the manner of a natural process and is essentially subject to the same laws of motion. But from the fact that the wills of individuals—each of whom desires what he is impelled to by his physical constitution and external, in the last resort economic, circumstances (either his own personal circumstances or those of society in general)—do not attain what they want, but are merged into an aggregate mean, a common resultant, it must not be concluded that they are equal to zero. On the contrary, each contributes to the resultant and is to this extent included in it.

I would furthermore ask you to study this theory from its original sources and not at second hand; it is really much easier. Marx hardly wrote anything in which it did not play a part. But especially *The Eighteenth Brumaire of Louis Bonaparte* is a most excellent example of its application. There are also many allusions to it in *Capital*. Then may I also direct you to my writings: *Herr Eugen Dühring's Revolution in Science* and *Ludwig Feuerbach and the End of Classical German Philosophy*, in which I have given the most detailed account of historical materialism that, as far as I know, exists.

Marx and I are ourselves partly to blame for the fact that the younger people sometimes lay more stress on the economic side than is due to it. We had to emphasize the main principle vis-à-vis our adversaries, who denied it, and we had not always the time, the place, or the opportunity to give their due to the other elements involved in the interaction. But when it came to presenting a section of history, that is, to making a practical application, it was a different matter and there no error was permissible. Unfortunately, however, it happens only too often that people think they have fully understood a new theory and can apply it without more ado from the moment they have assimilated its main principles, and even those not always correctly. And I cannot exempt many of the more recent "Marxists" from this reproach, for the most amazing rubbish has been produced in this quarter, too. . . .

ENGELS TO CONRAD SCHMIDT

London, October 27, 1890

I am taking advantage of the first free moments to reply to you. I think you would do very well to take the post in Zurich. You could always learn a good deal about economics there, especially if you bear in mind that Zurich is after all only a third-rate money and speculation market, so that the impressions which make themselves felt there are weakened by twofold or threefold reflection, or are deliberately distorted. But you will get a practical knowledge of the mechanism and be obliged to follow the stock exchange reports from London, New York, Paris, Berlin, and Vienna at first hand, and thus the world market, in its reflex as money and stock market, will reveal itself to you. Economic, political, and other reflections are just like those in the human eye: they pass through a condensing lens, and therefore appear upside down, standing on their heads. Only the nervous apparatus which would put them on their feet again for presentation to us is lacking. The money-market man sees the movement of industry and of the world market only in the inverted reflection of the money and stock market, and so effect becomes cause to him. I noticed that already in the forties in Manchester: the London stock exchange reports were utterly useless for understanding the course of industry and its periodic maxima and minima because these gentry tried to explain everything by crises on the money market, which of course were themselves generally only symptoms. At that time the point was to disprove temporary overproduction as the origin of industrial crises, so that the thing had in addition its tendentious side provocative of distortion. This point now ceases to exist—for us, at any rate, for good and all—besides which, it is indeed a fact that the money market can also have its own crises, in which direct disturbances of industry play only a subordinate part or no part at all. Here there is still much to be established and examined, especially in the history of the last twenty years.

Where there is division of labor on a social scale there the separate labor processes become independent of each other. In the last instance production is the decisive factor. But as soon as trade in products becomes independent of production proper it follows a movement of its own, which, while governed as a whole by that of production, still in particulars and within this general dependence again follows laws of its own inherent in the nature of this new factor; this movement has phases of its own and in its turn reacts on the movement of production. The discovery of America was due to the thirst for gold, which had previously driven the Portuguese to Africa (cf. Soetbeer's *Production of Precious Metals*), because the enormously extended European industry of the fourteenth and fifteenth centuries and the trade corresponding to it demanded more means of exchange than Germany, the great silver country from 1450 to 1550, could provide. The conquest of India by the Portuguese, Dutch, and English between 1500 and 1800 had *imports from* India as its object—nobody dreamed of exporting anything there. And yet what a colossal reaction these discoveries and conquests, brought about solely by trade interests, had upon industry: it was only the need for *exports to* these countries that created and developed modern large-scale industry.

So it is, too, with the money market. As soon as trade in money becomes separate from trade in commodities it has—under certain conditions imposed by production and commodity trade and within these limits—a development of its own, special laws determined by its own nature and separate phases. If to this is added that money trade, developing further, comes to include trade in securities and that these securities are not only government papers but also industrial and transport stocks, so that money trade gains direct control over a portion of the production by which, taken as a whole, it is itself controlled, then the reaction of money trading on production becomes still stronger and more complicated. The traders in money are the owners of railways, mines, ironworks, etc. These means of production take on a double aspect: their operation has to be directed sometimes in the interests of direct production, but sometimes also according to the requirements of the shareholders, so far as they are money traders. The most striking example of this is furnished by the North American railways, whose operation is entirely dependent on the daily stock exchange operations of a Jay Gould or a Vanderbilt, etc., which have nothing whatever to do with the particular railway and its interests as a means of communication. And even here in England we have seen contests lasting decades between different railway companies over the boundaries of their respective territories—contests on which an enormous amount of money was thrown away, not in the interests of production and communication, but simply because of a rivalry whose sole object usually was to facilitate the stock exchange transactions of the shareholding money traders.

With these few indications of my conception of the relation of production to commodity trade and of both to money trade, I have answered, in essence, your questions about "historical materialism" generally. The thing is easiest to grasp from the point of view of the division of labor. Society gives rise to certain common functions which it cannot dispense with. The persons appointed for this purpose form a new branch of the division of labor *within society*. This gives them particular interests, distinct, too, from the interests of those who empowered them; they make themselves independent of the latter and—the state is in being. And now things proceed in a way similar to that in commodity trade and later in money trade: the new independent power, while having, in the main, to follow the movement of production, reacts in its turn, by virtue of its inherent relative independence—that is, the relative independence once transferred to it and gradually further developed—upon the conditions and course of production. It is the interaction of two unequal forces: on the one hand, the economic movement; on the other, the new political power, which strives for as much independence as possible, and which, having once been established, is endowed with a movement of its own. On the whole, the economic movement gets its way, but it also has to suffer reactions from the political movement which it itself established and endowed with relative independence, from the movement of the state power, on the one hand, and of the opposition simultaneously engendered, on the other. Just as the movement of the industrial market is, in the main and with the reservations already indicated, reflected in the money market and, of course, in *inverted* form, so the struggle between the classes already existing and fighting with one another is reflected in the struggle between government and opposition, but likewise in inverted form, no longer directly but indirectly, not as a class struggle but as a fight for political principles, and so distorted that it has taken us thousands of years to get behind it.

The reaction of the state power upon economic development can be of three kinds: it can run in the same direction, and then development is more rapid; it can oppose the line of development, in which case nowadays it will go to pieces in the long run in every great people; or it can prevent the economic development from proceeding along certain lines, and prescribe other lines. This case ultimately reduces itself to one of the two previous ones. But it is obvious that in cases two and three the political power can do great damage to the economic development and cause a great squandering of energy and material.

Then there is also the case of the conquest and brutal destruction of economic resources, by which, in certain circumstances, a whole local or national economic development could formerly be ruined. Nowadays such a case usually has the opposite effect, at least with great peoples: in the long run the vanquished often gains more economically, politically, and morally than the victor.

Similarly with law. As soon as the new division of labor which creates professional lawyers becomes necessary, another new and independent sphere is opened up which, for all its general dependence on production and trade, has also a special capacity for reacting upon these spheres. In a modern state law must not only correspond to the general economic condition and be its expression, but must also be an *internally coherent* expression which does not, owing to inner contradictions, reduce itself to nought. And in order to achieve this the faithful reflection of economic conditions suffers increasingly. All the more so the more rarely it happens that a code of law is the blunt, unmitigated, unadulterated expression of the domination of a class—this in itself would offend the "conception of right." Even in the Code Napoléon the pure, consistent conception of right held by the revolutionary bourgeoisie of 1792–96 is already adulterated in many ways and, in so far as it is embodied there, daily has to undergo all sorts of attenuations, owing to the rising power of the proletariat. This does not prevent the Code Napoléon from being the statute book which serves as the basis of every new code of law in every part of the world. Thus to a great extent the course of the "development of right" consists only, first, in the attempt to do away with the contradictions arising from the direct translation of economic relations into legal principles, and to establish a harmonious system of law, and then in the repeated breaches made in this system by the influence and compulsion of further economic development, which involves it in further contradictions. (I am speaking here for the moment only of civil law.)

The reflection of economic relations as legal principles is necessarily also a topsy-turvy one: it goes on without the person who is acting being conscious of it; the jurist imagines he is operating with a priori propositions, whereas they are really only economic reflexes, so everything is upside down. And it seems to me obvious that this inversion, which, so long as it remains unrecognized, forms what we call *ideological outlook*, reacts in its turn upon the economic basis and may, within certain limits, modify it. The basis of the right of inheritance—assuming that the stages reached in the development of the family are the same—is an economic one. Nevertheless, it would be difficult to prove, for instance, that the absolute liberty of the testator in England and the severe restrictions in every detail imposed upon him in France are owing to economic causes alone. Both react, however, on the economic sphere to a very considerable extent, because they influence the distribution of property.

As to the realms of ideology which soar still higher in the air—religion, philosophy, etc.—these have a prehistoric stock, found already in existence by and taken over in the historical period, of what we should today call bunk. These various false conceptions of nature, of man's own being, of spirits, magic forces, etc., have for the most part only a negative economic element as their basis; the low economic development of the prehistoric period is supplemented and also partially conditioned and even caused by the false conceptions of nature. And even though economic necessity was the main driving force of the progressive knowledge of nature and has become ever more so, it would surely be pedantic to try to find economic causes for all this primitive nonsense. The history of science is the history of the gradual clearing away of this nonsense, or rather of its replacement by fresh but always less absurd nonsense. The people who attend to this belong in their turn to special spheres in the division of labor and appear to themselves to be working in an independent field. And to the extent that they form an independent group within the social division of labor, their productions, including their errors, react upon the whole development of society, even on its economic development. But all the same, they themselves are in turn under the dominating influence of economic development. In philosophy, for instance, this can be most readily proved true for the bourgeois period. Hobbes was the first modern materialist (in the eighteenth-century sense), but he was an absolutist in a period when absolute monarchy was at its height throughout Europe and in England entered the lists against the people. Locke, both in religion and politics, was the child of the class compromise of 1688. The English deists and their more consistent continuators, the French materialists, were the true philosophers of the bourgeoisie, the French even of the bourgeois revolution. The German Philistine runs through German philosophy from Kant to Hegel, sometimes positively and sometimes negatively. But as a definite sphere in the division of labor the philosophy of every epoch presupposes certain definite thought material handed down to it by its predecessors, from which it takes its start. And that is why economically backward countries can still play first fiddle in philosophy: France in the eighteenth century as compared with England, on whose philosophy the French based themselves, and later Germany as compared with both. But in France as well as Germany philosophy and the general blossoming of literature at that time were the result of a rising economic development. I consider the ultimate supremacy of economic development established in these spheres, too, but it comes to pass within the limitations imposed by the particular sphere itself: in philosophy, for instance, by the operation of economic influences (which again generally act only under political, etc., disguises) upon the existing philosophic material handed down by predecessors. Here economy creates nothing anew, but it determines the way in which the thought material found in existence is altered and further developed, and that, too, for the most part indirectly, for it is the political, legal, and moral reflexes which exert the greatest direct influence on philosophy.

About religion I have said what was most necessary in the last section on Feuerbach.

If therefore Barth supposes that we deny any and every reaction of the political, etc., reflexes of the economic movement upon the movement itself, he is simply tilting at windmills. He only has to look at Marx's *Eighteenth Brumaire,* which deals almost exclusively with the *particular* part played by political struggles and events, of course within their *general* dependence upon economic conditions. Or *Capital,* the section on the working day, for instance, where legislation, which is surely a political act, has such a trenchant effect. Or the section on the history of the bourgeoisie. (Chapter XXIV.) Or why do we fight for the political dictatorship of the proletariat if political power is economically impotent? Force (that is, state power) is also an economic power!

But I have no time to criticize the book now. I must

first get out Volume III, and besides, I think that Bernstein, for instance, could deal with it quite effectively.

What these gentlemen all lack is dialectics. They always see only here cause, there effect. That this is a hollow abstraction, that such metaphysical polar opposites exist in the real world only during crises, while the whole vast process goes on in the form of interaction—though of very unequal forces, the economic movement being by far the strongest, most primordial, most decisive—that here everything is relative and nothing absolute—this they never begin to see. As far as they are concerned, Hegel never existed . . .

ENGELS TO FRANZ MEHRING

London, July 14, 1893

Today is my first opportunity to thank you for the *Lessing Legend* you were kind enough to send me. I did not want to reply with a bare formal acknowledgment of receipt of the book, but intended at the same time to tell you something about it, about its contents. Hence the delay.

I shall begin at the end—the appendix on historical materialism, in which you have lined up the main things excellently and for any unprejudiced person convincingly. If I find anything to object to it is that you give me more credit than I deserve, even if I count in everything which I might possibly have found out for myself—in time—but which Marx with his more rapid *coup d'œil* and wider vision discovered much more quickly. When one has the good fortune to work for forty years with a man like Marx, one usually does not during his lifetime get the recognition one thinks one deserves. Then, when the greater man dies, the lesser easily gets overrated and this seems to me to be just my case at present; history will set all this right in the end, and by that time one will have quietly turned up one's toes and not know anything any more about anything.

Otherwise only one more point is lacking, which, however, Marx and I always failed to stress enough in our writings and in regard to which we are all equally guilty. That is to say, we all laid, and *were bound* to lay, the main emphasis, in the first place, on the *derivation* of political, juridical, and other ideological notions, and of actions arising through the medium of these notions, from basic economic facts. But in so doing we neglected the formal side—the ways and means by which these notions, etc., come about—for the sake of the content. This has given our adversaries a welcome opportunity for misunderstandings and distortions, of which Paul Barth is a striking example.

Ideology is a process accomplished by the so-called thinker consciously, it is true, but with a false consciousness. The real motive forces impelling him remain unknown to him; otherwise it simply would not be an ideological process. Hence he imagines false or seeming motive forces. Because it is a process of thought, he derives its form as well as its content from pure thought, either his own or that of his predecessors. He works with mere thought material, which he accepts without examination as the product of thought, and does not investigate further for a more remote source independent of thought; indeed, this is a matter of course to him, because as all action is *mediated* by thought it appears to him to be ultimately *based* upon thought.

The historical ideologist (historical is here simply meant to comprise the political, juridical, philosophical, theological—in short, all the spheres belonging to *society* and not only to nature) thus possesses in every sphere of science material which has formed itself independently out of the thought of previous generations and has gone through its own independent course of development in the brains of these successive generations. True, external facts belonging to one or another sphere may have exercised a co-determining influence on this development, but the tacit presupposition is that these facts themselves are also only the fruits of a process of thought, and so we still remain within that realm of mere thought, which apparently has successfully digested even the hardest facts.

It is above all this semblance of an independent history of state constitutions, of systems of law, of ideological conceptions in every separate domain that dazzles most people. If Luther and Calvin "overcome" the official Catholic religion or Hegel "overcomes" Fichte and Kant, or Rousseau with his republican *contrat social* indirectly "overcomes" the constitutional Montesquieu, this is a process which remains within theology, philosophy, or political science, represents a stage in the history of these particular spheres of thought, and never passes beyond the sphere of thought. And since the bourgeois illusion of the eternity and finality of capitalist production has been added as well, even the overcoming of the mercantilists by the physiocrats and Adam Smith is accounted as a sheer victory of thought; not as the reflection in thought of changed economic facts, but as the finally achieved correct understanding of actual conditions subsisting always and everywhere—in fact, if Richard Coeur de Lion and Philip Augustus had introduced free trade instead of getting mixed up in the Crusades we should have been spared five hundred years of misery and stupidity.

This aspect of the matter, which I can only indicate here, we have all, I think, neglected more than it deserves. It is the old story: form is always neglected at first for content. As I say, I have done that, too, and the mistake has always struck me only later. So I am not only far from reproaching you with this in any way—as the older of the guilty parties I certainly have no right to do so; on the contrary. But I would like all the same to draw your attention to this point for the future.

Hanging together with this is the fatuous notion of the ideologists that because we deny an independent historical development to the various ideological spheres which play a part in history we also deny them any *effect upon history*. The basis of this is the common undialectical conception of cause and effect as rigidly opposite poles, the total disregarding of interaction. These gentlemen often almost deliberately forget that once a historic element has been brought into the world by other, ultimately economic causes it reacts, can react on its environment and even on the causes that have given rise to it. For instance, Barth on the priesthood and religion, your page 475. . . .

ENGELS TO HEINZ STARKENBURG

London, January 25, 1894

Here is the answer to your questions:

1. What we understand by the economic relations, which we regard as the determining basis of the history of society, is the manner and method by which men in a given society produce their means of subsistence and exchange the products among themselves (in so far as division of labor exists). Thus the *entire technique* of production and transport is here included. According to our conception, this technique also determines the manner and method of exchange and, further, of the distribution of products, and with it, after the dissolution of gentile society, also the division into classes, and hence the relations of lordship and servitude and with them the state, politics, law, etc. Further included in economic relations are the *geographical basis* on which they operate and those remnants of earlier stages of economic development which have actually been transmitted and have survived—often only through tradition or by force of inertia; also of course the external environment which surrounds this form of society.

If, as you say, technique largely depends on the state of science, science depends far more still on the *state* and the *requirements* of technique. If society has a technical need, that helps science forward more than ten universities. The whole of hydrostatics (Torricelli, etc.) was called forth by the necessity for regulating the mountain streams of Italy in the sixteenth and seventeenth centuries. We have known anything reasonable about electricity only since its technical applicability was discovered. But unfortunately it has become the custom in Germany to write the history of the sciences as if they had fallen from the skies.

2. We regard economic conditions as that which ultimately conditions historical development. But race is itself an economic factor. Here, however, two points must not be overlooked:

a. Political, juridical, philosophical, religious, literary, artistic, etc., development is based on economic development. But all these react upon one another and also upon the economic basis. It is not that the economic situation is *cause, solely active*, while everything else is only passive effect. There is, rather, interaction on the basis of economic necessity, which *ultimately* always asserts itself. The state, for instance, exercises an influence by protective tariffs, free trade, good or bad fiscal system; and even the deadly inanition and impotence of the German Philistine, arising from the miserable economic condition of Germany from 1648 to 1830 and expressing themselves at first in pietism, then in sentimentality and cringing servility to princes and nobles, were not without economic effect. That was one of the greatest hindrances to recovery, and was not shaken until the revolutionary and Napoleonic wars made the chronic misery an acute one. So it is not, as people try here and there conveniently to imagine, that the economic situation produces an automatic effect. No. Men make their history themselves, only they do so in a given environment, which conditions it, and on the basis of actual relations already existing, among which the economic relations, however much they may be influenced by the other, the political and ideological relations, are still ultimately the decisive ones, forming the keynote which runs through them and alone leads to understanding.

b. Men make their history themselves, but not as yet with a collective will according to a collective plan, or even in a definite, delimited given society. Their aspirations clash, and for that very reason all such societies are governed by *necessity*, the complement and form of appearance of which is *accident*. The necessity which here asserts itself athwart all accident is again ultimately economic necessity. This is where the so-called great men come in for treatment. That such and such a man and precisely that man arises at a particular time in a particular country is, of course, pure chance. But cut him out and there will be a demand for a substitute, and this substitute will be found, good or bad, but in the long run he will be found. That Napoleon, just that particular Corsican, should have been the military dictator whom the French Republic, exhausted by its own warfare, had rendered necessary was chance; but that if a Napoleon had been lacking another would have filled the place is proved by the fact that the man was always found as soon as he became necessary: Caesar, Augustus, Cromwell, etc. While Marx discovered the materialist conception of history, Thierry, Mignet, Guizot, and all the English historians up to 1850 are evidence that it was being striven for, and the discovery of the same conception by Morgan proves that the time was ripe for it and that it simply *had* to be discovered.

So with all the other accidents, and apparent accidents, of history. The further the particular sphere which we are investigating is removed from the economic sphere and approaches that of pure abstract ideology, the more shall we find it exhibiting accidents in its development, the more will its curve run zigzag. But if you plot the average axis of the curve you will find that this axis will run more and more nearly parallel to the axis of economic development the longer the period considered and the wider the field dealt with.

In Germany the greatest hindrance to correct understanding is the irresponsible neglect by literature of economic history. It is so hard not only to disaccustom oneself to the ideas of history drilled into one at school but still more to rake up the necessary material for doing so. Who, for instance, has read at least old G. von Gülich, whose dry collection of material nevertheless contains so much stuff for the clarification of innumerable political facts!

For the rest, the fine example which Marx has given in *The Eighteenth Brumaire* should, I think, provide you fairly well with information on your questions, just because it is a practical example. I have also, I believe, already touched on most of the points in *Anti-Dühring* I, Chapters 9–11, and II, 2–4, as well as in III, 1, or Introduction, and also in the last section of *Feuerbach*.

Please do not weigh each word in the above too scrupulously, but keep the general connection in mind; I regret that I have not the time to word what I am writing to you as exactly as I should be obliged to do for publication. . . .

XVIII. *Excerpts from* The Peasant War in Germany

FRIEDRICH ENGELS

From his strict Pietist upbringing Engels retained a deeper interest in religion than Marx had. The failure of the Revolution of 1848, in which they both actively participated, led Engels to reflect historically on the similar suppression of their precursors of the Peasants' Revolt of 1525. During the summer of 1850, in the quiet of London, and "under the vivid impression of the counterrevolution that had just been completed," Engels wrote the articles which later composed his book, *The Peasant War in Germany*. It is outstanding for its insight into the conditions under which revolutionary aspirations take a religious form, and for its understanding of the political significance of mysticism, pantheism, and asceticism among the lower classes.—Ed.

II

The grouping of the then numerous and variegated estates into bigger entities was made virtually impossible by decentralization, local and provincial independence, the industrial and commercial isolation of the provinces from each other, and poor communications. It developed only with the general spread of revolutionary politico-religious ideas during the Reformation. The various estates that either embraced or opposed those ideas concentrated the nation, painfully and only approximately, into three large camps—the reactionary or Catholic camp, the Lutheran bourgeois reformist camp, and the revolutionary camp. And should we discover little logic in this great division of the nation, and find partly the same elements in the first two camps, this is explained by the dissolution of most of the official estates that came down from the Middle Ages, and by the decentralization, which, for the moment, gave these estates in different localities opposing orientations. In recent years we have so often encountered similar facts in Germany that this apparent jumble of estates and classes under the much more complicated conditions of the sixteenth century can scarcely surprise us.

In spite of the latest experiences the German ideology still sees nothing except violent theological bickering in the struggles that ended the Middle Ages. Should the people of that time, say our homebred historians and sages, have only come to an understanding concerning celestial things, there would have been no ground whatever to quarrel over earthly affairs. These ideologists are gullible enough to accept unquestioningly all the illusions that an epoch makes about itself, or that ideologists of some epoch make about that epoch. People of that kind, for instance, see in the Revolution of 1789 nothing but a somewhat heated debate about the advantages of a constitutional monarchy over absolutism, in the July revolution a practical controversy over the untenability of justice "by the grace of God," and in the February revolution an attempt at solving the problem: Republic or monarchy?, etc. They have hardly any idea to this day of the *class struggles* which were fought out in these upheavals, and of which the political slogan on the banner is every time a bare expression, although notice of them is audible enough not only from abroad, but also in the roar and rumble of many thousands of home proletarians.

Even the so-called religious wars of the sixteenth century involved positive material class interests; those wars were class wars, too, just as the later internal collisions in England and France. Although the class struggles of that day were clothed in religious shibboleths, and though the interests, requirements, and demands of the various classes were concealed behind a religious screen, this changed nothing in the matter, and is easily explained by the conditions of the time.

The Middle Ages had developed altogether from the raw. They wiped the old civilization, the old philosophy, politics, and jurisprudence off the slate, to begin anew in everything. The only thing they kept from the old shattered world was Christianity and a number of half-ruined towns divested of all their civilization. As a consequence the clergy obtained a monopoly on intellectual education, just as in every primitive stage of development, and education itself became essentially theological. In the hands of the clergy politics and jurisprudence, much like all other sciences, remained mere branches of theology, and were treated along the principles prevailing in the latter. Church dogmas were also political axioms, and Bible quotations had the validity of law in any court. Even as a special estate of jurists was taking shape, jurisprudence long remained under the patronage of theology. And this supremacy of theology in the entire realm of intellectual activity was at the same time an inevitable consequence of the place held by the Church as all-embracing synthesis and most general sanction of the existing feudal domination.

It is clear that, under the circumstances, all the generally voiced attacks against feudalism—above all, the attacks against the Church and all revolutionary social and political doctrines—had, mostly and simultaneously, to be theological heresies. The existing social conditions had to be stripped of their halo of sanctity before they could be attacked.

The revolutionary opposition to feudalism was alive all down the Middle Ages. It took the shape of mysticism, open heresy, or armed insurrection, all depending on the conditions of the time. As for mysticism, it is well known how much sixteenth-century reformers depended on it. Münzer himself was largely indebted to it. The heresies gave expression partly to the reaction of the patriarchal Alpine shepherds against the feudalism advancing upon them (Waldenses), partly to the opposition to feudalism of the towns that had outgrown it (the Albigenses, Arnold of Brescia, etc.), and partly to direct peasant insurrections (John Ball, the Hungarian teacher in Picardy, etc.). We can here leave aside the patriarchal heresy of the Waldenses, and the Swiss insurrection, which was, in form and content, a reactionary, purely local attempt at stemming the tide of history. In the other two forms of medieval heresy we find the twelfth-century precursors of the great antithesis between the burgher and peasant-plebeian oppositions, which caused the defeat of the Peasant War. This antithesis is evident all down the later Middle Ages.

The town heresies—and those are the actual official heresies of the Middle Ages—were turned primarily against the clergy, whose wealth and political importance they attacked. Just as the present-day bourgeoisie demands a "*gouvernement à bon marché* [cheap government]," the medieval burghers chiefly demanded an "*église à bon marché* [cheap church]." Reactionary in form, like any heresy that sees only degeneration in the further development of Church and dogma, the burgher heresy demanded the revival of the simple early Christian Church constitution and abolition of exclusive priesthood. This cheap arrangement would eliminate monks, prelates, and the Roman court, or, in short, everything in the Church that was expensive. The towns, republics themselves, albeit under the protection of monarchs, first enunciated in general terms through their attacks upon Papacy that a republic was the normal form of bourgeois rule. Their hostility to a number of dogmas and Church laws is explained partly by the foregoing, and partly by their living conditions. Their bitter opposition to celibacy, for instance, has never been better explained than by Boccaccio. Arnold of Brescia in Italy and Germany, the Albigenses in southern France, John Wycliffe in England, Huss and the Calixtines in Bohemia were the principal representatives of this trend. The towns were then already a recognized estate sufficiently capable of fighting lay feudalism and its privileges either by force of arms or in the estate Assemblies, and that explains quite simply why the opposition to feudalism appeared only as an opposition to *religious* feudalism.

We also find both in southern France and in England and Bohemia that most of the lesser nobility joined the towns in their struggle against the clergy, and in their heresies—a phenomenon explained by the dependence of the lesser nobility upon the towns, and by their community of interests as opposed to the princes and prelates. We shall encounter the same thing in the Peasant War.

The heresy that lent direct expression to peasant and plebeian demands, and was almost invariably bound up with an insurrection, was of a totally different nature. Though it shared all the demands of burgher heresy with regard to the clergy, the Papacy, and revival of the early Christian Church constitution, it also went infinitely further. It demanded the restoration of early Christian equality among members of the community, and the recognition of this equality as a prescript for the burgher world as well. It drew on the "equality of the children of God" to conclude civil equality, and partly even equality of property. Equality of nobleman and peasant, of patrician and privileged burgher, and the plebeian, abolition of compulsory labor, ground rents, taxes, privileges, and at least the most crying differences in property—those were demands advanced with more or less determination as natural implications of the early Christian doctrine. At the time when feudalism was at its zenith there was little to choose between this peasant-plebeian heresy, among the Albigenses, for example, and the burgher opposition, but in the fourteenth and fifteenth centuries it developed into a clearly defined party opinion and usually took an independent stand alongside the heresy of the burghers. That was the case with John Ball, preacher of Wat Tyler's Rebellion in England, alongside the Wycliffe movement, and with the Taborites alongside the Calixtines in Bohemia. The Taborites even showed a republican trend under a theocratic cloak, a view further developed by representatives of the plebeians in Germany in the fifteenth and early sixteenth century.

The fanaticism of mystically minded sects, of the Flagellants and Lollards, etc., which continued the revolutionary tradition in times of suppression, rallied round this form of heresy.

At that time the plebeians were the only class that stood outside the existing official society. They stood outside both the feudal and burgher associations. They had neither privileges nor property; they did not even have the kind of property the peasant or petty burgher had, weighed down as it was with burdensome taxes. They were unpropertied and rightless in every respect; their living conditions never even brought them into direct contact with the existing institutions, which ignored them completely. They were a living symptom of the decay of the feudal and guild-burgher society, and at the same time the first precursors of the modern bourgeois society.

This explains why the plebeian opposition even then could not stop at fighting only feudalism and the privileged burghers; why, in fantasy at least, it reached beyond the then scarcely dawning modern bourgeois society; why, an absolutely propertyless faction, it questioned the institutions, views, and conceptions common to all societies based on class antagonisms. In this respect the chiliastic dream visions of early Christianity offered a very convenient starting point. On the other hand, this sally beyond both the present and even the future could be nothing but violent and fantastic, and of necessity fell back into the narrow limits set by the contemporary situation. The attack on private property, the demand for common ownership, was bound to resolve into a primitive organization of charity; vague Christian equality could at best resolve into civil "equality before the law"; elimination of all authorities finally culminates in the establishment of republican governments elected by the people. The anticipation of communism nurtured by fantasy becomes in reality an anticipation of modern bourgeois conditions.

This violent anticipation of coming historical developments, easily explained by the living conditions of the plebeians, is first observed in *Germany*, in *Thomas Münzer* and his party. The Taborites had a kind of chiliastic common ownership, but that was a purely military measure. Only in the teachings of Münzer did these communist notions express the aspirations of a real fraction of society. It was he who formulated them with a certain definiteness, and they have since been observed in every great popular upheaval, until they gradually merge with the modern proletarian movement. It was all much like the struggles of free peasants in the Middle Ages against the increasing stronghold of feudal domination, which merged with the struggles of serfs and bondsmen for complete abolition of the feudal system.

While the first of the three large camps, the *conservative Catholic*, embraced all the elements interested in maintaining the existing conditions, i.e., the imperial authorities, the ecclesiastical and a section of the lay princes, the richer nobility, the prelates, and the city patricians, the camp of *Lutheran* reforms, *moderate in the burgher manner*, attracted all the propertied elements of the opposition, the bulk of the lesser nobility, the burghers, and even a portion of the lay princes who hoped to enrich themselves through confiscation of church estates and wanted to seize the opportunity of gaining greater independence from the empire. As to the peasants and plebeians, they formed a *revolutionary* party whose demands and doctrines were most clearly expressed by Münzer.

Luther and Münzer each fully represented his party by his doctrine as well as by his character and actions.

From 1517 to 1525, *Luther* underwent quite the same changes that the present-day German constitutionalists did between 1846 and 1849, and that are undergone by every bourgeois party which, placed for a while at the head of the movement, is overwhelmed by the plebeian-proletarian party standing behind it.

When, in 1517, Luther first opposed the dogmas and statutes of the Catholic Church, his opposition by no means possessed a definite character. While it did not overstep the demands of the earlier burgher heresy it did not, and could not, rule out any trend which went further. At that early stage all the oppositional elements had to be united, the most aggressive revolutionary energy displayed, and the sum of the existing heresies against the Catholic orthodoxy had to find a protagonist. In much the same way our liberal bourgeoisie of 1847 was still revolutionary, called itself socialist and communist, and clamored for the emancipation of the working class. Luther's sturdy peasant nature asserted itself in the stormiest fashion in that first period of his activities. "If the raging madness [of the Roman churchmen] were to continue, it seems to me no better counsel and remedy could be found against it than that kings and princes apply force, arm themselves, attack those evil people who have poisoned the entire world, and put an end to this game once and for all, *with arms, not with words*. Since we punish thieves with the halter, murderers with the sword, and heretics with fire, why do we not turn on all those evil teachers of perdition, those popes, cardinals, and bishops, and the entire swarm of the Roman Sodom *with arms in hand, and wash our hands in their blood?*"

But this revolutionary ardor was short-lived. Luther's lightning struck home. The entire German people was set in motion. On the one hand, peasants and plebeians saw the signal to revolt in his appeals against the clergy, and in his sermon of Christian freedom; and on the other, he was joined by the moderate burghers and a large section of the lesser nobility, and even princes were drawn into the maelstrom. The former believed the day had come to wreak vengeance upon all their oppressors, the latter only wished to break the power of the clergy, the dependence upon Rome, the Catholic hierarchy, and to enrich themselves on the confiscation of church property. The parties stood aloof from each other, and each found its spokesmen. Luther had to choose between them. He, the protégé of the Elector of Saxony, the revered professor of Wittenberg who had become powerful and famous overnight, the great man with his coterie of servile creatures and flatterers, did not hesitate a single moment. He dropped the popular elements of the movement and took the side of the burghers, the nobility, and the princes. His appeals for a war of extermination against Rome were heard no more. Luther now preached *peaceful progress* and *passive resistance* (cf., for example, *To the Nobility of the German Nation*, 1520, etc.). Invited by Hutten to visit him and Sickingen in the Castle of Ebern, the seat of the nobility's conspiracy against clergy and princes, Luther replied: "I do not wish the Gospel *defended by force and bloodshed*. The world was conquered by the Word, the Church is maintained by the Word, the Word will also put the Church back into its own, and Antichrist, who gained his own without violence, will fall without violence."

From this tendency, or, to be more exact, from this more definite delineation of Luther's policy, sprang that bartering and haggling over institutions and dogmas to be retained or reformed, that disgusting diplomatizing, conciliating, intriguing, and compromising, which resulted in the Augsburg Confession, the finally importuned articles of a reformed burgher church. It was quite the same kind of petty bargaining that was recently repeated in political form *ad nauseam* at the German national assemblies, conciliatory gatherings, chambers of revision, and Erfurt parliaments. The Philistine nature of the official Reformation was most markedly evident at these negotiations.

There were good reasons for Luther, henceforth the recognized representative of the burgher reform, to preach lawful progress. The bulk of the towns espoused the cause of moderate reform, the petty nobility became more and more devoted to it, and a section of the princes struck in, while another vacillated. Success was as good as won, at least in a large part of Germany. The remaining regions could not in the long run withstand the pressure of moderate opposition in the event of continued peaceful development. Any violent upheaval, meanwhile, was bound to bring the moderate party into conflict with the extremist plebeian and peasant party, to alienate the princes, the nobility, and certain towns from the movement, leaving the alternative of either the burgher party being overshadowed by the peasants and plebeians or the entire movement being crushed by Catholic restoration. And there have been examples enough lately of how bourgeois parties seek to steer their way by means of lawful progress between the Scylla of revolution and the Charybdis of restoration after gaining the slightest victory.

Under the general social and political conditions prevailing in that day the results of every change were necessarily advantageous to the princes, and inevitably increased their power. Thus it came about that the burgher reform fell the more completely under the control of the reformed princes the more sharply it broke away from the plebeian and peasant elements. Luther himself became more and more their vassel, and the people well knew what they were doing when they accused him of having become, as the others, a flunky of the princes, and when they stoned him in Orlamünde.

When the Peasant War broke out, Luther strove to adopt a mediatory attitude in regions where the nobility and the princes were mostly Catholic. He resolutely attacked the governments. He said they were to blame for the rebellion in view of their oppression; it was not the peasants, but God himself, who rose against them. Yet, on the other hand, he said, the revolt was ungodly and contrary to the Gospel. In conclusion he called upon both parties to yield and reach a peaceful understanding.

But in spite of these well-meaning mediatory offers the revolt spread swiftly, and even involved Protestant regions dominated by Lutheran princes, lords, and towns, rapidly outgrowing the "circumspect" burgher reform. The most determined faction of the insurgents under Münzer made its headquarters in Luther's immediate proximity at Thuringia. A few more successes, and the whole of Germany would be in flames, Luther surrounded and perhaps piked as a traitor, and the burgher reform swept away by the tide of a peasant-plebeian revolution. There was no more time for circumspection. All the old animosities were forgotten in the face of the revolution. Compared with the hordes of peasants, the servants of the Roman Sodom were innocent lambs, sweet-tempered children of God. Burgher and prince, noble and clergyman, Luther and the Pope, all joined hands "against the murderous and plundering peasant hordes." "They must be *knocked to pieces, strangled* and *stabbed, secretly* and *openly*, by everyone who can, just as one must kill a *mad dog!*" Luther cried. "Therefore, dear sirs, help here, save there, stab, knock, strangle them everyone who can, and should you lose your life, bless you, no better death canst thou ever attain." There should only be no false mercy for the peasant. Whoever hath pity on those whom God pities not, whom He wishes punished and destroyed, belongs among the rebels himself. Later the peasants would themselves learn to thank God when they would have to give up one cow in order to enjoy the other in peace, and the princes would learn through the revolution the spirit of the mob that must be ruled by force only. "The wise man says: *Cibus, onus, et virgam asino* [Food, pack, and lash to the ass]. The peasants must have nothing but chaff. They do not hearken to the Word, and are foolish, so they must hearken to the rod and the gun, and that serves them right. We must pray for them, that they obey. Where they do not, there should not be much mercy. *Let the guns roar among them*, or else they will do it a thousand times worse."

That was exactly what our late socialist and philanthropic bourgeoisie said when the proletariat claimed its share in the fruits of victory after the March events.

Luther had put a powerful weapon into the hands of the plebeian movement by translating the Bible. Through the Bible he contrasted the feudalized Christianity of his day with the moderate Christianity of the first century, and the decaying feudal society with a picture of a society that knew nothing of the ramified and artificial feudal hierarchy. The peasants had made extensive use of this instrument against the princes, the nobility, and the clergy. Now Luther turned it against them, extracting from the Bible such a veritable hymn to the God-ordained authorities as no bootlicker of absolute monarchy had ever been able to accomplish. Princedom by the grace of God, resigned obedience, even serfdom, were sanctioned with the aid of the Bible. Not the peasant revolt alone, but Luther's own mutiny against religious and lay authority was thereby disavowed; and not only the popular movement, but the burgher movement as well, were betrayed to the princes.

Need we name the bourgeois who recently also gave us examples of such a disavowal of their own past?

Let us now compare the plebeian revolutionary *Münzer* with Luther, the burgher reformist.

Thomas Münzer was born in *Stolberg*, in the Harz, in 1498. His father is said to have died on the scaffold, a victim of the obduracy of the Count of Stolberg. In his fifteenth year Münzer organized a secret union at the Halle school against the Archbishop of Magdeburg and the Roman Church in general. His learning in the theology of his time brought him an early doctor's degree and the position of chaplain in a Halle nunnery. Here he treated the Church dogmas and rites with the greatest contempt. At mass he omitted the words of the transubstantiation and ate, as Luther said, the almighty gods unconsecrated. Medieval mystics, and particularly the chiliastic works of

Joachim the Calabrese, were the main subject of his studies. The millennium and the Day of Judgment over the degenerated Church and corrupted world propounded and described by that mystic seemed to Münzer imminently close, what with the Reformation and the general unrest of his time. He preached in his neighborhood with great success. In 1520 he went to Zwickau as the first evangelist preacher. There he found one of those fanatical chiliastic sects that continued their existence on the quiet in many localities, and whose momentary humility and detachment concealed the increasingly rampant opposition of the lowest strata of society to the prevailing conditions, and who were now coming into the light of day ever more boldly and persistently with the growing unrest. It was the sect of the Anabaptists, headed by *Niklas Storch*. They preached the approach of the Day of Judgment and of the millennium; they had "visions, transports, and the spirit of prophecy." They soon came into conflict with the Council of Zwickau. Münzer defended them, though he never joined them unconditionally, and would have rather brought them under his own influence. The Council took drastic measures against them; they had to leave the town, and Münzer with them. This was at the close of 1521.

He went to Prague and sought to gain a foothold by joining the remnants of the Hussite movement. But his proclamation only had the effect of compelling him to flee from Bohemia as well. In 1522 he became preacher at Allstedt in Thuringia. Here he started with reforming the cult. Even before Luther dared to go so far, he entirely abolished the Latin language and ordered the entire Bible, and not only the prescribed Sunday Gospels and Epistles, to be read to the people. At the same time, he organized propaganda in his locality. People flocked to him from all directions, and Allstedt soon became the center of the popular anti-priest movement of all Thuringia.

Münzer was as yet theologian before everything else. He still directed his attacks almost exclusively against the priests. He did not, however, preach quiet debate and peaceful progress, as Luther had begun at that time, but continued Luther's earlier violent sermons, calling upon the princes of Saxony and the people to rise in arms against the

Roman priests. "Does not Christ say, 'I came not to send peace, but a sword'? What must you [the princes of Saxony] do with that sword? Only one thing if you wish to be the servants of God, and that is to drive out and destroy the evil ones who stand in the way of the Gospel. Christ ordered very earnestly: [Luke 19:27] 'Bring hither mine enemies and slay them before me.' Do not give us any empty phrases that the power of God will do it without the aid of your sword, since then it would rust in its sheath. . . . Those who stand in the way of God's revelation must be destroyed mercilessly, as Hezekiah, Cyrus, Josiah, Daniel, and Elias destroyed the priests of Baal, else the Christian Church will never come back to its source. We must uproot the weeds in God's vineyard at harvest time. . . . God said in the Fifth Book of Moses, 7, 'Thou shalt not show mercy unto the idolators, but ye shall destroy their altars, and break down their images and burn them with fire, that I shall not be wroth at you.'"

But these appeals to the princes were of no avail, whereas revolutionary sentiments among the people grew day by day. Münzer, whose ideas became ever more sharply defined and bolder, now broke resolutely away from the burgher reformation, and henceforth became an outright political agitator.

His philosophico-theological doctrine attacked all the main points not only of Catholicism, but of Christianity generally. Under the cloak of Christian forms he preached a kind of pantheism, which curiously resembles modern speculative contemplation, and at times even approaches atheism. He repudiated the Bible both as the only and the infallible revelation. The real and living revelation, he said, was reason, a revelation which existed, and still exists, among all peoples at all times. To hold up the Bible against reason, he maintained, was to kill the spirit by the letter, for the Holy Spirit of which the Bible speaks is not something that exists outside us; the Holy Spirit is our reason. Faith is nothing else but reason come alive in man, and pagans could therefore also have faith. Through this faith, through reason come to life, man became godlike and blessed. Heaven is, therefore, nothing of another world, and is to be sought in this life, and it is the task of believers to establish this heaven, the kingdom of God, here on earth. Just as there is no heaven in the beyond, there is also no hell, and no damnation. Similarly, there is no devil but man's evil lusts and greed. Christ was a man, as we are, a prophet and a teacher, and his supper is a plain meal of commemoration wherein bread and wine are consumed without any mystic garnish.

Münzer preached these doctrines mostly cloaked in the same Christian phraseology under which the new philosophy had to hide for some time. But the archheretical fundamental idea is easily discerned in all his writings, and he obviously took the biblical cloak much less in earnest than many a disciple of Hegel in modern times. And yet three hundred years separate Münzer from modern philosophy.

Münzer's political doctrine followed his revolutionary religious conceptions very closely, and just as his theology overstepped the current conceptions of his time, so his political doctrine went beyond the directly prevailing social and political conditions. Just as Münzer's religious philosophy approached atheism, so his political program approached communism, and even on the eve of the February revolution more than one present-day communist sect lacked as comprehensive a theoretical arsenal as was "Münzer's" in the sixteenth century. This program, less of a compilation of the demands of the plebeians of that day than a visionary anticipation of the conditions for the emancipation of the proletarian element that had scarcely begun to develop among the plebeians—this program demanded the immediate establishment of the kingdom of God, of the prophesied millennium, by restoring the Church to its original status and abolishing all the institutions that conflicted with this allegedly early Christian, but, in fact, very much novel church. By the kingdom of God, Münzer understood a society without class differences, private property, and a state authority independent of, and foreign to, the members of society. All the existing authorities, in so far as they refused to submit and join the revolution, were to be overthrown, all work and all property shared in common, and complete equality introduced. A union was to be established to realize all this, not only throughout Germany, but throughout all Christendom. Princes and lords were to be invited to join, and should they refuse, the union was to take up arms and overthrow or kill them at the first opportunity.

Münzer set to work at once to organize the union. His sermons became still more militant and revolutionary. He thundered forth against the princes, the nobility, and the patricians with a passion that equaled the fervor of his attacks upon the clergy. He pictured the prevailing oppression in burning colors, and countered it with his dream vision of the millennium of social republican equality. He published one revolutionary pamphlet after another, and sent emissaries in all directions, while personally organizing the union in Allstedt and its vicinity.

The first fruit of this propaganda was the destruction of St. Mary's Chapel in Mellerbach, near Allstedt, according to the command of the Bible (Deuteronomy 7:6): "Ye shall destroy their altars, and dash in pieces their pillars, and burn their graven images with fire." The princes of Saxony came in person to Allstedt to quell the unrest, and had Münzer come to the castle. There he delivered a sermon the like of which they had not heard from Luther, "that easy-living flesh of Wittenberg," as Münzer called him. Münzer maintained that ungodly rulers, especially priests and monks, who treated the Gospel as heresy, should be killed, and referred to the New Testament for confirmation. The ungodly had no right to live save by the mercy of God's elect. If the princes would not exterminate the ungodly, God would take their sword from them, *because the entire community had the power of the sword.* The princes and lords are the prime movers of usury, thievery, and robbery; they take all creatures into their private possession—the fish in the water, the birds in the air, and the plants in the soil—and still preach to the poor the commandment, "Thou shalt not steal," while they themselves take everything they find, rob and oppress the peasant and the artisan; but when one of the latter commits the slightest transgression he has to hang, and Dr. Lügner says to all this: Amen. "The masters themselves are to blame that the poor man becomes their enemy. If they do not remove the causes of the upheaval, how can things go well in the long run? Oh, dear sirs, how the Lord will smite these old pots with an iron rod! But for saying so I am regarded a rebel. So be it!" (Cf. Zimmermann's *Bauernkrieg*, II, page 75.)

Münzer had the sermon printed. His Allstedt printer was punished by Duke Johann of Saxony with banishment, while Münzer's writings were to be henceforth censored by the ducal government in Weimar. But he paid no heed to this order. He lost no time in publishing a highly inciting paper in the imperial city of Mühlhausen, wherein he called on the people "to widen the hole so that all the world may see and understand who our great personages are that have blasphemously turned our Lord into a painted mannikin," and which ended with the following words: "All the world must suffer a big jolt. There will be such a game that the ungodly will be thrown off their seats and the downtrodden will rise." Thomas Münzer, "the man with the hammer," wrote the following motto on the title page: "Beware, I have put my words into thy mouth, I have put you over the people and over the empire that thou mayest uproot, destroy, scatter, and overthrow, and that thou mayest build and plant. A wall of iron against the kings, princes, priests, and against the people hath been erected. Let them fight, for victory will wondrously lead to the perdition of the strong and godless tyrants."

Münzer's breach with Luther and his party had taken place long before that. Luther had to accept some of the church reforms, introduced by Münzer without consulting him. He watched Münzer's activities with a moderate reformer's nettled mistrust of a more energetic, fartheraiming party. Already in the spring of 1524, in a letter to Melanchthon, that model of a hectic stay-at-home Philistine, Münzer wrote that he and Luther did not understand the movement at all. He said they sought to choke it by the letter of the Bible, and that their doctrine was wormeaten. "Dear brethren," he wrote, "cease your procrastinations and vacillations. It is time; summer is knocking at the door. Do not keep friendship with the ungodly who hinder the Word from working its full force. Do not flatter your princes, or you may perish with them. Ye tender, bookish scholars, do not be wroth, for I can do nothing to change it."

Luther had more than once challenged Münzer to an open debate. The latter, however, always ready to take up the battle before the people, had not the least desire to let himself in for a theological squabble before the partisan public of Wittenberg University. He did not wish "to bring the testimony of the spirit exclusively before the high school of learning." If Luther were sincere he should use his influence to stop the chicaneries against his, Münzer's, printer, and lift the censorship, so that their controversy might be freely fought out in the press.

But now, when Münzer's above-mentioned revolutionary brochure appeared, Luther openly denounced him. In his *Letter to the Princes of Saxony against the Rebellious Spirit* he declared Münzer to be an instrument of Satan, and demanded of the princes to intervene and drive the instigators of the upheaval out of the country, since they did not confine themselves to preaching their evil doctrine, but incited to insurrection, to violent action against the authorities.

On August 1, Münzer was compelled to appear before the princes in the Castle of Weimar on the charge of incitement to mutiny. Highly compromising facts were available against him; they were on the scent of his secret union; his hand was detected in the societies of the miners and the peasants. He was threatened with banishment. No sooner had he returned to Allstedt than he learned that Duke Georg of Saxony demanded his extradition. Union letters in his handwriting had been intercepted, wherein he called Georg's subjects to armed resistance against the enemies of the Gospel. The Council would have extradited him had he not left the town.

In the meantime, the growing unrest among the peasants and plebeians had made Münzer's propaganda work incomparably easier. In the Anabaptists he found invaluable agents for that purpose. This sect, which had no definite dogmas, held together only by its common opposition to all ruling classes and by the common symbol of the second baptism, ascetic in their mode of living, untiring, fanatical and intrepid in carrying on propaganda, had grouped itself more and more closely around Münzer. Made homeless by persecutions, its members wandered all over Germany and carried word everywhere of the new teaching, in which Münzer had made clear to them their own demands and wishes. Countless Anabaptists were put on the rack, burned, or otherwise executed, but the courage and endurance of these emissaries were unshakable, and the success of their activities amidst the rapidly growing unrest of the people was enormous. Thus, on his flight from Thuringia, Münzer found the ground prepared wherever he turned.

Near Nuremberg, where Münzer first went, a peasant revolt had been nipped in the bud a month before. Münzer conducted his propaganda on the quiet; people soon appeared who defended his most audacious theological propositions on the non-obligatory nature of the Bible and the meaninglessness of sacraments, who declared Christ a mere man and the power of the lay authorities ungodly. "There is Satan stalking, the spirit of Allstedt!" Luther exclaimed. In Nuremberg, Münzer printed his reply to Luther. He accused him of flattering the princes and supporting the reactionary party through his insipid moderation. But the people would free themselves nonetheless, he wrote, and it would go with Dr. Luther as with a captive fox. The Council ordered the paper confiscated, and Münzer had to leave Nuremberg.

Now he went across Swabia to Alsace, then to Switzerland, and then back to the upper Black Forest, where an insurrection had broken out several months before, largely precipitated by his Anabaptist emissaries. This propaganda tour of Münzer's had unquestionably and substantially contributed to the establishment of the people's party, to a clear formulation of its demands, and to the final general outbreak of the insurrection in April 1525. It was through this trip that the dual effect of Münzer's activities appears particularly pronounced: on the one hand, on the people, whom he addressed in the only language they could then comprehend, that of religious prophecy; and, on the other hand, on the initiated, to whom he could disclose his ultimate aims. Even before his journey he had assembled in Thuringia a circle of resolute men from among the people and the lesser clergy, whom he had put at the head of his secret society. Now he became the soul of the entire revolutionary movement in southwestern Germany, organized ties between Saxony and Thuringia through Franconia and Swabia up to Alsace and the Swiss border, and counted such south German agitators as Hubmaier of Waldshut, Conrad Grebel of Zürich, Franz Rabmann of Griessen, Schappeler of Memmingen, Jakob Wehe of Leipheim, and Dr. Mantel in Stuttgart, who were mostly revolutionary priests, among his disciples and the heads of the union. He himself stayed mostly in Griessen on the Schaffhausen border, journeying from there across the Hegau, Klettgau, etc. The bloody persecutions undertaken by the alarmed princes and lords everywhere against this new plebeian heresy contributed not a little to fanning the spirit of rebellion and consolidating the ranks of the society. In this way Münzer conducted his agitation for about five months in upper Germany, and returned to Thuringia when the outbreak of the conspiracy was near at hand because he wished to lead the movement personally. There we shall find him later.

We shall see how truly the character and behavior of the two party leaders reflected the attitude of their respective parties, how Luther's indecision and fear of the movement, that was assuming serious proportions, and his cowardly servility to the princes fully corresponded to the hesitant and ambiguous policy of the burghers, and how Münzer's revolutionary energy and resolution were reproduced among the most advanced section of the plebeians and peasants. The only difference was that while Luther confined himself to expressing the conceptions and wishes of the majority of his class, and thereby won an extremely cheap popularity among it, Münzer, on the contrary, went far beyond the immediate ideas and demands of the plebeians and peasants and first organized a party of the elite of the then existing revolutionary elements, which, inasmuch as it shared his ideas and energy, always remained only a small minority of the insurgent masses.

III

The first signs of a budding revolutionary spirit appeared among the German peasants about fifty years after the suppression of the Hussite movement.

In 1476 the first peasant conspiracy occurred in the bishopric of Würzburg, a land impoverished by the Hussite wars, "by bad government, manifold taxes, payments, feuds, enmity, war, fire, murder, prison, and the like," and continually and shamelessly plundered by bishops, priests, and the nobility. A young shepherd and musician, *Hans Böheim of Niklashausen*, also called the Drum Beater and *Hans the Piper*, suddenly appeared in the Tauber Valley in the role of prophet. He declared that he had had a vision of the Virgin Mary, that she had commanded him to burn his drum, to cease serving the dance and sinful sensuality, and to exhort the people to do penance. Everyone should purge himself of sin and the vain lusts of the world, forsake all adornments and embellishments, and make a pilgrimage to the Madonna of Niklashausen to obtain forgiveness.

Already among these precursors of the movement we find an asceticism typical of all medieval uprisings tinged with religion, and, in modern times, of the early stages of every proletarian movement. This ascetic austerity of morals, this demand to forsake all joys of life and entertainments, opposes the ruling classes with the principle of Spartan equality, on the one hand, and is, on the other, a necessary transitional stage, without which the lowest stratum of society can never set itself into motion. In order to develop their revolutionary energy, to become conscious of their own hostile attitude towards all other elements of society, to concentrate themselves as a class, the lower strata of society must begin by stripping themselves of everything that could reconcile them to the existing social system; they must renounce the few pleasures that make their grievous position in the least tolerable for the moment, and of which even the severest oppression could not deprive them. This *plebeian and proletarian asceticism* differs both in its wild fanatical form and in its essence from the bourgeois asceticism of the Lutheran burgher morality and of the English Puritans (as distinct from the Independents and the more radical sects), whose entire secret lay in *bourgeois thrift*. It stands to reason that this plebeian-proletarian asceticism gradually sheds its revolutionary nature as the development of modern productive forces infinitely multiplies the luxuries, thus rendering Spartan equality superfluous, and as the position of the proletariat in society, and thereby the proletariat itself, becomes ever more revolutionary. This asceticism disappears gradually from among the masses, and in the sects which relied upon it, it degenerates into either bourgeois parsimony or a high-sounding virtuousness, which, in practice, also comes down to a Philistine, or guild-artisan, niggardliness. Besides, renunciation of pleasures need hardly be preached to the proletariat for the simple reason that it has almost nothing more to renounce.

Hans the Piper's call to penitence found a great response. All the prophets of rebellion started with appeals against sin, and, indeed, only a violent exertion, a sudden renunciation of all this habitual mode of existence could bring this disunited, widely scattered, sparsely sown peasant species, raised in blind submission, into concerted motion. The pilgrimages to Niklashausen began and rapidly increased, and the more massive the stream of pilgrims, the more openly the young rebel spoke out his plans. The Madonna of Niklashausen had told him, he preached, that henceforth there should be neither king nor prince, neither pope nor any other ecclesiastic or lay authority. Each should be a brother to the other, and win his bread by the toil of his own hands, and that none should have more than his neighbor. All tributes, ground rents, services, tolls, taxes, and other payments and duties should be forever abolished, and forest, water, and pasture should everywhere be free.

The people received this new gospel with joy. The fame of the prophet, "the message of our Lady," spread far and wide; pilgrim throngs flocked to him from Odenwald, from the Main, Kocher and Jagst, even from Bavaria and Swabia, and from the Rhine. Miracles were recounted that were to have been performed by the Piper; people fell to their knees before him, praying to him as to a saint, and then fought for the tufts from his cap as for relics or amulets. In vain did the priests speak against him, denouncing his visions as the devil's delusions and his miracles as diabolic swindles. The mass of the believers increased inordinately, a revolutionary sect began to take shape, the Sunday sermons of the rebel shepherd drew gatherings of forty thousand and more to Niklashausen.

Hans the Piper preached to the masses for a number of months, but he did not intend to confine himself to preaching. He had secret connections with the pastor of Niklashausen and with two knights, Kunz von Thunfeld and his son, who held to the new teaching and were to become the military leaders of the planned insurrection. Finally, on the Sunday before the day of St. Kilian, when his power appeared to be great enough, the shepherd gave the signal. "And now go home," he closed his sermon, "and weigh in your mind what our holiest Lady has announced to you, and on the coming Saturday leave your wives and children and old men at home, and you, men, come back to Niklashausen on the day of St. Margaret, which is next Saturday, and bring your brothers and friends, as many as they may be. Do not come with pilgrims' staves, however, but with armor and arms, a candle in one hand, and a sword, pike, or halberd in the other, and the Holy Virgin will then tell you what she wishes you to do."

But before the peasants arrived in their masses, the bishop's horsemen seized the rebel prophet at night and brought him to the Castle of Würzburg. On the appointed day thirty-four thousand armed peasants appeared, but the news crushed them. Most of them went home, while the more initiated kept about sixteen thousand together, with whom they marched to the castle under the leadership of Kunz von Thunfeld and his son Michael. The bishop persuaded them with promises to turn back, but no sooner had they begun to disperse than they were attacked by the bishop's horsemen, and many of them taken captive. Two were decapitated, and Hans the Piper was burned. Kunz von Thunfeld fled, and was allowed to return only after ceding all his estates to the bishopric. The pilgrimages to

Niklashausen continued for some time, but were finally also suppressed.

After this initial attempt Germany again remained quiet for some time. Only towards the close of the century new peasant revolts and conspiracies broke out. . . .

VI

. . . The worst thing that can befall a leader of an extreme party is to be compelled to take over a government in an epoch when the movement is not yet ripe for the domination of the class which he represents, and for the realization of the measures which that domination implies. What he *can* do depends not upon his will but upon the degree of contradiction between the various classes, and upon the level of development of the material means of existence, of the conditions of production and commerce upon which class contradictions always repose. What he *ought* to do, what his party demands of him, again depends not upon him or the stage of development of the class struggle and its conditions. He is bound to the doctrines and demands hitherto propounded, which, again, do not proceed from the class relations of the moment or from the more or less accidental level of production and commerce, but from his more or less penetrating insight into the general result of the social and political movement. Thus he necessarily finds himself in an unsolvable dilemma. What he *can* do contradicts all his previous actions, principles, and the immediate interests of his party, and what he *ought* to do cannot be done. In a word, he is compelled to represent not his party or his class, but the class for whose domination the movement is then ripe. In the interests of the movement he is compelled to advance the interests of an alien class, and to feed his own class with phrases and promises, and with the asseveration that the interests of that alien class are its own interests. Whoever is put into this awkward position is irrevocably lost. We have seen examples of this in recent times, and need only to recall the position taken in the last French provisional government by the representatives of the proletariat, though they themselves represented only a very low stage of development of the proletariat. Whoever can still speculate over official positions after the experiences of the February government—to say nothing of our own noble German provisional governments and imperial regencies—is either foolish beyond measure or only pays lip service to the extreme revolutionary party.

Münzer's position at the head of the "eternal council" of Mühlhausen was indeed much more precarious than that of any modern revolutionary regent. Not only the movement of his time, but the age itself was not ripe for the ideas of which he himself had only a faint notion. The class which he represented was only just in its birth throes, and far from being fully developed and capable of subjugating and transforming society. The social changes that he fancied in his imagination were little grounded in the then existing economic conditions, which even paved the way to a social system that was a direct opposite of what he aspired to. Nevertheless, he was bound to his early sermon of Christian equality and evangelical community of ownership, and was compelled at least to attempt its realization. Community of ownership, universal and equal labor, and abolition of all rights to exercise authority were proclaimed. But in reality Mühlhausen remained a republican imperial city with a somewhat democratized constitution, a senate elected by universal suffrage and controlled by a forum, and with a hastily improvised system of care for the poor. The social upheaval that so horrified its Protestant burgher contemporaries actually never went beyond a feeble and unconscious premature attempt to establish the bourgeois society of a later period.

Münzer himself seems to have sensed the abyss between his theories and the surrounding realities, an abyss that he must have felt all the more keenly, the more distortedly his visionary views were mirrored in the crude minds of his mass of followers. He devoted himself to extending and organizing the movement with a zeal rare even for him. He wrote letters and sent messengers and emissaries in all directions. His writings and sermons breathed a revolutionary fanaticism, astounding even when compared with his former works. The naïve youthful humor of Münzer's prerevolutionary pamphlets was gone completely. The placid scholastic language of the thinker, usual in his earlier years, appeared no more. Münzer became an out-and-out prophet of the revolution. He untiringly fanned the hatred against the ruling classes, he spurred the wildest passions, and used only the forceful language that religious and nationalist delirium put into the mouths of the Old Testament prophets. The style he had to adopt reflects the educational level of the public he was to influence. . . .

XIX. Letters and Essays on Political Sociology

KARL MARX AND FRIEDRICH ENGELS

[RUSSIA'S PATTERN OF DEVELOPMENT]

MARX TO THE EDITORIAL BOARD OF THE OTECHESTVENNIYE ZAPISKI [FATHERLAND NOTES]

[London], November 1877

The author of the article "Karl Marx before the Tribunal of Mr. Zhukovsky" is evidently a clever man, and if, in my account of primitive accumulation, he had found a single passage to support his conclusions he would have quoted it. In the absence of any such passage he finds himself obliged to seize upon an *hors d'œuvre*, a sort of polemic against a Russian "literary man," published in the Appendix to the first German edition of *Capital*. What is my complaint against this writer there? That he discovered the Russian community not in Russia but in the book written by Haxthausen, Prussian Counselor of State, and that in his hands the Russian community only serves as an argument to prove that rotten old Europe should be regenerated by the victory of Pan-Slavism. My estimate of this writer may be right or it may be wrong, but it cannot in any case furnish a clue to my views regarding the efforts "of Russians to find a path of development for their country which will be different from that which Western Europe pursued and still pursues," etc.

In the Afterword to the second German edition of *Cap-*

ital—which the author[1] of the article on Mr. Zhukovsky knows, because he quotes it—I speak of a "great Russian scholar and critic"[2] with the high consideration he deserves. In his remarkable articles this writer has dealt with the question whether, as her liberal economists maintain, Russia must begin by destroying the village community in order to pass to the capitalist regime or whether, on the contrary, she can without experiencing the tortures of this regime appropriate all its fruits by developing the historical conditions specifically her own. He pronounces in favor of this latter solution. And my honorable critic would have had at least as much reason for inferring from my consideration for this "great Russian scholar and critic" that I shared his views on the question as for concluding from my polemic against the "literary man" and Pan-Slavist that I rejected them.

To conclude, as I am not fond of leaving "anything to guesswork" I shall come straight to the point. In order that I might be specially qualified to estimate the economic development in Russia, I learned Russian, and then for many years studied the official publications and others bearing on this subject. I have arrived at this conclusion: If Russia continues to pursue the path she has followed since 1861, she will lose the finest chance ever offered by history to a people and undergo all the fatal vicissitudes of the capitalist regime.

II

The chapter on primitive accumulation does not pretend to do more than trace the path by which, in Western Europe, the capitalist order of economy emerged from the womb of the feudal order of economy. It therefore describes the historical movement which by divorcing the

[1] [N. K. Mikhailovsky, the leading philosopher among the Russian Populists, advocated a personalistic metaphysics and an ethics of freedom. He was the exemplar of the repentant nobleman. —Ed.]

[2] [N. G. Chernyshevsky, the inspirer of the Russian Populist Movement, and a disciple of Feuerbach, had spent many years in prison and exile.—Ed.]

producers from their means of production converts them into wage workers (proletarians in the modern sense of the word) while it converts those who possess the means of production into capitalists. In that history "all revolutions are epoch-making that act as levers for the advancement of the capitalist class in course of formation; above all, those which, by stripping great masses of men of their traditional means of production and subsistence, suddenly hurl them on the labor market. But the basis of this whole development is the expropriation of the agricultural producer. This has been accomplished in radical fashion only in England . . . but all the countries of Western Europe are going through the same movement," etc. (*Capital*, French edition, page 315.) At the end of the chapter the historical tendency of production is summed up thus: That it "itself begets its own negation with the inexorability which governs the metamorphoses of nature"; that it has itself created the elements of a new economic order, by giving the greatest impulse at once to the productive forces of social labor and to the integral development of every individual producer; that capitalist property, resting already, as it actually does, on a collective mode of production, cannot but transform itself into social property. At this point I have not furnished any proof, for the good reason that this statement is itself nothing else but a general summary of long expositions previously given in the chapters on capitalist production.

Now what application to Russia could my critic make of this historical sketch? Only this: If Russia is tending to become a capitalist nation after the example of the West European countries—and during the last few years she has been taking a lot of trouble in this direction—she will not succeed without having first transformed a good part of her peasants into proletarians; and after that, once taken to the bosom of the capitalist regime, she will experience its pitiless laws like other profane peoples. That is all. But that is too little for my critic. He feels he absolutely must metamorphose my historical sketch of the genesis of capitalism in Western Europe into a historico-philosophic theory of the general path every people is fated to tread, whatever the historical circumstances in which it finds itself, in order that it may ultimately arrive at the form of economy which ensures, together with the greatest expansion of the productive powers of social labor, the most complete development of man. But I beg his pardon. (He is both honoring and shaming me too much.) Let us take an example.

In several parts of *Capital* I allude to the fate which overtook the plebeians of ancient Rome. They were originally free peasants, each cultivating his own piece of land on his own account. In the course of Roman history they were expropriated. The same movement which divorced them from their means of production and subsistence involved the formation not only of big landed property but also of big money capital. And so one fine morning there were to be found on the one hand free men, stripped of everything except their labor power, and on the other, in order to exploit this labor, those who held all the acquired wealth in their possession. What happened? The Roman proletarians became not wage laborers but a *mob* of do-nothings more abject than the former "poor whites" in the South of the United States, and alongside of them there developed a mode of production which was not capitalist but based on slavery. Thus events strikingly analogous but taking place in different historical surroundings led to totally different results. By studying each of these forms of evolution separately and then comparing them one can easily find the clue to this phenomenon, but one will never arrive there by using as one's master key a general historico-philosophical theory, the supreme virtue of which consists in being super-historical.

[THE RUSSIAN MARXISTS AND MARXIST TEXTS]

ENGELS TO ISAAC A. HOURWICH[1]

1 [Hourwich, a Russian-born immigrant to the United States, sent his doctoral dissertation, *The Economics of the Russian Village*, to Engels with a request for comment. Engels' reply was written in English. Hourwich was the first Marxian economist to teach at an American university. His career at the University of Chicago was, however, terminated by the authorities.]

London, May 27, 1893

Dr. Isaac A. Hourwich

Dear Sir:

Many thanks for your interesting study on the *Economics of the Russian Village*, which I read, I hope, not without profit.

As to the burning questions of the Russian revolutionary movement, the part which the peasantry may be expected to take in it, these are subjects on which I could not conscientiously state an opinion for publication without previously studying over again the whole subject and completing my very imperfect knowledge of the facts of the case by bringing it up to date. But for that, I am sorry to say, I have not at present the time. And then, I have every reason to doubt whether such a public statement by me would have the effect you expect of it. I know from my own experience (1849–52) how unavoidably a political emigration splits itself up into a number of divergent factions so long as the mother country remains quiet. The burning desire to act, face to face with the impossibility of doing anything effective, causes in many intelligent and energetic heads an overactive mental speculation, an attempt at discovering or inventing new and almost miraculous means of action. The word of an outsider would have but a trifling, and at best a passing, effect. If you have followed the Russian emigration literature of the last decade, you will yourself know how, for instance, passages from Marx's writings and correspondence have been interpreted in the most contradictory ways, exactly as if they had been texts from the classics or from the New Testament, by various sections of Russian emigrants. Whatever I might say on the subject you mention would probably share the same fate, if any attention was paid to it. And so for all these various reasons, I think it best for all whom it may concern, including myself, to abstain.

Yours very truly,

F. Engels

[ANARCHISM AND CONSPIRATORIAL ETHICS]

ENGELS TO THEODOR CUNO

London, January 24, 1872

. . . Bakunin has a peculiar theory of his own, a medley of Proudhonism and communism. The chief point concerning the former is that he does not regard capital, i.e., the class antagonism between capitalists and wage workers which has arisen through social development, but the *state* as the main evil to be abolished. While the great mass of the social-democratic workers hold our view that state power is nothing more than the organization which the ruling classes—landowners and capitalists—have provided for themselves in order to protect their social privileges, Bakunin maintains that it is the *state* which has created capital, that the capitalist has his capital *only by the grace of the state*. As, therefore, the state is the chief evil, it is above all the state which must be done away with, and then capitalism will go to blazes of itself. We, on the contrary, say: Do away with capital, the concentration of all means of production in the hands of the few, and the state will fall of itself. The difference is an essential one: without a previous social revolution the abolition of the state is nonsense; the abolition of capital *is* precisely the social revolution, and involves a change in the whole mode of production. Now then, inasmuch as to Bakunin the state is the main evil, nothing must be done which can keep the state—that is, any state, whether it be a republic, a monarchy, or anything else—alive. Hence *complete abstention from all politics*. To commit a political act, especially to take part in an election, would be a betrayal of principle. The thing to do is to carry on propaganda, heap abuse upon the state, organize, and when *all* the workers, hence the majority, are won over, depose all the authorities, abolish the state, and replace it with the organization of the International. This great act, with which the millennium begins, is called *social liquidation*.

All this sounds extremely radical and is so simple that it can be learned by heart in five minutes; that is why the Bakuninist theory has speedily found favor also in Italy and Spain among young lawyers, doctors, and other doctrinaires. But the mass of the workers will never allow themselves to be persuaded that the public affairs of their countries are not also their own affairs; they are naturally *politically-minded*, and whoever tries to make them believe that they should leave politics alone will in the end be left in the lurch. To preach to the workers that they should in all circumstances abstain from politics is to drive them into the arms of the priests or the bourgeois republicans.

Now, as the International, according to Bakunin, was not formed for political struggle but to replace the old state organization as soon as social liquidation takes place, it follows that it must come as near as possible to the Bakuninist ideal of future society. In this society there will, above all, be no *authority*, for authority = state = absolute evil. (How these people propose to run a factory, operate a railway, or steer a ship without a will that decides in the last resort, without single management, they of course do not tell us.) The authority of the majority over the minority also ceases. Every individual and every community is autonomous, but as to how a society of even only two people is possible unless each gives up some of his autonomy Bakunin again maintains silence. . . .

The nucleus of the Bakunin crowd consists of a few dozen people in the Jura whose whole following amounts to scarcely two hundred workers. Their vanguard is made up of young lawyers, doctors, and journalists in Italy, who everywhere now act as spokesmen of the Italian workers; a few of their brand are in Barcelona and Madrid, and every now and then you will find one—hardly ever a worker—in Lyons or Brussels; here there is a single specimen, Robin.

The conference,[1] convoked under the pressure of circumstances in lieu of the congress that had become impossible, served them as a pretext; and since most of the French refugees in Switzerland went over to their side be-

[1] [The reference is to the London Conference of the First International, held in 1871.]

cause they (being Proudhonists) found many a kindred soul among them and for personal reasons, they sallied forth on their campaign. Malcontent minorities and unrecognized geniuses may naturally be found everywhere in the International, and these were counted upon, not without reason.

At present their fighting strength is as follows:

(1) Bakunin himself—the Napoleon of this campaign.

(2) The two hundred Jurassians and the forty–fifty members of the French Section (refugees in Geneva).

(3) In Brussels, Hins, editor of the *Liberté*, who, however, does *not* come out *openly* for them.

(4) Here, the remnants of the French Section of 1871, which we have never recognized and which has already split into three mutually hostile parts. . . .

And the General Council will certainly not call an extraordinary congress just to please a few bumptious intriguers. So long as these gentlemen keep within legal bounds, the General Council will gladly let them have their way. This coalition of the most diverse elements will soon fall apart, but as soon as they start anything against the Rules or the congress resolutions the General Council will do its duty.

If you reflect upon the fact that these people have launched their conspiracy precisely at the moment when a general hue and cry is being raised against the International you cannot help thinking that the International sleuths must have a hand in the game. And so it is. . . . How far the Russian police is involved in this I shall leave as a moot question for the present, but Bakunin was deeply embroiled in the Nechayev affair (he denies it, of course, but we have the original Russian reports here, and since Marx and I understand Russian he cannot put anything over on us). Nechayev is either a Russian *agent provocateur* or, anyhow, acted as if he were. Moreover, Bakunin has all kinds of suspicious characters among his Russian friends. . . .

I would also ask you to be rather discreet with *all* people connected with Bakunin. It is in all sects to stick together and intrigue. You may rest assured that *any information you give them* will immediately be passed on to Bakunin. It is one of his fundamental principles that keeping promises and the like are merely bourgeois prejudices, which a true revolutionary must treat with disdain to help along the cause. In Russia he says this openly, in Western Europe it is secret lore. . . .

Yours,
F. Engels

[ENGLISH FABIAN SOCIALISM]

ENGELS TO KARL KAUTSKY

Ryde, September 4, 1892

. . . If you had been here during the last elections you would talk differently about the Fabians. In our tactics one thing is thoroughly established for all modern countries and times: to bring the workers to the point of forming their own independent party, opposed to all bourgeois parties. During the last elections the English workers, for the first time and perhaps still only instinctively, pressed by the course of events, took a decided step in this direction; and this step has been surprisingly successful, and has contributed more to the development of the minds of the workers than any other event of the last twenty years. And what did the Fabians do, not just this or that Fabian but the Society as a whole? It preached and practiced: *affiliation of the workers to the Liberals,* and what was to be expected happened: the Liberals assigned them four seats impossible to win, and the Fabian candidates conspicuously failed. The paradoxical belletrist Shaw—very talented and witty as a belletrist but absolutely useless as an economist and politician, although honest and not a careerist—wrote to Bebel that if they did not follow this policy of forcing their candidates on the Liberals they would reap nothing but defeat and disgrace (as if defeat were not often more honorable than victory), and now they have pursued their policy and have reaped both.

That is the crux of the whole matter. At a juncture when the workers for the first time come out independently, the Fabian Society advises them to remain the tail of the Liberals. And the socialists on the Continent must be told that openly. To gloss this over would be to share the blame. That's why I was sorry that the final portion of the Avelings' article[1] did not appear. It was not *post festum*, not an afterthought. It had simply been overlooked in the rush to get the article off. The article is not complete without a description of the attitude of both socialist organizations towards the elections, and the readers of the *Neue Zeit* have a right to know about this.

I believe I told you myself in my last letter that both in the Social-Democratic Federation and in the Fabian Society the provincial members were better than the central body. But that is of no avail as long as the attitude of the central body determines that of the Society. I don't know any of the other fine chaps except Banner. Curiously enough, Banner has never come to see me since he joined the Fabian Society. I suppose his action was determined by his disgust with the S.D.F. and the need for some kind of organization, perhaps also some illusions. But this one swallow makes no summer.

You see something unfinished in the Fabian Society. On the contrary, this crowd is only *too* finished: a clique of bourgeois "socialists" of diverse calibers, from careerists to sentimental socialists and philanthropists, united only by their fear of the threatening rule of the workers and doing all in their power to spike this danger by making *their own* leadership secure, the leadership exercised by the "eddicated." If afterwards they admit a few workers into their central board in order that they may play there the role of the worker Albert of 1848, the role of constantly outvoted minority, this should not deceive anyone.

The means employed by the Fabian Society are just the same as those of the corrupt parliamentary politicians: money, intrigues, careerism. That is the English way, according to which it is self-understood that every political party (only among the workers it is supposed to be different!) pays its agents in some way or other or rewards

1 [An article by Eleanor and Edward Aveling, entitled, "Elections in Great Britain," had been published in the *Neue Zeit*. Eleanor was Marx's youngest daughter; she had entered into a "free alliance" with Edward Aveling, who was much disliked by the Fabians because of his notorious dishonesty and immorality.]

them with posts. These people are immersed up to their necks in the intrigues of the Liberal party, hold Liberal party jobs, as for instance Sidney Webb, who in general is a genuine British politician. These gentry do everything that the workers have to be warned against.

In spite of all this I do not ask you to treat these people as enemies. Neither ought you in my opinion to shield them from criticism, just as you don't shield anybody else. And that is precisely what the omission of the passages concerning them in the article by the Avelings looked like. . . .

[AUGUSTE COMTE]

ENGELS TO FERDINAND TÖNNIES

London, January 24, 1895

. . . Your observations on Auguste Comte interested me. As far as this "philosopher" is concerned, a substantial job of work has, in my opinion, still to be done. Comte was for five years secretary to St. Simon, and his intimate friend. The latter positively suffered from repleteness of thought. He was a genius and mystic in one. To establish clearness, order, system was not his forte. So in Comte he drew to his bosom a man who after his master's death would perhaps present these overbrimming ideas to the world in orderly fashion. Comte's mathematical schooling and method of thought seemed to render him peculiarly fit for this in contrast to other pupils, who were dreamers. Suddenly Comte broke with his "master" and withdrew from the school. Then, after a rather lengthy period of time, he came out with his "positive philosophy."

In this system there are three characteristic elements: (1) a series of brilliant thoughts, which however are almost always spoiled more or less because of insufficient development; (2) an accordingly narrow, Philistine mode of outlook, sharply contrasting with that brilliance of mind; (3) a hierarchically organized religious constitution, originating from a thoroughly St. Simonist source, but divested of all mysticism and sobered in the extreme, with a regular pope at the head, so that Huxley could say of Comtism that it was Catholicism without Christianity.[1]

Now I'll bet you No. 3 furnishes us the clue to the otherwise incomprehensible contradiction between No. 1 and No. 2; Comte took all his bright ideas from St. Simon, but mutilated them when grouping them in his own peculiar way; by divesting them of the mysticism that adhered to them he dragged them down to a lower level, reshaping them in Philistine fashion to the best of his ability. In very many of them the St. Simonist origin can easily be traced, and I am convinced that this would be possible in yet other cases if somebody could be found to tackle the job seriously. It would certainly have been discovered long ago if after 1830 St. Simon's own writings had not been completely stifled by the clamor of the St. Simonist school and religion, which stressed and developed certain aspects of the master's teaching to the detriment of the magnificent conception as a whole.

Then there is another point I should like to correct, the note on page 513. Marx never was Secretary-General of the International, but only Secretary for Germany and Russia. And none of the Comtists in London participated in the founding of the International. Professor E. Beesly deserves great credit for his defense of the International in the press at the time of the Commune against the vehement attacks of that day. Frederic Harrison, too, publicly took up the cudgels for the Commune. But a few years later the Comtists cooled off considerably toward the labor movement. The workers had become too powerful, and it was now a question of maintaining a proper balance between capitalists and workers (both producers, after all, according to St. Simon), and to that end of once more supporting the former. Ever since then the Comtists have wrapped themselves in complete silence as regards the labor question.

Yours very truly,
F. Engels

1 [Thomas Henry Huxley, *Lay Sermons, Addresses, and Reviews*, New York, 1871, p. 140.]

[SOCIALIST IMPERIALISM IN JAVA]

ENGELS TO KARL KAUTSKY

London, February 16, 1884

. . . It would be a good thing for somebody to take the pains to elucidate the state socialism now rampant by using the example of it in *Java,* where its practice is in full bloom. All the material for that will be found in *Java, or How to Manage a Colony,* by I. W. B. Money, Barrister at Law, London 1861, two volumes. Here it will be seen how, on the basis of the old community communism, the Dutch organized production under state control and secured for the people what they considered a quite comfortable existence. The result: the people are kept at the stage of primitive stupidity, and seventy million marks (now surely more) are annually collected by the Dutch national treasury. This case is highly interesting, and can easily be turned to practical use. Incidentally, it is proof of how today primitive communism furnishes there, as well as in India and Russia, the finest and broadest basis of exploitation and despotism (so long as it is not aroused by some element of modern communism), and how in the conditions of modern society it turns out to be a crying anachronism (to be removed or further developed) as much as were the independent mark associations of the original cantons. . . .

[DEFENCE OF PROGRESSIVE IMPERIALISM IN ALGERIA]

FRIEDRICH ENGELS

This excerpt is from an article written by Engels, as Paris correspondent for the English Chartist newspaper *Northern Star,* Vol. XI, January 22, 1848, No. 535, p. 7. —ED.

Upon the whole it is, in our opinion, very fortunate that the Arabian chief [Abd-el-Kader] has been taken. The struggle of the Bedouins was a hopeless one, and though the manner in which brutal soldiers, like Bugeaud, have carried on the war is highly blamable, the conquest of Algeria is an important and fortunate fact for the progress of civilization. The piracies of the Barbaresque states, never interfered with by the English government as long as they did not disturb their ships, could not be put down but by the conquest of one of these states. And the conquest of Algeria has already forced the Beys of Tunis and Tripoli, and even the Emperor of Morocco, to enter upon the road of civilization. They were obliged to find other employment for their people than piracy, and other means of filling their exchequer than tributes paid to them by the smaller states of Europe. And if we may regret that the liberty of the Bedouins of the desert has been destroyed, we must not forget that these same Bedouins were a nation of robbers, whose principal means of living consisted of making excursions either upon each other or upon the settled villagers, taking what they found, slaughtering all those who resisted, and selling the remaining prisoners as slaves. All these nations of free barbarians look very proud, noble, and glorious at a distance, but only come near them and you will find that they, as well as the more civilized nations, are ruled by the lust of gain, and only employ ruder and more cruel means. And after all, the modern *bourgeois*, with civilization, industry, order, and at least relative enlightenment following him, is preferable to the feudal lord or to the marauding robber, with the barbarian state of society to which they belong.

[SOCIALIST COLONIAL POLICY]

ENGELS TO KARL KAUTSKY

London, November 12, 1882

. . . In my opinion, the colonies proper, i.e., the countries occupied with a European population, Canada, the Cape, Australia, will all become independent; on the other hand, the countries inhabited by a native population, which are simply subjugated, India, Algiers, the Dutch,

Portuguese, and Spanish possessions, must be taken over for the time being by the proletariat and led as rapidly as possible towards independence. How this process will develop is difficult to say. India will perhaps, indeed very probably, produce a revolution, and as the proletariat emancipating itself cannot conduct any colonial wars this would have to be allowed; it would not pass off without all sorts of destruction, of course, but that sort of thing is inseparable from all revolutions. The same might also take place elsewhere, e.g., in Algiers and Egypt, and would certainly be the best thing *for us*. We shall have enough to do at home. Once Europe is organized, and North America, that will furnish such colossal power and such an example that the semi-civilized countries will follow in their wake of their own accord. Economic needs alone will be responsible for this. But as to what social and political phases these countries will then have to pass through before they likewise arrive at socialist organization, we today can only advance rather idle hypotheses, I think. One thing alone is certain: the victorious proletariat can force no blessings of any kind upon any foreign nation without undermining its own victory by so doing. Which of course by no means excludes defensive wars of various kinds. . . .

[SOCIOLOGY OF THE BIBLE]

ENGELS TO MARX

[Manchester, approximately May 24, 1853]

. . . Yesterday I read the book about the Arabian inscriptions of which I told you. The thing is not devoid of interest, although priest and Bible apologist are written disgustingly all over it. His greatest triumph consists in being able to prove that *Gibbon* committed some blunders in ancient geography, from which it may be deduced that Gibbon's theology is also unsound. The thing is called *The Historical Geography of Arabia*, by the Reverend Charles Forster. The best one can get out of it is the following:

1. The genealogy given in Genesis, purporting to be that of Noah, Abraham, etc., is a fairly exact enumeration of the

Bedouin tribes of that time, according to their major or minor dialectal kinship, etc. As we know, the Bedouin tribes have to the present day always called themselves Beni Saled, Beni Jussuff, and so on, i.e., the sons of so-and-so. This appellation, which springs from the ancient patriarchal mode of existence, leads in the end to this kind of genealogy. The enumeration in Genesis is corroborated more or less by the ancient geographers and the more recent travelers prove that the old names, with dialectal changes, still exist in their majority. However, it follows from this that the Jews themselves were nothing more than a small Bedouin tribe, just like the rest, which local conditions, agriculture, and so forth, placed in opposition to the other Bedouins.

2. With regard to the great Arabian invasion, of which we spoke previously: that the Bedouins made periodic invasions, just like the Mongols, that the Assyrian Empire as well as the Babylonian was founded by Bedouin tribes, on the same spot where later the Caliphate of Baghdad arose. The founders of the Babylonian Empire, the Chaldeans, still exist under the same name, Beni Chaled, in the same locality. The rapid rise of big cities like Nineveh and Babylon occurred in exactly the same way as only three hundred years ago similar giant cities, such as Agra, Delhi, Lahore, and Muttan, in the East Indies, were created by an Afghan or Tatar invasion. Thus the Mohammedan invasion loses much of its distinctive character.

3. It seems that the Arabians, where they had settled down, in the Southwest, were just as civilized a people as the Egyptians, Assyrians, etc., as is proved by the buildings they erected. This, too, explains much in the Mohammedan invasion. As far as that fake, religion, is concerned, it seems to follow from the ancient inscriptions in the South, in which the old national Arabian tradition of monotheism still predominates (as it does among the American Indians) and of which tradition the Hebrew constitutes only a *small part*, that Mohammed's religious revolution, like *every* religious movement, was *formally a reaction*, an alleged return to the old, the simple.

That Jewish so-called Holy Scripture is nothing more than a record of the old Arabian religious and tribal traditions, modified by the early separation of the Jews from their consanguineous but nomadic neighbors—that is now perfectly clear to me. The circumstance that Palestine is surrounded on the Arabian side by nothing but deserts, Bedouin land, explains the separate exposition. But the old Arabian inscriptions, traditions, and the Koran, and the ease with which all genealogies, etc., can now be unraveled evidence the fact that the main content was Arabic, or rather Semitic, in general, as with us the Edda and German heroic saga.

Yours,
F. E.

[ORIENTAL CITIES]

MARX TO ENGELS

London, June 2, 1853

. . . With regard to the Hebrews and Arabians, your letter interested me very much. By the way: (1) a *general* relationship can be proved, since history began, among all Oriental tribes, between the settlement of one part of the tribes and the continued nomadic life of the others. (2) In Mohammed's time the trade route from Europe to Asia had been considerably modified and the cities of Arabia, which had taken a great part in the trade with India, etc., were in a state of commercial decay; this in any case also lent impetus. (3) As to religion, the question resolves itself into the general and therefore easily answered one: Why does the history of the East *appear* as a history of religions?

On the formation of Oriental cities one can read nothing more brilliant, graphic, and striking than old François Bernier (nine years physician to Aurung-Zebe): *Travels Containing a Description of the Dominions of the Great Mogul, etc.* He also describes the military system, the way these great armies were fed, etc., very well. On these two points he remarks, among other things: "The cavalry forms the principal section, the infantry is not so big as is generally rumored, unless all the servants and people from the bazaars or markets who follow the army are mixed in with the real fighting force; for in that case I could well believe that they would be right in putting the number of men in the army accompanying the king alone at two hundred thousand or three hundred thousand, and sometimes even more, when for example it is certain that he will be a long time absent from the capital. And this will not appear so very astonishing to one who knows the strange encumbrance of tents, kitchens, clothes, furniture, and quite frequently even of women, and consequently also the elephants, camels, oxen, horses, porters, foragers, provisioners, merchants of all kinds, and servitors whom these armies carry in their wake; or to one who understands the particular condition and government of the country, namely that the *king is the one and only proprietor of all the land* in the kingdom, from which it follows as a necessary consequence that a whole *capital city*, like Delhi or Agra, lives almost entirely on the army and is therefore obliged to follow the king if he takes the field for any length of time. For these towns neither are nor can be anything like a Paris, *being virtually nothing but military camps*, only a little better and more conveniently situated than in the open country."

On the occasion of the march of the Great Mogul into Kashmir with an army of four hundred thousand men, etc., he says: "The difficulty is to know whence and how such a great army, such a great number of men and animals, can subsist in the field. For this it is only necessary to suppose what is perfectly true, that the Indians are very sober and very simple in their food, and that of all that great number of horsemen not the tenth, nor even the twentieth, part eats meat during the march. So long as they have their *kicheri*, or mixture of rice and other vegetables, over which when it is cooked they pour melted butter, they are satisfied. Further, it is necessary to know that camels are possessed of extreme endurance at work, and can long resist hunger and thirst, live on little and eat anything, and that as soon as the army has arrived the camel drivers lead them to graze in the open country, where they eat whatever they can find. Moreover, the same merchants who keep the bazaars in Delhi are forced to maintain them during campaigns, too, and so do the small merchants, etc. . . . And finally, with regard to forage, all these poor folks go roaming all over the countryside to buy such and thus earn something. Their great and common resort is to rasp whole fields with a sort of small trowel, thrash or cleanse the small herb rasped, and bring it along to sell to the army. . . ."

Bernier rightly considered the basis of all phenomena in the East—he refers to Turkey, Persia, Hindustan—to be the *absence of private property in land.* This is the real key, even to the Oriental heaven. . . .

[SOCIAL CLASSES IN AMERICA]

MARX TO JOSEPH WEYDEMEYER

London, March 5, 1852

. . . How far bourgeois society in the United States still is from being mature enough to make the class struggle obvious and comprehensible is most strikingly proved by *C. H. Carey* (of Philadelphia), the only American economist of importance. He attacks *Ricardo,* the most classic representative (interpreter) of the bourgeoisie and the most stoical adversary of the proletariat, as a man whose works are an arsenal for anarchists, socialists, and all the enemies of the bourgeois order of society. He reproaches not only him, but Malthus, Mill, Say, Torrens, Wakefield, McCulloch, Senior, Whately, R. Jones, and others, the masterminds among the economists of Europe, with rending society asunder and preparing civil war because they show that the economic bases of the different classes are bound to give rise to a necessary and ever growing antagonism among them. He tried to refute them, not indeed like the fatuous Heinzen by connecting the existence of classes with the existence of *political* privileges and *monopolies,* but by attempting to make out that *economic* conditions—rent (landed property), *profit* (capital), and wages (wage labor), instead of being conditions of struggle and antagonism, are rather conditions of association and harmony. All he proves, of course, is that he is taking the "undeveloped" conditions of the United States for "normal conditions."

And now as to myself, no credit is due to me for discovering the existence of classes in modern society or the struggle between them. Long before me bourgeois historians had described the historical development of this class struggle and bourgeois economists the economic anatomy of the classes. What I did that was new was to prove: (1) that the *existence of classes* is only bound up with *particular historical phases in the development of production,* (2) that the class struggle necessarily leads to the *dictatorship of the proletariat,* (3) that this dictatorship itself constitutes only the transition to the *abolition of all classes* and to a *classless society*. Ignorant louts like Heinzen, who deny not merely the class struggle but even the existence of classes, only prove that, despite all their bloodcurdling yelps and the humanitarian airs they give themselves, they regard the social conditions under which the bourgeoisie rules as the final product, the *non plus ultra* of history, and that they are only the servitors of the bourgeoisie. And the less these louts realize the greatness and transient necessity of the bourgeois regime itself, the more disgusting is their servitude. . . .

[WHY THERE IS NO LARGE SOCIALIST PARTY IN AMERICA]

ENGELS TO FRIEDRICH A. SORGE

London, December 2, 1893

Dear Sorge:

. . . The repeal of the silver-purchase law has saved America from a severe money crisis and will promote industrial prosperity. But I don't know whether it wouldn't have been better for this crash to have actually occurred. The phrase "cheap money" seems to be bred deep in the bone of your Western farmers. . . .

The German socialists in America are an annoying business. The people you get over there from Germany are usually not the best—they stay here—and in any event, they are not at all a fair sample of the German party. And as is the case everywhere, each new arrival feels himself called upon to turn everything he finds upside down, turning it into something *new*, so that a new epoch may date from himself. Moreover, most of these greenhorns remain stuck in New York for a long time or for life, continually reinforced by new additions and relieved of the necessity of learning the language of the country or of getting to know American conditions properly. All of that certainly causes much harm, but, on the other hand, it is not to be denied that American conditions involve very great and peculiar difficulties for a steady development of a workers' party.

First, the Constitution, based as in England upon party government, which causes every vote for any candidate not put up by one of the two governing parties to appear to be *lost*. And the American, like the Englishman, wants to influence his state; he does not throw his vote away.

Then, and more especially, immigration, which divides the workers into two groups: the native-born and the foreigners, and the latter in turn into (1) the Irish, (2) the Germans, (3) the many small groups, each of which understands only itself: Czechs, Poles, Italians, Scandinavians, etc. And then the Negroes. To form a single party out of these requires quite unusually powerful incentives. Often there is a sudden violent *élan*, but the bourgeois need only wait passively and the dissimilar elements of the working class fall apart again.

Third, through the protective tariff system and the steadily growing domestic market the workers must have been exposed to a prosperity no trace of which has been seen here in Europe for years now (except in Russia, where, however, the bourgeois profit by it and not the workers).

A country like America, when it is really ripe for a socialist workers' party, certainly cannot be hindered from having one by the couple of German socialist doctrinaires. . . .

Your

F. Engels

HISTORY OF THE COMMUNIST LEAGUE

FRIEDRICH ENGELS

This essay was first published by Engels in 1885 as the Introduction to the third edition of Marx's pamphlet, *Revelations Concerning the Cologne Communist Trial*. Its vivid narrative emphasizes how Marx and Engels refused to join the Federation of the Just until it had rid itself of the character of a conspiracy. Under Marx's influence, the German workingmen abandoned ethical socialism and adopted the ideology of class struggle.—ED.

In 1836 the most extreme, chiefly proletarian elements of the secret democratic-republican Outlaws' League, which was founded by German refugees in Paris in 1834, split off and formed the new secret *League of the Just*. The parent League, in which only sleepy-headed elements à la Jakobus Venedey were left, soon fell asleep altogether: when in 1840 the police scented out a few sections in Germany, it was hardly even a shadow of its former self. The new League, on the contrary, developed comparatively rapidly. Originally it was a German outlier of the French worker communism, reminiscent of Babouvism and taking shape in Paris at about this time; community of goods was demanded as the necessary consequence of "equality." The aims were those of the Parisian secret societies of the time: half propaganda association, half conspiracy, Paris, however, being always regarded as the central point of revolutionary action, although the preparation of occasional Putsches in Germany was by no means excluded. But as Paris remained the decisive battleground, the League was at that time actually not much more than the German branch of the French secret societies, especially the Société des Saisons, led by Blanqui and Barbès, with which a close connection was maintained. The French went into action on May 12, 1839; the sections of the League marched with them, and thus were involved in the common defeat.

Among the Germans arrested were *Karl Schapper* and *Heinrich Bauer*; Louis Philippe's government contented itself with deporting them after a fairly long imprisonment. Both went to London. Schapper came from Weilburg in Nassau, and while a student of forestry at Giessen in 1832 was a member of the conspiracy organized by Georg Büchner; he took part in the storming of the Frankfort constable station on April 3, 1833, escaped abroad, and in February 1834 joined Mazzini's march on Savoy. Of gigantic stature, resolute and energetic, always ready to risk civil existence and life, he was a model of the professional revolutionist who played a certain role in the thirties. In spite of a certain sluggishness of thought he was by no means incapable of profound theoretical understanding, as is proved by his development from "demagogue" to communist, and he held then all the more rigidly to what he had once come to recognize. Precisely on that account his revolutionary passion sometimes got the better of his understanding, but he always afterwards realized his mistake and openly acknowledged it. He was fully a man and what he did for the founding of the German workers' movement will not be forgotten.

Heinrich Bauer, from Franconia, was a shoemaker; a lively, alert, witty little fellow, whose little body, however, also contained much shrewdness and determination.

Arrived in London, where Schapper, who had been a compositor in Paris, now tried to earn his living as a teacher of languages, they both set to work gathering up the broken threads and made London the center of the League. They were joined over here, if not already earlier in Paris, by *Joseph Moll*, a watchmaker from Cologne, a medium-sized Hercules—how often did Schapper and he victoriously defend the entrance to a hall against hundreds of onrushing opponents—a man who was at least the equal of his two comrades in energy and determination, and intellectually superior to both of them. Not only was he a born diplomat, as the success of his numerous trips on various missions proved; he was also more capable of theoretical insight. I came to know all three of them in London in 1843. They were the first revolutionary proletarians whom I met, and however far apart our views were at that time in details—for I still owned, as against their narrow-minded equalitarian communism,[1] a goodly dose of just as narrow-minded philosophical arrogance—I shall never forget the deep impression that these three real men made upon me, who was then still only wanting to become a man.

In London, as in a lesser degree in Switzerland, they had the benefit of freedom of association and assembly. As early as February 7, 1840, the legally functioning German Workers' Educational Association, which still exists, was founded. The Association served the League as a recruiting ground for new members, and since, as always, the communists were the most active and intelligent members of the Association, it was a matter of course that its leadership lay entirely in the hands of the League. The League soon had several communities, or, as they were then still called, "lodges," in London. The same obvious tactics were followed in Switzerland and elsewhere. Where workers' associations could be founded, they were utilized in like manner. Where this was forbidden by law, one joined choral societies, athletic clubs, and the like. Connections were to a large extent maintained by members who were continually traveling back and forth; they also, when required, served as emissaries. In both respects the League obtained lively support through the wisdom of the governments which, by resorting to deportation, converted any objectionable worker—and in nine cases out of ten he was a member of the League—into an emissary.

The extent to which the restored League spread was considerable. Notably in Switzerland, *Weitling, August Becker* (a highly gifted man who, however, like so many Germans, came to grief because of innate instability of character), and others created a strong organization more or less pledged to Weitling's communist system. This is not the place to criticize the communism of Weitling. But as regards its significance as the first independent theoretical stirring of the German proletariat, I still today subscribe to Marx's words in the Paris *Vorwärts* of 1844: "Where could the [German] bourgeoisie—including its philosophers and learned scribes—point to a work *relating to the*

[1] By equalitarian communism I understand, as stated, only that communism which bases itself exclusively or predominantly on the demand for equality.

emancipation of the bourgeoisie—its political emancipation—comparable to Weitling's *Guarantees of Harmony and Freedom?* If one compares the insipid mealymouthed mediocrity of German political literature with this immeasurable and brilliant debut of the German workers, if one compares these *gigantic children's shoes of the proletariat* with the dwarf proportions of the worn-out political shoes of the bourgeoisie, one must prophesy an athlete's figure for this Cinderella." This athlete's figure confronts us today, although still far from being fully grown.

Numerous sections existed also in Germany; in the nature of things they were of a transient character, but those coming into existence more than made up for those passing away. Only after seven years, at the end of 1846, did the police discover traces of the League in Berlin (Mentel) and Magdebourg (Beck), without being in a position to follow them further.

In Paris, Weitling, who was still there in 1840, likewise gathered the scattered elements together again before he left for Switzerland.

The tailors formed the central force of the League. German tailors were everywhere: in Switzerland, in London, in Paris. In the last-named city German was so much the prevailing tongue in this trade that I was acquainted there in 1846 with a Norwegian tailor who had traveled directly by sea from Trondhjem to France and in the space of eighteen months had learned hardly a word of French but had acquired an excellent knowledge of German. Two of the Paris communities in 1847 consisted predominantly of tailors, one of cabinetmakers.

After the center of gravity had shifted from Paris to London, a new feature grew conspicuous: from being German, the League gradually became *international*. In the workers' society there were to be found, besides Germans and Swiss, also members of all those nationalities for whom German served as the chief means of communication with foreigners, notably, therefore, Scandinavians, Dutch, Hungarians, Czechs, southern Slavs, and also Russians and Alsatians. In 1847 the regular frequenters included a British grenadier of the Guards in uniform. The society soon called itself the *Communist* Workers' Educational Association, and the membership cards bore the inscription "All Men Are Brothers," in at least twenty languages, even if not without mistakes here and there. Like the open Association, so also the secret League soon took on a more international character; at first in a restricted sense, practically through the varied nationalities of its members, theoretically through the realization that any revolution to be victorious must be a European one. One did not go any further as yet, but the foundations were there.

Close connections were maintained with the French revolutionists through the London refugees, comrades in arms of May 12, 1839. Similarly with the more radical Poles. The official Polish *émigrés*, as also Mazzini, were, of course, opponents rather than allies. The English Chartists, on account of the specific English character of their movement, were disregarded as not revolutionary. The London leaders of the League came in touch with them only later, through me.

In other ways, too, the character of the League had altered with events. Although Paris was still—and at that time quite rightly—looked upon as the mother city of the revolution, one had nevertheless emerged from the state of dependence on the Paris conspirators. The spread of the League raised its self-consciousness. It was felt that roots were being struck more and more in the German working class and that these German workers were historically called upon to be the standard-bearers of the workers of the North and East of Europe. In Weitling was to be found a communist theoretician who could be boldly placed at the side of his contemporary French rivals. Finally, the experience of May 12 had taught us that for the time being there was nothing to be gained by attempts at *Putsches*. And if one still continued to explain every event as a sign of the approaching storm, if one still preserved intact the old, semi-conspiratorial rules, that was mainly the fault of the old revolutionary defiance, which had already begun to collide with the sounder views that were gaining headway.

However, the social doctrine of the League, indefinite as it was, contained a very great defect, but one that had its roots in the conditions themselves. The members, in so far as they were workers at all, were almost exclusively artisans.

Even in the big metropolises, the man who exploited them was usually only a small master. The exploitation of tailoring on a large scale, what is now called the manufacture of ready-made clothes, by the conversion of handicraft tailoring into a domestic industry working for a big capitalist, was at that time even in London only just making its appearance. On the one hand, the exploiter of these artisans was a small master; on the other hand, they all hoped ultimately to become small masters themselves. In addition, a mass of inherited guild notions still clung to the German artisan at that time. The greatest honor is due to them, in that they, who were themselves not yet full proletarians but only an appendage of the petty bourgeoisie, an appendage which was passing into the modern proletariat and which did not yet stand in direct opposition to the bourgeoisie, that is, to big capital—in that these artisans were capable of instinctively anticipating their future development and of constituting themselves, even if not yet with full consciousness, the party of the proletariat. But it was also inevitable that their old handicraft prejudices should be a stumbling block to them at every moment, whenever it was a question of criticizing existing society in detail, that is, of investigating economic facts. And I do not believe there was a single man in the whole League at that time who had ever read a book on political economy. But that mattered little; for the time being "equality," "brotherhood" and "justice" helped them to surmount every theoretical obstacle.

Meanwhile a second, essentially different communism was developing alongside that of the League and of Weitling. While I was in Manchester, it was tangibly brought home to me that the economic facts, which have so far played no role or only a contemptible one in the writing of history, are, at least in the modern world, a decisive historical force; that they form the basis of the origination of the present-day class antagonisms; that these class antagonisms, in the countries where they have become fully developed, thanks to large-scale industry, hence especially in England, are in their turn the basis of the formation of political parties and of party struggles, and thus of all political history. Marx had not only arrived at the same view, but had already, in the *German-French Annuals* (1844), generalized it to the effect that, speaking generally, it is not the state which conditions and regulates civil society, but civil society which conditions and regulates the state, and, consequently, that policy and its history are to be explained from the economic relations and their development, and not vice versa. When I visited Marx in Paris in the summer of 1844, our complete agreement in all theoretical fields became evident, and our joint work dates from that time. When, in the spring of 1845, we met again in Brussels, Marx had already fully developed his materialist theory of history in its main features from the above-mentioned basis, and we now applied ourselves to the detailed elaboration of the newly won mode of outlook in the most varied directions.

This discovery, which revolutionized the science of history and, as we have seen, is essentially the work of Marx—a discovery in which I can claim for myself only a very insignificant share—was, however, of immediate importance for the contemporary workers' movement. Communism among the French and Germans, Chartism among the English now no longer appeared as something accidental, which could just as well not have occurred. These movements now presented themselves as a movement of the modern oppressed class, the proletariat, as the more or less developed forms of its historically necessary struggle against the ruling class, the bourgeoisie; as forms of the class struggle, but distinguished from all earlier class struggles by this one thing, that the present-day oppressed class, the proletariat, cannot achieve its emancipation without at the same time emancipating society as a whole from division into classes and, therefore, from class struggles. And communism now no longer meant the concoction, by means of the imagination, of an ideal society as perfect as possible, but insight into the nature, the conditions, and the consequent general aims of the struggle waged by the proletariat.

Now we were by no means of the opinion that the new scientific results should be confided in large tomes exclusively to the "learned" world. Quite the contrary. We were, both of us, already deeply involved in the political movement, and possessed a certain following in the educated world, especially of western Germany, and abundant contact with the organized proletariat. It was our duty to provide a scientific foundation for our view, but it was equally important for us to win over the European and in the first place the German proletariat to our conviction. As soon as we had become clear in our own minds, we set about the task. We founded a German workers' society in Brussels and took over the *Deutsche Brüsseler Zeitung*, which served us as an organ up to the February revolution. We kept in touch with the revolutionary section of the English Chartists through Julian Harney, the editor of the central organ of the movement, *The Northern Star*, to which I was a contributor. We entered likewise into a sort of cartel with the Brussels democrats (Marx was vice-president of the Democratic Society) and with the French social democrats of the *Réforme*, which I furnished with news of the English and German movements. In short, our connections with the radical and proletarian organizations and press organs were quite what one could wish.

Our relations with the League of the Just were as follows: The existence of the League was, of course, known to us; in 1843, Schapper had suggested that I join it, which I at that time naturally refused to do. But we not only kept up our continuous correspondence with the Londoners but remained on still closer terms with Dr. Everbeck, then the leader of the Paris communities. Without going into the League's internal affairs we learned of every important happening. On the other hand, we influenced the theoretical views of the most important members of the League by word of mouth, by letter, and through the press. For this purpose we also made use of various lithographed circulars, which we dispatched to our friends and correspondents throughout the world on particular occasions, when it was a question of the internal affairs of the communist party in process of formation. In these the League itself sometimes came to be dealt with. Thus a young Westphalian student, Hermann Kriege, who went to America, came forward there as an emissary of the League and associated himself with the crazy Harro Harring for the purpose of using the League to turn South America upside down. He founded a paper in which, in the name of the League, he preached an extravagant communism of love dreaming, based on "love" and overflowing with love. Against this we let fly with a circular that did not fail of its effect. Kriege vanished from the League scene.

Later Weitling came to Brussels. But he was no longer the naïve young journeyman tailor who, astonished at his own talents, was trying to clarify in his own mind just what a communist society would look like. He was now the great man, persecuted by the envious on account of his superiority, who scented rivals, secret enemies, and traps everywhere—the prophet, driven from country to country, who carried a recipe for the realization of heaven on earth ready-made in his pocket, and who was possessed with the idea that everybody intended to steal it from him. He had already fallen out with the members of the League in London; and in Brussels, where Marx and his wife welcomed him with almost superhuman forbearance, he also could not get along with anyone. So he soon afterwards went to America to try out his role of prophet there.

All these circumstances contributed to the quiet revolution that was taking place in the League, and especially among the leaders in London. The inadequacy of the previous conception of communism, both the simple French equalitarian communism and that of Weitling, became more and more clear to them. The tracing of communism back to primitive Christianity introduced by Weitling—no matter how brilliant certain passages to be found in his *Gospel of Poor Sinners*—had resulted in delivering the movement in Switzerland to a large extent into the hands first of fools like Albrecht, and then of exploiting fake prophets like Kuhlmann. The "true socialism" dealt in by a few literary writers—a translation of French socialist phraseology into corrupt Hegelian German, and sentimental love dreaming (see the section on German or "True" Socialism in the *Communist Manifesto*)—that Kriege and the study of the corresponding literature introduced in the League was found soon to disgust the old revolutionists of the League, if only because of its slobbering feebleness. As against the untenability of the previous theoretical views, and as against the practical aberrations resulting therefrom, it was realized more and more in London that Marx and

I were right in our new theory. This understanding was undoubtedly promoted by the fact that among the London leaders there were now two men who were considerably superior to those previously mentioned in capacity for theoretical knowledge: the miniature painter Karl Pfänder from Heilbronn and the tailor Georg Eccarius from Thuringia.[2]

It suffices to say that in the spring of 1847 Moll visited Marx in Brussels and immediately afterwards me in Paris, and invited us repeatedly, in the name of his comrades, to enter the League. He reported that they were as much convinced of the general correctness of our mode of outlook as of the necessity of freeing the League from the old conspiratorial traditions and forms. Should we enter we would be given an opportunity of expounding our critical communism before a congress of the League in a manifesto, which would then be published as the manifesto of the League; we would likewise be able to contribute our quota towards the replacement of the obsolete League organization by one in keeping with the new times and aims.

We entertained no doubt that an organization within the German working class was necessary, if only for propaganda purposes, and that this organization, in so far as it would not be merely local in character, could only be a secret one, even outside Germany. Now there already existed exactly such an organization in the shape of the League. What we previously objected to in this League was now relinquished as erroneous by the representatives of the League themselves; we were even invited to co-operate in the work of reorganization. Could we say no? Certainly not. Therefore we entered the League; Marx founded a League community in Brussels from among our close friends, while I attended the three Paris communities.

In the summer of 1847 the First League Congress took place in London, at which W. Wolff represented the Brus-

[2] Pfänder died about eight years ago in London. He was a man of peculiarly fine intelligence, witty, ironical, and dialectical. Eccarius, as we know, was later for many years Secretary of the General Council of the International Workingmen's Association, in the General Council of which the following old League members were to be found, among others: Eccarius, Pfänder, Lessner, Lochner, Marx, and myself. Eccarius subsequently devoted himself exclusively to the English trade union movement.

sels and I the Paris communities. At this Congress the reorganization of the League was carried through first of all. Whatever remained of the old mystical names dating back to the conspiratorial period was now abolished; the League now consisted of communities, circles, leading circles, a Central Committee and a Congress, and henceforth called itself the "Communist League." "The aim of the League is the overthrow of the bourgeoisie, the rule of the proletariat, the abolition of the old, bourgeois society based on class antagonisms, and the foundation of a new society without classes and without private property"—thus ran the first article. The organization itself was thoroughly democratic, with elective and always removable boards. This alone barred all hankering after conspiracy, which requires dictatorship, and the League was converted—for ordinary peacetimes at least—into a pure propaganda society. These new Rules were submitted to the communities for discussion—so democratic was the procedure now followed—then once again debated at the Second Congress, and finally adopted by the latter on December 8, 1847. They are to be found reprinted in Wermuth and Stieber, Volume I, page 239, Appendix X.

The Second Congress took place during the end of November and beginning of December of the same year. Marx also attended this time and expounded the new theory in a fairly long debate—the Congress lasted at least ten days. All contradiction and doubt were finally set at rest, the new basic principles were unanimously adopted, and Marx and I were commissioned to draw up the *Manifesto*. This was done immediately afterwards. A few weeks before the February revolution it was sent to London to be printed. Since then it has traveled round the world, has been translated into almost all languages, and today still serves in numerous countries as a guide for the proletarian movement. In place of the old League motto, "All Men Are Brothers," appeared the new battle cry, "Workingmen of All Countries, Unite!" which openly proclaimed the international character of the struggle. Seventeen years later this battle cry resounded throughout the world as the watchword of the International Workingmen's Association, and today the militant proletariat of all countries has inscribed it on its banner.

Excerpt from ON SOCIAL CONDITIONS IN RUSSIA

FRIEDRICH ENGELS

This essay was written by Engels during the course of a controversy with a Russian critic, Peter Nikitich Tkachov. It was published in the *Volksstaat* in 1875. Engels traces the source of "Oriental despotism" to the system of isolated village communities. He asserts that the Russian peasantry can skip the bourgeois stage in their development only if supported by a successful socialist revolution in Western Europe. This problem of "skipping stages" became the central issue in the theoretical debates between Lenin and Kautsky, and Trotsky and Stalin.—ED.

. . . In reality communal ownership of the land is an institution which is to be found on a low level of development among all Indo-Germanic races from India to Ireland and even among the Malays who have developed under Indian influence, for instance, in Java. . . . In Western Europe, including Poland and Little Russia, at a certain stage in the social development this communal ownership became a fetter, a brake on agricultural production, and was more and more eliminated. In Great Russia (i.e., Russia proper), on the other hand, it has persisted until today, thereby proving in the first place that agricultural production and the social conditions in the countryside corresponding to it are there still on a very undeveloped level, as is also actually the case. The Russian peasant lives and has his being only in his village, the rest of the world exists for him only in so far as it affects his village. This is so much the case that in Russian the same word "*mir*" means on the one hand "world" and on the other "peasant community." "*Ves mir*," the whole world, means for the peasant the meeting of the community members. Hence when Mr. Tkachov speaks of the "*world* outlook" of the Russian peasants he has obviously translated the Russian *mir* incorrectly. Such a complete isolation of the individual communities from one another, which creates throughout the country, it is true, similar, but the very opposite of common, interests, is the natural basis for *Oriental despotism*, and from India to Russia this form of society, wherever it has prevailed, has always produced it and always found its complement in it. Not only the Russian state in general, but even its specific form, czarist despotism, instead of hanging in the air, is the necessary and logical product of the Russian social conditions with which, according to Mr. Tkachov, it has "nothing in common"! Further development of Russia in a *bourgeois* direction would here also destroy communal ownership little by little, without its being necessary for the Russian Government to intervene with "bayonet and knout." And this all the more because the communally owned land in Russia is not cultivated by the peasants collectively and only the product divided, as is still the case in some districts in India; on the contrary, from time to time the land is divided up among the various heads of families, and each cultivates his allotment for himself. Consequently great differences in prosperity are possible among the members of the community, and also actually exist. Almost everywhere, there are a few rich peasants among them—here and there millionaires—who play the usurer and suck the blood of the mass of the peasants. No one knows this better than Mr. Tkachov. While he wishes to fool the German workers into thinking that the "idea of collective ownership" can be driven out of the Russian peasants, these instinctive, traditional communists, only by bayonet and knout he writes on page 15 of his Russian pamphlet: "Among the peasants a class of usurers [kulaks] is making its way, a class of people who *buy up* and lease the lands of farmers and nobles—a peasant aristocracy." These are the same kind of bloodsuckers as we described more fully above.

What dealt the severest blow to communal ownership was again the redemption of the *corvée*. The greater and better part of the land was allotted to the nobility; for the peasant there remained scarcely enough, often not enough, to live on. In addition, the forests were given to the nobles; the wood for fuel, building, and implements, which the peasant formerly could fetch there for nothing, he has now to buy. Thus the peasant has nothing now but his house and the bare land, without means to cultivate it, and on the average without land enough to support him and his family from one harvest to the next. Under such circumstances and under the pressure of taxes and usurers communal ownership of the land is no blessing, it becomes a fetter. The peasants often run away, with or without their family, to earn their living as wandering laborers, and leave their land behind them.[1]

It is clear that communal ownership in Russia is long past its flourishing period and to all appearances is moving towards its dissolution. Nevertheless, the possibility undeniably exists of transforming this social form into a higher one, if it should last until circumstances are ripe for that, and if it shows itself capable of development in such a way that the peasants no longer cultivate the land separately, but collectively;[2] and to transform it into this higher form, without it being necessary for the Russian peasants to go through the intermediate stage of bourgeois small ownership. This, however, can happen only if, before the complete breakup of communal ownership, a proletarian revolution is successfully carried out in Western Europe, creating for the Russian peasant the pre-conditions necessary for such a transformation, in particular, the material conditions which he needs in order to carry through the reconstruction of his whole agricultural system, thereby necessarily involved. It is therefore sheer bounce for Mr. Tkachov to say that the Russian peasants, although "own-

[1] On the position of the peasants compare *inter alia* the official report of the Government Commission on Agricultural Production (1873), and further Skaldin, *V Zakholustye i v Stolitse* [*In the Remote Provinces and in the Capital*], St. Petersburg, 1870; the latter publication by a liberal conservative. [Note by F. Engels.]

[2] In Poland, in particular in the Grodno gubernia, where the nobility for the most part was ruined by the rebellion of 1863, the peasants now frequently buy or rent estates from the nobles and cultivate them as a whole and *on a collective account*. And these peasants for centuries past have not had communal ownership any more and are not Russians, but Poles, Lithuanians, and White Russians. [Note by F. Engels.]

ers," stand "nearer to socialism" than the propertyless workers of Western Europe. Exactly the contrary is the case. If anything can still save Russian communal ownership and give it a chance of growing into a new form really capable of life, it is a proletarian revolution in Western Europe. . . .

There is no doubt Russia is on the eve of a revolution. Her finances are in extreme disorder. Increasing taxation proves of no avail, the interest on old state loans is paid by means of new loans, and every new loan meets with greater difficulties; money can now be raised only under the pretext of building railways! The administration, as of old, corrupt from top to bottom, the officials living more from theft, bribery, and extortion than from their salaries. The entire agricultural production—by far the most essential for Russia—thrown into complete disorder by the redemption settlement of 1861; the big landowners without sufficient labor, the peasants without sufficient land, oppressed by taxation and sucked dry by usurers, the yield from agriculture declining from year to year. The whole held together with great difficulty and only outwardly by an Oriental despotism whose arbitrariness we in the West simply cannot imagine; a despotism which not only from day to day comes into more glaring contradiction with the views of the enlightened classes, and in particular with those of the rapidly developing bourgeoisie of the capital cities, but which, under its present bearer, has lost faith in itself, one day making concessions to liberalism and the next canceling them again in terror, and thus bringing itself more and more into disrepute. With all that, a growing recognition among the enlightened strata of the nation concentrated in the capital that this position is untenable, that a revolution is imminent, and the illusion that it will be possible to guide this revolution into a smooth, constitutional channel. Here we have united all the conditions of a revolution, of a revolution which, possibly started by the upper classes of the capital, even perhaps by the government itself, must be rapidly carried further, beyond the first constitutional phase, by the peasants; of a revolution which will be of the greatest importance for the whole of Europe if only because it will destroy at one blow the last, so far intact, reserve of the entire European reaction. This revolution is surely approaching. Only two events can delay it: a successful war against Turkey or Austria, for which money and firm alliances are necessary, or a premature attempt at insurrection, which would drive the property-owning classes back into the arms of the government.

THE BRITISH RULE IN INDIA

KARL MARX

At the request of Charles A. Dana, its managing editor, Marx became the European correspondent of the New York *Tribune* in 1851. During the next eleven years many of Marx's articles were published in that leading radical newspaper of its time. "The British Rule in India" appeared in the *Tribune* on June 25, 1853. It was written by Marx in English.—Ed.

Telegraphic dispatches from Vienna announce that the pacific solution of the Turkish, Sardinian, and Swiss questions is regarded there as a certainty.

Last night the debate on India was continued in the House of Commons, in the usual dull manner. Mr. Blackett charged the statements of Sir Charles Wood and Sir J. Hogg with bearing the stamp of optimistic falsehood. A lot of ministerial and directorial advocates rebuked the charge as well as they could, and the inevitable Mr. Hume summed up by calling on ministers to withdraw their bill. Debate adjourned.

Hindustan is an Italy of Asiatic dimensions, the Himalayas for the Alps, the Plains of Bengal for the Plains of Lombardy, the Deccan for the Apennines, and the Isle of Ceylon for the Island of Sicily. The same rich variety in the products of the soil, and the same dismemberment in the political configuration. Just as Italy has, from time to time, been compressed by the conqueror's sword into different national masses, so do we find Hindustan, when not under the pressure of the Mohammedan, or the Mogul, or the Briton, dissolved into as many independent and conflicting states as it numbers towns, or even villages. Yet, in a social point of view, Hindustan is not the Italy, but the Ireland of the East. And this strange combination of Italy and Ireland, of a world of voluptuousness and of a world of woes, is anticipated in the ancient traditions of the religion of Hindustan. That religion is at once a religion of sensualist exuberance and a religion of self-torturing asceticism, a religion of the Lingam and of the Juggernaut, the religion of the Monk and of the Bayadere.

I share not the opinion of those who believe in a golden age of Hindustan, without recurring, however, like Sir Charles Wood, for the confirmation of my view, to the authority of Khuli-Khan. But take, for example, the times of Aurang-Zebe; or the epoch when the Mogul appeared in the North and the Portuguese in the South; or the age of Mohammedan invasion, and of the heptarchy in southern India; or, if you will, go still more, back to antiquity: take the mythological chronology of the Brahman himself, who places the commencement of Indian misery in an epoch even more remote than the Christian creation of the world.

There cannot, however, remain any doubt but that the misery inflicted by the British on Hindustan is of an essentially different and infinitely more intensive kind than all Hindustan had to suffer before. I do not allude to European despotism, planted upon Asiatic despotism, by the British East India Company, forming a more monstrous combination than any of the divine monsters startling us in the Temple of Salsette. This is no distinctive feature of British colonial rule, but only an imitation of the Dutch, and so much so that in order to characterize the working of the British East India Company it is sufficient to literally repeat what Sir Stamford Raffles, the *English* Governor of Java, said of the old Dutch East India Company:

"The Dutch Company, actuated solely by the spirit of gain, and viewing their subjects with less regard or consideration than a West India planter formerly viewed a gang upon his estate, because the latter had paid the purchase money of human property, which the other had not, employed all the existing machinery of despotism to squeeze from the people their utmost mite of contribution, the last dregs of their labor, and thus aggravated the evils of a capricious and semi-barbarous government by working it with all the practiced ingenuity of politicians and all the monopolizing selfishness of traders."

All the civil wars, invasions, revolutions, conquests, famines, strangely complex, rapid, and destructive as the successive action of Hindustan may appear, did not go deeper than its surface. England has broken down the entire framework of Indian society, without any symptoms of reconstitution yet appearing. This loss of his old world, with no gain of a new one, imparts a particular kind of melancholy to the present misery of the Hindu, and separates Hindustan, ruled by Britain, from all its ancient traditions, and from the whole of its past history.

There have been in Asia, generally, from immemorial times, but three departments of government: that of Finance, or the plunder of the interior; that of War, or the plunder of the exterior; and, finally, the Department of Public Works.

Climate and territorial conditions, especially the vast tracts of desert, extending from the Sahara, through Arabia, Persia, India, and Tartary, to the most elevated Asiatic highlands, constituted artificial irrigation by canals and waterworks the basis of Oriental agriculture. As in Egypt and India, inundations are used for fertilizing the soil in Mesopotamia, Persia, etc.; advantage is taken of a high level for feeding irrigative canals. This prime necessity of an economical and common use of water, which, in the Occident, drove private enterprise to voluntary association, as in Flanders and Italy, necessitated in the Orient, where civilization was too low and the territorial extent too vast to call into life voluntary association, the interference of the centralizing power of government. Hence an economic function devolved upon all Asiatic government: the function of providing public works. This artificial fertilization of the soil, dependent on a central government and immediately decaying with the neglect of irrigation and drainage, explains the otherwise strange fact we now find: whole territories barren and desert that were once brilliantly cultivated, as Palmyra, Petra, the ruins of Yemen, and large provinces of Egypt, Persia, and Hindustan; it also explains how a single war of devastation has been able to depopulate a country for centuries, and to strip it of all its civilization.

Now the British in East India accepted from their predecessors the Department of Finance and of War, but they have neglected entirely that of Public Works. Hence the deterioration of an agriculture which is not capable of being conducted on the British principle of free competition, of *laissez-faire* and *laissez-aller*. But in Asiatic empires we are quite accustomed to see agriculture deteriorating under one government and reviving again under some other government. There the harvests correspond to good or bad government, as they change in Europe with good or bad seasons. Thus the oppression and neglect of agriculture, bad as it is, could not be looked upon as the final blow dealt to Indian society by the British intruder, had it not been attended by a circumstance of quite different importance, a novelty in the annals of the whole Asiatic world. However changing the political aspect of India's past must appear, its social condition has remained unaltered since its remotest antiquity, until the first decennium of the nineteenth century. The hand loom and the spinning wheel, producing their regular myriads of spinners and weavers, were the pivots of the structure of that society. From immemorial times Europe received the admirable textures of Indian labor, sending in return for them her precious metals, and furnishing thereby his material to the goldsmith, that indispensable member of Indian society, whose love of finery is so great that even the lowest class, those who go about nearly naked, have commonly a pair of golden earrings and a gold ornament of some kind hung round their necks. Rings on the fingers and toes have also been common. Women as well as children frequently wore massive bracelets and anklets of gold or silver, and statuettes of divinities in gold and silver were met with in the households. It was the British intruder who broke up the Indian hand loom and destroyed the spinning wheel. England began with driving the Indian cotton from the European market; it then introduced twist into Hindustan, and in the end inundated the very mother country of cotton with cottons. From 1818 to 1836 the export of twist from Great Britain rose in the proportion of one to fifty-two hundred. In 1824 the export of British muslins to India hardly amounted to a million yards, while in 1837 it surpassed sixty-four million yards. But at the same time the population of Dacca decreased from a hundred and fifty thousand inhabitants to twenty thousand. This decline of Indian towns celebrated for their fabrics was by no means the worst consequence. British steam and science uprooted, over the whole surface of Hindustan, the union between agricultural and manufacturing industries.

These two circumstances—the Hindu, on the one hand, leaving, like all Oriental peoples, to the central government the care of the great public works, the prime condition of his agriculture and commerce; dispersed, on the other hand, over the surface of the country, and agglomerated in small centers by the domestic union of agricultural and manufacturing pursuits—these two circumstances had brought about, since the remotest times, a social system of particular features—the so-called "village system," which gave to each of these small unions their independent organization and distinct life. The peculiar character of this system may be judged from the following description, contained in an old official report of the British House of Commons on Indian affairs:

> A village, geographically considered, is a tract of country comprising some hundred or thousand acres of arable and wastelands; politically viewed, it resembles a corporation or township. Its proper establishment of officers and servants consists of the following descriptions: The *potail*, or head inhabitant, who has generally the superintendence of the affairs of the village, settles the disputes of the inhabitants, attends to the police, and performs the duty of collecting the revenue within his village, a duty which his personal influence and minute acquaintance with the situation and concerns of the people render him the best qualified to discharge. The *kurnum* keeps the accounts of cultivation, and registers everything connected with it. The *tallier* and the *totie*, the duty of the former of which consists in gaining information of crimes and offenses, and in escorting and protecting persons traveling from one village to another; the province of the latter appearing to be more immediately confined to the village, consisting, among other

duties, in guarding the crops and assisting in measuring them. The *boundaryman,* who preserves the limits of the village, or gives evidence respecting them in cases of dispute. The Superintendent of Tanks and Watercourses distributes the water for the purposes of agriculture. The Brahman, who performs the village worship. The schoolmaster, who is seen teaching the children in a village to read and write in the sand. The calendar Brahman, or astrologer, etc. These officers and servants generally constitute the establishment of a village; but in some parts of the country it is of less extent, some of the duties and functions above described being united in the same person; in others it exceeds the above-named number of individuals. Under this simple form of municipal government the inhabitants of the country have lived from time immemorial. The boundaries of the villages have been but seldom altered; and though the villages themselves have been sometimes injured, and even desolated, by war, famine, or disease, the same name, the same limits, the same interests, and even the same families have continued for ages. The inhabitants gave themselves no trouble about the breaking up and divisions of kingdoms; while the village remains entire, they care not to what power it is transferred, or to what sovereign it devolves; its internal economy remains unchanged. The potail is still the head inhabitant, and still acts as the petty judge or magistrate, and collector or renter of the village.

These small stereotype forms of social organism have been to the greater part dissolved, and are disappearing, not so much through the brutal interference of the British taxgatherer and the British soldier as through the working of English steam and English free trade. Those family communities were based on domestic industry, in that peculiar combination of hand weaving, hand spinning, and hand-tilling agriculture which gave them self-supporting power. English interference having placed the spinner in Lancashire and the weaver in Bengal, or sweeping away both Hindu spinner and weaver, dissolved these small, semi-barbarian, semi-civilized communities by blowing up their economic bases, and thus produced the greatest and, to speak the truth, the only *social* revolution ever heard of in Asia.

Now, sickening as it must be to human feeling to witness those myriads of industrious patriarchal and inoffensive social organizations disorganized and dissolved into their units, thrown into a sea of woes, and their individual members losing at the same time their ancient form of civilization, and their hereditary means of subsistence, we must not forget that these idyllic village communities, inoffensive though they may appear, had always been the solid foundation of Oriental despotism, that they restrained the human mind within the smallest possible compass, making it the unresisting tool of superstition, enslaving it beneath traditional rules, depriving it of all grandeur and historical energies. We must not forget the barbarian egotism which, concentrating on some miserable patch of land, had quietly witnessed the ruin of empires, the perpetration of unspeakable cruelties, the massacre of the population of large towns, with no other consideration bestowed upon them than on natural events, itself the helpless prey of any aggressor who deigned to notice it at all. We must not forget that this undignified, stagnatory, and vegetative life, that this passive sort of existence evoked on the other part, in contradistinction, wild, aimless, unbounded forces of destruction and rendered murder itself a religious rite in Hindustan. We must not forget that these little communities were contaminated by distinctions of caste, and by slavery, that they subjugated man to external circumstances instead of elevating man into the sovereign of circumstances, that they transformed a self-developing social state into never changing natural destiny, and thus brought about a brutalizing worship of nature, exhibiting its degradation in the fact that man, the sovereign of nature, fell down on his knees in adoration of Hanuman, the monkey, and Sabbala, the cow.

England, it is true, in causing a social revolution in Hindustan, was actuated only by the vilest interests, and was stupid in her manner of enforcing them. But that is not the question. The question is: Can mankind fulfill its destiny without a fundamental revolution in the social state of Asia? If not, whatever may have been the crimes of England, she was the unconscious tool of history in bringing about that revolution.

Then, whatever bitterness the spectacle of the crumbling of an ancient world may have for our personal feelings, we have the right, in point of history, to exclaim with Goethe:

> "*Sollte diese Qual uns quälen*
> *Da sie unsere Lust vermehrt,*
> *Hat nicht myriaden Seelen*
> *Timur's Herrschaft aufgezehrt?*"[1]

ON AUTHORITY

FRIEDRICH ENGELS

Engels wrote this essay to discredit the anarchists, but in doing so he gave expression more clearly than he had elsewhere to an authoritarian principle latent in his and Marx's philosophy. When a worker enters a factory, says Engels, be it a socialist or capitalist one, he leaves behind him all freedom, at least during his working hours. Modern technology imposes upon men "a veritable despotism independent of all social organization." The dialectical standpoint is superseded in this notion of a social necessity which cannot be removed by changes in the social system. At most what can be done is to keep the workings of this authoritarian principle to the minimum. Lenin made extensive use of this essay in his *The State and Revolution* to buttress his argument for dictatorship. Engels' article had a curious history. It was first published in Italian in 1874 under the title "Dell' Autorità" in the *Alamanacco Repubblicano*; when rediscovered, it was translated by David Riazanov in *Die Neue Zeit*, Volume XXXII, Band 1, 1913–14, pages 37–39.—ED.

A number of socialists have latterly launched a regular crusade against what they call the *principle of authority*.

1 ["*Since they thus have swelled our joy,*
Should such torments grieve us, then?
Doth not Timur's rule destroy
Myriad souls of living men?"
To Suleika, Book of Timur, 1815, *The Poems of Goethe*, translated by Edgar Alfred Bowring, London, 1874.]

It suffices to tell them that this or that act is *authoritarian* for it to be condemned. This summary mode of procedure is being abused to such an extent that it has become necessary to look into the matter somewhat more closely. Authority, in the sense in which the word is used here, means the imposition of the will of another upon ours; on the other hand, authority presupposes subordination. Now since these two words sound bad and the relationship which they represent is disagreeable to the subordinated party, the question is to ascertain whether there is any way of dispensing with it, whether—given the conditions of present-day society—we could not create another social system, in which this authority would be given no scope any longer and would consequently have to disappear. On examining the economic, industrial, and agricultural conditions which form the basis of present-day bourgeois society, we find that they tend more and more to replace isolated action by combined action of individuals. Modern industry with its big factories and mills, where hundreds of workers supervise complicated machines driven by steam, has superseded the small workshops of the separate producers; the carriages and wagons of the highways have been replaced by railway trains, just as the small schooners and sailing feluccas have been by steamboats. Even agriculture falls increasingly under the dominion of the machine and of steam, which slowly but relentlessly put in the place of the small proprietors big capitalists, who with the aid of hired workers cultivate vast stretches of land. Everywhere combined action, the complication of processes dependent upon each other, displaces independent action by individuals. But whoever mentions combined action speaks of organization; now is it possible to have organization without authority?

Supposing a social revolution dethroned the capitalists, who now exercise their authority over the production and circulation of wealth. Supposing, to adopt entirely the point of view of the anti-authoritarians, that the land and the instruments of labor had become the collective property of the workers who use them. Will authority have disappeared or will it only have changed its form? Let us see.

Let us take by way of example a cotton-spinning mill.

The cotton must pass through at least six successive operations before it is reduced to the state of thread, and these operations take place for the most part in different rooms. Furthermore, keeping the machines going requires an engineer to look after the steam engine, mechanics to make the current repairs, and many other laborers, whose business it is to transfer the products from one room to another, and so forth. All these workers, men, women, and children, are obliged to begin and finish their work at the hours fixed by the authority of the steam, which cares nothing for individual autonomy. The workers must, therefore, first come to an understanding on the hours of work; and these hours, once they are fixed, must be observed by all, without any exception. Thereafter particular questions arise in each room and at every moment concerning the mode of production, distribution of materials, etc., which must be settled at once on pain of seeing all production immediately stopped; whether they are settled by decision of a delegate placed at the head of each branch of labor or, if possible, by a majority vote, the will of the single individual will always have to subordinate itself, which means that questions are settled in an authoritarian way. The automatic machinery of a big factory is much more despotic than the small capitalists who employ workers ever have been. At least with regard to the hours of work one may write upon the portals of these factories: *Lasciate ogni autonomia, voi che entrate!*[1] If man, by dint of his knowledge and inventive genius, has subdued the forces of nature, the latter avenge themselves upon him by subjecting him, in so far as he employs them, to a veritable despotism, independent of all social organization. Wanting to abolish authority in large-scale industry is tantamount to wanting to abolish industry itself, to destroy the power loom in order to return to the spinning wheel.

Let us take another example—the railway. Here, too, the co-operation of an infinite number of individuals is absolutely necessary, and this co-operation must be practiced during precisely fixed hours, so that no accidents may happen. Here, too, the first condition of the job is a dominant

[1] [Leave, ye that enter in, all autonomy behind!]

will that settles all subordinate questions, whether this will is represented by a single delegate or a committee charged with the execution of the resolutions of the majority of persons interested. In either case there is very pronounced authority. Moreover, what would happen to the first train dispatched if the authority of the railway employees over the honorable passengers were abolished?

But the necessity of authority, and of imperious authority at that, will nowhere be found more evident than on board a ship on the high seas. There, in time of danger, the lives of all depend on the instantaneous and absolute obedience of all to the will of one.

When I submitted arguments like these to the most rabid anti-authoritarians, the only answer they were able to give me was the following: Yes, that's true, but here it is not a case of authority which we confer on our delegates, *but of a commission entrusted!* These gentlemen think that when they have changed the names of things they have changed the things themselves. This is how these profound thinkers mock at the whole world.

We have thus seen that, on the one hand, a certain authority, no matter how delegated, and, on the other hand, a certain subordination are things which, independent of all social organization, are imposed upon us together with the material conditions under which we produce and make products circulate.

We have seen, besides, that the material conditions of production and circulation inevitably develop with large-scale industry and large-scale agriculture, and increasingly tend to enlarge the scope of this authority. Hence it is absurd to speak of the principle of authority as being absolutely evil and of the principle of autonomy as being absolutely good. Authority and autonomy are relative things, whose spheres vary with the various phases of the development of society. If the autonomists confined themselves to saying that the social organization of the future would restrict authority solely to the limits within which the conditions of production render it inevitable, we could understand each other; but they are blind to all facts that make the thing necessary and they passionately fight the word.

Why do the anti-authoritarians not confine themselves to crying out against political authority, the state? All socialists are agreed that the political state, and with it political authority, will disappear as a result of the coming social revolution, that is, that public functions will lose their political character and be transformed into the simple administrative functions of watching over the true interests of society. But the anti-authoritarians demand that the authoritarian political state be abolished at one stroke, even before the social conditions that gave birth to it have been destroyed. They demand that the first act of the social revolution shall be the abolition of authority. Have these gentlemen ever seen a revolution? A revolution is certainly the most authoritarian thing there is; it is the act whereby one part of the population imposes its will upon the other part by means of rifles, bayonets, and cannon—authoritarian means, if such there be at all; and if the victorious party does not want to have fought in vain, it must maintain this rule by means of the terror which its arms inspire in the reactionaries. Would the Paris Commune have lasted a single day if it had not made use of this authority of the armed people against the bourgeois? Should we not, on the contrary, reproach it for not having used it freely enough?

Therefore, either one of two things: either the anti-authoritarians don't know what they are talking about, in which case they are creating nothing but confusion, or they do know, and in that case they are betraying the movement of the proletariat. In either case they serve the reaction.

CAPITAL PUNISHMENT

KARL MARX

New York *Daily Tribune*
February 18, 1853

LONDON, Friday, January 28, 1853

The Times of January 25 contains the following observations under the head of "Amateur Hanging":

It has often been remarked that in this country a public execution is generally followed closely by instances of death by hanging, either suicidal or accidental, in consequence of the powerful effect which the execution of a noted criminal produces upon a morbid and unmatured mind.

Of the several cases which are alleged by *The Times* in illustration of this remark, one is that of a lunatic at Sheffield, who, after talking with other lunatics respecting the execution of Barbour, put an end to his existence by hanging himself. Another case is that of a boy of fourteen years, who also hanged himself.

The doctrine to which the enumeration of these facts was intended to give its support is one which no reasonable man would be likely to guess, it being no less than a direct apotheosis of the hangman, while capital punishment is extolled as the *ultima ratio* of society. This is done in a leading article of the "leading journal."

The Morning Advertiser, in some very bitter but just strictures on the hanging predilections and bloody logic of *The Times*, has the following interesting data on forty-three days of the year 1849:

Executions of	Murders and Suicides
Millan ....March 20	Hannah Saddles . March 22
Petley ....March 20	M. G. Newton .. March 22
	J. G. Gleeson—4 Murders at Liverpool .... March 27
Smith ....March 27	Murder and Suicide at Leicester ....April 2
Howe ....March 31	Poisoning at Bath .. April 7
	W. Bailey ....April 8
	J. Ward murders his mother ....April 13
Landish ....April 9	Yardley ....April 14
Sarah Thomas ......May 9	Doxy, parricide ...April 14
	J. Bailey kills his two children and himself ....April 17
J. Griffiths ....April 18	Chas. Overton ...April 18
J. Rush ....April 21	Daniel Holmston ...May 2

This table, as *The Times* concedes, shows not only suicides, but also murders of the most atrocious kind, following closely upon the execution of criminals. It is astonishing that the article in question does not produce even a single argument or pretext for indulging in the savage theory therein propounded; and it would be very difficult, if not altogether impossible, to establish any principle upon which the justice or expediency of capital punishment could be founded in a society glorying in its civilization. Punishment in general has been defended as a means either of ameliorating or of intimidating. Now what right have you to punish me for the amelioration or intimidation of others? And besides, there is history—there is such a thing as statistics—which prove with the most complete evidence that since Cain the world has been neither intimidated nor ameliorated by punishment. Quite the contrary. From the point of view of abstract right, there is only one theory of punishment which recognizes human dignity in the abstract, and that is the theory of Kant, especially in the more rigid formula given to it by Hegel. Hegel says:

> Punishment is the *right* of the criminal. It is an act of his own will. The violation of right has been proclaimed by the criminal as his own right. His crime is the negation of right. Punishment is the negation of this negation, and consequently an affirmation of right, solicited and forced upon the criminal by himself.

There is no doubt something specious in this formula, inasmuch as Hegel, instead of looking upon the criminal as the mere object, the slave of justice, elevates him to the position of a free and self-determined being. Looking, however, more closely into the matter, we discover that German idealism here, as in most other instances, has but given a transcendental sanction to the rules of existing society. Is it not a delusion to substitute for the individual with his real motives, with multifarious social circumstances pressing upon him, the abstraction of "free will"—one among the many qualities of man for man himself? This theory, considering punishment as the result of the criminal's own will, is only a metaphysical expression for the old *jus talionis*; eye against eye, tooth against tooth, blood against blood. Plainly speaking, and dispensing with all paraphrases, punishment is nothing but a means of society to defend itself against the infraction of its vital conditions, whatever may be their character. Now what a state of society is that which knows of no better instrument for its own defense than the hangman, and which proclaims, through the "leading journal of the world," its own brutality as eternal law?

Mr. A. Quételet, in his excellent and learned work, *L'Homme et ses Facultés*, says:

> There is a *budget* which we pay with frightful regularity—it is that of prisons, dungeons, and scaffolds. . . . We might even predict how many individuals will stain their hands with the blood of their fellow men, how many will be forgers, how many will deal in poison, pretty nearly the same way as we may foretell the annual births and deaths.

And Mr. Quételet, in a calculation of the probabilities of crime published in 1829, actually predicted with astonishing certainty not only the amount but all the different kinds of crimes committed in France in 1830. That it is not so much the particular political institutions of a country as the fundamental conditions of modern *bourgeois* society in general which produce an average amount of crime in a given national fraction of society may be seen from the following table, communicated by Quételet, for the years 1822–24. We find in a number of one hundred condemned criminals in America and France:

Age.	Philadelphia.	France.
Under twenty-one years	19	19
Twenty-one to thirty	44	35
Thirty to forty	23	23
Above forty	14	23
Total	100	100

Now, if crimes observed on a great scale thus show, in their amount and their classification, the regularity of physical phenomena—if, as Mr. Quételet remarks: "It would be difficult to decide in respect to which of the two [the physical world and the social system] the acting causes produce their effect with the utmost regularity"—is there not a necessity for deeply reflecting upon an alteration of the system that breeds these crimes, instead of glorifying the hangman who executes a lot of criminals to make room only for the supply of new ones?

THE LABOR MOVEMENT IN THE UNITED STATES

FRIEDRICH ENGELS

This essay was written by Engels as the Preface to the American edition of *The Condition of the Working Class in England in 1844*, published in New York in 1887. Florence Kelley Wischnewetzsky was the translator. Her subsequent career and important contribution to social reforms in America are narrated in Josephine Clara Goldmark's *Impatient Crusader: Florence Kelley's Life Story*, Urbana, University of Illinois Press, 1953.—ED.

Ten months have elapsed since, at the translator's wish, I wrote the Appendix to this book; and during these ten months a revolution has been accomplished in American society such as in any other country would have taken at least ten years. In February 1885, American public opinion was almost unanimous on this one point: that there was no working class, in the European sense of the word, in America; that consequently no class struggle between workmen and capitalists, such as tore European society to pieces, was possible in the American republic; and that, therefore, socialism was a thing of foreign importation, which could never take root on American soil. And yet, at that moment, the coming class struggle was casting its gigantic shadow before it in the strikes of the Pennsylvania coal miners, and of many other trades, and especially in the preparations, all over the country, for the great eight-hour movement, which was to come off and did come off in the May following. That I then duly appreciated these symptoms, that I anticipated a working-class movement on a national scale, my Appendix shows; but no one could then foresee that in such a short time the movement would burst out with such irresistible force, would spread with the rapidity of a prairie fire, would shake American society to its very foundations.

The fact is there, stubborn and indisputable. To what an extent it had struck with terror the American ruling classes was revealed to me, in an amusing way, by American journalists who did me the honor of calling on me last summer; the "new departure" had put them into a state of helpless fright and perplexity. But at that time the movement was only just on the start; there was but a series of confused and apparently disconnected upheavals of that class which, by the suppression of Negro slavery and the rapid development of manufactures, had become the lowest stratum of American society. Before the year closed, these bewildering social convulsions began to take a definite direction. The spontaneous, instinctive movements of these vast masses of working people, over a vast extent of country, the simultaneous outburst of their common discontent with a miserable social condition, the same everywhere and due to the same causes, made them conscious of the fact that they formed a new and distinct class of American society: a class of—practically speaking—more or less hereditary wage workers, proletarians. And with true American instinct this consciousness led them at once to take the next step towards their deliverance: the formation of a political workingmen's party, with a platform of its own, and with the conquest of the Capitol and the White House for its goal. In May the struggle for the eight-hour working day, the troubles in Chicago, Milwaukee, etc., the attempts of the ruling class to crush the nascent uprising of labor by brute force and brutal class justice; in November the new Labor party organized in all great centers, and the New York, Chicago, and Milwaukee elections. May and November have hitherto reminded the American bourgeoisie only of the payment of coupons of U.S. bonds; henceforth May and November will remind them, too, of the dates on which the American working class presented *their* coupons for payment.

In European countries it took the working class years and

years before they fully realized the fact that they formed a distinct and, under the existing social conditions, a permanent class of modern society; and it took years again until this class consciousness led them to form themselves into a distinct political party, independent of, and opposed to, all the old political parties formed by the various sections of the ruling classes. On the more favored soil of America, where no medieval ruins bar the way, where history begins with the elements of the modern bourgeois society as evolved in the seventeenth century, the working class passed through these two stages of its development within ten months.

Still, all this is but a beginning. That the laboring masses should feel their community of grievances and of interests, their solidarity as a class in opposition to all other classes; that in order to give expression and effect to this feeling they should set in motion the political machinery provided for that purpose in every free country—that is the first step only. The next step is to find the common remedy for these common grievances, and to embody it in the platform of the new Labor party. And this—the most important and the most difficult step in the movement—has yet to be taken in America.

A new party must have a distinct positive platform, a platform which may vary in details as circumstances vary and as the party itself develops, but still one upon which the party, for the time being, is agreed. So long as such a platform has not been worked out, or exists but in a rudimentary form, so long the new party, too, will have but a rudimentary existence; it may exist locally, but not yet nationally; it will be a party potentially, but not actually.

That platform, whatever may be its first initial shape, must develop in a direction which may be determined beforehand. The causes that brought into existence the abyss between the working class and the capitalist class are the same in America as in Europe; the means of filling up that abyss are equally the same everywhere. Consequently the platform of the American proletariat will, in the long run, coincide as to the ultimate end to be attained with the one which, after sixty years of dissensions and discussions, has become the adopted platform of the great mass of the

European militant proletariat. It will proclaim as the ultimate end the conquest of political supremacy by the working class, in order to effect the direct appropriation of all means of production—land, railways, mines, machinery, etc.—by society at large, to be worked in common by all for the account and benefit of all.

But if the new American party, like all political parties everywhere, by the very fact of its formation aspires to the conquest of political power, it is as yet far from agreed upon what to do with that power when once attained. In New York and the other great cities of the East the organization of the working class has proceeded upon the lines of trade societies, forming in each city a powerful Central Labor Union. In New York the Central Labor Union, last November, chose for its standard-bearer Henry George, and consequently its temporary electoral platform has been largely imbued with his principles. In the great cities of the Northwest the electoral battle was fought upon a rather indefinite labor platform, and the influence of Henry George's theories was scarcely, if at all, visible. And while in these great centers of population and of industry the new class movement came to a political head, we find all over the country two widespread labor organizations: the Knights of Labor and the Socialist Labor party, of which only the latter has a platform in harmony with the modern European standpoint, as summarized above.

Of the three more or less definite forms under which the American labor movement thus presents itself, the first, the Henry George movement in New York, is for the moment of a chiefly local significance. No doubt New York is by far the most important city of the States, but New York is not Paris and the United States are not France. And it seems to me that the Henry George platform, in its present shape, is too narrow to form the basis for anything but a local movement, or at least for a short-lived phase of the general movement. To Henry George the expropriation of the mass of the people from the land is the great and universal cause of the splitting up of the people into rich and poor. Now this is not quite correct historically. In Asiatic and classical antiquity the predominant form of class oppression was slavery, that is to say, not so much the expropriation of the masses from the land as the appropriation of their persons. When, in the decline of the Roman Republic, the free Italian peasants were expropriated from their farms they formed a class of "poor whites" similar to that of the Southern slave states before 1861; and between slaves and poor whites, two classes equally unfit for self-emancipation, the old world went to pieces.

In the Middle Ages it was not the expropriation of the people *from,* but, on the contrary, their appropriation *to* the land which became the source of feudal oppression. The peasant retained his land, but was attached to it as a serf or villein, and made liable to tribute to the lord in labor and in produce. It was only at the dawn of modern times, towards the end of the fifteenth century, that the expropriation of the peasantry on a large scale laid the foundation for the modern class of wage workers who possess nothing but their labor power and can live only by the selling of that labor power to others. But if the expropriation from the land brought this class into existence, it was the development of capitalist production, of modern industry and agriculture on a large scale which perpetuated it, increased it, and shaped it into a distinct class with distinct interests and a distinct historical mission. All this has been fully expounded by Marx (*Capital,* Part VIII: "The So-called Primitive Accumulation"). According to Marx, the cause of the present antagonism of the classes and of the social degradation of the working class is their expropriation from *all* means of production, in which the land is of course included.

If Henry George declares land monopolization to be the sole cause of poverty and misery he naturally finds the remedy in the resumption of the land by society at large. Now the socialists of the school of Marx, too, demand the resumption, by society, of the land, and not only of the land but of all other means of production likewise. But even if we leave these out of the question, there is another difference. What is to be done with the land? Modern socialists, as represented by Marx, demand that it should be held and worked in common and for common account, and the same with all other means of social production, mines, railways, factories, etc.; Henry George would confine himself to letting it out to individuals as at present, merely regulating its distribution and applying the rents for public instead of, as at present, for private purposes. What the socialists demand implies a total revolution of the whole system of social production; what Henry George demands leaves the present mode of social production untouched, and has, in fact, been anticipated by the extreme section of Ricardian bourgeois economists, who, too, demanded the confiscation of the rent of land by the state.

It would of course be unfair to suppose that Henry George has said his last word once for all. But I am bound to take his theory as I find it.

The second great section of the American movement is formed by the Knights of Labor. And that seems to be the section most typical of the present state of the movement, as it is undoubtedly by far the strongest. An immense association spread over an immense extent of country in innumerable "assemblies," representing all shades of individual and local opinion within the working class; the whole of them sheltered under a platform of corresponding indistinctness and held together much less by their impracticable constitution than by the instinctive feeling that the very fact of their clubbing together for their common aspiration makes them a great power in the country; a truly American paradox, clothing the most modern tendencies in the most medieval mummeries, and hiding the most democratic and even rebellious spirit behind an apparent, but really powerless, despotism—such is the picture the Knights of Labor offer to a European observer. But if we are not arrested by mere outside whimsicalities, we cannot help seeing in this vast agglomeration an immense amount of potential energy evolving slowly but surely into actual force. The Knights of Labor are the first national organization created by the American working class as a whole; whatever be their origin and history, whatever their shortcomings and little absurdities, whatever their platform and their constitution, here they are, the work of practically the whole class of American wage workers, the only national bond that holds them together, that makes their strength felt to themselves not less than to their enemies, and that fills them with the proud hope of future victories.

For it would not be exact to say that the Knights of Labor are liable to development. They are constantly in full process of development and revolution, a heaving, fermenting mass of plastic material seeking the shape and form appropriate to its inherent nature. That form will be attained as surely as historical evolution has, like natural evolution, its own immanent laws. Whether the Knights of Labor will then retain their present name or not makes no difference, but to an outsider it appears evident that here is the raw material out of which the future of the American working-class movement, and along with it, the future of American society at large, has to be shaped.

The third section consists of the Socialist Labor party. This section is a party but in name, for nowhere in America has it, up to now, been able actually to take its stand as a political party. It is, moreover, to a certain extent foreign to America, having until lately been made up almost exclusively of German immigrants, using their own language and, for the most part, little conversant with the common language of the country. But if it came from a foreign stock, it came, at the same time, armed with the experience earned during long years of class struggle in Europe, and with an insight into the general conditions of working-class emancipation far superior to that hitherto gained by American workingmen. This is a fortunate circumstance for the American proletarians, who thus are enabled to appropriate and to take advantage of the intellectual and moral fruits of the forty-year struggle of their European classmates, and thus to hasten on the time of their own victory. For, as I said before, there cannot be any doubt that the ultimate platform of the American working class must and will be essentially the same as that now adopted by the whole militant working class of Europe, the same as that of the German-American Socialist Labor party. In so far this party is called upon to play a very important part in the movement. But in order to do so they will have to doff every remnant of their foreign garb. They will have to become out and out American. They cannot expect the Americans to come to them; they, the minority and the immigrants, must go to the Americans, who are the vast majority and the natives. And to do that they must, above all things, learn English.

The process of fusing together these various elements of the vast moving mass—elements not really discordant, but indeed mutually isolated by their various starting points—will take some time, and will not come off without a deal of friction, such as is visible at different points even now. The Knights of Labor, for instance, are here and there, in the Eastern cities, locally at war with the organized trade unions. But then this same friction exists within the Knights of Labor themselves, where there is anything but peace and harmony. These are not symptoms of decay, for capitalists to crow over. They are merely signs that the innumerable hosts of workers, for the first time set in motion in a common direction, have as yet found out neither the adequate expression for their common interest nor the form of organization best adapted to the struggle, nor the discipline required to ensure victory. They are as yet the first *levées en masse* of the great revolutionary war, raised and equipped locally and independently, all converging to form one common army, but as yet without regular organization and common plan of campaign. The converging columns cross each other here and there; confusion, angry disputes, even threats of conflict arise. But the community of ultimate purpose in the end overcomes all minor troubles; ere long the struggling and squabbling battalions will be formed in a long line of battle array, presenting to the enemy a well-ordered front, ominously silent under their glittering arms, supported by bold skirmishers in front and by unshakable reserves in the rear.

To bring about this result the unification of the various independent bodies into one national labor army, with no matter how inadequate a provisional platform, provided it be a truly working-class platform—that is the next great step to be accomplished in America. To effect this, and to make that platform worthy of the cause, the Socialist Labor party can contribute a great deal, if they will only act in the same way as the European socialists acted at the time when they were but a small minority of the working class. That line of action was first laid down in the *Communist Manifesto* of 1848 in the following words:

"The communists [that was the name we took at the time and that even now we are far from repudiating] do not form a separate party opposed to other working-class parties.

"They have no interests separate and apart from those of the proletariat as a whole.

"They do not set up any sectarian principles of their own, by which to shape and mold the proletarian movement.

"The communists are distinguished from the other working-class parties by this only: 1. In the national struggles of the proletarians of the different countries they point out and bring to the front the common interests of the entire proletariat, independent of all nationality; 2. In the various stages of development which the struggle of the working class against the bourgeoisie has to pass through, they always and everywhere represent the interests of the movement as a whole.

"The communists, therefore, are on the one hand, practically, the most advanced and resolute section of the working-class parties of every country, that section which pushes forward all others; on the other hand, theoretically, they have over the great mass of the proletariat the advantage of clearly understanding the line of march, the conditions, and the ultimate general results of the proletarian movement. . . .

"The communists fight for the attainment of the immediate aims, for the enforcement of the momentary interests of the working class, but in the movement of the present they also represent and take care of the future of that movement."

That is the line of action which the great founder of modern socialism, Karl Marx, and with him I and the socialists of all nations who worked along with us have followed for more than forty years, with the result that it has led to victory everywhere, and that at this moment the mass of European socialists, in Germany and in France, in Belgium, Holland, and Switzerland, in Denmark and Sweden, as well as in Spain and Portugal, are fighting as one common army under one and the same flag.

London, January 26, 1887